Cubase® 6 Power!: The Comprehensive Guide

Michael Miller and Robert Guérin

Course Technology PTR
A part of Cengage Learning

COURSE TECHNOLOGY
CENGAGE Learning™

Australia • Brazil • Japan • Korea • Mexico • Singapore • Spain • United Kingdom • United States

COURSE TECHNOLOGY
CENGAGE Learning

Cubase® 6 Power!: The Comprehensive Guide
Michael Miller and Robert Guérin

Publisher and General Manager, Course Technology PTR: Stacy L. Hiquet

Associate Director of Marketing: Sarah Panella

Manager of Editorial Services: Heather Talbot

Marketing Manager: Mark Hughes

Acquisitions Editor: Orren Merton

Project Editor and Copy Editor: Kim Benbow

Technical Reviewer: Steve Pacey

Interior Layout Tech: MPS Limited, a Macmillan Company

Cover Designer: Mike Tanamachi

Indexer: Larry Sweazy

Proofreaders: Gene Redding and Sue Boshers

> For product information and technology assistance, contact us at
> **Cengage Learning Customer & Sales Support, 1-800-354-9706**
>
> For permission to use material from this text or product, submit all requests online at **www.cengage.com/permissions**
> Further permissions questions can be emailed to
> **permissionrequest@cengage.com**

Steinberg, Cubase, VST, and ASIO are registered trademarks of Steinberg Media Technologies GmbH.

Record, Reason, ReCycle, ReBirth, ReWire, REX, ReFill, Remote, and ReGroove are trademarks of Propellerhead Software AB.

Microsoft, Windows, Windows logo, and Internet Explorer are either registered trademarks or trademarks of Microsoft Corporation in the United States and/or other countries.

Apple, Mac, the Mac logo, Mac OS, and FireWire are either registered trademarks or trademarks of Apple Computer, Inc. in the United States and/or other countries.

All other trademarks are the property of their respective owners.

All images © Cengage Learning unless otherwise noted.

Library of Congress Control Number: 2011930896

ISBN-13: 978-1-4354-6022-5

ISBN-10: 1-4354-6022-7

Course Technology, a part of Cengage Learning
20 Channel Center Street
Boston, MA 02210
USA

Cengage Learning is a leading provider of customized learning solutions with office locations around the globe, including Singapore, the United Kingdom, Australia, Mexico, Brazil, and Japan. Locate your local office at **international.cengage.com/region**

Cengage Learning products are represented in Canada by Nelson Education, Ltd.

For your lifelong learning solutions, visit **courseptr.com**

Visit our corporate website at **cengage.com**

Printed in the United States of America
1 2 3 4 5 6 7 13 12 11

To my stepchildren, Kristi, Laura, Amy, and Ben—it's great having you all in my life.

Acknowledgments

For this edition of the book, Michael would like to thank Orren Merton, Kim Benbow, and everyone else at Course Technology for their assistance in turning this manuscript into a finished book.

For previous editions, Robert would like to give big thanks to Sang Hee Park, for all her support, gentle words of encouragement, love, and affection. I am truly blessed to share this path with you.

Thank you to Colin MacQueen: You have definitely elevated this book with your collaborative views, words of wisdom, and hard labor.

I would like to give thanks to Arnd Kaiser and Martin Gente at Steinberg, who have provided me with the necessary tools and help when needed.

To all of you, *merci beaucoup*. Your help is truly appreciated, and this book would not have been possible without your support.

About the Authors

Michael Miller has written more than 100 non-fiction books over the past two decades. Collectively, his books have sold more than one million copies. Many of his books—including this one—build on his experience as a musician, which includes a stint at the Indiana University School of Music's prestigious Jazz Studies program, as well as many years as a working musician. He uses Cubase to create the CDs that are included with many of his music books.

Learn more about Michael and his books at www.molehillgroup.com. He can be contacted via email at cubase@molehillgroup.com.

Robert Guérin is a composer and music enthusiast. He has worked on different personal and professional projects, such as feature and short films, television themes, and educational and corporate videos. Composing, arranging, playing, recording, and mixing most of his material, he has developed working habits that allow him to be creative without losing his sense of efficiency.

As a professor, Robert has put together several courses covering a wide range of topics, such as computer software for musicians, digital audio technologies, sound on the Web, sound in multimedia productions, hard disk recording, and many more. He has been program coordinator at Trebas Institute in Montreal and a part-time professor at Vanier College, also in Montreal. Robert has developed online courses on sound integration in Web pages and has written several articles, tutorials, and software reviews for audio- and music-related online magazines.

In addition to this book, Robert has also written two editions of *MIDI Power!*, co-wrote *Nuendo Power!*, and has worked on a number of Course Technology Cengage Learning CSi CD-ROM products, including *Sound Forge 7 CSi Starter*, *ACID 5 CSi Starter*, and *Cubase SX 3 CSi Starter* and *Master*.

Contents

Introduction xix

PART I
SETUP   1

Chapter 1
Introducing Cubase   3
What Is Cubase? 3
A Brief History of Cubase 4
Understanding the Cubase Toolset 5
What's New in Cubase 6 6
Understanding the Different Versions of Cubase 6 6

Chapter 2
Understanding Cubase Recording Technology   9
A Brief Overview of Digital Audio 9
    What Is Analog Sound? 10
    What Is Digital Audio? 11
    How Sampling Works 11
    About 32-Bit and Floating-Point Recording 12
What Is MIDI? 13
    Data, Not Notes—How MIDI Works 13
    Anatomy of a MIDI Message 14
    MIDI Connectors 15
Understanding Audio Connections 18
    Input Busses 20
    Output Busses 20
    Audio Track 20
    Audio Channels 21
Understanding MIDI Connections 22
    MIDI Ports 22
    MIDI Channel 23
    MIDI Track 24
Understanding the Cubase Environment 25

Understanding Cubase Audio Terminology 25
    Audio Clips and Audio Events 25
    Audio Regions 26
    Audio Slices 26
    Audio Parts 26
Understanding Nondestructive Editing 28

Chapter 3
Setting Up Peripherals   31

Connecting an Audio Interface 32
    Audio Interface Devices 32
    MIDI Interface Devices 33
    Control Surfaces 33
Working with Audio Drivers 34
    ASIO Drivers and Latency 35
    ASIO DirectX Full Duplex Drivers 35
MIDI Interfaces and Drivers 36
Setting Up Devices in Cubase 38
    Setting Up MIDI Ports 39
    Setting Up a Remote Device 40
    Setting Up Audio Ports 41
Running Other Applications Simultaneously 44
    Background Processes 44
    Other Audio Applications 44
Getting It All Working 45

Chapter 4
Monitoring and Connecting Audio   47

Monitoring Methods 48
    Monitoring Through Cubase 48
    Monitoring Externally 50
    Direct Monitoring 50
Setting Up VST Connections 51
    Input Connections 51
    Output Connections 53
    Group/FX Connections 54
    External FX Connections 54
    External Instrument Connections 56
    Studio Connections 57
Saving Connections 58
    Saving Connections in a Template 59
    Saving Connection Presets 60

Chapter 5
Creating a New Project   61

Understanding Cubase Projects 61
    Creating a Project 62
    Configuring Project Settings 63
Creating Audio Tracks 66
Creating an Audio Track with a Preset Configuration 67
    Setting Up an Audio Track 69
Creating an Instrument Track 70
Creating a MIDI Track 71
Setting Up a MIDI or Instrument Track 72

PART II
RECORDING   73

Chapter 6
Using the Control Room Mixer   75

Understanding the Control Room 76
Monitoring with the Control Room 77
    External Inputs 79
    Monitoring Options 79
    Listen Mode 80
    Talkback Options 81
    Dim and Reference Levels 81
    CRM Extended View 82
    Studio Sends 83

Chapter 7
Managing Your Media   85

Using the MediaBay 85
    Define Locations 85
    Locations 86
    Filters 86
    Results 87
    Previewer 87
VST Instrument Presets 87
    Applying Instrument Presets 87
    Using Other VST Presets 87
    Saving Your Own Presets 89

Importing Audio Content 90

Importing Audio Files 90

Importing Audio CD Tracks 91

Importing MIDI Files 92

Importing Audio from Video Files 93

Importing Video Files 93

Chapter 8
Recording Audio   95

Recording an Audio Track 95

Click Track, Tempo, and Time Signature 98

Click Settings 98

Tempo and Time Signature 100

Chapter 9
Overdubbing   103

Adding a New Track 103

Punch-In/Punch-Out Recording 104

Pre-Roll/Post-Roll 106

Punching In New Tracks 107

Recording Multiple Takes 108

Recording in Cycle Mode 108

Working with Lanes 109

Assembling a Master Take 109

Chapter 10
Using VST and MIDI Instruments   111

Using VST Instruments 111

Setting Up an Instrument Track 112

Setting Up a VSTi 114

Saving Presets 118

VSTi and Latency 118

Adding MIDI Devices with the Device Manager 119

Adding a MIDI Device 120

Managing a MIDI Device 121

Using Devices in the Inspector 124

Chapter 11
Recording MIDI   127

Record Modes 127

Linear Record Mode 127

Cycle Record Mode 128

Auto-Quantize 129

Left and Right Locators 129
MIDI and Audio Activity Indicators 130
Recording MIDI.. 132
Recording Multiple Takes 133
    Recording MIDI in Cycle Mode... 133
    Working with MIDI Lanes.. 134
    Assembling a Master MIDI Take 134
Virtual MIDI Keyboard.. 135

Chapter 12
Using ReWire

137

ReWire Setup 137
VSTi and ReWire Channels... 139
Exporting VSTi and ReWire Channels 140

Chapter 13
Using Insert Effects

143

How Plug-In Effects Work 143
    Applying Effects... 144
    Inserts versus Sends.. 144
Cubase's Audio Plug-In Effects.. 146
Audio Track Inserts.. 149
    How Track Inserts Work 149
    Insert Effect Controls 150
    Applying Insert Effects 152
    Processing Power.. 154
Inserts on Control Room Connections 154

Chapter 14
Using the Pool

157

Understanding the Pool 157
Understanding the Information 160
Using the Pool Functions.. 162
    Dealing with Missing Files 163
    Optimizing the Pool 164
    Archiving and Exporting a Pool 165
Pool Interaction.. 166
Applying Offline Processes in the Pool 167

PART III
NAVIGATION   169

Chapter 15
Navigating the Project Window   171

Project Window Areas... 171
    Toolbar 173
    The Inspector 180
    The Track List 182
    Transport Panel 183
Track Classes 184
Adding Tracks 185

Chapter 16
Mastering Project Navigation   187

Changing Your Focus 187
    Using the Overview Line 188
    Using the Zoom Tools 189
The Transport Panel 190
    Main Transport 191
    Shuttle, Jog, and Nudge 191

Chapter 17
Navigating MIDI Tracks   193

MIDI Events in Cubase 193
Setting Up a MIDI Track 194
    Notepad 198
    Quick Controls 198
MIDI Fader 199
MIDI Channel Settings... 201
Converting MIDI to Audio Track 203

Chapter 18
Navigating Audio Tracks   205

Setting Up an Audio Track 205
    Controls and Parameters 206
    Inspector Sections 208
The Channel Section 209
    Channel Section Controls 210
    Channel Settings Panel 210
Overlapping Audio Events 211

PART IV
EDITING   213

Chapter 19
Using the Sample Editor   215

Sample Editor Areas.. 215
    Main Areas 216
    Toolbar 217
    Thumbnail and Waveform Displays 220
Basic Editing Functions 220
    Trimming Start and End Points....................................... 220
    Cutting and Pasting.. 221
    Inserting Silence 221
    Erasing Individual Notes 221
Musical Mode 222
Working with Regions 223
Snap Point... 224

Chapter 20
Using Audio Processing Options   227

Audio Processing Options 227
    Online vs. Offline Processing 227
    Using Audio Processes and Effects 228
    Cubase 6 Offline Processes... 230
Managing Offline Process History.. 237
Changing Tempo and Pitch with AudioWarp 239
    Time-Stretching 239
    Pitch Shifting... 240

Chapter 21
Editing Vocals   243

Recording Vocals 243
    The Recording Space... 243
    Vocal Microphones 244
    Microphone Placement 244
    Equalization 245
Using Popular Plug-Ins 245
    Compressor 245
    DeEsser 247
    Gate 248
    Reverb.. 249
    Pitch Correct 250

Editing Vocals with VariAudio..251
  Changing Pitch...251
  Changing Timing 252
  Editing Notes 253

Chapter 22
Editing MIDI Events with the In-Place Editor   **255**
Using the In-Place Editor...255
Zooming 256
Moving MIDI Events 257
Muting Events 258
Splitting and Resizing Note Events..258
Merging Note Events 259
Using the Draw Tool..260
Using the Line Tool 260

Chapter 23
Using the Key Editor and Note Expression   **265**
Using the Key Editor...265
  Solo Editor and Acoustic Feedback...266
  Tool Buttons 267
  Auto Select Controllers 268
  Note Expression Data 268
  Part Editing Options 268
  Indicate Transpositions and Insert Velocity 269
  Snap and Quantize 269
  Step Input and MIDI Edit Buttons 270
Key Editor Display Areas 271
Using Step Input...273
Editing Multiple Tracks 274
Editing Controller Data with Note Expression................................275
  Activating Note Expression 275
  Mapping Controllers for Note Expression 276
  Recording Note Expression Data 277
  Editing Note Expression Data 278

Chapter 24
Editing MIDI Drum Tracks   **279**
Understanding the Drum Editor 279
Editing Drum Parts 282
Working with Drum Maps 282
  Understanding Drum Maps 282
  Remapping Drum Maps 284
Quantizing MIDI Drum Parts 285

Chapter 25
Understanding MIDI Menu Options   287
Using the MIDI Transpose Command...287
Merge MIDI in Loop 289
Using the Dissolve Parts Function 290
Using the O-Note Conversion Tool...291
Using MIDI Functions...292

Chapter 26
Quantizing Events   295
Understanding and Configuring Quantize Methods 295
Setting Up a Quantize Grid..298
Setting Quantize Parameters...299
Applying MIDI Quantization 300
Creating MIDI Groove Quantize Presets 302
Quantizing Audio Events 303
   Understanding Hitpoints 303
   Creating Hitpoints 304
   Other Hitpoint Functions 305
   Applying Quantization 306
   Applying Quantization to Multiple Audio Tracks 307

Chapter 27
Adding MIDI Track Effects   309
Cubase 6's MIDI Effects 309
MIDI Inserts..310
MIDI Sends...312

PART V
ARRANGING   315

Chapter 28
Arranging in the Project Window   317
Splitting Events 318
   Split at Cursor...318
   Split Loop 319
   Split Range..319
   Range Crop...319
Inserting Silence 320
Pasting Functions 320
Copying Events 322
   Duplicate Command 322

Repeat Command 322
Fill Loop Function 324
Resizing Objects... 325
Normal Sizing 325
Sizing Moves Contents Mode 326
Sizing Applies Time Stretch Mode....................................... 327
Shifting Events Inside an Object 328
Muting Objects 329
Locking Events 329
Undoing Steps Using the Edit History 329

Chapter 29
Using the Arranger Track

331

Creating an Arranger Project.. 331
Creating an Arranger Track 332
Working with Arranger Controls 332
Creating Arranger Events 333
Arranger Track Inspector 335
Using the Arranger Editor 336
Populating a Chain.. 337
Navigating the Arranger Chain 337
Changing the Order of Events 337
Managing Arranger Chains 338
Flattening a Chain... 338

Chapter 30
Working with Tempo

341

Using the Tempo Track Editor... 341
Time Warping... 345
Changing Tempo with Time Warp.. 346
Locking Tempo with Warp Tabs 347
Automatic Tempo Detection 348

Chapter 31
Working with Beats and Loops

351

Working with Loops 352
Obtaining Samples and Loops 352
Matching Tempo 353
Matching Pitch... 353
Extending Loops 354
Creating and Manipulating Drum Tracks 356
Enhancing Drum Loops 356
Replacing Drum Hits in an Audio Track 357

Using Groove Agent ONE...358
Using Beat Designer 360
Using LoopMash2..362

PART VI
MIXING AND MASTERING   365

Chapter 32
Using the Mixer   367

Understanding the Mixer Areas..368
    Common Panel..369
    Channel Strips..372
    Extended Mixer Panel...373
    Routing Panel..375
Working with Mixer Settings 375
Editing the Input Bus Channels..376
Editing the Output Bus Channels...377
Using the Can Hide Function 378
What Makes a Great Mix?..379

Chapter 33
Working with FX Channel Tracks   381

Understanding the FX Channel Options...381
Using Audio Track Sends 382
    Understanding Send Effects 383
    Managing Audio Track Sends 383
Managing FX Channels Through VST Connections 386

Chapter 34
Adding Equalization   389

Understanding Equalization 389
    Frequency...390
    Gain..390
    Q...390
Adding EQ...391
    EQ in the Channel Settings Window...391
    EQ in the Track Inspector..393
    EQ in the Extended Mixer 393
Applying Filter Types 393
Using EQ Presets...395
Carving EQ Holes...395

Chapter 35
Working with Group Channel Tracks   397

Anatomy of a Group Track.. 397
Using Group Channels 398

Chapter 36
Writing and Reading Automation   401

Using the Read and Write Buttons 402
Writing Channel Track Automation... 403
Writing Parameter Automation 404
About Automation Modes.. 405
Managing Automation with the Automation Panel 406
Drawing Automation 407
    Adding Additional Automation Events.. 408
    Drawing Shapes 409
Hiding and Removing Automation Subtracks 409
Editing Automation... 410
    Using Write Automation 410
    Using Automation Subtracks 411

Chapter 37
Mixing for Surround Sound   413

Multichannel Configurations... 413
Creating a Surround Bus 415
Surround Routing Options 416
SurroundPanner V5 417
Routing Effects in Surround Outputs 418
Exporting a Surround Mix 420

Chapter 38
Mastering and Exporting the Final Mix   421

Audio Exporting Options 421
Choosing an Audio Format 424
Adding Metadata 425
About Mastering 426
About Dithering 429
Backing Up Your Work 431
OMF Export Options 432

PART VII
MANAGING   435

Chapter 39
Customizing Your Project   437

Creating and Organizing Workspaces 437
Creating Templates 439
Customizing Key Commands 441
Using Cubase Macros... 442
Customizing Toolbars 444
Customizing Your Transport Panel 445
Customizing Track Controls 445

Chapter 40
Optimizing Your Project   449

Disabling Audio Tracks... 449
Processing VST Plug-Ins Offline 450
Using the Freeze Function 451
    Freezing an Audio Channel 451
    Freezing Edits.. 452
    Freezing VSTi.. 452
Using Folder Tracks 454

Index 457

Introduction

The recording industry today isn't what it used to be. And that's a good thing. In the old days, to make a record (is the word "record" old technology now?) you had to spend big bucks to rent a professional recording studio. You also probably had to hire a gaggle of expensive studio musicians. This made recording pretty much the province of the independently wealthy or, more often, those artists backed by major record labels.

Today, however, any musician can create professional recordings in the comfort of his own home. All you need is a standard-issue personal computer, some cables and microphones, and digital recording software, such as Cubase. This puts recording technology in the hands of virtually every musician, and has helped to fuel the independent music business.

Not that Cubase is new software; it's been around in one form or another since the late 1980s. But it's only recently that increased computing power at affordable prices has enabled the level of recording fidelity that we find today. Those early versions of Cubase (first available on the Atari ST, if anyone can remember that old machine) were really nothing more than MIDI sequencers. Since then, many things have changed, and Cubase has evolved into a full-fledged recording, mixing, and mastering application, complete with its own virtual instruments.

The current version of the program, Cubase 6, builds on the knowledge that Steinberg has acquired from years of experience and user feedback. If you are new to Cubase, you can expect this software to help you through your entire musical creation process. If you are a veteran Cubase user, you will find many of the things you loved and a few new features, as usual, that have made their way into the standard music-producer toolbox over the years. Hopefully, in both cases, this book will help you to get the most out of this great tool.

There's a lot you can do with Cubase 6—more than we can cover in this book, in fact. Steinberg supplies extensive documentation on the installation disc provided with the software, but that requires you to sift through thousands of pages of PDF-format documentation to find the one piece of information you want. For most users, this might seem like an overwhelming task.

To that end, *Cubase 6 Power!* focuses on only the most important and most-used features of the program; we don't waste space (or your time) on those features most readers will never use. And, unlike the official documentation, we cover those features in an easy-to-read, step-by-step format. The focus is on the practical uses of Cubase—how you will use the program in a typical recording project.

Versions Covered

While this book targets the full-featured Cubase 6 version of the program, much of the information and advice also apply to the lesser-featured versions of Cubase Artist 6 and Cubase Elements 6. But since these are trimmed-down versions of the full application, some features described in this book won't apply to those versions. You can find a complete list of feature differences on Steinberg's website.

Likewise, if you're using an older version of the program—Cubase 5 or 4, for example—much of the advice in this book still applies. Many of the specific instructions, however, will differ, as Steinberg has made significant changes to how the program works over the years.

In addition, this book covers both the Windows and Macintosh versions of the program. In reality, it doesn't really matter which platform you're using; the way you use the features and functions are the same in both the PC and Mac worlds. That said, Mac users are strongly encouraged to purchase a two-button mouse; although it is possible to use the Mac alternative Control-click for single-button devices, many of the features available in Cubase are available through context menus, and the second button simply makes them easier and more convenient to access.

How This Book Is Organized

It's important to understand that this book and Cubase itself are tools that will hopefully help you jumpstart your imagination. We can give you paint and a brush and show you creative techniques, but what you do with that is all up to you.

With this in mind, the book is organized into 40 chapters that address specific topics. At the beginning of each chapter, you will find a summary of what you will be learning. These chapters are organized into seven parts that follow a typical production workflow. You can read this book from beginning to end, or you can quickly jump to the topics that interest you the most if you are already familiar with some of the features discussed.

Here's a summary of what you can expect to find:

- **Part I: Setup.** Chapters 1 through 5 help you get started using Cubase 6. In addition to addressing basic concepts related to digital audio recording and MIDI, this section also looks at what needs to be done to connect peripherals to Cubase and to monitor your recordings. In other words, this part covers getting sound in and out of Cubase and making sure your project is properly configured to handle these connections.

- **Part II: Recording.** Chapters 6 through 14 address recording preparations, monitoring setups through the Control Room Mixer, managing the various media in your projects, configuring and using physical and virtual instruments, and, most important, recording both audio and MIDI data. We also discuss the ReWire application, plug-in insert effects, audio content management through the Pool, and overdubbing techniques.

- **Part III: Navigation.** Chapters 15 through 18 address project navigation and similar functions, along with the most common operations performed in Cubase's main interface, the Project window. In addition, we take a close look at the components and controls provided in Cubase's audio and MIDI tracks—both essential to almost every Cubase project.

- **Part IV: Editing.** Chapters 19 through 27 address editing environments outside the Project window: the Sample Editor for audio events, and the In-Place, Key, and Drum Editors for MIDI events. We also explore a number of editing features and commands found in the MIDI and Audio menus, as well as Cubase's new features for recording and editing vocal and drum tracks.

- **Part V: Arranging.** Chapters 28 to 31 address techniques and tools associated with organizing your content and arranging your compositions. Specifically, you'll learn how to rearrange the events in a project, use Cubase's Arranger Track to build a project non-linearly, synchronize and change tempo within a project, and create beat- and loop-based recordings.

- **Part VI: Mixing and Mastering.** Chapters 32 to 38 are all about the final stages of your project —mixing and mastering your final recording. These chapters show you how to use the Mixer panel, work with plug-in effect tracks and send effects, and create group channels for submixes. This part of the book also investigates Cubase's automation features, surround mixing, equalization, and audio export options.

- **Part VII: Managing.** The final two chapters (39 and 40) look at ways to customize Cubase to better fit your working style, as well as techniques that make a project more resource-efficient.

Keeping the Book's Content Current

Everyone involved with this book has worked hard to make it complete and accurate. But as we all know, technology changes rapidly, and a small number of errors may have crept in besides. If you find any errors, have suggestions for future editions, or have questions about the book or other topics, please contact Michael at cubase@molehillgroup.com. You're also invited to check out Michael's website at www.molehillgroup.com for any corrections or updates to this book—as well as to find out more about Michael's other books and projects.

Setup

1 Introducing Cubase

Digital recording has forever changed the music industry. Instead of spending big bucks to rent a large recording studio and hire professional studio musicians to record the basic tracks, musicians today can record a song or an entire album in their homes on a shoestring budget. The results can be every bit as professional as what used to be achieved with pro-studio recording—or sound horribly amateurish, if you don't do everything right.

What do you need to get started with digital recording today? It's a short list: a personal computer, a couple of monitor speakers or a good set of keyboards, a MIDI keyboard or electric guitar, and a microphone or two. Plus a quality digital recording and mixing application, of course—such as Steinberg's Cubase 6.

Here's a summary of what you will learn in this chapter:

- What Cubase is and what it does

- How Cubase evolved through the years

- What's new in Cubase 6

What Is Cubase?

Cubase 6 is a digital audio workstation (DAW) program that enables you to create your own professional audio recordings. But what does that mean—and how can you use Cubase for your recording projects?

You use Cubase to perform all the discrete steps involved in a typical recording project:

- **Recording.** This is the actual recording of musicians singing and playing their instruments—whether those instruments are acoustic (acoustic guitars, piano, trumpet, violin, voice), electric (electric piano, electric guitar, electric bass), or electronic (synthesizers and samplers). Cubase enables you to record digital audio or MIDI performances.

- **Editing.** This is the changing of recorded tracks to make them more appropriate for the final music release. You can cut sections of music, splice together multiple takes, remove or fix wrong notes, fix errant pitch and erratic tempo, and so forth.

- **Mixing.** This is the process of blending all your recorded tracks together into a single recording. You'll need to adjust volume levels between tracks, add effects (such as reverb), and generally work to make all the tracks work together as a whole.

- **Mastering.** This final process readies your final mix into a form suitable for physical or digital distribution.

You can think of Cubase, then, as a musician's toolbox with all the tools necessary to record, edit, mix, and master audio and MIDI information. But the Cubase we know today is much changed from the initial version of the program; from its beginnings as a simple MIDI sequencer, Cubase has undergone many transformations.

A Brief History of Cubase

The history of Cubase goes all the way back to 1984 and a sequencing program called Steinberg Pro 16. Created by German programmers Karl Steinberg and Manfred Rürup, Pro 16 was available on floppy diskette for the popular Commodore 64 and Apple II computers of the day. A newer version, Pro 24, was released a year later with more advanced features.

By 1989, Pro 16/24 evolved into the program called Cubase and gained more advanced groove quantizing, sound editing, and scoring features. Interestingly, Steinberg intended to call the program Cubit, but changed the name due to copyright reasons.

With the 1996 release of Cubase VST, Steinberg's program expanded beyond MIDI sequencing to add traditional audio recording and editing so that regular musical instruments and microphones could be recorded. With this major addition, Cubase became a full audio production tool, contributing in many ways to the development and democratization of the creative process that lies inside every musician. Cubase VST also introduced Virtual Studio Technology (VST) instruments, which made it possible to replace hardware devices with their software equivalents; you could now play a musical pattern on a keyboard synthesizer, for example, and have that pattern assigned the sound of a flute or violin or some other virtual instrument.

The third major version of the Cubase program was introduced in 2002. Cubase SX was based on Nuendo, Steinberg's professional post-production software. This version of Cubase dramatically changed the way the program operated, but brought with it more sophisticated audio and MIDI editing. It also added real-time audio stretching and the ability to adjust a track's tempo.

Further small upgrades to the program have been released since Cubase SX on pretty much an every-other-year basis. The latest version of the program, Cubase 6, was introduced in 2010, adding a number of new and useful features to the application. It's this latest version that I discuss in this book.

Understanding the Cubase Toolset

Cubase is a robust recording, mixing, and mastering environment for use by both professional and hobbyist recordists. In formal terms, that means Cubase is a digital audio workstation, or DAW application, offering a variety of tools for the following recording and editing tasks:

- **Audio and MIDI recording environments.** Cubase records and plays back both digital audio and MIDI. It also records and plays back any automation (called *parameter automation events*) you use while recording a performance. The program also includes a studio control room–type of interface, which makes recording live musicians and performing overdubs easier than ever.

- **Audio and MIDI editing environments.** Once audio or MIDI is recorded, you can edit these events using one of many editing windows.

- **Virtual instruments.** If you don't own external sound modules, Cubase provides the technology necessary to transform your computer into a "virtual instrument" through VST instruments. VST instruments are software synthesizers installed on your computer that use your audio interface to generate their sounds. You no longer need to purchase expensive synthesizer modules, because they are part of your virtual studio environment. Cubase 6 includes eight of these virtual instruments.

- **Effects.** Cubase allows you to use its built-in audio and MIDI effects, add third-party effects, and even connect external effect devices. Effects allow you to process audio in a number of ways, such as controlling the dynamic and harmonic content of audio through compressors, filters, or other types of signal processing. Cubase integrates this potential within its Virtual Studio Technology and gives you the necessary tools to control every aspect effects can provide. Cubase 6 includes 60 of these real-time audio effects, including the new VST Amp Rack guitar tone suite.

- **Mixing environment.** While you're recording, editing, and manipulating MIDI and audio events, you can mix every track by using a virtual mixer not unlike its hardware counterpart. This virtual mixer accommodates as many inputs, output busses, effects, MIDI tracks, virtual instrument tracks, groups, and audio tracks as your project needs. Then, you can automate your mix easily and create complex mixes without leaving your computer. You can also connect third-party hardware controllers to get a more interesting tactile experience during your mixing process.

- **Multimedia production environment.** You can synchronize your Cubase audio project for use in multimedia and video productions, making it a great post-production environment for today's producers. Cubase now supports more import and export formats than ever, making it easy to prepare content for the Web, as well as for high-quality surround sound audio and video productions—including TV, movie, and video game soundtracks.

What's New in Cubase 6

Cubase 6 is an evolution, not a revolution, from previous versions of the program. There are several new and evolved features in this version of Cubase, including the following:

- **Improved audio editing.** Perhaps the most important development in Cubase 6 is in the way it enables you to edit your digital audio files. Cubase 6 features intelligent transient detection, which provides for easier editing of drum tracks. In addition, you get advanced tempo detection, multi-track audio quantization, and more.

- **Redesigned graphical user interface.** The Cubase 6 workspace is cleaner and more intuitive, which makes it easier to work with. Color and contrast optimization help to minimize eyestrain and viewing fatigue, while also helping you distinguish between what's important and what's less so in a project. The main toolbar has also been reorganized, with several options and controls renamed, all with an eye toward making the program easier to understand and use.

- **Lane Tracks.** The new Lane Track concept allows for ultrafast multi-take recording. Cubase records a separate Lane Track for each take; you can then swipe across the best parts of each take to automatically create a master take.

- **Track Edit Groups.** The new Track Edit Groups tool allows multi-track editing with a single click. Related tracks are tied together so they can be edited at the same time.

- **VST Expression 2.** The revised Note Expression tool takes MIDI editing to the next level, making it easier to assign, create, and edit multiple controller values on a single-note level.

- **VST Amp Rack.** This new VST effect is a suite of guitar amplifiers and effects, delivering a comprehensive collection of guitar tones at the press of a button.

- **HALion Sonic SE.** This is a streamlined version of HALion Sonic, Steinberg's premiere VST workstation, with more than 900 production-ready virtual instruments and sounds.

- **LoopMash 2.** This is a revised version of the popular VST instrument used for creating and remixing loop-based recordings, with more than 20 new MIDI-controllable live and slice-based effects.

Understanding the Different Versions of Cubase 6

As noted, Cubase 6 is the latest version of Steinberg's digital audio workstation application. But there are actually three different versions of Cubase 6, with slightly different feature sets:

- **Cubase 6** is the flagship member of the Cubase family. This is the fully featured version of Cubase, with the largest number of included plug-ins, virtual instruments, inputs and outputs, and the like. Cubase 6 is priced at $499.99.

- **Cubase Artist 6** is a slightly less fully featured version of the basic Cubase program. It does everything that Cubase 6 does, but with fewer plug-ins, virtual instruments, available tracks, and such. It also lacks the Control Room feature found in the main Cubase 6 program, but otherwise functions almost identically to the higher-priced Cubase 6, which makes it ideal for musicians to use in their project studios. Cubase Artist 6 is priced at $249.99.

- **Cubase Elements 6** is a "lite" or entry-level version of the Cubase program. This version of Cubase is limited to just 48 audio tracks per project, whereas Cubase Artist 6 has 64 available tracks, and Cubase 6 offers an unlimited number of tracks. The number of available inputs and outputs, VST instrument slots, FX return channels, and the like is also limited; this version also has less recording functionality and flexibility, and it includes fewer plug-ins and virtual instruments. At the time of this writing, the price for Cubase Elements 6 is $99.99.

You use most of the same techniques for recording, mixing, and mastering across all three versions of Cubase—knowing, of course, that the lower-priced versions of the program lack some of the features found in the higher-priced versions. So, although this book covers the full-featured Cubase 6 version, most of the advice and instructions offered here will also work with Cubase Artist 6 and Cubase Elements 6.

2 Understanding Cubase Recording Technology

Cubase accommodates two similar-but-different types of recording—the recording of traditional audio tracks and the recording of MIDI tracks. There's a lot of technology involved in both types of recording and a lot of equipment to deal with. In fact, one of the biggest challenges most musicians face when starting their journey into the music production arena is understanding how they can record performances in Cubase.

Even though Cubase 6 is surprisingly simple to start using, at least on a basic level, it's easy to get lost in the shuffle if you don't understand the technology and terminology involved with a typical recording project. This chapter lays down some of these issues and describes the concepts behind such terms as ports, inputs, outputs, and channels.

Here's a summary of what you will learn in this chapter:

- A brief introduction to digital audio and MIDI fundamentals

- How sound is digitized and what the parameters are that affect the quality of your digital audio recording

- How MIDI and digital audio are handled inside Cubase

- How MIDI tracks, ports, channels, inputs, and outputs function

- What audio tracks, channels, inputs, and outputs are

- What the differences are between windows, dialog boxes, and panels

- What the Project window components are

A Brief Overview of Digital Audio

Musical instruments and voices used to be recorded in analog fashion, on acetate discs or magnetic tape or even thin wires. Today, however, music is recorded digitally—that is, the analog sounds generated by the instruments and voices are converted into digital signals. Understanding how analog sound is transformed into digital audio will put you in a better position to predict and control the results of your Cubase recordings—and help you produce better results.

9

What Is Analog Sound?

A musical instrument vibrates when played. Examples of this include the string of a violin, the skin of a drum, and even the cone of a loudspeaker. This vibration is transferred to the molecules of the air, which carry the sound to our ears. Receiving the sound, our eardrums vibrate, moving back and forth anywhere between 20 and 20,000 times every second. A sound's rate of vibration is called its *frequency* and is measured in Hertz. (The human range of hearing is typically from 20 Hz to 20 kHz (kilohertz).) If the frequency of the vibration is slow, we hear a low note; if the frequency is fast, we hear a high note. If the vibration is gentle, making the air move back and forth only a little, we hear a soft sound. This movement is known as *amplitude*. If the amplitude is high, making the windows rattle, we hear a loud sound!

If you were to graph air movement against time, you could draw a picture of the sound. This is called a *waveform*. You can see a very simple waveform at low amplitude on the left in Figure 2.1. The middle waveform is the same sound, but much louder (higher amplitude). Finally, the waveform on the right is a musical instrument that contains harmonics—a wider range of simultaneous frequencies. In all of these waveforms, there is one constant: The horizontal axis always represents time, and the vertical axis always represents amplitude.

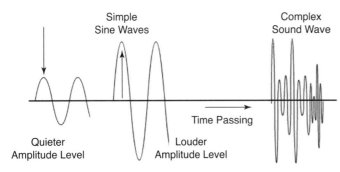

Figure 2.1 The vertical axis represents the amplitude of a waveform, and the horizontal axis represents time.

Complex Waveforms: In the real world, sounds don't consist of just one frequency, but of many frequencies mixed together at different levels of amplitude (loudness). This is what makes a musical sound interesting. Despite its complexity, every waveform can be represented by a graph. At any given time, the waveform has a measurable amplitude. If we can capture this "picture" and then reproduce it, we've succeeded in our goal of recording sound.

The second dimension of sound is *amplitude*, or the intensity of molecule displacement. When many molecules are moved, the sound will be louder. Inversely, if few molecules are moved in space, the sound is softer. Amplitude is measured in volts because this displacement of molecules creates energy. When the energy is positive, it pushes molecules forward, making the line in Figure 2.1 move upward. When the energy is negative, it pushes the molecules backward, making the line go downward. When the line is near the center, it means that fewer molecules are being moved around. That's why the sound appears to be quieter.

Space is a third dimension to sound. This dimension does not have its own axis because it is usually the result of amplitude variations through time, but the space will affect the waveform itself. In other words, the space will affect the amplitude of a sound through time. This will be important when we talk about effects and microphone placement when recording or mixing digital audio. But suffice it to say now that the environment in which sound occurs has a great influence on how we will perceive the sound.

What Is Digital Audio?

Where analog sound is a continuous variation of the molecules of air traveling through space, creating a sound's energy, digital sound consists of a discrete— non-continuous—sampling of this variation. In digital audio, there is no such thing as continuous—only the illusion of continuum.

Digital audio works on the theory that a wave form can be reproduced if one samples the variation of sound at least twice in every period of that waveform. A *period* is a full cycle of the sound, measured in Hertz (Hz). So, if you have a sound at a frequency of 20 Hz, you need at least 40 samples per second to reproduce it. The value captured by each audio sample is the voltage of that sound at a specific point in time.

How Sampling Works

In the analog world, amplitude is measured as a voltage value. In the digital world, this value is quantified and stored as a number. In the computer world, numbers are stored as binary memory units called *bits*—and the more bits you have, the longer this number will be. Longer numbers are also synonymous with more precise representations of the original voltage values the digital audio was meant to store. In other words, every digital audio sample stores the value of the amplitude (or voltage) as a binary number. The more bits per sample, the more values you can represent.

Because digital audio records in discrete units rather than smooth curves, recordings literally jump from one digital value to the next. This creates noise-like artifacts, a kind of digital distortion known as *quantization error*, which is not something you want in your sound. So, the more values you have to represent different amplitudes, the more closely your sound will resemble the original analog signal in terms of amplitude variation.

The sampling *frequency* (measured in Hertz) represents the number of times a voltage value is recorded each second, using bits to store this (voltage) value once it has been converted into a binary number. As with amplitude values in bits, the sampling frequency greatly affects the quality of your sound—in particular because it directly affects the highest frequencies that can be captured and played back. Because most audio components, such as amplifiers and speakers, can reproduce sounds ranging from 20 Hz to 20 kHz, the sampling frequency standard for compact disc digital audio was fixed at 44.1 kHz—a little bit more than twice the highest frequency produced by your monitoring system.

The first thing you notice when you change the sampling frequency of a sound is that with higher sampling frequencies—or greater numbers of samples per second—you get a sharper, crisper sound with better definition and fewer artifacts. With lower sampling frequencies (fewer samples), you get a duller, mushier, and less-defined sound. Why is this? Because you need twice as many samples as there are frequencies in your sound, higher sampling frequencies allow you to capture higher harmonic components in the source audio—and that's where the sound qualities mentioned previously are found. When you reduce the sampling frequency, you also reduce the frequency bandwidth captured by the digital audio recording system. If your sampling frequency is extremely low, you not only lose harmonics, but fundamentals as well. And this will change the tonal quality of the sound altogether.

About 32-Bit and Floating-Point Recording

Digital audio recordings, like analog audio recordings, are not all created equal. Recording with higher digital resolutions and superior equipment will allow you to create better-sounding results; that's because the higher the recording resolution, the more accurate the resulting sound. To that end, all professional audio hardware available today supports at least 16-bit resolution. Better-quality audio interfaces also support 20- and 24-bit resolutions.

With 16-bit resolution, the vertical steps corresponding to voltage values are few and far between. In the 24-bit resolution, there are many more steps than in 16-bit recordings. In 32-bit, the binary word is twice as long; instead of having 65,535 steps, you have more than four billion steps. This dramatically increases the dynamic range (the range between the loudest sound before digital clipping and the minimum level) of a digital audio recording. On the minus side, it also increases the hard disk space required to record digital audio as well as processing time when applying changes, such as adding an effect to a sound. Ultimately, to record using precisions higher than 24-bit resolutions, you'll need a fast computer, a fast hard drive, and lots of memory, both in disk space and in RAM.

Up until recently, recording audio was limited to fixed integer values, as mentioned previously. With *floating-point* recording, the computer adds a decimal value and can move that decimal point wherever it needs it to get greater precision. The steps in the digital recording are not fixed, but rather variable points that adjust themselves according to the needs of the audio waveform.

It's important to know that the bit depth (resolution) of the recording's final mix does not have to be the same as the recorded tracks. Cubase allows you to select a different format to mix down your tracks when you are finished working on them; you can record at a higher quality and then mix down to the lower quality used in compact discs and online downloads.

You see, Cubase records in a format that is superior to CD or digital download formats. As a rule of thumb, always work with the best quality your entire system supports (all devices involved in the recording process especially), and decrease the quality to a more common 44.1-kHz, 16-bit format only when rendering a CD- or online-compatible mix. (Cubase itself uses 32-bit processing for all its operations; you mix down to 16 bits later in the process.) As long as your hardware and software can handle it, go for it. But remember this: Audio CD format supports only 44.1-kHz, 16-bit stereo files. So, if you don't convert your audio beforehand, either in Cubase or in another audio-conversion application, you won't be able to write it in audio CD format unless your CD-writing software specifically offers tools for converting source audio files from higher resolutions.

Likewise with digital downloads; set the audio quality too high, and you'll create files that are simply too large for today's music download services. You need to convert Cubase's high-quality audio to lower-quality compressed files, such as those in the MP3 format, for optimal downloading convenience.

What Is MIDI?

As noted in the previous chapter, Cubase was initially conceived as a MIDI sequencer named Pro 16. The latest version of Cubase retains this MIDI functionality, along with the ability to record traditional instruments and voices.

Data, Not Notes—How MIDI Works

MIDI is an acronym that stands for Musical Instrument Digital Interface. As such, this interface provides a way to digitally represent musical notes.

With traditional audio recording, you're recording actual sounds—those waveforms that travel through the air and are captured by the microphone (or in the case of direct-injected instruments, the waveforms generated by the instrument's electrical impulses). MIDI, in contrast, doesn't record sounds. Instead, MIDI records computerized instructions. These instructions tell any computer what sounds to generate in terms of frequency (musical pitch), velocity (volume level), and duration (note length).

MIDI, then, is a communication system used to transmit information from one MIDI-compatible device to another. These devices can include musical instruments (keyboard controllers, samplers, synthesizers, sound modules, drum machines) and computers or other hardware devices, such as MIDI control surfaces or synchronizers.

The key to understanding what MIDI does and how it works is to recognize that MIDI transmits performance *data*, not sound. You can think of MIDI as an old player piano using a paper roll. The holes in the paper roll marked the moments at which the musician played the notes, but the holes themselves were not the sounds. MIDI information is transmitted in much the same way, capturing the performance of the musician but not the sound of the instrument on which he or she played.

To hear the notes that MIDI data signifies, you will always need some kind of sound module that can reproduce the musical events recorded as MIDI data. This sound module could be an external synthesizer, a sampler, a virtual synthesizer inside your computer software, or even the synthesizer chip on your audio interface. This is precisely one of the types of information Cubase allows you to work with—recording a musical performance through your computer, using a keyboard to trigger MIDI events, and using Cubase as the recording device *and* the sound generator, thus creating a virtual paper roll inside the application.

Anatomy of a MIDI Message

MIDI transmits digital data in the form of *messages*. MIDI messages are sent at a rate of 31,250 bps (*bits per second*); this is called MIDI's *baud rate*. Because MIDI is transferred through a serial port, it sends information one bit at a time. Every MIDI message uses 10 bits of data (8 bits for the information and 2 bits for error correction), which means that MIDI sends about 3,906 bytes of data every second (31,250 bps divided by 8 bits). If you compare this to the 176,400-byte (or 172.3-kilobyte) transfer rate that digital audio requires when recording or playing back CD-quality sound without compression, MIDI may seem very slow. But, in reality, it's fast enough for what it needs to transfer. At this speed, you can transmit approximately 500 MIDI note events per second.

MIDI sends or receives the following information:

- Data related to the performance being recorded. This includes when a note starts and how long it lasts, as well as the velocity of the note—how loud or soft it sounds.

- Parameters for these actions, such as the channel settings. Each MIDI cable or port can support up to 16 channels of information, much like having up to 16 separate instruments playing at once.

- Wheels and pedal controls, such as pitch bend and modulation wheels or levers, sustain pedals, and switch pedals.

- Key pressures of pressed keys, also known as *aftertouch* information, sent by the controller keyboard or by the sequencer to a sound module. Note that not all keyboards support this function, but when they do, the information is sent as MIDI data.

- Program changes or patch changes, as well as sound bank selections.

- Synchronization for MIDI devices that have built-in timing clocks. These timing clocks may determine the desired tempo of a drum machine, for example. Through synchronization, MIDI devices can also follow or trigger other devices or applications, such as sequencers or drum machines, making sure each one stays in sync with the "master" MIDI clock.

- System Exclusive messages used to alter synthesizer parameters and control the transport of System Exclusive–compatible multi-track recorders.

- MIDI Timecode or MTC, which is a way for MIDI-compatible devices to lock to an SMPTE device—a translation of SMPTE timecode into something MIDI devices can understand.

MIDI Connectors

MIDI devices come in many flavors, shapes, and sizes. Manufacturers have adapted the MIDI format to fit today's needs and market. Earlier devices would typically have either two or three MIDI-connector plugs: In and Out; or In, Out, and Thru. Two-port configurations were reserved for computer-related hardware (see the left side of Figure 2.2), as well as software-based synthesizers because the output connector could be switched within a software application. Soft-switching allows users to transform the MIDI output into a MIDI Thru connection.

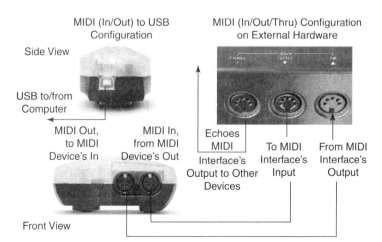

Figure 2.2 On the left is an example of a two-connector configuration typical of a USB-to-MIDI interface for computers. On the right is a typical three-connector configuration found on keyboards and sound modules.

On most newer hardware devices, a single USB port is used in place of the two (more expensive to produce) MIDI connectors. As a result, many devices now communicate MIDI events to and from a computer workstation using a USB connector, which can be configured via the computer's operating system.

MIDI Out

MIDI does not transmit sound over cables the way audio components in a sound system do. Instead, MIDI sends a message that contains an identifier portion and its associated parameters. For example, when you play a note, the identifier would be that this is a "note on" event, whose parameters would be the note number for the key you pressed, plus a velocity parameter indicating how hard you hit that note.

As you play on a MIDI keyboard or other type of MIDI controller, the internal processor in that device examines your performance, converting it into a stream of MIDI events that represents your actions. That information is sent out over the instrument's MIDI output to other synthesizers that reproduce the performance using their own sounds—and/or to Cubase in order to be recorded as part of your project.

A device's MIDI output will not echo (retransmit) any MIDI events received at its MIDI input. If you want to do this, you need to use the MIDI Thru connector, which is described later in the chapter.

MIDI In

Many freestanding MIDI synthesizers can be viewed as two machines in one (see Figure 2.3):

- **A sound module.** The electronics that actually produce the sounds in a MIDI device, as directed by the onboard processor.

- **A MIDI interface.** The computer processor that monitors the keyboard, front panel displays, and program memory to send events to the sound module or out through the device's MIDI ports.

The MIDI input receives incoming MIDI information and sends it to the instrument's processor, which will act upon it in much the same way as a performance on the instrument itself, such as pressing a key to play notes. It makes no difference to the sound-making parts of a synthesizer whether the command to play notes comes from a key press on the instrument's local keyboard or as a command from other MIDI devices and programs.

When you are working with a program that offers MIDI sequencing, as does Cubase, it is recommended that you set your MIDI instrument's local switch parameter to off, as both Cubase and the local keyboard would be sending MIDI information to the sound module portion of your instrument if it were connected to Cubase through MIDI.

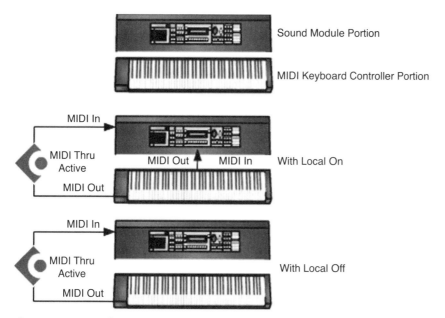

Sound Module Portion

MIDI Keyboard Controller Portion

With Local On

With Local Off

Figure 2.3 Configuring your keyboard's MIDI input.

When the local switch is enabled, your instrument plays sounds directly when you press keys on its keyboard; when the local switch is set to off, the instrument responds only to incoming events on its MIDI In port. In other words, setting it to off will disconnect the bridge between the actual MIDI playing surface (the keyboard) and the sound module part that allows you to hear the keyboard's sounds as you play the keys.

When using Cubase, you will use your keyboard or other MIDI controller to send MIDI to the host computer through the instrument's MIDI Out port. As Cubase records the information you play it can also send it back out to your keyboard's MIDI In connector. If your keyboard's MIDI setting isn't set to Local Off, the sound module portion of your instrument would play the sounds twice—once when you play the notes on your keyboard, and once when Cubase sends the MIDI information back to it. Note that this precaution also applies to MIDI controllers that serve as a tactile mixing interface when mixing in Cubase.

On the other hand, if you have a sound module without a keyboard, you will not need to take this precaution because there is no MIDI being sent to the device's MIDI input besides what is connected to this input.

MIDI Thru

MIDI data can be chained from one device to another. As such, the MIDI Thru port retransmits the MIDI data received at the MIDI input of a device so that it can be received by another device in a chain.

When putting together a MIDI-based music system, know that anything played on a MIDI controller goes only to the MIDI Out port and not to the MIDI Thru port. This third port is very useful when you want to avoid MIDI loops when hooking together your MIDI devices. (A MIDI loop occurs when MIDI information is sent from one instrument to another and ends up being routed back to the MIDI In initial instrument; this causes the instrument to play each note twice and, in some cases, causes a feedback of MIDI data that could potentially cause your sequencer to crash.)

If you have a MIDI patch bay or a multiport MIDI interface—MIDI devices with multiple MIDI inputs and outputs—you are better off using a separate MIDI output for each connected device, thus reducing the amount of information flowing through a single MIDI cable. Each MIDI port in a MIDI setup sends or receives up to 16 MIDI channels. For example, if you are using a MIDI interface with four MIDI ports, you will have four MIDI inputs and four MIDI outputs, and you will have independent control over 64 MIDI channels. If you do not own a multiport or MIDI patch bay, daisy-chaining MIDI devices using the MIDI Thru socket is your best bet (see Figure 2.4).

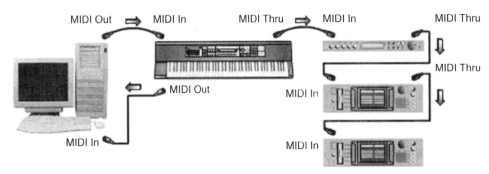

Figure 2.4 Using the MIDI Thru connector to hook together multiple MIDI devices.

Understanding Audio Connections

An audio connection creates a link between your audio interface's physical inputs and outputs (for microphones and other instruments, such as guitars and keyboards) and the Cubase program. Before sound can reach Cubase, it needs to enter your computer through an audio interface. This audio interface, typically an outboard hardware box, is then identified by your computer's operating system through an ASIO driver or, in the Mac OS, an optional Core Audio driver. This driver is what Cubase uses to identify the inputs and outputs of the audio interface installed on your system.

ASIO Technology: ASIO is the acronym for Audio Stream Input/Output, a technology developed by Steinberg that allows audio hardware to process and synchronize inputs and introduces the least amount of latency, or delay, between the inputs and the outputs of the audio hardware. You will find additional information about ASIO drivers in Chapter 3, "Setting Up Peripherals."

When dealing with audio connections, there's a lot of technical terminology to deal with. Let's take a look at the technology and terminology involved, starting outside your computer and moving upstream into the Cubase program.

- The audio *device port* is where you make the physical connection to your audio interface—where you plug in your bass guitar, mixer, microphone, synth, or whatever. A device port is typically an input or output on your audio interface device. How many device ports your interface has depends on the model itself and the number of physical ports it offers. You will need a minimum of one mono input and one mono output to get sound into Cubase and out of it, but if you plan to record live musicians, additional inputs are recommended. (For example, if you want to record eight instruments at the same time, you'll need an audio interface with eight device ports—one for each instrument.)

- These device ports are identified by the *audio device driver* installed on your system. The driver lets you tell Cubase which audio device to use. Once Cubase knows which audio device to use, it then displays the available ports mentioned previously. There may be several types of drivers on your computer, but on both Windows and Mac computers, Cubase works best with ASIO drivers.

- *Busses* are created to group together ports on an audio device to create mono, stereo, or, in Cubase 6, surround recordings. If necessary, you can change the name of a bus to give it meaning inside your own studio setup. By selecting a mono input bus when recording, for example, you decide that the content will be recorded in mono. You can create multiple bus configurations using the same ports on your audio interface for different purposes, reducing the need for a complex patch bay to change how ports are used by Cubase.

- An *audio channel* is created in Cubase whenever an audio, effect, VST instrument, or group track is created. The audio channel offers controls over several audio-related and routing parameters. When you want to record audio on an audio channel, for example, you need to select which input bus to use as its source. The bus selection depends on where the sound source you want to record is actually connected. To monitor during recording, or to play it back, you need to assign the audio output from that channel to an output bus.

By creating connections within Cubase, you can use the same physical connections in multiple configurations; for example, if your hardware audio interface offers four audio inputs, you can either use inputs 1 and 2 as a single stereo input bus or as two mono input busses. You could also create an external effect bus, using an additional output to send a signal to an external reverb or other device and two inputs to receive the stereo signal back from the effect device.

Bus configurations are saved with each Cubase project file, and you can also save them as templates to be recalled later and used when creating new recording projects. If you find yourself using certain configurations each time you begin a new project, then you can simply set the connections once at the beginning of a project; Cubase will save these connection configurations along with the project file so that you don't need to repeat the configuration every time you open the project.

Let's examine these items in more detail.

Input Busses

An input bus is a bridge between the physical inputs of an audio interface and the source for the audio that you want to record onto an audio track (represented by a channel in the Mixer). By selecting an input bus, you also decide whether the audio track will record mono, stereo, or surround content, depending on how you configured this input bus in the first place. You can also adjust the input level coming from the input bus.

Output Busses

Output busses enable you to monitor the content of an audio track through one or several audio outputs on an audio interface and/or send the signal to an external hardware effect or a headphone amplifier. As with input busses, you can create multiple output bus connections, depending on your needs. You need a minimum of one master stereo output bus, but you can create as many output busses as you need.

Audio Track

An audio track in Cubase is similar to an audio track in a traditional multi-track audio recorder. It has, however, the advantage of being mono, stereo, or multichannel to support surround sound, depending on the configuration of the input/output audio busses you choose for it. You can create as many audio tracks as you need in Cubase. That said, there will be practical limits related to your computer's speed, disk access, or memory capacity, so working within these limits will be your only concern.

Your project's settings determine the audio properties of audio tracks (record format in bits per sample and sample rate in Hertz); however, the number of audio channels each track will support is determined when it is created. Cubase will ask you which configuration you want to use: mono, stereo, or one of many multichannel setups. This will ultimately influence your available choices for assigning input and output busses on this track later. For example, if you want to create a vocal track, you would typically create a mono track and then select a mono input bus.

As a rule of thumb, you should:

- Record mono signals on mono tracks using a mono input bus, and then monitor through either a mono or stereo bus.

- Record stereo signals on stereo tracks using a stereo input bus, and then monitor through a stereo bus.

■ Record multichannel signals on equivalent multichannel audio tracks, using the same type of input bus, and monitor through the same type of multichannel output bus.

Audio Channels

Whenever you create an audio track, an audio channel is also created. This audio channel is visible in the Mixer (see the Strings channel in Figure 2.5), as well as in the Inspector area of a selected track in the Project window under the Channel section (shown in Figure 2.6).

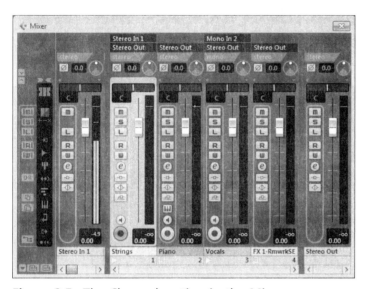

Figure 2.5 The Channel section in the Mixer.

Figure 2.6 The Channel section in the Inspector area of the Project window.

An audio channel in Cubase is similar to a mixer channel on a hardware mixer—with some notable exceptions:

- If you set a track to record or play stereo or multichannel events, a single mixer channel will display information for all the subchannels that comprise its signal path. On hardware mixers, stereo channels often require two channel strips.

- Adding an FX channel or a Group channel track also creates its own channel in the Mixer. Obviously, this can't happen in a hardware mixer.

Because this is a virtual mixing environment, the Mixer will change as you create more tracks in a project. Unlike with hardware mixers, you're not limited to a fixed number of tracks.

Understanding MIDI Connections

Although MIDI and audio handle recording quite differently, the two technologies follow similar philosophies regarding connections. That is, connecting hardware and software devices to record or play back MIDI is similar to how you connect audio devices.

With audio recording, you have an audio signal connected to an audio port that's associated with an input bus assigned as the source for a track; with MIDI recording, you have MIDI events coming from a MIDI port on the selected MIDI input channel for a MIDI track, which plays through a MIDI instrument. The MIDI instrument, of course, can be either a software-based virtual instrument or an external device (such as a MIDI keyboard) connected to the selected physical MIDI output for the track.

MIDI Ports

A MIDI port is a hardware (physical) or software (virtual) point of entry or exit for your MIDI data. The number of physical MIDI ports that will be available is determined by your computer's MIDI interface. This might be a standalone MIDI interface box or MIDI connectors included on an audio interface device. If your interface has four MIDI inputs and four MIDI outputs, you will have four MIDI ports available for this interface in Cubase.

On the other hand, if you are using Cubase to send or receive MIDI information to or from another application inside your computer, you will also be using *virtual* MIDI ports. Why virtual? Because they do not require additional hardware. This is the case when you are using VST instruments (which will be discussed further in Chapter 10, "Using VST and MIDI Instruments") or when using separate, third-party programs in conjunction with Cubase, such as Reason, Ableton Live, or others. Whenever you load virtual instruments, they create virtual ports that can be addressed in Cubase much like external MIDI instruments that are plugged into your computer through an actual MIDI port. The virtual ports will, in other words, allow you to receive MIDI from these applications or send MIDI to them.

The MIDI port determines which physical or virtual MIDI socket the events on a MIDI track are coming from and going to. Each MIDI port can carry up to 16 independently addressable MIDI channels.

View/change a MIDI track's input and output port settings:

1.   Select the MIDI track you want to view in the Inspector, as shown in Figure 2.7.

2.   To view/change input settings, click the MIDI Input Routing field in the Inspector, then select the appropriate port from the list.

3.   To view/change output settings, click the Instrument field in the Inspector, then select the appropriate device from the list.

Figure 2.7 Accessing the MIDI port settings.

Each MIDI track has its own MIDI input and output port settings. The available MIDI input ports that appear in your MIDI Input Routing field depend on which ports that are currently set as active in Cubase's MIDI Device Setup window. You can record MIDI from multiple MIDI sources directly in your project as long as you have a MIDI input device, such as a keyboard or other MIDI controller, connected to these input ports. The MIDI output can then be sent to various MIDI or VST instruments.

MIDI Channel

Each MIDI port will support up to 16 simultaneous MIDI channels. The channel used by a MIDI device connected to the MIDI input has little effect over the result, unless the MIDI track's channel setting is set to Any, which implies that incoming MIDI events are re-transmitted to any channels at the output. As a result, incoming signals coming on channel 2, for example, would be re-transmitted on channel 2 as well. Otherwise, the MIDI track's channel setting re-transmits the events through the channel number you choose.

It is the MIDI output channel you assign to the track that determines how the incoming MIDI data is routed and which sound is applied. For example, suppose you have connected a multitimbral instrument to the MIDI output port of this track. A multitimbral instrument can play one sound per MIDI channel. So you might configure a piano sound on channel 1 of this instrument, a guitar on channel 2, and a bass on channel 3. If you change the output MIDI channel on the piano track to channel 2, a guitar sound will play what the piano was previously playing.

Once your MIDI channel is selected, you can assign to it any preset sound (sometimes called a *patch*). This type of audio preset is merely a reference to a particular instrument sound, such as a bass or a trumpet. When you assign a preset, the MIDI signals are sent to the selected instrument or sound.

Each MIDI channel playing over a device or virtual instrument plug-in has the capacity to play one MIDI program at a time. You can change the preset along the way, but you can have only one patch or preset assigned to that channel at a time. In other words, you can have up to 16 sounds/presets/MIDI devices playing simultaneously on one MIDI port.

If you run out of MIDI channels for one MIDI port, you will need to use another MIDI port to play the MIDI events. Each virtual instrument loaded into a project will create its own virtual MIDI port, so running out of MIDI channels because of MIDI events is unlikely. It might become an issue when you are using MIDI controllers that require several MIDI channels to transfer control data through a MIDI port.

Whenever the channel is set to Any, the MIDI channel assignment is determined by either the channel information recorded on the track or the channel information being sent by the input device connected to your MIDI interface, such as a MIDI keyboard or other controller, for example. It's common to send MIDI performance data to multiple MIDI channels simultaneously, especially with guitar and drum set controllers. This enables you, for example, to create a "fatter" guitar or drum sound by having multiple instruments sound the same notes. In this instance, MIDI channel Any setting is the appropriate choice.

MIDI Track

A MIDI track contains MIDI events for a single MIDI port. When you play on a MIDI controller (such as a keyboard), it sends out MIDI events on a MIDI channel that is recorded into a MIDI track. Before recording a MIDI part, you assign a MIDI channel and program number to the MIDI track to get the appropriate sound at the output, as mentioned previously. (You can also reassign the MIDI channel and program number after the track has been recorded; the notes played remain the same, but the output device changes.)

Each track has its own MIDI input and output port settings, as well as its channel setting. You can also record from multiple input sources and multiple channels simultaneously on a single track by selecting the appropriate settings for this track; however, it is recommended that you keep each musical part on a separate track for easier editing later. Because you can create as many MIDI tracks as you need in Cubase, you don't really need to worry about running out of them.

Understanding the Cubase Environment

Cubase uses a number of windows, dialog boxes, context menus, and panels to display settings and options. I will refer to these elements throughout this book, so to be sure you understand the terminology, make a note of these elements that set them apart:

- A *window* contains a toolbar at the top and sometimes a toolbar on one side. It may also have a local menu bar at the top of the window. You can edit information inside a window (as with other elements). You don't need to press any buttons to accept or apply changes made to windows. When you make changes to information within a window, the window is automatically updated.

- A *dialog box* appears when you want to apply a process or transformation that requires you to accept or apply this process. It is usually associated with a function, such as the Save function or a setting of some sort, such as the Metronome Setup or the Project Setup dialog box. When a dialog box is open, you most likely have to close this dialog box by accepting or rejecting the changes (via OK and Cancel buttons, for instance) before doing anything else in your project.

- A *panel* is similar in nature to a front panel of a device. Panels have controls or fields in which you can make selections. Panels do not have any menus or toolbars and do not have any confirmation or cancel button. An example is the Mixer panel, which enables you to mix channels, route signals, assign effects to channels, and modify their parameters, as well as perform other mix-related tasks.

- A *context menu* appears only through a right-click action on a PC or a Control-click action on a Mac. Context menus often provide a quick contextual set of options. As the name implies, the options found in this type of menu are context-sensitive, so right-clicking/Control-clicking over an audio track will reveal different options, depending on the object found underneath the cursor.

Understanding Cubase Audio Terminology

To work with audio inside a Cubase project, it is important to understand the associated audio terminology. In Cubase, audio is referred to as *audio clips*, *events*, *parts*, *regions*, and *slices*. This section describes how, when, and why these terms are used.

Audio Clips and Audio Events

In the Project window, recorded audio is referred to as an *audio event*. In essence, when you edit an audio event inside Cubase, you edit the graphic representation of all or part of an actual audio file on your media drive (called an *audio clip*), without changing the original content of that file. When an audio clip is placed on a track in a project, it becomes an audio event. So the difference between an audio clip and an audio event is that the event has been positioned (either manually or through recording) in order to play at a specific time in the Project window's timeline, whereas clips don't have a playback time associated with them and are viewed outside the Project window, in the Pool, MediaBay, and SoundFrame Browser windows.

Audio Regions

Audio clips in the Pool also can contain *regions*. Regions can be created automatically when recording in Cycle mode, or you can create regions manually inside the Sample Editor. Regions represent a portion of a single audio clip or audio event.

When placing an audio event that contains several regions in an audio track, it is possible to change which region will play without changing the event's location. You simply need to tell Cubase to play another region instead. For example, if you have recorded three takes of a solo performance in Cycle recording mode, each time the recording started a new lap, a region might have been created. (This depends on the recording preferences found under File (PC)/Cubase (Mac) > Preferences > Record > Audio > Audio Cycle Record Mode options.) You can later decide which lap you want to listen to by selecting which region is active (on top).

Audio Slices

Another type of event/region combination found in Cubase is called an *audio slice*. Slices are used with rhythmic parts, such as drum loops. Using the Hitpoints tool enables you to define where important beats or slices occur in rhythmic or percussive musical content. For example, you can cut a drum loop into individual hits. Each hit is what Cubase then calls a *slice*.

When you place a drum loop sample containing slices onto an audio track, Cubase creates an audio *part* that holds this drum loop, and each event in the part corresponds to a slice of the audio clip. By dividing rhythmic audio events using slices, you can later quantize these events the same way you would quantize MIDI events. Furthermore, if you change the tempo of a project, the position of each slice's start point will be adjusted to maintain its relation to the beat. If an audio file containing a rhythmic loop is not time-sliced, changing the tempo would not affect the bar/beat location of this loop's start point, but the rhythmic accuracy will suffer because the tempo of the audio loop won't match the project anymore.

Audio Parts

Finally, you can have audio parts in your project. Audio parts are containers for multiple audio events, regions, or slices. An audio part does not represent a recorded or imported audio event, but you can place audio events inside of a part. You also can convert an event into a part, and you can place additional audio events inside an existing part. In other words, audio parts are similar to MIDI parts in that they hold information that can be moved across other audio tracks or in time. Audio parts are useful when you want to move together multiple related audio events, such as the ones found when using slices.

Each of these three types of audio objects offers different editing properties when placed on a track. Table 2.1 takes a look at how different these objects are.

Table 2.1 Differences Between Events, Regions, and Part Objects on an Audio Track

Events	Regions	Parts
You can modify the length of an event on a track, but you can't extend the event beyond the limit of the source disk file to which it refers.	You can modify the length of a region on a track and extend it beyond the original limits of the region itself, but not beyond the limit of the clip to which the region refers.	You can extend the boundaries of a part as much as you want because a part is simply a container that does not refer to a particular audio clip, event, or region.
Audio events have envelopes (fade in, sustain level, fade out). You can use these envelopes to control the level of the event. The envelope is locked with the event, so when you move the event, the envelope follows.	Audio regions also have envelopes (fade in, sustain level, fade out). You can use these envelopes to control the level of the event (refer to Figure 2.6). The envelope is locked with the region, so when you move it, the envelope follows.	Audio parts do not have envelopes associated with them, but the events and regions they contain have individual envelopes that can be edited inside the Audio Part Editor.
The default editing window for events is the Sample Editor.	The default editing window for regions is the Sample Editor.	The default editing window for parts is the Audio Part Editor.
On an audio track, you can convert an event into a region or a part using the Audio > Events to Part option.	On an audio track, you can also convert a region into a part using the Audio > Events to Part option. Also, if you have resized a region in the Project window beyond the original region's boundaries, you can bring back the region to its original size using the Audio > Advanced > Events From Regions option.	You can dissolve an audio part containing several events and regions to create independent objects on a track using the Audio > Dissolve Part command.

Figure 2.8 shows the relationship between the various audio parts available in Cubase 6. The figure is divided into three sections. On the left, you can see where to find the different types of audio terms mentioned in this section. In the center, you can see the hierarchy of relationships between these terms, and on the right, a diagram displaying how this hierarchy works in your project. By default, when you double-click an audio part in the Project window, it launches the Audio Part Editor. Once a part is opened in the Audio Part Editor, you can drag other regions, events, or sliced events into it. When you double-click on an individual audio event or a region inside the Audio Part Editor or in the Project window, it launches the Sample Editor. You can't drag anything into the Sample Editor.

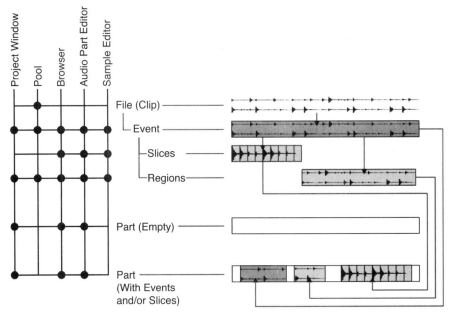

Figure 2.8   The hierarchy of audio parts in Cubase 6.

This hierarchy allows for nondestructive editing because what you normally edit is the audio clip, its associated event, regions, and slices, not the audio file itself. When a portion of the audio event is processed, Cubase creates an additional audio clip on the media drive containing the newly processed section of your audio. The audio parts containing references to processed audio material update themselves to correspond to this new link.

Understanding Nondestructive Editing

It's quite common to get a musical idea that requires you to take risks or to try out things and listen to them to see how they sound. If you don't like how they sound, it's nice to be able to put things back the way they were. To facilitate this type of experimentation, Cubase offers a way to reorganize the musical information inside the application without affecting the saved data on the disk—in effect, to undo any changes you make. In fact, Cubase doesn't even change the content of the files it refers to unless you specifically tell it to.

In Cubase, media files are called *clips*. These clips are on the media drive, usually inside a project subfolder appropriately called Audio. When you save a Cubase project file (with the .CPR extension), that file itself does not contain the audio, but merely links to or references the original audio clips. When you split an audio event and place it somewhere else in your project, you are changing the reference points found in the project file to the audio clip, but not editing or transforming the original clip in any way. The same applies to effects or volume changes you might add to a project; none of these transformations affect the original audio file. This type of editing is referred to as *non-destructive editing*.

If we push the editing further and decide to apply a time stretch, a normalize, or fade out to a portion of an audio clip, Cubase still does not touch the original content of the file. Instead, Cubase creates additional files inside the Edits subfolder of your project folder to store the results.

If this is not enough to convince you that Cubase is a completely nondestructive environment, you also can use multiple undo levels through the History option in the Edit menu. In addition, the Offline Process History option in the Edit menu allows you to select processing that you applied to an audio file—let's say, seven steps ago—and edit the parameters of that processing without affecting the other six steps you did after that . . . even *after* the project file has been saved various times!

The primary downside to Cubase's nondestructive editing is that it requires more space than traditional destructive editing—where changes are made to the original files. When you work on large project files, every processed audio bit in your project is retained unless you decide to clean up the audio (through another function called Remove Unused Media, which I discuss later). Keep in mind that a project can grow quickly, and you should prepare sufficient media drive space when working with a digital audio multi-track project using high-resolution recordings. If space is not an issue, enjoy the benefits of working in an environment that allows you to undo large numbers of steps that may have led your music in the wrong direction and to take creative risks with the audio files you record.

3 Setting Up Peripherals

One of the major challenges for new Cubase users is getting everything set up and ready to go. This means making sure that your computer's operating system, audio hardware, and MIDI interface are installed properly and configured for optimal audio operations. Getting all these software and hardware items to work nicely with each other can take a bit of doing.

In addition, running an application such as Cubase requires a stable computer environment and lots of available computer resources, especially when you are using effects and software instruments. Making these resources available to Cubase will help you get the most out of your working session—even if that means changing your computer's configuration to emphasize performance rather than appearance.

This chapter, then, explores how to set up peripheral devices both inside and outside the Cubase environment. Remember, though, that every system is different; the general advice presented here may need to be tweaked for your particular combination of hardware and software.

Here's a summary of what you will learn in this chapter:

- How to choose and connect audio and MIDI interface devices to your computer
- How to choose the right driver for your audio hardware when working in Cubase
- The difference between hardware-specific ASIO drivers and generic ASIO drivers
- Setting up MIDI interfaces and drivers in your system
- Setting up MIDI ports, remote devices, and audio ports inside Cubase
- The impact background processes have on Cubase performance
- The implications of loading other audio applications when running Cubase

---

Optimize Your System for Cubase Performance:
Before you can do anything in Cubase, you should make sure of the following:

- Your software is properly installed on your system.
- You have a stable operating system.

- The latest drivers for all your peripherals are installed, including those peripherals that you think are not related, such as video and network drivers.

- All non-related applications and utilities are closed. This includes any programs or services running in the background, including networking adapters.

Connecting an Audio Interface

You can run Cubase 6 on any Windows or Mac computer that meets Steinberg's system requirements for processing power, memory, and hard disk storage. But most computers don't have inputs to connect microphones, keyboards, MIDI synthesizers, and the like. For this reason, you need to connect an external audio interface device to your computer; this device provides all the inputs and outputs you need to record instruments and vocals.

Audio Interface Devices

To record a vocalist singing into a microphone, an acoustic instrument playing into a mic, an electric guitar, an electronic keyboard, or other instruments, you need an audio interface device. This is a box that includes one or more microphone or line audio inputs. You will need to connect your instrument(s) or microphone(s) to the input box, and then connect the input box to your computer via either USB or FireWire.

There are a variety of input boxes available. Some have just a single 1/4-inch or balanced XLR microphone input; others have four, eight, or even 16 different inputs, along with a complement of MIDI inputs and outputs. Obviously, the more inputs that are available, the more instruments and voices you can record simultaneously. (Multiple inputs are also necessary when recording drums, where each drum typically has its own microphone.)

You'll find audio interface devices from many of the same manufacturers who offer MIDI interface boxes. Figure 3.1 shows Steinberg's own MR816x interface box, designed specifically to work with Cubase.

Figure 3.1 Steinberg's MR816x audio interface device, complete with eight XLR mic inputs, eight balanced line/instrument inputs, one Hi-Z input for electric guitar or bass, and all manner of outputs.

MIDI Interface Devices

To make a MIDI recording, you'll need some sort of MIDI instrument or input device, such as a MIDI keyboard or synthesizer, as well as some way to connect that instrument to your computer. Most of today's audio interface devices include MIDI input and output connections in addition to the traditional audio inputs and outputs, which makes this a good all-around solution. In addition, many newer MIDI instruments/controllers actually connect to your computer via USB, so you don't have to worry about physical MIDI connections at all.

You can also connect MIDI instruments to a freestanding MIDI interface, which is an external device that connects to your computer via either USB or FireWire; the MIDI instrument connects to the MIDI interface, which then connects to your computer. Most of these MIDI interface devices have one or two MIDI inputs and a corresponding number of MIDI outputs (to connect back to your MIDI instrument). These interface devices are available from Cakewalk, M-Audio, MOTU, and other manufacturers. (Figure 3.2 shows the connections on M-Audio's popular MIDISport 2x2 interface box.)

Figure 3.2 The back panel of the MIDISport 2x2 MIDI interface—two MIDI inputs (one on the front) and two MIDI outputs.

Other MIDI Connections: Many audio interface devices also include MIDI input and output connections, thus negating the need for a separate MIDI interface box. In addition, many newer MIDI instruments/controllers actually connect to your computer via USB, eliminating the need for a separate MIDI interface box.

Control Surfaces

To better control large numbers of mic and instrument inputs, some recordists prefer to use an external control surface. Most control surfaces blend the functionality of an audio interface with an external mixer. You connect the appropriate instruments and microphones to the control surface, and then connect the control surface to your computer via either USB or FireWire. (Some control surfaces, however, do not contain audio and MIDI inputs and function solely as external mixers for inputs from a separate input device.)

When you use an external control surface, you have the option of adjusting the volume faders and other controls on the external mixer itself or in Cubase's virtual mixer interface. You can also connect external effects processors directly to the control surface and manage them as Send or Insert effects in Cubase.

There are a number of different mixer/control surfaces available from M-Audio, Steinberg, TASCAM, Yamaha, and other manufacturers. Figure 3.3 shows the Alesis MasterControl product.

Photo courtesy of Alesis.

Figure 3.3 The Alesis MasterControl mixer/control surface, with slider control of eight input channels. (Photo courtesy of Alesis.)

Working with Audio Drivers

Connecting an audio or MIDI interface to your computer is relatively simple; just connect the appropriate USB or FireWire cable to an open port on your computer. But that's just part of the process—you also need to make sure you have the proper device driver for the interface installed on your computer.

In general, both Windows and Mac users should always use the ASIO driver provided by the audio hardware manufacturer. Macintosh users can also use the Core Audio driver in order to use the computer's built-in audio for Cubase—although certain other audio devices can optionally be assigned for audio input/output via the operating system itself, in the Sound section of System Preferences.

Windows users can also choose to use a generic ASIO multimedia driver provided by Cubase; if you're running Windows Vista or Windows 7, the Generic Low Latency ASIO driver is also a good choice. Know, however, that using such a generic driver will not provide the best performance, as the generic driver has not been specifically optimized to work with your specific hardware device. You can find a list of recommended audio interfaces offering ASIO drivers on Steinberg's website or by performing a search on Google.

ASIO Drivers and Latency

Using the proprietary ASIO driver supplied by the manufacturer of your audio interface device is *strongly recommended*. That's because the driver has been optimized for this particular piece of hardware; it's simply going to work better and faster, with lower *latency*. Latency measures the amount of time between what you record and what you hear from Cubase after the signal has been processed by your computer. The lower the latency, the shorter the delay between what you record and what you hear. Obviously, low latency is desirable.

High latencies are often troublesome when recording live material. There is always a delay when monitoring audio through software, and the greater the latency time, the more noticeable this delay will be. Better ASIO drivers have a lower latency, which lets you record music while playing back previously recorded tracks without any noticeable differences.

A typical latency for audio hardware using a dedicated ASIO driver should be around or below 10 milliseconds. Note also that latency affects the response time of VST instruments and the output and input monitoring in a channel.

Most audio interfaces today support the ASIO format, but if in doubt, consult both Steinberg's website and the audio hardware manufacturer's website for information about ASIO compatibility.

ASIO DirectX Full Duplex Drivers

If you're a Windows user who doesn't have an audio interface offering a dedicated ASIO driver, you'll need to use Microsoft's DirectSound technology, which is part of DirectX. If your audio interface has an ASIO driver, or if you're using a Mac, you can skip this section.

The DirectX driver is included with your Windows operating system, and you can find free DirectX updates on Microsoft's website. Steinberg provides the ASIO DirectX Full Duplex driver on the Cubase installation DVD. In the absence of a soundcard-specific ASIO driver, the ASIO DirectX driver provides the next best (but by far not the most desirable) solution. This driver allows Cubase to communicate with DirectX and allows full duplex communication with your audio hardware.

Full duplex means that you can record and play back simultaneously through the audio hardware. In contrast, *half duplex* allows only one operation at a time: play or record. Because Cubase has to communicate with DirectX through the ASIO DirectX driver, and then DirectX communicates with the audio hardware, expect higher latencies when using this type of driver setup.

To set up this driver, you need to use the ASIO DirectSound Full Duplex Setup window to configure your audio hardware properly. This window lists all DirectSound-compatible input and output ports on your system. Devices that are checked are available inside Cubase. You can find the ASIO DirectX Full Duplex setup utility in a special ASIO folder under the Cubase program folder. To launch it, simply locate its icon or alias and launch it from there.

Configure your DirectSound drivers:

1. From the ASIO DirectX Full Duplex setup window, activate the device ports you want to use by adding a check mark in the box next to them.

2. To change the buffer size, double-click in the corresponding column and enter a new value. The buffer size is used when audio data is transferred between Cubase and the audio hardware. Larger buffer sizes will ensure that playback will occur without glitches with relatively larger numbers of tracks and plug-ins, whereas smaller buffer sizes will reduce the latency. The default buffer size appearing in this column should be fine in most cases; however, if you want to solve crackling sounds in your audio when using this driver, you can increase the buffer size by increments of 64 samples or greater.

3. To change the Offset value, double-click in the corresponding column and enter a new value. If you hear a constant offset (delay) during playback of audio and MIDI recordings, you can adjust the output or input latency time by using an offset value. In most cases, you should leave this at its default zero value. If you are noticing a delay at the output, increase the output offset, and if you are noticing a delay at the input, increase the input offset.

4. The Sync Reference option lets you determine how MIDI is synchronized with the audio. You can choose to synchronize MIDI to the audio input or audio output. This also determines which offset value you should adjust, as mentioned earlier.

5. The Card Options should be left with the Full Duplex option selected; however, if you are noticing problems while this is selected, you can check the Start Input First option.

MIDI Interfaces and Drivers

Most MIDI interfaces available today are installed in two simple steps—physically connect the device (don't forget the power supply, if required) and then install its drivers on your computer. This is usually quite simple and is explained in the documentation that comes with your MIDI interface. Hardware specifics will not be discussed here because there are too many MIDI and audio interfaces out there to cover them thoroughly. But to make sure everything is set up properly, one good starting point is to verify that your MIDI port appears in your system configuration.

Verify installed MIDI ports (under Windows):

1. Open the Start menu, right-click on Computer or My Computer, and select Manage from the context menu.

2. In the Computer Management window, select the Device Manager entry under System Tools.

3. Locate the Sound, Video and Game Controllers entry and expand the list to view the items under this entry.

4. Double-click on your MIDI interface or audio hardware if you have a MIDI port on it to view its properties.

5. The device's Properties dialog box will appear. In the General tab, make sure the Device Status reads, "This device is working properly." If not, click on the Properties tab.

6. Select your installed MIDI port and click on the Properties button to see whether there are any messages warning you that the device is not installed properly or whether this device is in conflict with another peripheral.

At this point, if you have not seen any question marks or exclamation marks next to your device, and if there are no indications that it is not installed properly, you should be able to use this port in Cubase. If, on the other hand, you have found a problem, you should try reinstalling the driver for this peripheral and following the installation procedure provided by your device's manufacturer.

Consult the Manufacturer: Consult your manufacturer's website for specific settings related to your MIDI or audio hardware device. This website will probably provide you with a driver update and tips on configuring your device with Cubase and other software.

Verify installed MIDI ports (under Mac OS X):

1. After installing any Macintosh drivers that were provided with your MIDI interface from its installation disk, open the Audio-MIDI Setup utility. The Utilities folder can be opened via the Go > Utilities menu command, or by using the keyboard shortcut Shift+Command+U.

2. In the Audio-MIDI Setup utility program, an icon for your MIDI interface (or the MIDI interface features of your audio interface if a single device provides both functions in your setup) should now appear.

3. Now you need to indicate to the operating system what external MIDI devices are in your studio configuration. Click the Add Device button in this utility's toolbar.

4. Double-click the new device icon, and in its Properties dialog box, select the manufacturer name and device model from the preconfigured pop-up lists. If the device you want to add doesn't appear, simply type in this information, which can be edited at any time to make the naming conventions in your studio setup more self-explanatory.

5. If using a preexisting device definition, an appropriate icon and other information about this device's properties will be filled in automatically. Otherwise, the most important thing is to indicate on what MIDI channels the device can transmit or receive (many sound modules may not transmit on any MIDI channel at all, and some controllers don't respond to any incoming MIDI channels since they don't have any sound-generation capabilities), and whether it is strictly a General MIDI (GM)–compatible device. If the device responds to MIDI Time Code or MIDI Beat Clock (which is common for drum machines and some onboard hardware sequencers), this property can also be indicated here. You can also assign an icon from the selection provided by the Macintosh operating system.

6. Arrow graphics at the bottom of the icons for your MIDI interface and each external MIDI device that you have defined indicate their available MIDI inputs and outputs. Click on these to drag virtual "cables" between the devices, to mirror how they are physically cabled together in your studio setup.

7. Your devices will now appear by name when you open the Cubase program and start selecting input sources or external output destinations for your MIDI tracks. One of the advantages of the preexisting MIDI device definitions is that they already come associated with patchname scripts (which allow you to specify program and bank changes by name rather than by number). If a particular device in your studio doesn't appear in the preconfigured list, you may also be able to locate patchname scripts (a text file in XML format) on the Internet. The Macintosh forums at www.cubase.net are an excellent place to start, since a fairly sizeable collection of device maps and patchname scripts has been compiled there.

Setting Up Devices in Cubase

At this point, the audio and MIDI devices are properly installed on your system, and you are now ready to tell Cubase which devices to use. The Device Setup dialog box, found under the Devices menu, lets you configure MIDI, Transport controls, remote control devices, video device drivers, and audio hardware, as well as VST System Link settings. VST System Link networks multiple computers through a digital audio connection. In this chapter, I will discuss only the MIDI and audio settings and leave the other settings for later, as they become relevant to the topic under discussion.

USB and FireWire Devices: Always make sure your USB or FireWire devices are connected and powered up before launching Cubase; otherwise, the device will not show up in the Device Setup dialog box, and you won't be able to configure it or use it properly.

When you launch Cubase, it scans all installed peripherals and plug-ins—both audio and MIDI—in order to make them available in a Cubase project. All successfully recognized devices appear in the Device Setup dialog box. Selecting the appropriate entry in the Devices tree (see the left side of the dialog box in Figure 3.4) reveals this device's setup options on the right side. Here, the MIDI Port Setup is visible.

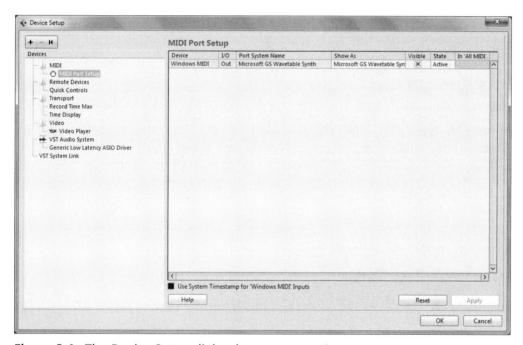

Figure 3.4   The Device Setup dialog box.

Setting Up MIDI Ports

Because the MIDI devices appear at the top of the list, let's start there. MIDI ports connect external MIDI devices, such as MIDI keyboards, synthesizers, and multitimbral sound modules, to Cubase through your MIDI interface's MIDI Input port and transmit MIDI events to these devices through its MIDI Output port. The Device, I/O (input/output), and Port System Name columns display system-related information over which you have no control. However, the Show As, Visible, and In All MIDI Inputs columns let you set up how these ports appear in a project.

The Show As column displays how the MIDI port appears when selecting MIDI ports. To rename a MIDI port, click in the Show As column and type a new name. The Visible option hides a MIDI port from the pop-up selector on MIDI tracks when it is not checked.

Monitoring Active MIDI Ports: The State column lets you know whether a port is currently active in your project. A port is active when a MIDI track is assigned to it, so avoid hiding MIDI ports that are active.

By the way, the Inspector's MIDI Input selector for MIDI tracks offers an All MIDI Inputs choice. When this option is selected, the track records or echoes all MIDI events coming from all currently active MIDI inputs. To filter out an input port from this All MIDI Inputs mode, uncheck that port here in the Device Setup window.

Click the Reset button to make all ports visible and include all ports in the In All MIDI Inputs column.

Setting Up a Remote Device

A remote device is a hardware device that can be programmed to offer a physical, tactile interface for Cubase's virtual controls. Remote devices come in many shapes, formats, and functions, and the setup options will vary from one device to the next. Without going into detail on how each remote is implemented inside Cubase, here's a look at how you can set up a remote control surface inside Cubase.

Install a MIDI remote control device:

1. Select Devices > Device Setup.

2. Click the plus sign above the Devices list in the dialog box (see Figure 3.5).

3. Select the appropriate device from the supported devices list. If your device is not in this list, select the Generic Remote device. The device is added under the Remote Devices folder in the Device Setup dialog box.

4. Select the device in the list.

5. Select the appropriate MIDI input and output ports connecting the controller to Cubase, and be sure these ports are well connected to this device.

6. Enable the Auto Select option if your device supports this option. (A channel is automatically selected when the corresponding fader on the remote is touched.)

7. Click OK when you are finished.

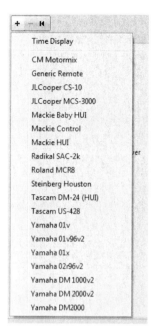

Figure 3.5 Adding a MIDI device controller to your device setup.

Once a remote device is installed, its name appears in the Devices menu. Selecting its name brings up the device's control panel. Use the control panel to determine which Cubase virtual controls are affected by incoming controller messages generated by this device.

Setting Up Audio Ports

The VST Audio System section of the Device Setup window determines how Cubase interfaces with your system's audio peripheral. You can tell Cubase which drivers to use and which ports should be visible, save these settings, and never worry about it again. On the other hand, you can change any of these settings when needed.

Remember that audio ports correspond to physical inputs or outputs; you will need to associate these ports with input and output busses later. When selecting the source or input for a track, you will be selecting the bus associated with the port, not the port itself.

Set up audio ports in Cubase:

1. Select Devices > Device Setup.

2. Select VST Audio System in the Devices list to view its properties (see Figure 3.6).

3. In the ASIO Driver field, select the appropriate driver for your audio interface. If you have a dedicated ASIO driver for your interface, it is strongly recommended that you use it. Cubase uses this driver by default (although on the Macintosh your ASIO Driver selection may default to Built-In Audio), but it's always good to confirm this the first time you run Cubase after it has been installed.

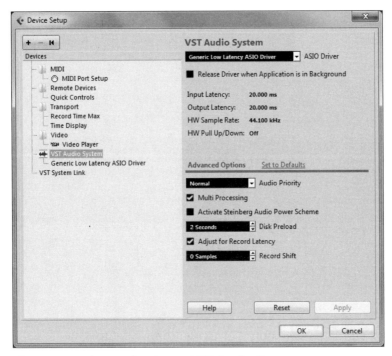

Figure 3.6 The Device Setup VST Audio System setup page.

4. Click Apply to update the ASIO driver displayed under VST Audio System if you've made any changes.

5. Return to the Devices list and select the ASIO driver under the VST Audio System item; this displays the driver's settings (see Figure 3.7).

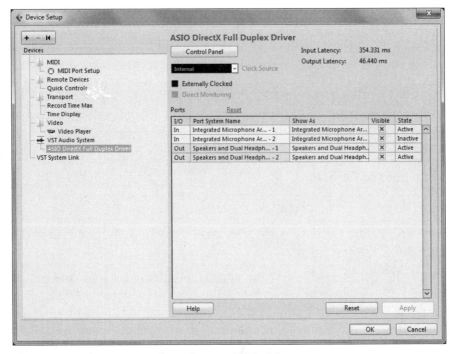

Figure 3.7 The port settings for an ASIO driver.

Different ASIO drivers and devices have different numbers of available ports. If you have more than one audio interface with ASIO drivers installed on your system, additional selections will appear under VST Audio System. Each has its own settings page.

As with MIDI ports described earlier in this chapter, the I/O column identifies whether the port is an input or output, whereas the Port System Name column shows all the ports available in this interface. You can also rename the ports in the Show As column to change the way they appear whenever busses are created in the VST Connections panel (select Devices > VST Connections).

To hide certain audio ports when working inside Cubase, uncheck their Visible check boxes. Ports that are not visible will not appear when you are associating ports to busses in the VST Connections panel later. You can change these settings at any time, but hiding ports that are currently used within a project will force Cubase to discard any routing information associated with this port. The State column plays a similar role as described for MIDI ports earlier in this chapter. Whenever an audio port is connected to a bus, its state will become active.

If you are using a dedicated ASIO driver, you can set the clock source of the audio device by clicking on the device's control panel in Windows, or by using the pop-up Clock Source selector within the Device Setup dialog box on Macintosh computers. The clock source determines whether the sampling frequency of your audio peripheral is controlled by its own internal clock or some other external source. Once again, the number of settings found in this dialog box varies from one device to the next.

You should set the clock source of your audio device to master (internal) when:

■ You don't have any other digital audio devices in your studio setup.

■ You want the clock of your audio device to serve as the master clock reference for other devices.

You should set the clock source of the audio device to slave/external sync or auto-sync when:

■ You want the digital clock of another device to control your computer's audio hardware clock.

Adjusting the Buffer Size: You should set the input and output latencies as low as possible. This produces the best results when playing VST instruments in real time or when monitoring source audio through Cubase during the recording process—especially if you're applying plug-in effects. Latency won't affect the quality of the sound or the timing of a performance once it's inside a project, but with larger amounts of latency, you will hear a delay between what is being played back from Cubase and the part you're currently recording. This delay can throw off your timing while recording a performance.

Because latency is directly related to the Audio Buffer Size setting, increasing the buffer's size will also increase the latency. But you may need to increase the buffer size to get rid of some crackling noise in the audio when working on projects with many audio tracks and/or a large number of plug-ins that may be taxing the processing power of your CPU. You can always reduce the buffer size later, if you need lower monitoring latency while recording performances with VST instruments or live audio, for example.

Running Other Applications Simultaneously

Most digital audio workstation applications, such as Cubase, require a lot of memory and CPU power. Running other applications simultaneously will prevent Cubase from using these resources. For example, some background applications might start doing a hard drive scan in the middle of a recording—which could interfere with Cubase's operation. A good example of this is real-time scanning from an anti-virus program or file indexing with a file search utility.

Background Processes

Any background applications that make intensive use of memory or hard drive resources should be disabled when using Cubase. A good rule of thumb for improving your performance is to not run *any* other nonessential applications while using Cubase.

To find out which background applications are running in Windows, right-click the Taskbar and select Start Task Manager, which opens the Windows Task Manager; select the Processes tab to view how much memory a given application uses. If you're running OS X on a Macintosh computer, you can view the active processes with the Activity Monitor; open the Finder menu and select Go > Applications > Utilities Folder, then double-click the Activity Monitor icon.

When you find an application using too much background memory, you can then configure the application to not launch automatically or run in the background. It's important to keep the number of background applications to a minimum. This may mean deleting all non-essential applications. This is why many serious Cubase owners use a dedicated computer for recording, and thus avoid doing office work and Internet browsing on their recording system.

Other Audio Applications

The situation is different if you try to run another audio-related application. When Cubase is loaded, it generally assumes control of the audio hardware, leaving it unusable for other applications that would also need it to run concurrently with Cubase. To run other audio-related applications simultaneously with Cubase, then, you need audio hardware that provides a multi-client driver.

A multi-client driver shares access to the audio hardware between audio applications. Think of it this way: A single-client access is like going to the grocery store and having only one cash register open. Everybody has to line up and wait their turn to pay for their groceries. A multi-client driver is like having two or three cash registers open so people can go to a second or even a third cash register if the first is busy.

Steinberg provides an engine developed by Propellerhead Software, called ReWire. ReWire lets you share audio resources between ReWire-compatible applications, such as Ableton Live, Propellerhead Reason, Cakewalk Sonar, Sony Media Software ACID, and so on. (Working with ReWire applications is discussed in Chapter 12, "Using ReWire.")

For other types of audio software, you will have to load that software first and set Cubase as your default sequencer from within the application's environment. After this has been configured, you can launch Cubase from within the other application when needed. If you have problems doing this, try disabling any audio outputs in that application that you intend to use in Cubase (for good measure, keep outputs 1 and 2 available for Cubase) and disabling audio inputs and outputs in Cubase that you want to use in the other application. By doing this, you are effectively assigning certain outputs of your audio hardware to Cubase and the remainder to the other application.

Know, however, that running such a dual-application setup imposes a huge load on your computer resources, and you are also testing many compatibility issues between different software and hardware manufacturers. If you are experiencing difficulties, here are a couple of places to look for information:

- Visit Steinberg's website to see whether there is any additional information on the difficulty you are having.

- Visit your other software manufacturer's website; it also might have some answers for you.

- Check on your audio hardware manufacturer's website to confirm that you have the latest drivers for your audio hardware, and you can take a look at the support, troubleshooting, or FAQ section to find additional help.

- Use discussion forums (such as www.cubase.net and others) to share your problems with other users; there is a good chance that someone else has had the same problem and can suggest a workaround for you.

Getting It All Working

One last thing about setting up an audio system for digital recording—it's complicated. The reality is, even the pros spend a lot of time hooking up and configuring all the pieces and parts, and things often don't work the first time around.

The most common question I get from readers is, "How do I get equipment XYZ to work with Cubase?" This is, unfortunately, a question I can't answer. That's because every setup is different, and every piece of equipment from every manufacturer has its own requirements and quirks. When a complicated audio system isn't working—when you're not getting any sound out of your speakers or not registering any audio input from your other equipment—the cause could be in any individual piece of the chain. It's simply impossible to troubleshoot, especially from a distance.

With that said, I always recommend taking a step back, taking a deep breath, and rechecking all your connections and configurations. You'd be surprised how many problems are caused by cables that aren't connected properly—or not connected to where they're supposed to be connected. To that end, it also helps to revisit all your virtual connections within Cubase and within your computer's operating system. It's just possible that something is switched off that should be switched on, or vice versa.

Beyond this basic advice, I have to direct you to the manufacturer's technical support. That is, you should contact the manufacturer of the equipment in question, or contact Steinberg for Cubase-related issues. Most manufacturers (including Steinberg) have robust online help systems and support communities, which means you can find a lot of answers over the Internet. You can also call most manufacturers to talk to a real live tech support representative. It's in each company's best interest to get you up and running so that you can get maximum value out of the products they sell.

4 Monitoring and Connecting Audio

Monitoring is essential to the recording process; you need to hear what you're recording in order to make sure not only that the recording levels are appropriate, but also that you're capturing a good performance. To monitor what your record, however, you need to properly route the input signal within Cubase to the desired audio output.

This signal path routing differs, depending on how you're making the recording, and sometimes needs to change from one project to another. It also depends on the external equipment you're using; setting up this equipment to fulfill your production needs is just as important as where the signal is or where it can be routed inside Cubase.

Proper signal routing is important for many other practical reasons—for example, if you want to add a click track to a musician's headphones without sending it to the control-room monitors or to the audio track being recorded. It's also necessary if you want the producer to be able to communicate with the guitarist in another room, without the drummer hearing what's being said.

In Cubase, signal routing is accomplished via the VST Connections panel. No matter what your signal routing needs are, VST Connections will make them happen.

Here's a summary of what you will learn in this chapter:

- How to monitor music productions through Cubase's VST audio engine
- How to monitor audio through an external mixer
- How to use direct monitoring mode to reduce latency effects
- How to make simple to complex hardware setup connections
- How to set up input and output busses
- How to set up group and plug-in effects busses
- How to set up external effect and instrument busses
- How to save VST Connections

47

Monitoring Methods

Audio monitoring refers to listening to an audio signal as it enters the computer hosting Cubase and as it exits Cubase to a monitoring setup. There are three basic audio monitoring methods available when working with Cubase (see Figure 4.1): monitoring through Cubase, monitoring through an external mixer, and direct monitoring.

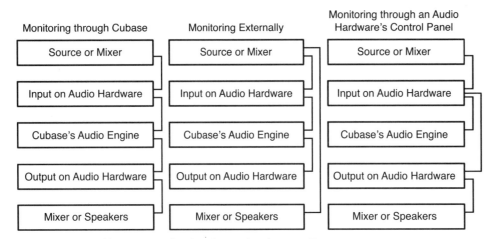

Figure 4.1 Different methods of monitoring audio.

Monitoring Through Cubase

Monitoring through Cubase is the recommended mode because it lets you add processing and control the sound inside Cubase at every step of the production process. When monitoring through Cubase, the signal enters the VST audio system, is routed and processed inside Cubase, and then is sent to the audio interface's output port. For this to work well, however, you need an audio interface with a low latency.

Latency is the delay between the actual input signal and when it is heard coming back out through the audio hardware. The signal coming out of Cubase, once it has been processed, panned, leveled, and equalized, is delayed by the amount of latency in the audio interface. With lower latencies, this delay will not be noticeable, but with higher latencies, it will definitely throw off someone trying to record a new track while listening to what has been previously recorded.

Set up auto monitoring preferences:

1. Select File > Preferences (Application > Preferences on the Mac).

2. Select VST at the bottom of the list on the left (see Figure 4.2).

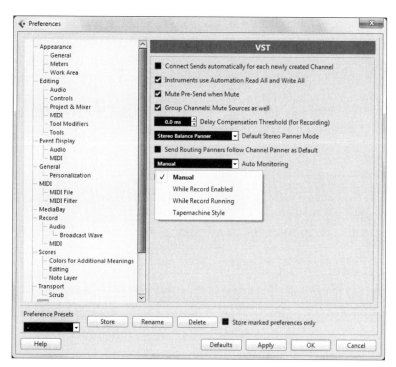

Figure 4.2 Changing the auto monitoring options in the VST Preferences.

3. From the Auto Monitoring drop-down list on the right, select one of the four auto monitoring options: Manual, While Record Enabled, While Record Running, and Tapemachine Style.

   ■ **Manual** monitoring enables you to switch to input monitoring by pressing the Monitor button in the track's channel mixer or the Mixer panel (see Figure 4.3). When this button is active, signals coming into Cubase are monitored through the Mixer panel, and then sent out to the channel's output bus. This is the default setting in Cubase.

   ■ **While Record Enabled** switches the channel to input monitoring as soon as you enable the Record Enable button for this channel. This is the button below the Monitor button shown in Figure 4.3.

Monitor Button

Record Enabled Button

Figure 4.3 The Monitor and Record Enabled buttons in the Mixer.

- **While Record Running** switches all the record-enabled channels to input monitoring when you click the Record button on the Transport panel.
- **Tapemachine Style** switches a selected audio track to input monitoring automatically when recording or when the project is stopped, but it will revert to output monitoring when you press Play. This mode is similar to traditional analog tape recorder behavior.

4. Click Apply, and then OK.

Monitoring Externally

This monitoring technique requires the following setup:

- You use an external audio interface or control surface for monitoring.

- What you are monitoring is routed and processed through the external audio interface or through an audio hardware mixer application, not inside Cubase.

Think of external monitoring as a direct output on a mixer—a point going back out right after coming into Cubase, but before any type of control or processing can occur. When monitoring through an external mixer, you should avoid also monitoring through Cubase simultaneously because you will hear two different signals with a delay between them. You can monitor an audio signal that has been previously recorded without any problem, but make sure to mute the track being recorded inside Cubase to avoid this double-monitoring problem when using an external mixer.

Direct Monitoring

Direct monitoring (with ASIO 2.0–compatible audio devices) controls the monitoring from the audio interface device's control panel. The options available to you will therefore be device-dependent. Cubase 6 users can also use the input bus faders to adjust input levels, but because the signal is sent back out right away, monitoring the input through the track's audio channel will not be possible. You can't apply processing, such as EQ or insert effects, and monitor these effects while recording when direct monitoring is active. The sound is sent directly to Cubase, but you are monitoring the input, not what's going into Cubase. In other words, you are monitoring the sound coming in through the audio device's mixer utility, bypassing the VST audio engine that sends the signal into the Cubase mixer for processing. This is an advantage when using audio devices with higher latencies, because you monitor what is coming into Cubase directly through your device's outputs, without adding any delay between the input and the output. On lower-latency audio devices, monitoring through Cubase is preferred because it gives you access to the controls and routing possibilities Cubase offers.

Enable direct monitoring mode:

1. Select Devices > Device Setup.

2. Select the appropriate ASIO driver under VST Audio System in the Devices pane.

3. Check the Direct Monitoring option, if available, in the ASIO driver settings page.

4. Click Apply, and then OK.

Setting Up VST Connections

The concept of connections was introduced in Chapter 2 as a way to connect busses to ports—busses being what you select inside Cubase as the source or destination for audio. A bus can be mono, stereo, or multi-channel. A port, on the other hand, is a single (mono) physical connection. By adding the concept of a bus to connections, Cubase makes it possible to use the same inputs and outputs for different purposes, offering much more flexibility in studio setups of any type.

Most of this discussion will center on options found in the VST Connections panel, which can be opened by selecting Devices > VST Connections, or by pressing the F4 keyboard shortcut.

The VST Connections panel offers six tabs: Inputs, Outputs, Group/FX, External FX, External Instruments, and Studio. The following sections describe the purpose of each tab and how to configure connections according to your needs. Because you need at least one output bus, you should configure the VST Connections before you begin a new project.

Input Connections

The Inputs tab in the VST Connections panel lets you create input busses manually or select from a list of presets. Once busses are created, you can connect audio device input ports to these busses (see Figure 4.4).

Input busses are used to record audio, and you need an input bus for each microphone or instrument you want to record simultaneously—although a single bus can record different instruments at different times. You can create as many input busses as you need and in the desired channel format: mono, stereo, or multi-channel. For example, if you do a lot of rock band recordings, you'll need a number of mono input busses for the bass, guitar, and vocals; a combination of mono and stereo busses for the drum kit; and possibly a stereo bus to record keyboards.

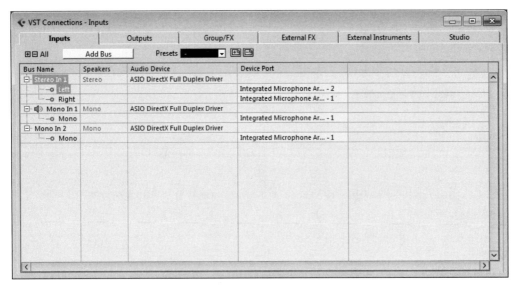

Figure 4.4 The Inputs tab on the VST Connections panel.

Create input busses:

1. Open the VST Connections panel (press F4 or select Devices > VST Connections).

2. Select the Inputs tab.

3. Click the Add Bus button (refer to Figure 4.4).

4. In the Add Input Bus dialog box, select the bus configuration from the drop-down menu. For example, select Mono to create a bus for recording mono instruments, such as bass, vocal, trumpet, and so on.

5. Adjust the number of busses you want to create, if needed.

6. Click OK.

7. In the Audio Device column, select the appropriate audio device driver for this bus. The names of devices that appear here will depend on your VST Audio System setting, as described earlier in this chapter.

8. In the Device Port column, select the port on the audio device that you want to use for this bus. By assigning a device port to a bus, you effectively tell Cubase where the sound is coming from when you select an input bus on a channel's Input Bus selection menu.

9. Select the bus name, and then click on it a second time to rename it if necessary. A rectangle appears around the name when you can edit it. The name you enter here appears in the bus selection menu in the track Inspector (see Figure 4.5).

Figure 4.5 The Input drop-down menu, found in the audio track Inspector area, lists available busses.

10. Repeat these steps for each input bus you want to create.

11. Close the VST Connections panel when you are finished. Once the busses are created, the Speakers column in the VST Connections panel will display their configuration.

Output Connections

The Outputs tab in the VST Connections panel lets users create output busses manually or select from a list of presets. Once busses are created, users can assign audio device output ports to these busses. Outputs are used to monitor a track or channel's playback or to send the signal to an external multi-track recorder, for example.

Create output busses:

1. Open the VST Connections panel (press F4 or select Devices > VST Connections).

2. Select the Outputs tab.

3. Click the Add Bus button.

4. In the Add Input Bus dialog box, select the bus configuration from the drop-down menu.

5. Adjust the number of busses you want to create, if needed.

6. Click OK.

7. In the Audio Device column, select the appropriate audio device driver for this bus.

8. In the Device Port column, select the port on the audio device that you want to use for this bus.

9. Select the bus name, and then click on it a second time to rename it if necessary.

10. Use the Click column to toggle the click track on or off for each output bus.

Although the Transport panel provides a Click button, which is convenient when you need to generate a click track during the recording process, you might not want to send this click sound to all output busses. This is where the Click column comes in handy. When the Click function is enabled in the Transport panel (see Figure 4.6), busses with the word "Click" will hear the click through the device port connected to this bus.

Figure 4.6 Click track assignment for output busses.

Group/FX Connections

The Group/FX tab lets you add group busses/channels that allow you to combine and control the main audio output from several other channels. You could apply the same EQ to the signal from all channels in that group, control their overall volume with a single fader, or control the position of an entire group through a single pan control. FX (short for *effects*) can be added to a project to process audio channels, such as adding a filter or reverb effect to one or several tracks.

On traditional mixers, this type of effect is often called a *send effect*, as opposed to an *insert effect*. Send effects are called this because audio from multiple channels can be "sent" through an FX bus to an effect. Use the Group/FX page in the VST Connections panel to keep track of these types of tracks in your project or add new ones. You can also create groups and effects from the main project window as well, which is not the case with the rest of the connections in this panel. Look for additional ways to use FX channels in Chapter 33, "Working with FX Channel Tracks," or create groups in Chapter 35, "Working with Group Channel Tracks."

External FX Connections

If you have external effect units and would like to integrate them into your Cubase environment, use the External FX bus tab. For example, suppose you have a good analog preamp you like because it warms things up, and you wonder how it would sound on your mix. By creating an external FX bus, you can make the necessary connections. The External FX tab lets you connect Cubase to an external effect by configuring both the *send to effect* and the *effect return* pathways. Once the connection between the external effect and Cubase is established, you can use external effects the same way you would use a VST plug-in effect inside Cubase.

Create an External FX bus:

1. In the VST Connections External FX tab, click on the Add External FX button.

2. In the Add External FX dialog box, type a name for the effect, as shown in Figure 4.7.

Figure 4.7 Renaming an external effect.

3. Select a Send and Return channel configuration. These settings depend on the external effect's input and output configuration and on the number of inputs and outputs available on the audio device. Quite often you might have a stereo pair going to an effect and a stereo pair coming back. Selecting a stereo configuration would be advisable in this case.

4. Click OK. The External FX bus name is now visible in the FX Plug-in selection list whenever you want to use it.

5. Return to the External FX tab in the VST Connections panel and set the Audio Device for both the Send and Return busses. Sends use audio outputs, whereas returns use inputs. Once an output port is used by an Output, External FX, External Instruments or Studio bus, it can't be used as an External FX bus.

6. Adjust the delay value, if necessary. The Delay value compensates in milliseconds for external devices that may have inherent latency once the signal returns. When using reverbs and delays, for example, it may be okay to leave this set to 0 ms. It would definitely *not* be okay to leave it at 0 ms for a compressor, harmonizer, preamp, and other time-sensitive processes in which the resultant delay would cause phase cancellation or other time-alignment issues.

Dealing with Audio Alignment Issues When connecting external devices to Cubase through the External FX bus, understand that an audio signal gets sent outside Cubase, is processed by this external device, and returns inside Cubase before it is sent to the project's output. This little trip in the outside world can sometimes cause a time shift in the signal and potentially create time-alignment issues with the rest of your mix. This is due in part to the I/O conversion (if any) or the internal processing latency of the external device itself. When this is the case, use the Delay value to adjust the amount of delay needed to restore the timing of the signal. Adjusting the delay works better when the project is playing because you will hear the result of the change in value and the effect it has on the audio as it is moved in time to fit with the rest of your mix.

7. Enter the desired amount of Send Gain and Return Gain. The Send and Return Gain values let you adjust the gain level for the signal being sent to or received from the device.

8. If the external effect is MIDI-compatible and you want to associate a MIDI port with it, select an existing one from the MIDI Device column or create one if needed.

Once an external effect device is connected to a MIDI port and properly configured in the MIDI Device Manager, you can record MIDI messages in Cubase and play them back to change presets or parameter values in your device. This is a very nice feature when you want to get the most out of your external devices.

External Instrument Connections

Similar to external FX, the External Instruments tab lets you connect external hardware sound modules so that you can use them in your project as with any other virtual instrument. External instrument connections offer a very convenient way to set up MIDI and audio for these devices simultaneously in Cubase. Because you can save these settings to a template file, you won't have to redo the same setup steps every time you want to use your external MIDI gear in a new project.

Create an external instrument:

1. In the VST Connections panel External Instruments tab, click the Add External Instrument button.

2. In the Add External Instrument dialog box, type a name for this effect. Because this name will appear in the instrument selection menu, it's recommended that you give it an easily recognizable name, such as "MOTIF ES8" if you own a Yamaha MOTIF ES8 synth.

3. Set up the instrument returns appropriately. These settings depend on the output configuration on your external device and the number of audio

inputs on your computer you want to use for this setup. With many synths/samplers, a single stereo return should work fine. You can change this setting later, if necessary, by creating an additional instrument.

4. Click the Associate MIDI Device button and select an existing MIDI device. In order for the device's patch names to show up in the Inspector, it is recommended that you create the MIDI device inside the MIDI Device Manager beforehand. For more information on how to install a MIDI device in the Manager, check out Chapter 10, "Using VST and MIDI Instruments."

5. Adjust the Delay value, if necessary. As with an external FX, the Delay value compensates in milliseconds for external devices that may have inherent latency once the signal returns. Here again, I recommend that you start by leaving this value at 0 ms.

6. Enter the desired amount of return gain, if necessary. The Return Gain values let you adjust the gain level received from the device.

Once both MIDI and audio port connections are made, your external MIDI devices will appear in the VST Instruments panel and in the instrument selection field of the Add Instrument Track dialog box.

Studio Connections

The Studio connection tab lets you configure a number of additional discrete cue mixes, from a control-room mono monitoring setup to a multi-channel monitoring setup, headphone mixes, or a studio talkback microphone when you need to communicate instructions through musician's headphones in a recording booth. In a simpler setup, cue mixes added in this tab allow you to cue sounds you're about to import to a project through a separate audio port, even though they haven't been assigned to a track yet. Think of it as creating a preview bus.

With that said, if you are using Cubase as a project or home studio production tool, have all your gear in a single room and record most of your tracks while sitting in front of the computer, you probably won't need to create any studio connections. If this case applies to you, disable the Control Room Mixer by pressing the Disable Control Room button, as displayed in Figure 4.8. Disabling the Control Room Mixer is also recommended if you only have a stereo pair of inputs and outputs. When the Control Room Mixer is disabled, the audio generated when previewing files being imported to your project passes through the output bus.

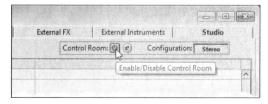

Figure 4.8 Disabling the Control Room Mixer.

For additional information about signal routing options associated with the different studio connections, check out the discussion of the Control Room Mixer in Chapter 6, "Using the Control Room Mixer."

Create a studio connection:

1. In the Studio tab of the VST Connections panel, click on the Add Channel button.

2. From the pop-up menu, select the type of studio connection you want to create.

3. In the Add Channel dialog box, type a name for the studio connection and select the desired channel configuration.

4. Click OK.

5. Expand the channel to display the device ports connection assignment, as seen in Figure 4.9.

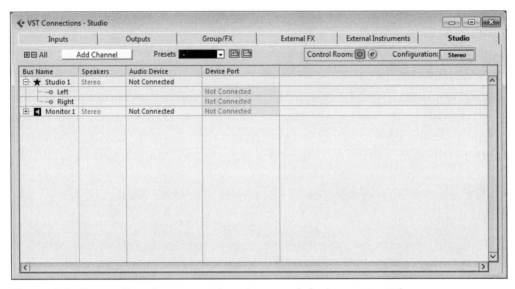

Figure 4.9 Expanding the connections to reveal device port settings.

6. Click in the Device Port column to assign this channel to unused audio ports.

Saving Connections

The connection settings discussed in this chapter can be saved and recalled later. Saving connections makes setting up work sessions a breeze. It's also convenient to save connections when the number of available audio ports is limited. The audio ports on your audio device become your patch bay, and Cubase handles all signal routing tasks internally. There are two ways to save connections:

- By setting everything up and saving the project as a template (File > Save As Template)

- By saving the connections as presets

Saving Connections in a Template

Templates appear when you are creating a new project, as displayed in Figure 4.10. When a project is saved as a template, all connections are saved with templates. You can create different connection configurations using all your inputs to feed tracks when you know the project involves mostly live musicians in a studio. You can also save another template in which connections are optimized for projects with external effects and MIDI sound modules.

Working with Templates: Templates can include much more than just connections; you can also define the number and types of tracks, EQ settings, effects, levels, and the like. Learn more about working with templates in Chapter 39, "Customizing Your Project."

Figure 4.10 The Project Assistant displays the available templates.

Saving Connection Presets

You can also save connections as presets. Connection presets work much the same as other presets in Cubase, as you can see in Figure 4.11.

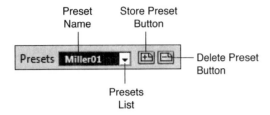

Figure 4.11 VST Connections: connection preset tools.

Manage connection presets:

- To save a connection preset, click on the Store Preset button and give the preset a name in the Preset Name dialog box.

- To recall a preset configuration, select it from the Presets list.

- To delete a connection preset, click on the Delete Preset button.

- To rename a connection preset, double-click on the preset name.

---

5 Creating a New Project

Projects in Cubase 6 are the equivalent of documents in Microsoft Word, image files in Adobe Photoshop, or any other software-specific file format. A project holds all the information needed to re-create the work, with the exception of media files, which are saved as separate entities on your media drive and referred to by the project file when you are editing it.

In theory, you can have as many projects open in Cubase as you want (although only one can be active and playable at a time). In practice, however, your system's resources will most likely dictate how many projects you can load into memory simultaneously. The more tracks and plug-ins loaded into a project, the more memory it tends to use up in your computer.

Dragging Events: When you have more than one Project window open in Cubase, you can drag events from one project to another.

Here's a summary of what you will learn in this chapter:

- What a Cubase project file is

- How to set up a project's display, audio, and timecode properties

- How to create audio tracks

- How to apply a preset configuration for an audio track

- How to set up audio tracks for recording

- How to create instrument and MIDI tracks

- How to set up instrument and MIDI tracks for recording

Understanding Cubase Projects

Each Cubase project you create is saved as a Cubase *PR*oject file (CPR file). Cubase projects contain all MIDI data, automation, plug-in effect settings and assignments, and overall mixer and connection settings. Although audio and video clips are not saved within the project file, the position and other playback parameters for audio events placed on the timeline inside Cubase tracks are also saved with the project file.

When you reload a project file, it will find these media files where you left them. If you changed any of the media files' locations between saves, Cubase will prompt you for a new location before loading them in your project. Furthermore, if you delete a folder containing media files used in a project without backing them up beforehand, you will no longer be able to use this audio or video in your project, and Cubase will warn you that it could not load certain files.

Creating a Project

Now that you understand the relationship between a project and its media files references, let's create a new project.

Create a new project:

1. Select File > New Project or press the keyboard shortcut Ctrl+N (PC)/ Command+N (Mac).

2. This opens the Project Assistant, shown in Figure 5.1, which you use to easily create common types of projects. The tabs along the top of this window (Recent, Recording, Scoring, Production, Mastering, and More) each contain templates for different types of projects. For example, when you select the Recording tab, you see various types of

Figure 5.1 Creating a new project with the Project Assistant.

recording projects—Acoustic Guitar + Vocal, Clean E-Guitar + Vocal, Distortion Guitar + Vocal, Piano + Vocal, and Stereo Acoustic Guitar. Each of these templates automatically creates the right number and types of tracks for the specified type of recording.
You can click any of these templates to create a project of that specific type, or select the More tab and click Empty to create a new empty project—one that does not yet have any tracks created.

Project Templates: Templates are project files with specific combinations of tracks and other features that were saved as templates in the Cubase 6 program folder. To learn more about how to create templates, see Chapter 39, "Customizing Your Project."

---

3. If the Use Default Location option is selected at the bottom of the Project Assistant window, Cubase will create this new project in the default location it uses for all new projects. (This default folder is displayed to the right of the Use Default Location option.) If you prefer to specify a different location for this project, select the Prompt for Project Location option; when you create the project, Cubase will prompt you for the location for this project.

4. Click the Create button to create the new project.

If you have chosen to create a new empty project, Cubase opens an empty Project window. If you have selected to create a project based on an existing template, Cubase will automatically create a project with tracks corresponding to the template's default settings. For example, if you selected the Hip-Hop Production template (on the Production tab), you will see five tracks in the Project Assistant window: Drums, Bass, Clavinet, Lead Synth, and Vocals.

Configuring Project Settings

Before you add content to a project, you need to configure some basic settings for that project. You do this from the Project Setup dialog box, which you open by selecting Project > Project Setup.

The Project Setup dialog box contains five groups of settings:

- The author and company associated with the project.

- The start time and total length of the project.

- The frame rate (when creating soundtracks for video projects).

- The display format, display offset value, and bar offset.

■ Key digital audio properties, including sample rate, bit resolution, record file type, and stereo pan law.

The digital audio properties are probably the most important settings here; in general, the higher the settings, the higher the recording quality. So, for example, if you plan to do most of your work in 48 kHz, you should make sure your project is set up to record audio using this sample rate.

The sample rate also influences how files are imported into the project. For example, if you import audio files recorded at 44.1 kHz into a 48-kHz project, Cubase will prompt you to convert the files to the project's sample rate before importing them.

Changing Numeric Values: Whenever you see numeric values—such as a time location or a volume level below a fader—clicking on the value box to highlight it will allow you to change the value in one of several ways.

If you have a mouse with a scroll wheel, you can use the scroll wheel to increase or decrease the value. In addition, when you point the pop-up arrow toward the top or bottom of a time display, the cursor will change into a plus or minus sign; clicking when this pointer is displayed will increase or decrease the value by single units, whereas holding the mouse button down will scroll the selected value up or down. Finally, you can always type new values whenever a value box is selected and editable.

Set up a project:

1. Select Project > Project Setup or press Shift+S to open the Project Setup dialog box, shown in Figure 5.2.

2. Enter your name into the Author field, and your company name (if you have one) into the Company field.

3. Leave the Start field at its default setting. If you want your project to start at a different time location, enter the proper value in this field in hours, minutes, seconds, and frames format. This adds the entered value to the time displayed in the project. For example, set the Start time to 01:00:00:00, and the project will begin at that time rather than at the usual 00:00:00:00.

4. Set the Length field to the approximate length of your project. Setting up the length influences the proportion of time displayed in the overview area of the current project and speeds up any freezing or rendering processes, which are discussed in Chapter 40, "Optimizing Your Project."

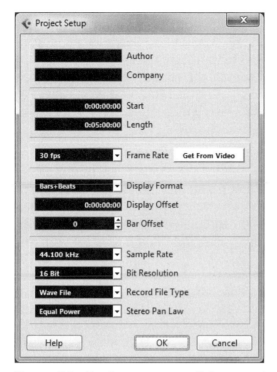

Figure 5.2 Setting up a new Cubase project.

5.   If you are working with a video file, set the Frame Rate field to this media's frame rate. (You can more easily do this by clicking the Get From Video button.) This ensures that the timecode displayed in Cubase corresponds to the timecode format of the synchronizing media.

6.   In the Display Format field, select Bars+Beats to determine how time is displayed on your project's Transport Control bar. This setting displays your project as musical measures and beats, which is useful when recording music; other settings may be better for spoken-word or other non-music projects. You can change this later while working in your project.

7.   The Display Offset value can be left at its default, in most cases. If you are synchronizing a project to an external video that starts at a frame other than zero—for example, if the tape starts at 01:59:45:00—you might still want the timeline display in your project to start at the position 00:00:00:00. Then you would set the Display Offset value at 01:59:45:00 for the start position (00:00:00:00) to correspond to this time.

8.   If you selected Bars+Beats, you can then select a Bar Offset value. This works much like the Display Offset, in that you can use it to compensate for recordings starting at a point other than bar 1, beat 1. In most instances, you can leave this field at 0.

9.   Set the Sample Rate field to the desired rate.

10.   Set the Bit Resolution to the desired bit depth from the drop-down menu. You can select any resolution supported by your audio hardware. Unlike the sample rate, you can import or record audio files with different bit depths in a single project. However, the record format selected here will determine the number of bits per sample in any digital audio files created in this project by new recordings or other audio-related operations.

11.   From the Record File Type field, select the desired audio file type. In most cases you'll select Wave File, although the Broadcast Wave file format is a viable option. Broadcast Wave is identical to normal Wave (WAV-format files) with one exception: It enters text strings that will be embedded in the audio files. These text strings can contain information about your project, its creators, and audio time stamping information. By using this file type, you don't have to enter this information later because it will be done automatically. Another option is the Wave 64 format; this is a Sony (formerly Sonic Foundry) proprietary format that supports files larger than 2 GB. Wave 64 files are better suited for live-concert recordings in surround format, in which file size can reach the limit of regular Wave file capacity fairly easily. And, if you're recording on a Mac, the AIFF format is an option, as it's the standard format on the Mac platform, much as Wave is the standard format in Windows.

12.   In the Stereo Pan Law field, select the default –3 dB from the drop-down list. When panning a channel, you want the left, center, and right pan positions to sound equally loud. Selecting 3 dB or 6 dB will ensure this. Otherwise, a setting of 0 dB will cause a channel panned to the center position to sound louder. When two similar signals are panned to the center, they double up, causing the perceived loudness to be 3 dB louder than a single audio signal.

13.   Click OK when you are finished.

Creating Audio Tracks

To record audio information in a project, you will need to start by adding audio tracks. When you add audio tracks to a project, you make a choice about how you want them configured. In Cubase 6, you can pick between mono, stereo, or multi-channel tracks (up to six channels). Events recorded on a mono track are recorded in mono format, and events recorded on a stereo track are recorded in stereo interleaved format. *Stereo interleaved* means that both channels (left and right) are recorded into the same file. With multi-channel tracks, the choice widens to include surround-sound formats such as LCRS (left, center, right, and surround), 5.0, 5.1, or one of many other multi-channel formats, as shown in Figure 5.3.

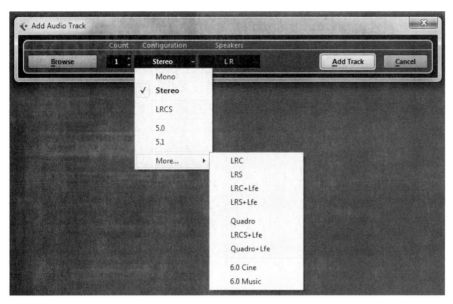

Figure 5.3 Multi-channel audio track configurations.

After an audio track is created, you can record and import or move audio from the Pool into this track.

Add audio tracks:

1. Select Project > Add Track > Audio from the Project menu, or right-click (PC)/Control-click (Mac) in the Track List area of the Project window and choose Add Audio Track from the context menu.

2. In the Add Audio Track dialog box, specify the number of tracks to create. Note that all of these tracks will have the same configuration.

3. Select a track configuration from the drop-down menu.

4. Click OK.

Creating an Audio Track with a Preset Configuration

You can also create a new audio track with preset effects, processing, and the like suited for specific instruments or voices. Cubase 6 includes a large number of audio track presets, and they're ideal for setting up a new track with a minimum of fuss and muss.

Audio presets are available for instruments from A (accordion) to W (woodwinds). You browse the presets by general instrument category first, then by subcategory, then by musical style, then by sonic character, and then by number of channels.

For example, if you want to record an acoustic piano track, you might select Piano for the main category, A. Piano for the subcategory, Pop for style, Acoustic for character, and Stereo for channels. This displays two possible presets—Bright Delta Blues Piano and Bright Piano for a Little Ambiance. If you choose the second preset, you create a track with a variety of insert effects (VintageCompressor, Roomworks SE, and Limiter) and EQ settings pre-applied, to best achieve the sound that you selected. You can further tweak the track's settings, of course, but this provides a good head start in achieving the desired sound for that instrument.

You can apply a preset to a track after it's been created, although it's easiest to choose the preset as you're creating the track.

Create an audio track with a preset configuration:

1. Select Project > Add Track > Audio from the Project menu, or right-click (PC)/Control-click (Mac) in the Track List area of the Project window and choose Add Audio Track from the context menu.

2. In the Add Audio Track dialog box, specify the number of tracks to create from the Count control.

3. Select a track configuration from the Configuration control.

4. Click the Browse button to expand the Add Audio Track dialog box, as shown in Figure 5.4.

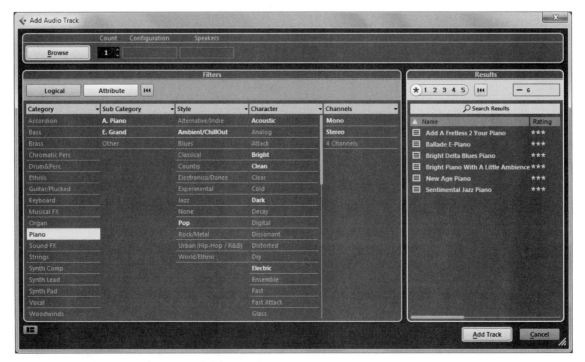

Figure 5.4 Choosing from available track presets.

5. Select the Category, Sub Category, Style, Character, and Channels options you want for this track. (You don't have to select any or all of these options; selecting more options helps to fine-tune the available track presets.)

6. Select the preset you want from the Search Results list.

7. Click OK.

Setting Up an Audio Track

Once an audio track exists in a project, it can receive audio from a source, such as a mic, the audio of a keyboard, or the output of a turntable, and it can play existing audio events through an output bus. By default, audio tracks are labeled Audio 01, Audio 02, and so on. Naming a track makes it easier to manage and find its content later. More importantly, because audio files are given the name of the track where they were recorded, it makes sense to rename them before recording anything. Notice the audio event names on the right; they both correspond to their respective tracks.

Most of the operations described here take place in the Inspector panel of the Project window, as shown in Figure 5.5.

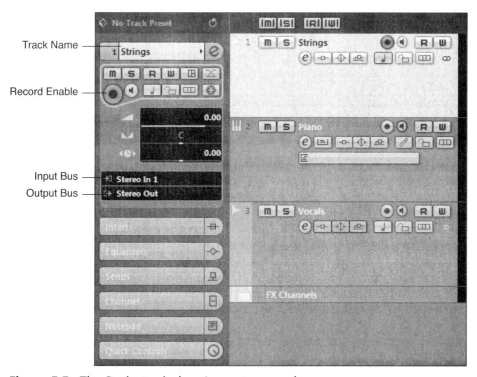

Figure 5.5 The Project window Inspector panel.

Set up an audio track for recording:

1. If the Inspector panel is not visible, click the Show Inspector button in the Project window toolbar.

2. From the Inspector, as shown in Figure 5.5, select the input bus from the track's input routing field.

3. Select the output bus from the track's output routing field.

4. Double-click in the Track Name field and type a new name for the track.

5. To apply a preset configuration for this track, click the Load/Save Track Preset button and then select Load Track Preset to display the Presets pane; click the preset you want to apply.

6. Click the Record Enable button if you intend to record new content into this track.

Creating an Instrument Track

As a composer, producer, or audio engineer, if you're not recording a live instrument or microphone, chances are you're triggering synths, samplers, or a drum machine through MIDI. In Cubase 6, there are two ways to set up a MIDI track, and which one you choose depends on how you intend to use MIDI in the project.

Perhaps the quickest and easiest way is to set up a track for MIDI is to create what Cubase calls an *instrument track*. You can then assign any installed VST plug-in instrument or configured MIDI device as the destination for the MIDI input for this track.

Cubase Instruments   This method of adding an instrument track works for the VST instruments included with Cubase. You'll need to create standard MIDI tracks for most third-party VST instruments, as discussed later in this chapter.

Add an instrument track:

1. Select Project > Add Track > Instrument, or right-click (PC)/Control-click (Mac) in the Track List area of the Project window and choose Add Instrument Track.

2. In the Add Instrument Track dialog box, use the Count control to specify the number of tracks to create. For example, to use two separate instances of the same plug-in, use the small arrows in the Count field to increase the value to 2. Each instrument instance creates a track and its corresponding instrument channel in the Mixer.

3. Select the desired instrument as the track's MIDI destination. The list in Figure 5.6 displays the instruments installed on your computer.

4. To apply a preset configuration for this instrument track, click the Browse button to expand the Add Instrument Track dialog box. Select Category, Sub Category, Style, Character, and Instrument options, and then click the desired preset in the Results list.

Figure 5.6 Loading an instrument plug-in into an instrument track.

5. Click the Add Track button.

The instrument track is now created, and the specified plug-in instruments or external devices are automatically configured to receive any MIDI events being played from or coming through the track. Finally, audio instrument channels are created in the Mixer panel for the output from the specified instruments.

Creating a MIDI Track

You can create additional MIDI tracks to hold different MIDI events that will play through this same device or plug-in. This might be applicable when you need to use several MIDI channels playing through a single external multi-timbral instrument, or a single multi-timbral plug-in instrument.

Add a MIDI track:

1. Select Project > Add Track > MIDI, or right-click (PC)/Control-click (Mac) in the Track List area of the Project window and choose Add MIDI Track.

2. In the Add MIDI Track dialog box, shown in Figure 5.7, use the Count control to specify the number of tracks to create. For example, to use two separate MIDI channels to separate a synth pad track from a percussion track playing through the same plug-in, increase the track count to 2.

3. Click OK.

Figure 5.7 Adding a new MIDI track.

Setting Up a MIDI or Instrument Track

MIDI and instrument tracks share a content type: MIDI events. The parameters that can be changed are also quite similar—the input source, the output destination, and the program or patch name associated with the instrument's internal settings. In Chapter 13, "Using Insert Effects," you'll learn how insert effects can transform the sound of a MIDI instrument; for now, let's learn how to set up these kinds of tracks for MIDI recording.

Set up a MIDI or instrument track for MIDI recording:

1. From the Inspector, select the track you want to configure.

2. Select the MIDI input port connected to your MIDI controller, or leave the MIDI input port set to All MIDI Inputs.

3. Select the MIDI output port, connecting to an external device or VST instrument of your choice. (The VST instrument must be loaded before you can select it from the MIDI output.) The MIDI output determines what will actually generate the audio produced by MIDI events.

4. Select the appropriate MIDI channel for the track's MIDI output, if necessary.

5. Double-click in the Track Name field and type a new name for the track.

6. Click the Record Enable button if you intend to record new content into this track.

Recording

6 Using the Control Room Mixer

For users working in a studio with a separate recording booth and control room, Cubase 6 provides the Control Room Mixer panel, which provides additional routing possibilities. The Control Room Mixer is fully customizable and supports up to four separate studio cue mixes, four separate monitor mixes, six external inputs, one control room headphone mix, and a talkback channel to communicate instructions to musicians from the control room without having to walk over to the booth or yell your lungs out.

For project studio producers, the Control Room Mixer and its studio connections, combined with multi-I/O audio hardware for use with Cubase, provide a flexible monitoring system without having to use an external mixer.

Creating the studio connections is discussed in Chapter 4, "Monitoring and Connecting Audio." This chapter discusses some of the applications and benefits associated with the Control Room Mixer panel and its Control Room Overview panel.

Here's a summary of what you will learn in this chapter:

- How the Control Room Mixer settings are represented in the Control Room Overview

- How to configure and monitor external input busses

- How to Control Room–monitoring options

- How to use the Listen Enable bus functionality

- How to use the Control Room's Talkback functionality

- How to use the Dim button and Use Reference Level button

- How to display the Control Room Mixer Extended panel

- How to add inserts to Control Room busses

- How to use studio sends to create discrete mixes

Understanding the Control Room

Before I begin discussing Control Room features, here are a few beginning pointers:

- If you are monitoring through an external mixer, you probably don't need to enable the Control Room Mixer (CRM) features. You can disable the Control Room functionalities by clicking on the Disable Control Room button in the Studio tab of the VST Connections window. Settings that are in effect when the CRM is disabled will be reestablished once it is enabled again.

- To avoid any routing confusion when using the Control Room Mixer, set all output busses to Not Connected or set the VST Mixer's main stereo output to act as the main mix on the CRM. You will be controlling what you hear in the control room through the CRM instead, which will provide you with additional monitoring and routing functionalities. Cubase displays the main stereo output bus corresponding to the CRM's main mix with a red speaker icon next to the connection's name in the VST Connections window. Right-click (PC)/Control-click (Mac) in the right column for another bus in the Outputs tab of the VST Connections panel, and select the Set *<This Output's Name>* as Main Mix option if you ever need to use that bus as the main mix.

- Like Cubase's Mixer panel, the CRM adapts itself to the connections created in the VST Connections panel. If you create a talkback connection, it will be available, but if you don't create one, those features will not be visible.

- In Cubase, the same audio ports can be used for different input and output busses, depending on your requirements at a given phase in the project. However, audio inputs and outputs used for studio connections can't be used for anything else. Once a port has been assigned to a studio connection, consider it unavailable for other uses. That's why you need an audio hardware device with multiple inputs and outputs to fully take advantage of the CRM features. There are a few exceptions to this rule. Using the same speakers in a stereo configuration and also in a surround configuration, with the same outputs on the audio hardware assigned to both monitor configurations is one of those exceptions. Sharing the inputs between an input bus and an external input device is another exception in which using the same ports for both purposes makes sense when creating connections.

Here's a typical project studio example in which the CRM comes in handy. Let's say that you're recording guitar and vocal overdub tracks over a stereo mix of a groove a friend has sent over the Internet, and you've already loaded the audio mix in a track. You're the guitarist, and you need to hear this mix along with a click track, but the vocalist wants to hear the mix without the click. The guitar is connected to an external preamp, which feeds an input on the audio interface. The lead singer's microphone is also connected to an external preamp feeding another input.

Because this is a project studio, I'll assume everyone is in the same room, so monitoring is done through headphones during recording. You'll need the following connections:

■ Two mono *input busses*—one for the guitar and another for the vocals.

■ One *monitor* connection to connect two audio output (stereo) ports on your audio hardware to control room monitors in the studio. Click the Monitor switch in the Control Room Mixer, as shown in Figure 6.1, to switch between the two sets of monitors at any point in time.

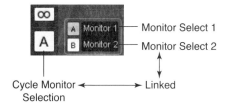

Figure 6.1 The Cycle Monitor Selection button in the Monitor channel of the Control Room Mixer.

Nearfield Monitors: If you use nearfield monitors in addition to headphones, create additional monitor connections in the Studio tab of the VST Connections panel.

■ One *headphone* connection for the guitarist/producer. (To create headphone or cue mixes for musicians in different recording booths, use the studio channels described later.)

■ One *studio channel* for an independent vocal headphone mixes. (The vocalist doesn't want to hear the click track.)

Monitoring with the Control Room

To work with the Control Room function, you need to display both the Control Room Mixer and Control Room Overview (CRO) panels; you enable both these panels from Cubase's Devices window. Both of these panels are shown in Figure 6.2; on the left is the CRO panel, and the CRM is on the right side of the figure.

Let's look at the CRO panel from top to bottom and describe what's happening. The CRO displays all the external inputs and studio, monitor, and talkback connections available. When a connection has been created, the CRO displays it in a darker shade. The channel mixer is summed and sent to the active "studios."

In the CRM, this channel is represented by the first channel on the left, labeled as "Studio 1." The Mix button at the top of this channel also indicates that the signal monitored through this channel comes from the main mix. The CLIK (Activate Metronome

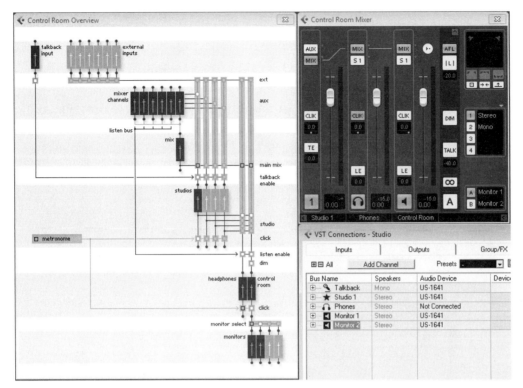

Figure 6.2 Example of a typical project studio Control Room setup, as viewed through the CRO and CRM panels.

Click) button in the center of the channel enables the metronome click for this channel. In the CRO, this is represented by the small white square below the active studios channel. You get the same result in the CRO by enabling the CLIK button in this channel or clicking to enable the corresponding small square button (labeled "click") where the metronome line meets the studios line will offer the same result. (When the click is activated, the box turns green.)

Moving along to the headphones at the bottom of the CRO display, in the second channel to the left of the CRM (labeled Phones), you can see that it also monitors the main mix, but in this example, the CLIK button is enabled in both locations (the CRO and the CRM).

Set up a click (metronome) track in the CRM:

1. Enable the CLIK button in the desired CRM channel.

2. Click on the Metronome Level display (just below the CLIK button) to adjust the volume of the click in this channel.

3. Press C to enable the click in Cubase.

External Inputs

At the top of each CRM channel is the Input Selector button, which controls the source of the audio signal entering each channel. When an external input is created, an additional EXT button shows up at the top. If more than one external input is created, you can click on the Show Left Strip button to expand the CRM's left strip, which reveals an external input selection.

Monitoring Options

There is also a similar strip on the right of the CRM that offers a number of monitoring options, which vary depending on the studio connections you have created (from top to bottom in Figure 6.3):

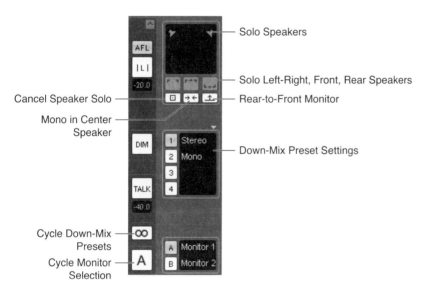

Figure 6.3 The monitoring options of the CRM.

- Click on any speaker to mute all other speakers. (In a 5.1 surround configuration, the plus sign in the center allows you to solo the LFE channel.)

- Click on Cancel Speaker Solo to unmute all channels at once. There are also a number of additional solo functions, depending on the active monitoring setup.

- Click any down-mix preset buttons to automatically switch between different down-mix options. A down-mix option lets you hear different mixes through the same monitors. For example, clicking on a stereo mix while monitoring in surround lets you hear how your surround mix will translate to stereo; clicking on a mono mix for a stereo recording lets you hear how your stereo recording will sound in a monophonic environment. Clicking on the Open MixConvert Settings down arrow opens the settings panel for the MixConvert plug-in, shown in Figure 6.4, where you can change the down-mix configuration if necessary.

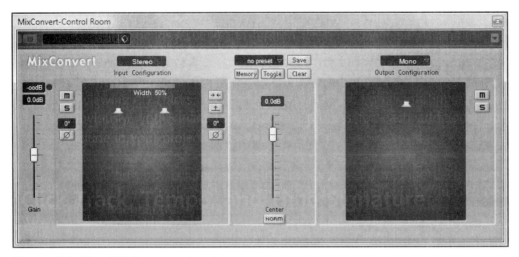

Figure 6.4 The MixConvert plug-in.

- The Cycle Downmix Preset button lets you quickly cycle through all the preset down-mixes.

Listen Mode

The CRM's Listen mode lets you send the signal of all audio-related Mixer channels that have their Listen buttons enabled to the Control Room monitors without interrupting the signal flow, overriding the normal signal being monitored. On many hardware consoles, this is also called the Pre Fader Listen (PFL) bus, because the levels that will be heard are unaffected by that channel's main volume fader. The Listen mode bypasses the Mixer's Volume Level control, the studio monitoring options, and the metronome options. When enabled, the signal is routed to this bus directly after the signal enters the channel, before any phase, trim, inserts, EQ, volume, or pan controls.

Use the Listen mode:

1. In the Mixer panel, enable the channels you want to include in the Listen bus.

2. In the CRM, click on the Listen Enable for Output (LE) button found in any of the monitor channels or in the headphones channels. From this point on, all channels that have their Listen button enabled will be summed with the rest of the signal on the listen-enabled bus.

3. By default, you're listening to the pre-fader output. To switch the listen-enabled channels to After Fader Listen (AFL), click on the PFL button to enable the AFL mode. This button toggles between both modes.

4. To change the level of the summed LE bus, click on the Listen bus level value, and a fader will pop up.

Talkback Options

The CRM's Talkback mono connection provides a way to communicate with musicians in a different room through a studio connection by connecting a microphone to one of the input ports on your audio hardware and creating a talkback connection in the VST Connections panel. Talkback options are displayed in the CRM only when a talkback channel has been created in the Studio tab of the VST Connections panel.

Use the Talkback functions:

1. Enable the Talkback button on each studio connection to which you want the talkback to be distributed.

2. Adjust the talkback level for each enabled studio connection.

3. Activate Talkback functionality by pressing the Talk button.

4. Adjust the overall talkback level.

Switching Between Talkback Modes   The Talkback button has two modes. By default, clicking on the Talk button enables the Talkback function, and clicking on it again disables it. This is called the *Latch mode*. You can also set the Talkback button to only be active when the button is pressed. In other words, the button doesn't latch; it simply switches to Talkback mode whenever you need it. Double-click once on the Talk button to toggle between the two modes. Manually enabling the Talk button is very convenient during a recording session when you just want to interject comments, and you don't want to leave the talkback on by mistake.

Dim and Reference Levels

The Dim button lets you quickly reduce the Control Room level by 30 dB without having to change the fader's position, which makes it very convenient when the producer wants to comment on a recording or mixing pass, and you want to make sure you heard the comments properly. Click the Dim button again to return the control room level to where it was. You can change the actual amount of reduction applied by the Dim button in the Preferences dialog box, on the Control Room panel.

The reference level lets you set the Control Room monitoring level to a calibrated mix, essential to most film-dubbing stages. By default, this value is set to –20 dB, but you can change this value by setting the Control Room fader to a new level and holding down the Alt (PC)/Option (Mac) key when clicking on the Reference Level button. When the reference level is used, the button is lit.

CRM Extended View

You can add insert effects to all channels found in the CRM as well as display output level metering through the CRM's extended view. Click the Show Extended Panel button, as shown in Figure 6.5, to display this panel. The Show Meters button toggles the display between inserts and output level meters.

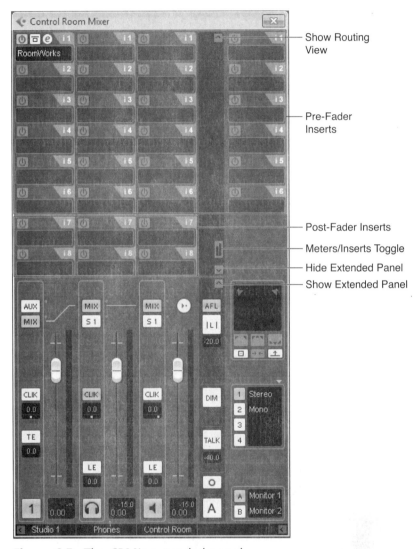

Figure 6.5 The CRM's extended panel.

As you can see, all channels can have up to six pre-fader inserts and, with the exception of external inserts and monitors, they also can have two additional post-fader inserts (numbers 7 and 8). By default, the external input inserts are displayed, but you also can add inserts to the talkback connection. To do so, simply enable the Talk button. Cubase displays the talkback inserts where the external input inserts are currently displayed. The talkback connection can have up to eight inserts.

You will find more on using insert effects in Chapter 13, "Using Insert Effects," but understand that you can use dynamic inserts, such as a gate or compressor, on the talkback connection, for example, to protect your performers' ears or to reduce the noise level leaking when talkback is enabled, or to add some reverb to the mix sent to the singer in the example I described at the beginning of this chapter.

Studio Sends

Studio sends are intended as discrete mixes that can be used to send a customized head-phone mix through a studio connection. By creating a mix using studio sends, you can make sure the bass player hears the kick drum well without forcing the singer or pianist to hear the same mix. Like many functionalities available in the CRM, the number of studio sends available is tied to the number of studio connections you created, so you can have up to four studio send mixes or four discrete headphone mixes. The way studio sends work is very similar to the way FX channels work. However, FX channels are better suited to process audio being sent from a number of audio or instrument channels (with a reverb or delay send effect on one of their inserts, for example) and can be used outside the CRM. You'll find more on FX channel tracks in Chapter 33, "Working with FX Channel Tracks."

Set up a discrete mix using studio sends:

1. In the Mixer panel (F3), display the extended panel.

2. In the extended panel's common area, click on the Show Studio Sends button. The studio sends controls will appear as shown in Figure 6.6.

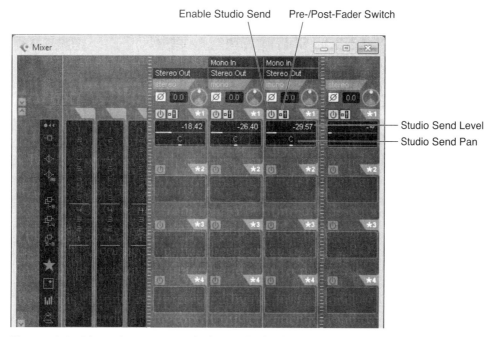

Figure 6.6 The Mixer's extended panel, displaying the studio sends setting.

3. Enable the studio sends for each channel you want to include in the mix.

4. Set the amount of signal sent from the channel to the studio connection by dragging the horizontal line displayed under the level value. You also can Alt-click (PC)/Option-click (Mac) on the value to use the pop-up fader.

5. Adjust the panning of the signal in the mix. As with the volume level, the pan value only affects the studio send mix.

6. By default, studio sends are set to Post-Fader, but to change the studio send level setting to Pre-Fader (so that its level will not be affected by changes to the channel's main volume fader), enable the option.

7. In the CRM, set the studio connection's source to AUX. From this point on, all signals being sent to studio sends 1 will be heard through the studio 1 connection.

7 Managing Your Media

A typical Cubase recording project incorporates multiple media files. Each track you record is its own file; each preset you apply is also a separate file. You manage all these media files from Cubase's MediaBay utility; managing MediaBay is essential to efficient Cubase operation.

Here's a summary of what you will learn in this chapter:

- How to use the MediaBay's browser to locate and manage folders containing media

- How to use the MediaBay's filtering options

- How to load and save VST and track presets

- How to import different file formats into a Cubase project

Using the MediaBay

The MediaBay represents the core of the Cubase VST Sound system. It's where you browse and manage all your Cubase-related media files. You open the MediaBay by selecting Media > MediaBay, or by pressing F5.

Media Browsers: Cubase 6 actually includes three separate media browsers: MediaBay, Loop Browser, and Sound Browser. You can access all these browsers from the Media menu.

Figure 7.1 shows what the MediaBay looks like in Cubase 6. (If you're familiar with MediaBay in previous versions of Cubase, it's been extensively redesigned.) There are several defined areas of the MediaBay: Define Locations, Locations, Filters, Results, and Previewer.

Define Locations

The left panel of the MediaBay window, labeled Define Locations, is where you select the location to browse for media. Disks, folders, and subfolders are displayed in a tree structure, similar to what you find in Windows Explorer or the Mac's Finder.

Figure 7.1 The MediaBay.

There are a few differences between the Define Locations pane and these other file-browsing utilities, however. For example, the Define Locations pane scans only for content that can be used in a Cubase project—in other words, files in compatible formats. These formats include a number of audio and MIDI file formats, as well as track presets (.trackpreset files), VST presets (.vstpreset files), Nuendo or Cubase project files, as well as video files such as QuickTime or MPEG.

Saving Locations: You can save specific locations by clicking on the Add button at the top of the Define Locations pane. Once a location is saved, it can be recalled from the Location drop-down menu in the Locations panel. This offers a convenient way to create a list of commonly accessed locations.

Locations

The Locations pane is located at the top of the main section of the MediaBay window. This pane essentially displays the location currently selected in the Define Locations pane. You can click the Location button to display a drop-down menu of saved locations.

Filters

The Filters pane is located just below the Locations pane in the main part of the Media-Bay window. You use this pane to filter the content in the selected location by a variety of parameters.

When you select the Attribute button, you can filter the content based on associated categories—essentially, tags or keywords associated with the VST Sound–compatible media formats described previously. By default, Cubase displays six columns of filters: Category, Sub Category, Style, Sub Style, Character, and Key. Select one or more options from these columns to display media content that matches the filters in the Results pane.

Alternatively, click the Logical button to search for specific media files. By default, Cubase searches all file attributes for the keywords you enter, but you can click the Attribute field to display the Select Filter Attributes dialog box, and then select specific file attributes to search. Enter your keywords into the search field to the right of this row; matching files will appear in the Results pane as you type.

Results

This pane displays the results of your filtering or searching in the Filters pane. That is, all matching files are displayed here.

Previewer

This final pane, located at the bottom of the MediaBay window, displays the content inside the selected file or folder in the Results area.

VST Instrument Presets

Instrument tracks provide a quick and convenient way to combine both the creative flexibility MIDI events provide and the power VST instrument plug-ins offer. You will learn more about setting up VST instruments and using external MIDI devices in instrument or MIDI tracks in Chapter 10, "Using VST and MIDI Instruments," but for now, let's look at the topic of instrument presets.

Applying Instrument Presets

As you already learned, you add an instrument track by selecting Project > Add Track > Instrument. By default, the Add Instrument Track window appears. To display available presets while creating the track, click the Browse button.

As you can see in Figure 7.2, the Filters section of the Add Instrument Track window is similar to the Filters pane in the MediaBay, where the selected filter hides all values not corresponding to the current selection. To hear what this preset sounds like before loading the instrument plug-in, select the preset in the Results pane, then click the Play button in the Previewer pane.

To apply an instrument preset, select the preset in the Results pane, then click the Add Track button. This creates an instrument track, with its MIDI output automatically routed to the VST instrument plug-in; the preset is loaded into the plug-in, and the track is ready to be used in a recording.

Using Other VST Presets

Thanks to Cubase's VST technology, preset configurations exist for many settings within the Cubase program and for various VST plug-ins. For example, when you load the MonoDelay VST plug-in as an insert on an instrument track, the MonoDelay

Figure 7.2 Using filters to find the right instrument preset.

panel appears by default. Click the VST Sound button next to the Name field and select Load Preset. You'll see a Results window that displays only the presets for this plug-in, as shown in Figure 7.3. Selecting a preset changes the setting of the plug-in automatically, making it possible to preview the result if the signal is passing through the plug-in as you select presets.

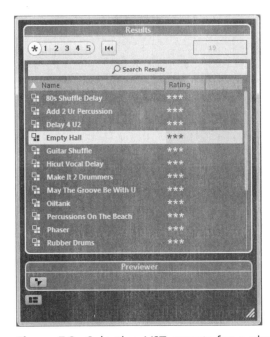

Figure 7.3 Selecting VST presets for a plug-in effect.

Saving Your Own Presets

Presets included with Cubase offer a great starting point, but you might want to save your own customized presets as well. You can save presets for VST plug-ins and for the various instrument and audio tracks you create.

Save a custom preset:

1.   From any field that allows presets, click the Load/Save Preset button and choose Save Preset from the pop-up menu.

2.   In the Save Preset dialog box, shown in Figure 7.4, enter a file name for the preset.

Figure 7.4 Saving a new preset with the Attribute Inspector panel displayed.

3.   To associate specific attributes with this custom preset, click the Show Attribute Inspector button; this expands the dialog box to display the Attribute Inspector panel. Enter the appropriate values next to the corresponding attribute.

4.   Click OK when you are finished.

Importing Audio Content

When working on a recording project, not only can you record events, but you also can import audio and MIDI files. All the import functions of Cubase can be found in the File menu under the Import submenu—or you can drag MIDI and audio files from Windows Explorer or the Mac Finder directly into a project.

When importing an audio file, Cubase will prompt you to copy the file into the active project folder. It is recommended that you keep all your audio files inside this project folder and that you accept that a copy of the audio file be created there. You can always work with audio files from different locations on your hard disk, but keep in mind that backing up a project with all its associated files will be easier if you keep all content in one folder.

Importing Audio Files

Cubase supports many of today's common audio formats: WAV, AIFF, WMA (Windows Media Audio), and MP3 files, for example, can be dragged directly from folders in the Windows Explorer or Macintosh Finder onto a track, or into the empty space below the last track in the Project window's Event Display area to create a new track. When importing WMA or MP3 files (which use audio data compression to reduce file size), Cubase creates a WAV or AIFF copy on your media drive, rather than using the source WMA or MP3 file directly; the resulting file is of the same audio quality as the original, however. Just remember that WAV and AIFF files can be much larger than their WMA or MP3 counterparts, but they have significantly higher audio quality.

You also can import ReCycle files (which become slices within your Cubase project), and Cubase will recognize any tempo and pitch metadata usually associated with ACID loops. ReCycle files are generated by the software called ReCycle, which was developed by Propellerhead Software. ReCycle cuts drum loops into smaller time slices to be reused as samples at different tempos without changing the pitch. This process is similar to the hit point and music mode processes found in the Sample Editor. Sony applications, such as ACID or Sound Forge, embed this time-slice information into standard WAV files as metadata. This information is interpreted by Cubase, which makes it possible to match the loop's tempo to the project's tempo on the fly.

Import audio files:

1. Select File > Import > Import Audio File.

2. Browse to the location of the file you want to import.

3. Select the file and click the Open button.

You can also import audio from inside the Pool window by selecting the Import button or by right-clicking (PC)/Control-clicking (Mac) in the Pool and selecting the Import Audio File option. When you import audio into a project, keep a copy of media files inside the audio folder of the project whenever possible to avoid mistakenly changing a sample that you might need for another project later.

Importing Audio CD Tracks

You can grab audio tracks directly from an audio CD by using the Import Audio CD option in Cubase. This lets you add samples from your favorite songs, or from CDs that offer drum loops, hits, and the like.

Import audio tracks from an audio CD:

1. Create an empty audio track and select it in the Track List area.

2. Position the cursor at the location where you want the event to be inserted.

3. Select File > Import > Import Audio CD.

4. The Import from Audio CD dialog box will appear, as shown in Figure 7.5. Choose the appropriate drive that contains the audio CD.

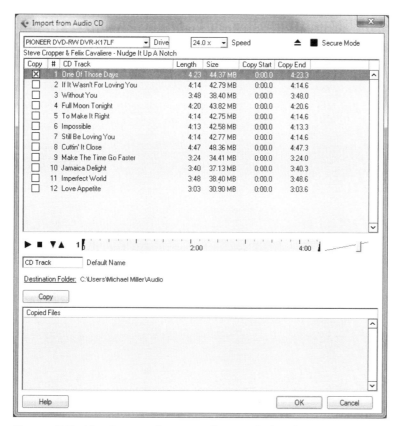

Figure 7.5 The Import from Audio CD dialog box.

5. Select the transfer speed you want to use to import these files. Note that faster speeds result in a faster transfer, but slower speeds limit the potential for errors that can occur during the transfer.

Previewing CD Tracks: You can preview a track before importing it by using the Play button at the middle left of the dialog box.

---

6. In the Copy column, select the track you want to import. To import more than one track, hold the Ctrl (PC)/⌘ (Mac) key while you click on non-sequential tracks.

7. If you don't want to import an entire track, move the Copy Start and Copy End arrows to the right of the Play button. This changes the values in the Copy Start and End columns, allowing you to import only sections of the audio.

8. Type a new name in the Default Name field to give a different name to the imported track.

9. Click the Destination Folder link to change the folder destination, browse your computer's hard drive, and select a new destination folder.

10. Click the Copy button at the bottom of the dialog box to begin the extraction process. The files will appear in the Copied Files section when the extraction is completed.

11. Click the OK button when you are finished.

Alternatively, you can import a CD track from the Pool by right-clicking (PC)/ Control-clicking (Mac) inside the window and choosing the Import Audio CD option. In this case, the audio track is imported into the Pool only, and no events appear in the project's Event Display area. This might be the method of choice when you start building a Pool of good drum loops for your new project.

Using Secure Mode   If you're running into read errors when importing content from an audio CD, try enabling the Secure Mode option. This mode takes more processing time, but it will help you get better results from a drive if it's having a hard time reading the data from the CD.

Importing MIDI Files

Cubase lets you either import MIDI files into an existing project or create a new project from the imported MIDI files. In a Type 0 MIDI file, all MIDI events in any channel are contained in one single track; after importing such a file, you need to make sure the MIDI track hosting this imported track is set to play out through *any* MIDI channels. In contrast, a Type 1 MIDI file contains as many MIDI tracks as there are MIDI channels actually used in the file; Cubase creates a corresponding number of separate MIDI tracks to host the newly imported Type 1 MIDI file. When you import any MIDI file, it is imported at the beginning of the project.

Import a MIDI file into an existing project:

1. In the project's timeline, position the project cursor where you want the MIDI file to begin.

2. Select File > Import > Import MIDI File.

3. At the prompt, click the No button.

4. Browse to the location of the file you want to import.

5. Select the file and click the Open button.

This prompts Cubase to create the new MIDI tracks necessary to place the imported MIDI content in the current project.

Importing Audio from Video Files

Cubase also offers the option of recording the audio track from a video file. If that's what you want, the Import Audio from Video File option will create a separate audio file from the selected video and place it in your project. The format of the audio file will be converted to the project's settings, and a copy of this audio track can be found in the project's folder. In other words, the original video file will not be used once you've imported the audio file from it.

Importing Video Files

Cubase is a popular program not just for recording and mixing pure audio files, but also for editing the audio portions of video files. You can use Cubase to "punch up" an existing soundtrack or create original soundtracks and musical scores.

Import a video file into a Cubase project:

1. Select File (PC)/Cubase (Mac) > Import > Video File.

2. Browse to the location of your file, select it, and then click Open. This adds the video file to the Media Pool.

3. Right-click (PC)/Control-click (Mac) in the Track List area and select Add Video Track from the context menu.

4.   From this point, you can use one of two methods to add your video to the video track. First, you can right-click the video in the Pool and select the Insert into Project option in the context menu. Then you can choose whether you want to insert it at the current cursor position or at the video's original time. Second, you can drag the video, as you would for an audio event, into the video track at the desired location.

8 Recording Audio

Without content, there is no project—and recording audio is the most common way to create content for your recording project, which means connecting a microphone or electric instrument to your computer (or audio input device) and getting ready to record.

It used to be the musician's job to get the notes right, and it was up to the recordist or sound engineer to get the performance recorded properly. In today's computer-based production environment, chances are you'll be doing both jobs, playing your instrument with one hand and triggering the recording device with the other. Cubase is there to make your job look easy and to make you feel confident about getting the most out of a recording session.

Here's a summary of what you will learn in this chapter:

■ How to set up Cubase to record digital audio

■ How to record a basic audio track

■ How to configure the click track (metronome)

■ How to set the tempo and time signature for a project

Recording an Audio Track

Before you begin your first audio recording, make sure your audio connections are configured properly. Your project settings should also be completed at this point, especially the sample rate. Check the Project Setup dialog box (the default key command is Shift+S) if you haven't done so already; all audio files in a project have to be recorded (or imported) at the same sampling rate.

Set the Clock Source: As a final checklist item before recording audio, make sure the clock source of your audio hardware is set up correctly. The clock defines the exact sampling rate (frequency) of the audio hardware; if the audio hardware is acting as a slave to another digital audio device, it should be set to match this device's sampling frequency. If your audio interface is not a slave to other devices in your studio setup, your audio hardware should always follow its own internal clock source.

For any project, the recording process consists of two parts: setting the input levels and making the recording. You set the input levels *before* the recording begins; this lets you make the recording with a minimum amount of knob twiddling.

Record a single track of audio in Cubase:

1. Select Project > Add Track > Audio to add a new audio track to your project.

2. When the Add Audio Track dialog box appears, pull down the Configuration list and select Mono (if it's a mono instrument or microphone) or Stereo (if it's a stereo instrument, like some electronic keyboards). If you want to use a preset template for this track, click the Browse button and browse for the preset you want. Click the Add Track button to create the new track.

3. The new track now appears in the Track List; make sure this track is selected.

4. In the selected track's Inspector, click the Input Routing field and select the input you want to record, as shown in Figure 8.1.

Figure 8.1   Readying a track for recording.

5. Click the Record Enable button for the selected track.

6. If the Monitor button is disabled, activate it to monitor the input level of the audio signal.

7. You now need to set the input level for this recording. Start by playing or singing as you would during the actual recording, at the same planned volume levels.

Adjust Your Source Levels First: The longer an audio signal chain is, the more likely it will pick up noise along the way. Increasing the audio's amplitude level later in the audio chain also increases any noise that has been added at previous points in this chain. As a rule of thumb, it's always better to increase a signal's amplitude at the source than at the input bus level (once it has already been converted or passed through electronic components).

8.   Next, adjust the level fader in the Mixer's input channel for the selected track, as shown in Figure 8.2. Do *not* use the fader in the audio channel itself, as it doesn't affect the input level; it only affects the output (monitored) level. Make sure you monitor the level using the input meter in the Mixer; get the levels as high as possible without going into the red.

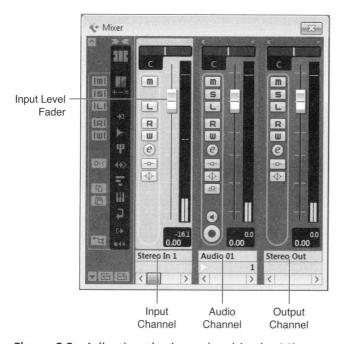

Figure 8.2 Adjusting the input level in the Mixer.

9.   In the Transport panel, select the appropriate recording mode. When recording audio, Normal is usually the appropriate choice.

10.   To start and stop a recording at a specific point in time, position the left and right locators appropriately and enable the Punch-In and Punch-Out buttons on the Transport panel.

11.   Place the project cursor at the position where you want your recording to begin.

12. When everything is ready, click the Record button and begin recording the audio.

13. Click the Stop button or press the spacebar to manually stop the recording if you haven't enabled the Punch-Out button.

Obviously, you'll want to repeat this process for each additional track you include in your project.

Click Track, Tempo, and Time Signature

When you want to hold a steady tempo throughout your recording, all the musicians need to play to what is called a *click track*. Now, this might sound formidable (and, in fact, might scare some inexperienced musicians), but it's nothing more than an electronic metronome. Setting the click track is an important part of any recording project.

> **Click:** A click track, sometimes just called a *click*, isn't actually a track within a Cubase project. It's just a constant click that Cubase generates; musicians play along with the click to keep in tempo.

Playing to a click track helps musicians play at the right tempo, without speeding up or slowing down throughout the piece. It's especially important if you're recording multiple tracks at different times; the click track enables each musician to play to the same beat, even though they may not be playing together.

In addition, the click track makes post-recording editing much easier. After you've recorded all the tracks and want to edit your project, you use Cubase's bars and beat markings the project provides as reference points to cut, move, copy, or resize events along the timeline. When your musicians play to a click track while recording, you can precisely edit the resulting recording.

Click Settings

To help you keep the beat while you are recording, you can activate the Click button on the Transport panel, as shown in Figure 8.3. The Click button enables or disables the metronome click. To generate the metronome click, you can use a MIDI device, your audio hardware output, or both. When the metronome click is enabled, the word "click" is lit, and the field next to the button displays the word "on."

Figure 8.3 The Click, Tempo, and Sync options on the Transport panel.

Configure the metronome settings:

1. Ctrl-click (PC) /⌘-click (Mac) the Click button on the Transport panel, or select Transport > Metronome Setup. The Metronome Setup dialog box will appear, as shown in Figure 8.4.

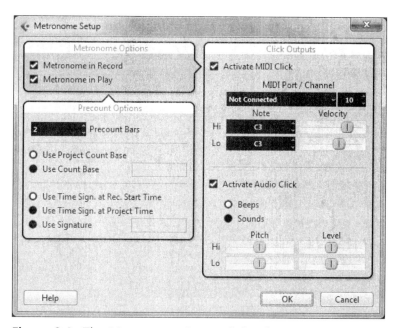

Figure 8.4   The Metronome Setup dialog box.

2. Check the Activate MIDI Click and/or the Activate Audio Click check boxes, depending on which type of click you want to hear. The MIDI click plays through a MIDI device or plug-in, whereas the audio click plays through an audio output.

3. If you've selected the Activate MIDI Click check box, make sure to select a MIDI port connected to a device that will play the MIDI click and an appropriate MIDI channel.

    You can change the MIDI note value of the high and low notes. High notes are played on the first beat of a bar, whereas low notes are played on the other beats. Finally, you can adjust the MIDI velocity of these notes in the same area.

4. For the audio click, if you want to hear beep sounds automatically generated by Cubase, select Beeps. If you prefer to hear a click sound played from an audio file, select the Sounds option; load different click sounds for both Hi and Lo clicks by clicking inside the field. Use the corresponding level controls to adjust the volume for each sound.

5. If you only want to hear the click sound while in record mode, select the Metronome in Record option. If you also want to hear the click sound during playback, select the Metronome in Play option.

6. If you want your metronome clicks on a different value than your time signature setting, such as every eighth note rather than every quarter note in a 4/4 bar, check the Use Count Base option (*not* Use Project Count Base). This displays a count box to the right of this option; use the up and down arrows in this box to adjust the beat subdivision for your metronome's click.

7. In the Precount Bars field, enter the appropriate number of bars you want Cubase to click through before it actually starts playing or recording. For example, if you want a two-bar lead in, enter **2** in the Precount Bars field. (This will have no influence on the metronome if the Precount button is disabled in the Transport panel.)

8. The Use Signature option affects the time signature of the metronome during the precount. This technique is convenient to hear a different time signature from the project's tempo track time signature. For example, if your project switches from a 4/4 to 3/4 time at the exact point you're punching in a new recording, you may want the count-in metronome to be in 3/4 as well. On the other hand, if you don't want to use the signature values associated with the tempo track of a project, enter a custom signature here. For example, it can sometimes be more natural to use a 4/4 count-in, even though the figure you're about to play is in 7/8.

9. When you have completed setting these options, click OK.

Avoid Recording the Metronome: To hear a metronome click while you are recording (but not in the recorded signal), be sure the metronome click is not somehow routed into the recorded signal (for example, because you are recording audio from a keyboard or MIDI sound module that is also the source for your MIDI metronome sound, or because the click sound has been inadvertently routed into your record input path via an external mixer). See Chapter 6, "Using the Control Room Mixer," for more on this topic. You can configure your metronome click through the Metronome Setup dialog box. After your settings are made, close the dialog box and enable or disable the metronome click from the Transport panel. (The default key command is C.)

Tempo and Time Signature

The tempo of a project is counted in beats per minute (BPM) and determines the speed of the project. The project's current tempo and time signature are displayed to the right of the Tempo button in the Transport panel.

When the Tempo button is enabled, the tempo track controls the tempo of the project. To open the Tempo Track window, Ctrl-click (PC)/⌘-click (Mac) the Tempo button. When the tempo track is enabled, the project's tempo follows tempo changes in the tempo track. When the Tempo button is not active, the project tempo remains fixed at the tempo value entered in the Transport panel. (Learn more about the tempo track in Chapter 30, "Working with Tempo.")

While a tempo track is useful when a song changes tempo mid-stream, most songs consist of a single tempo throughout. To that end, you can use Cubase to set the tempo and time signature for a project.

Set a fixed tempo and time signature for the project:

1. Disable the Tempo Track button on the Transport panel.

2. Select the Tempo value box in the Transport panel and type a new tempo for the project. Once this value box is selected, you can also use a mouse scroll wheel to change the value.

3. Select the Time Signature value box in the Transport panel and type a new value or use your mouse's scroll wheel.

Changing Tempo   Entering a new tempo after a recording has been made overrides the original tempo setting, effectively playing back all MIDI tracks at the new tempo. (It doesn't affect the tempo of audio tracks, however, unless they're set to Musical mode.) If you want to change the tempo at a specific location in a project, use the tempo track instead.

9 Overdubbing

Overdubbing is a recording term for the process of adding new recordings to previously recorded basic tracks. For example, consider the common situation where you've already recorded the drum, bass, and rhythm guitar parts, but now you need to lay down the lead guitar after the fact. The lead guitar track, then, is overdubbed on top of the existing tracks.

Because you can create as many tracks as you need during a recording session, overdubbing is an essential part of the modern recording process. Fortunately, Cubase makes it relatively easy to overdub new tracks into an existing recording. You can even overdub part of an *existing* track—which is useful when you need to fix a bad note or two. To create these types of overdubs, you use Cubase's Punch-In/Punch-Out feature—and, if you like, pre- and post-roll.

Here's a summary of what you will learn in this chapter:

- How to add new tracks to an existing recording

- How to overdub existing tracks using punch-in and punch-out techniques

- How to use the Pre-Roll and Post-Roll functions

- How to record multiple takes

Adding a New Track

Few recordings are made in a single take. Most songs involve multiple takes, often with additional instruments added long after the original recording was made.

The concept of building a recording one track at a time was popularized by The Beatles, but actually existed well before that in the 1950s recordings of Les Paul and Mary Ford, with their layered, multi-tracked vocals. Since tape recording equipment of that era was rather primitive, with no more than two or three tracks available in total, engineers had to "bounce" multiple previously recorded tracks onto a single track on a new tape, which made the entire process quite cumbersome.

Fortunately for all involved, 4-, 8-, 16-, 32-, and even 64-track recorders were eventually developed, thus enabling artists to expand their recording horizons. With the advent of hard disk–based digital recording, such as what you have with Cubase 6, you now have an unlimited number of tracks at your disposal. You can add as many new tracks—and as many instruments—as your music requires.

Multi-pass recording in this fashion is fairly easy, especially when the musicians are playing throughout the entire piece. For the musicians, it's just like playing along to the recording. When you're done, your original recording has been enhanced by the new tracks you've added.

Assuming that you've already added the new tracks to the Track List in the Project window, recording additional tracks is a relatively easy process. You can add tracks that last the entire length of the recording, or that pop in during specific segments of the recording.

Adding a new full-length track:

1. Disable recording for those tracks you've previously recorded by clicking off the red Record Enable button for those channels in the Mixer.

2. Enable recording for your new tracks by clicking on the Record Enable button for those channels in the Mixer.

3. Set the input levels for the new tracks you'll be adding.

4. Activate monitoring for those channels you want to hear in the monitor mix for your new recording pass.

5. Turn on the click track by clicking on the Click control in the Transport panel.

6. Ready your musicians for recording.

7. Click the Record button in the Transport panel.

8. The click track counts off the standard two-measure precount, and then recording starts.

9. When the musicians have finished recording, click the Stop button.

Punch-In/Punch-Out Recording

Another common situation occurs when you need to replace part of an existing track. Let's say you recorded a great guitar solo, except for a wrong note in one measure. Instead of re-recording the existing track (and risking losing the excitement of the original solo), you can have the guitarist punch in the right notes for that single measure. You keep the bulk of the original track but overdub the corrections you need.

To replace a section of an existing track, you use the *punch-in* technique, essentially recording a new event over part of an existing track. The new recording event is placed over the previous event, without deleting that event, due to Cubase's use of non-destructive editing. So if you end up liking the original track better than the re-recording, you can revert to the original. Nothing you record is ever lost, unless you deliberately delete it.

The place where you insert the new recording is called the *punch-in point*. The place where the new recording stops (and the previous one resumes) is called the *punch-out point*. You set your punch-in and punch-out points using Cubase's Transport panel. The Punch-In and Punch-Out buttons are in the Locator section of the panel, below the L and R buttons shown in Figure 9.1. These buttons transform the left locator into a punch-in point (where recording will begin) and the right locator into a punch-out point (where recording will stop).

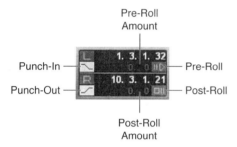

Figure 9.1 Setting the Punch-In and Punch-Out options on the Transport panel.

For example, to start playback at bar 1 of the project but only record over the content starting at bar 3 and ending at bar 4, set the left locator to 3.01.01.000 and the right locator to 4.01.01.000. You'll also want to activate the Punch-In and Punch-Out buttons.

The result is a new event recorded on top of the existing event, between the punch-in and punch-out points, like the one shown in Figure 9.2. Remember, Cubase only plays back the top-most events—in this instance, the new event you recorded.

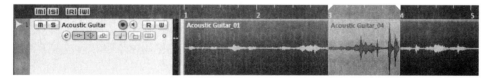

Figure 9.2 A new audio event punched into an existing track.

Replacing Sustaining Instruments: Be careful about punching in instruments that have a long sustain or resonance, such as a cymbal crash or trumpet blast. If you punch out before the sound dissipates, the edit will be quite noticeable to astute listeners.

Pre-Roll/Post-Roll

When you use punch-in recording, you also want to activate Cubase's Pre-Roll function. This tells Cubase to start playback a set amount of time before the punch-in recording begins so that the musicians can hear what they'll be playing to, in context.

The Pre-Roll and Post-Roll fields to the right of the Punch-In and Punch-Out buttons enable you to enter a time value for how long Cubase will play back before dropping into Record mode at the punch-in location. The Post-Roll field lets you determine how long Cubase continues playing after dropping out of Record mode at the punch-out location.

That said, you don't *have* to use the Pre-Roll and Post-Roll functions for punch-in/-out recording; you can start and stop your overdubs cold. But you should use the Pre-Roll and Post-Roll functions when you want Cubase to automatically start playback slightly before the punch-in point and end slightly after the overdub is complete.

Overdubbing an existing track:

1. Set your left locator to the time location where you want to punch in to your existing events.

2. Set your right locator to the time location where you want to punch out of the Record mode.

3. Enable the Punch-In and Punch-Out buttons on the Transport panel. If you want Cubase to replace all existing events from a specific location forward, leave the Punch-Out button disabled.

4. Set a value for the pre-roll. This is the amount of time in bars or beats (depending on the ruler format displayed) that Cubase will play before the left locator.

Exceeding Available Time: If the amount of pre-roll time you select exceeds the amount of time from the left locator to the beginning of the project, Cubase will simply pause for the necessary extra amount of time prior to starting playback at the beginning of the project timeline. For example, if you enter a value of 10 bars and you want to punch in at bar 5, Cubase will count five bars before bar 1 and will then start to play until it reaches bar 5, at which point it will go into Record mode.

---

5. If needed, set the post-roll time as well (found below the pre-roll time).

6. Disable the Click button in the Transport panel; otherwise, Cubase will use the metronome's precount setting rather than the pre-roll setting.

7. Enable the Pre-Roll/Post-Roll buttons on the Transport panel.

8. If you want Cubase to stop automatically after the punch-out time, select File (PC)/Cubase (Mac) > Preferences, and then select the Transport tab of the Preferences dialog box and enable the Stop after Automatic Punch-Out option.

9. Disable recording for all other previously recorded tracks, except the one you want to replace, by clicking off the red Record Enable button for those channels in the Mixer.

10. Enable recording for the track you want to overdub by clicking on that track's Record Enable button in the Mixer.

11. Set the input level for the track you're overdubbing.

12. Activate monitoring for those channels you want to hear in the monitor mix for your new recording pass. (It's often best to hear all or part of the rest of the mix, even if you're only overdubbing a single track.)

13. Click the Record button. Cubase will go into Play mode until it reaches the punch-in time, and then switch to Record mode.

14. Play the replacement part when it comes up in the playback.

15. If you have enabled the Punch-Out button, it will revert to Play mode when the playback reaches the punch-out point. If you have checked the Stop after Automatic Punch-Out option, it will also stop playing after any additional amount of post-roll time value that you have entered.

Punching In New Tracks

You can also use punch-in recording to create new tracks for an existing recording, as shown in Figure 9.3. This is a good approach for adding instruments or vocals that don't play throughout the entire recording; instead of having the musicians sit in silence for a number of minutes, you can punch them into the middle of a recording.

In this instance, you create a new track rather than select an existing one, and set the punch-in and punch-out points where you want the recording to take place. It's desirable to use a fair amount of pre-roll before the recording starts, as it helps the musicians get into the track before they have to start playing.

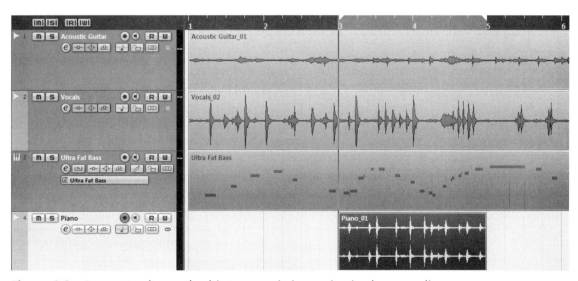

Figure 9.3 A new track punched into an existing point in the recording.

Recording Multiple Takes

Some musicians like to record multiple takes of various instrumental and vocal parts, and then use the take that sounded the best. This is particularly useful when recording instrumental solos. Just have the soloist make several passes through the chord changes, recording or punching in each new pass in turn. You can then audit each of the passes and keep the one you like best for your final recording.

When you record multiple passes in a single track, you create multiple audio events. These events are arranged in a stack, with the earliest events at the back and the latest ones at the front. When you initiate playback, only the front-most (most recent) event is played; the other takes are still there, however.

Recording in Cycle Mode

If you plan on recording multiple takes of a song, it's helpful to use Cubase's Cycle mode. Working in Cycle mode allows you to repeat a section of your song over and over again; while the selected section repeats, you can try different musical approaches and record each lap through the repeated section. When you're finished, you can edit together portions of the different takes.

When you record in Cycle mode, you loop a portion of the project timeline between the left and right locators. The selected section is repeated over and over until you hit Stop or deactivate Cycle mode. Cubase then creates a single long audio file that contains events associated with each lap; these takes are automatically numbered for you.

To record multiple takes in this fashion, you must first activate Cycle mode and set the section of your project to repeat. You can then start recording multiple takes until you get one you like.

Activate and record in Cycle mode:

1. Click the Cycle button on the Transport panel, shown in Figure 9.4.

Figure 9.4 Activating Cycle mode.

2. Click the Audio Record Mode section of the Transport panel and select Keep History.

3. Ctrl-click/Command-click on the point in the project timeline where you want the cycle to begin.

4. Alt-click/Option-click on the point in the project timeline where you want the cycle to end.

5. Click the Record button to begin recording. The recording runs through the selected portion of the project timeline and then automatically repeats, with no space between. The recording continues to repeat until you click the Stop button.

6. Click the Stop button to end the recording.

Working with Lanes

Each pass of the repeated section is recorded as a separate event on the selected track. These events are stacked on top of one another. The last recorded pass is on top and active, but all the other events are still on the track, in layers underneath the most-recent event.

Because you can hear only one event at a time on a track, you need the To Front option found in the Project window's context menu. This option appears when you right-click (PC)/Control-click (Mac) over the overlapping events. You should create and work with events when you want to split up the events to create a composite version using parts of each take.

To view all the takes you recorded, click the Show Lanes button in the Inspector for that track. As you can see in Figure 9.5, the first lane shown is the active lane; the other lanes are "unfolded" beneath that lane, each lane representing a separate take. Only the "top" lane that is currently activated for playback is heard.

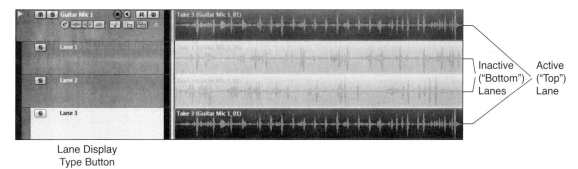

Lane Display
Type Button

Figure 9.5 Displaying all the lanes for multiple takes.

Assembling a Master Take

The process of assembling a single "perfect" master take from multiple lanes is referred to as *comping*. You can comp your takes using the Object Selection or Range Selection tool, although the latter is the most efficient approach.

Assemble a master take:

1. Select the Range Selection tool.

2. Swipe the Range Selection tool to select a range on a specific take, then double-click that range to bring it to the front.

3. Select ranges, in order, from multiple lanes to assemble the master take, as shown in Figure 9.6.

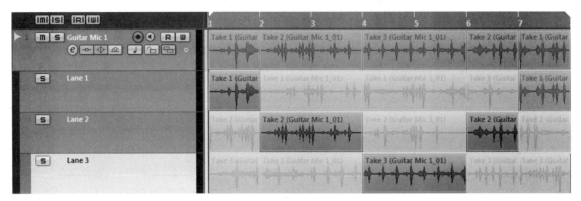

Figure 9.6 Selecting multiple ranges from multiple lanes.

4. If necessary, apply fades or crossfades to any overlapping ranges.

5. When all ranges have been selected, select Audio > Advanced > Delete Overlaps. This puts all the selected events in the top lane and resizes the events so that overlapping sections are removed.

The goal is to select the best portions of each take. The master take, then, consists of the best parts of each take, played in order. The result should sound as if it were a single take.

10 Using VST and MIDI Instruments

For years, recordings documented performances played on acoustic or electric instruments. That changed in the 1980s, when MIDI-based synthesizers added a different type of electronic sound to the mix—and defined the sound of that decade. In the 1990s, sampled loops arrived on the scene, and they still remain an important part of the creative set of tools used by many musicians today.

Today, technology has evolved to encompass and move beyond all the previous types of recorded music. The processing power provided by computers makes it practical to use virtual instruments that can be programmed to produce a wide variety of sounds, emulating both physical instruments and classic synths—or creating entirely new sounds. In this aspect, the computer has become the new musical instrument of the 21st century.

This chapter focuses on these software-based virtual instruments. You'll learn how Cubase communicates with these plug-ins, as well as how to reproduce your favorite MIDI devices inside the Cubase program. Here's a summary of what you will learn in this chapter:

- How to create and set up an instrument track
- How to create and set up an instance of a VST instrument
- How to load and save presets
- How to add a MIDI device in the MIDI Device Manager
- How to manage external MIDI device presets
- How to use installed devices in the Inspector
- How to use filter options to find the desired preset in the Inspector

Using VST Instruments

VST instruments (VSTi) are software-based synthesizers that use the ASIO 2 protocol to generate an audio output through the audio mixing/routing environment of the host program, which then sends this signal to the audio outputs of the computer's audio interface. These software instruments take the form of special audio plug-ins working within Cubase. They can be used to generate sounds triggered by MIDI events recorded in a project when the MIDI output of a track is routed into a VSTi plug-in that has been loaded in your project.

Using VST instruments opens up a whole world of exciting possibilities for any music enthusiast, as well as for hardcore music veterans. They are activated through the VST Instrument panel, which can be opened via the Devices menu or by pressing F11 on your computer keyboard. The VST Instruments panel (see Figure 10.1) is like an empty rack of instruments in which you load instruments as you need them. Each slot in the panel offers plug-in controls for the loaded instruments. Cubase comes with a number of its own VST instruments, but you also can install others; just follow the instructions provided by the plug-in manufacturer when you do so.

Figure 10.1 The VST Instruments panel.

A VSTi can be added to a project in one of two ways—via a new instrument track or by assigning the VSTi to an existing MIDI track.

Setting Up an Instrument Track

When a VSTi is loaded into a project through creating an instrument track, it will be checked in the MIDI Output selector for that track in the Inspector (as shown in Figure 10.2), and a stereo instrument channel for that VST instrument's audio output is added to the Mixer panel.

Figure 10.2   The HALion Sonic SE VSTi loaded into an instrument track.

Create an instrument channel:

1. Select Project > Add Track > Instrument, or right-click (PC)/Control-click (Mac) in the Track List area of the Project window and select Add Track > Add Instrument Track from the context menu.

2. In the Count field in the Add Instrument Track dialog box, shown in Figure 10.3, enter how many instances of a VSTi you want to create. Each instance loads in its own instrument track, with its corresponding stereo channel in the Mixer.

3. By default, Cubase 6 enables the Browse Presets option, which displays a number of filter options. These options are discussed in greater detail in Chapter 5, "Creating a New Project." Here, you'll set up the instrument without loading any presets into it, so click the Browse button to collapse the bottom half of the window.

Figure 10.3   The Add Instrument Track dialog box.

4. From the Instrument drop-down menu, select the appropriate VST instrument. This list contains all compatible VST instrument plug-ins installed on your system, along with external MIDI devices that have been configured through the MIDI Device Manager, discussed later in this chapter.

5. Click OK.

Cubase automatically creates the instrument track(s) per the number of instances you indicated in the Count field.

It's really a matter of preference whether you use instrument tracks or MIDI tracks for your VST instruments. Table 10.1 describes a few advantages and disadvantages of creating instrument tracks this way.

Table 10.1 Advantages and Disadvantages of Using VSTi Through Instrument Tracks

Advantages	Disadvantages
Offers the most convenient way to load a VST instrument plug-in into a project.	No support for multiple MIDI output channels.
No need to assign a MIDI output channel because it automatically routes MIDI events through the VSTi plug-in and its audio outputs.	No support for multiple audio output channels.
Creates a single channel in the Mixer instead of separate channels for the MIDI track and VSTi audio output, which makes it easier to manage.	When the plug-in offers multi-timbral support, loading multiple instances of this plug-in through the instrument track will use up more computer resources (both CPU and memory).
Both MIDI and audio inserts can be added to the same track in the Inspector.	

Setting Up a VSTi

If you want to use a multi-timbral and/or multi-output instrument, you'll need to load the instrument in the VST Instruments panel first. By doing so, you can route any number of MIDI tracks to the VSTi.

Furthermore, if the VSTi offers multiple audio outputs, each of its active outputs will be visible in the Mixer panel as well as in the Project window inside the instrument's folder tracks. In this case, you will deal with separate channels in the Mixer—one MIDI channel for each MIDI track from which MIDI events are routed to the VSTi, and one instrument channel for each active audio output on the VSTi.

Unlike instrument tracks, a VSTi loaded in the VST Instruments panel creates its own folder track where automation events are stored, as shown in Figure 10.4. VSTi folder tracks do not contain any MIDI or audio events, but they contain all the automation associated with a VSTi. (See Chapter 36, "Writing and Reading Automation," for more on automation.) Table 10.2 offers a few advantages and disadvantages of loading a VSTi in a MIDI track. By comparing this table with Table 10.1, you should get a good idea as to which technique is more convenient for your needs.

Figure 10.4 Instrument track (top) vs. MIDI+VST instruments (below)—with VSTi folder tracks beneath that.

Table 10.2 Advantages and Disadvantages of Using VSTi Through the VST Instruments Panel

Advantages	Disadvantages
Offers support for multiple MIDI output channels.	You must load the VSTi in the VST Instruments panel first, and then create individual MIDI channels that are routed to it.
Offers support for multiple audio output channels.	You must make the appropriate output settings for MIDI tracks as well as the VSTi channel itself.
Consumes fewer computer resources than a configuration using multiple instances of a VSTi.	MIDI/audio routing and representation can be confusing for beginners.
Each audio output from the VSTi can have its own EQ, inserts, and automation.	
Each MIDI track routed to the VSTi can have its own MIDI inserts, track settings, and modifiers, such as transpose or velocity compression.	

Let's set up a VSTi so that you can try it out (if you haven't done so already). The hardest part is choosing the sounds to use in the new project.

Set up a VSTi in a project:

1. Select Devices > VST Instruments, or press F11, to open the VST Instruments panel.

2. From the VST Instruments panel, select the first available slot in the rack and click anywhere on the drop-down menu where it currently says "no instrument." This will reveal the installed VST instruments on your computer, as shown in Figure 10.5.

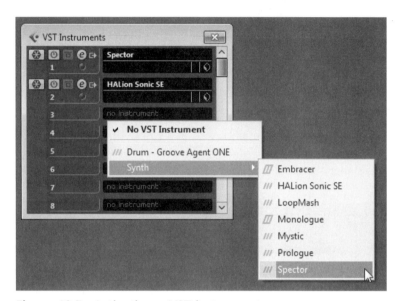

Figure 10.5 Activating a VST instrument.

3. Choose a VSTi from the list to activate it. The blue active button next to the selected instrument reveals that this instrument is ready to be assigned to a MIDI track.

4. Cubase prompts you to create a new MIDI track to control this instrument. Click Create to create a new MIDI track. Cubase will automatically route this MIDI track's output to the VSTi and create a stereo audio channel in the Mixer for the audio output from this software instrument.

5. Cubase opens the instrument's panel, where you can build a patch from scratch or select from a variety of presets. To use a preset, click the Preset selection field and select Load Preset.

6. From the VST Preset selection window, shown in Figure 10.6, select a preset from the list. As you scroll down the list and select each preset, you can preview the result by playing a few notes on your MIDI keyboard or other controller.

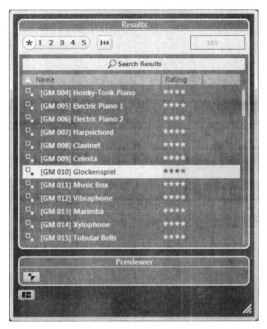

Figure 10.6 The list of presets available for the HALion Sonic SE virtual instrument included with Cubase 6.

7. When you have made your selection, close the instrument's panel to leave the instrument with these preset settings, or click outside the Preset selection box and tweak the instrument's controls to get the desired sound.

At this point, you should be able to hear the sound of the selected VSTi. If you can't hear anything, make sure the MIDI track's MIDI input selector is set to receive MIDI events from the port where your controller is connected, and that the output of the audio hardware is connected to your monitoring system.

If you change your mind about the preset or sound on a VST instrument that is playing MIDI events received from one or more MIDI tracks, or you want to select a different VSTi preset, you can always use the Patch Selector field in the Inspector, shown in Figure 10.7. Clicking this field redisplays the VSTi Preset selection window; you can make a new patch selection there.

To route MIDI events from additional MIDI tracks to the same VSTi, simply create additional MIDI tracks and select that VSTi in each track's MIDI output selection field, either in the Inspector or in the Mixer's routing panel.

Some VST instruments support multiple audio outputs, which makes it possible to set up each of their output channels in the Mixer with different compression settings, EQ, or send effects, among other things. By default, Cubase 6 will enable the first stereo pair

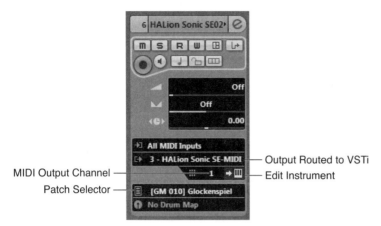

MIDI Output Channel

Patch Selector

Output Routed to VSTi

Edit Instrument

Figure 10.7 The Patch Selector field in a MIDI track playing through a VSTi plug-in.

for a new VST instrument, but it is possible to enable as many audio channels as the VSTi supports.

Saving Presets

With most VST instruments, you also can create your own preset patches and save them for later use. Use the VST Instruments panel's Save Preset option to store custom presets and the Load Preset option to recall presets that were previously saved. You will also find the same options at the top of the instrument's editing panel.

VSTi and Latency

All VST instruments play through your audio hardware, which means that latency plays a great role in how effective the instruments are on your system. Because latency introduces a delay between the time a key is played and the time a sound is heard from the VSTi, shorter delays make the experience more realistic.

To reduce latency to an acceptable level, your system needs to be configured properly, as outlined in Chapter 3, and always use the ASIO driver provided by the audio hardware manufacturer. If the latency is greater than about 25 milliseconds, you might find it disconcerting to play a VSTi, especially when you are playing parts with high rhythmic content, because there will always be a delay between the moment you press the keys on your keyboard and when you hear the sound. The smallest theoretical latency is 0 milliseconds, but in reality, you can expect at least a 1.5- to 3-millisecond latency, which is pretty good. For the best experience when playing through a VSTi, try setting your audio hardware driver preferences (if you have a dedicated ASIO driver for your audio hardware) and Cubase to have less than 10 milliseconds of latency.

Working with High-Latency Setups: If your audio hardware doesn't provide an ASIO driver with low latency, you can always monitor MIDI events through an external MIDI device temporarily while recording these events into a project.

Once the events have been recorded, you can then reassign the MIDI output of the recorded track to the VSTi. That way, you don't deal with the latency delay during recording and, because latency does not affect the timing of your performance, the recorded events are will be properly in sync with other events in the project. Obviously, this is just a workaround. Consider investing in an audio interface with low latency if you intend to use plug-in instruments on a regular basis.

Adding MIDI Devices with the Device Manager

It is possible to create program changes or tell a MIDI track to play a specific program and bank from the MIDI Settings section of the Inspector and the Track List. When working with a VSTi, this is quite easy to deal with because when you select a VSTi as the MIDI output for the track, the track's settings display the available parameters for that instrument. So, for example, if you load the Mystic VSTi, the Inspector will display a list of this plug-in's available presets when you click inside the Inspector's Programs field.

Working with external MIDI devices is a bit trickier because Cubase can't see which device is connected to it. To access the functionalities provided by external devices inside Cubase, you should add these devices to the MIDI Device Manager; this enables Cubase to know how and what to communicate with them. Many common MIDI device definitions are provided on Cubase's installation disc. You do need to install the devices in your personal setup through the MIDI Device Manager, to let Cubase know what is in your studio and how to address it properly.

> **Working with External MIDI Devices:** While I recommend you add MIDI devices via the Device Manager and create device maps for each device you add, this isn't strictly necessary. You can use an external MIDI keyboard without this sort of complex installation, as long as you assign your MIDI channels correctly and don't need to access all of the device's bells and whistles.

When you open up the MIDI Device Manager for the first time, it will be empty because you have not defined any devices in your setup yet. You access the MIDI Device Manager by selecting Devices > MIDI Device Manager or by clicking the MIDI Device Manager button on the Devices panel.

In Cubase 6, you also can use the MIDI Device Manager to create or edit existing panels, which are virtual representations of your external device. These panels are called *device maps*, and they let you control specific parameters on your external device from within each Cubase project, without touching its front panel. Think of these device maps as customizable remote controls.

Adding a MIDI Device

After you have identified your external MIDI devices, you can proceed with their installation inside the MIDI Device Manager. This section looks at how you can install an existing device definition in the MIDI Device Manager.

Add a MIDI device:

1. Select Devices > MIDI Device Manager to open the MIDI Device Manager panel.

2. Click the Install Device button. The Add MIDI Device dialog box will appear, displaying a list of existing device definitions (see Figure 10.8).

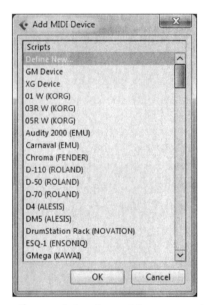

Figure 10.8 The Add MIDI Device dialog box.

3. Select the device you want to install and click OK. Your selected device will now appear in the MIDI Device Manager panel.

The name of each installed device appears in the Inspector's Output Routing selection menu for any MIDI track, with the MIDI port associated with it on the right.

If your MIDI device is not included in the default list in the Add MIDI Device dialog box, you might have to create a definition for it yourself. Remember, however, that if you are using a MIDI sampler, creating such a device definition in the MIDI Device Manager is pointless because a sampler generally does not have a fixed set of programs it loads by default when turned on. In fact, that might be why your device is not listed in Cubase's list of devices!

With that said, if you *do* have a MIDI device with programs and banks that are not defined already in Cubase, or if you want to create a panel that allows you to send parameter change messages to any external device that supports MIDI, you can create your own MIDI device in the Device Manager. Because creating a device from scratch is intricately linked to the device in your setup, you need to refer to your owner's manual and the online documentation (under the "MIDI Devices and Patches" section) provided with Cubase to find out how to create your own custom device with patches, banks, and specific MIDI messages associated with those, as well as customized panels that appear in the User Panel section of the Inspector.

Finding Resources on the Web: Before writing your own script or customizing an existing one from the installation CD, try searching on the Web. Google will certainly point you to sites that may already contain what you are looking for. Most of these sites offer free downloads. The Cubase.net forum is also a good starting point for device maps and patch name scripts.

Managing a MIDI Device

After a device is installed, you can reorganize its Patch Bank list, export or import other devices, and rename items in the patch banks. For example, the Roland JV-1080 patch list is organized in patches, performances, and drums. Inside the Patches folder, there are some 20 groups in which all the actual preset names of this MIDI device are found (see Figure 10.9). However, if you've ever used or seen the JV-1080, programs can also

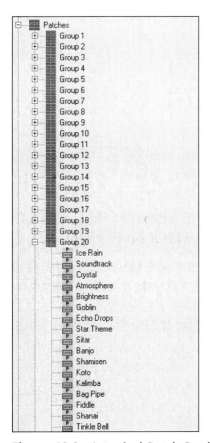

Figure 10.9 A typical Patch Bank list provided by Cubase.

be grouped by type of sounds rather than taking programs 0 to 31 and putting them in a group. So, you can start from the original instrument definition and create your own structure to better suit your needs. This makes it easier when you want to find the right sound for your track.

Add a patch bank to your device's setup:

1. In the MIDI Device Manager panel, select the device in the Installed Devices section for which you want to add the content.

2. Click the Open Device button.

3. When the panel for this device opens, click the Options drop-down menu on the toolbar and select Patch Banks, as shown in Figure 10.10.

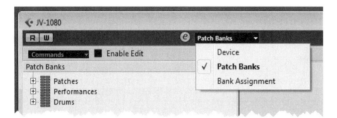

Figure 10.10 Accessing additional device-related options.

4. In the device's Patch Bank mode, check the Enable Edit box to enable the Commands field to its left.

5. Select the Create Bank option from the Commands menu.

6. A new bank will be created, called New Bank. Double-click this new entry and type a new name for this bank.

7. From the Options drop-down menu in the toolbar, select Bank Assignment. (If your device doesn't have patch banks, this option will not be available.) The Bank Assignment function associates MIDI channels with specific banks. For example, if you have a drums bank, you might want to assign this to Channel 10. When you select this device as the MIDI output port from a MIDI track and select Channel 10, the programs listed in the Inspector correspond to associated drum banks. Simply select the banks from the drop-down menu next to each channel to associate a bank with a channel.

If you want to add a bit more order in the presets listing, making them easier to find when the time comes, you can create folders for different types of presets, such as by putting all your piano-related sounds under a Piano group.

Add a preset or a folder to your device's setup:

1. In the Devices panel, be sure the Enable Edit option is checked and that the toolbar displays patch banks.

2. Select the bank or folder in which you want to add the preset or (sub) folder.

3. Select the New Preset or New Folder option from the Commands menu.

4. Double-click the new entry to rename it.

5. If you have added a preset, you need to add the relevant program change information (a type of MIDI message) associated with your device in the Value column found in the right portion of this window. With previously created templates, you won't need to know which MIDI message corresponds to each patch/preset, but when you create a MIDI device from scratch, you will need this information from the MIDI Implementation section of your external MIDI device's manual.

To create more than one device preset at a time in the Device Manager, select the Add Multiple Presets option in the Commands drop-down menu.

When you select the bank or folder in which you have created multiple presets, you will find a list of preset names. For example, there can be 64 presets numbered from Patch 0-0 to Patch 0-7 for the first bank, and then Patch 1-0 to Patch 1-7 for the second bank, and so on. Selecting any of these presets reveals (in the right side of the MIDI Device Manager panel) the actual MIDI message sent to the device.

If you made a mistake or you are not satisfied with an entry in the patch banks, you can simply click the entry and press the Delete key to remove it from the list. You also can change the order in which items appear and rearrange the list to better suit your needs by clicking and dragging the desired entry to a new location.

If you've made some adjustments to your MIDI device listings in the MIDI Device Manager patch banks, Devices panel, or Bank Assignment panel, export these changes to a file so you can retrieve them later if you ever have to reinstall your software or simply use your device setup with Cubase in another studio.

Export a MIDI device setup file:

1. In the MIDI Device Manager panel, select the currently installed device setup you want to export.

2. Click the Export Setup button.

3. Choose an appropriate folder and name for your file.

4. Click the Save button. This will create an XML file.

Import a MIDI device setup file:

1.   Open the MIDI Device Manager panel.

2.   Click the Import Setup button.

3.   Browse to the location of the file you want to import.

4.   Select the file and click the Open button. This will add the device to your MIDI Device Manager panel.

Adding a new device to a setup does not change or influence how existing devices are handled, so you don't have to worry about messing things up by installing an additional device, even temporarily. You can always remove any device you no longer use or need.

Remove a MIDI device from the MIDI Device Manager:

1.   Select the device in the MIDI Device Manager's Installed Device section.

2.   Click the Remove Device button.

Using Devices in the Inspector

After you've installed devices in the MIDI Device Manager, you can use the Program field in the Inspector or the Track List area of a MIDI track to select a program by name. If you have created a panel or imported a device configuration that contains one or several device panels, you also can load these in the User Panel area of the Inspector. When selecting an entry in one of the aforementioned fields or in the Devices panel, Cubase sends the appropriate MIDI message to your external MIDI device in order for you to hear the appropriate sound from that device as it responds to incoming MIDI events.

Assign a program to a MIDI track:

1.   Start by setting your MIDI track's output to a device defined in the MIDI Device Manager.

2.   In the Track Settings section of the Inspector or in the Track Controls area, click the Program Selector field to reveal its content.

3.   This field reveals the patch bank structure as defined in the MIDI Device Manager. Use the Filter field if you are looking for a specific name.

4. Select the program by clicking on its name. When you do so, Cubase sends a MIDI message to your device on that track's selected MIDI channel, causing it to change its program. You can listen to the sound if you want, or select another entry if you want to hear another sound.

5. Clicking once again on the selected sound or clicking outside this drop-down menu selects the sound and hides the menu.

11 Recording MIDI

MIDI offers the possibility of capturing a set of performance events without recording the audio output of the performance. By recording MIDI events, you capture the essence of a musical performance, which can later be edited creatively or aesthetically with great detail. Because the sound isn't part of what has been recorded, you can try a number of different sound, tempo, and pitch permutations. Although recording MIDI is often about recording note events, it's also about recording program changes, pitch bend values, or sustain pedal messages.

Here's a summary of what you will learn in this chapter:

- How to choose the appropriate Record mode

- How to use Cycle and Linear recording

- How to use and navigate with locators in a recording context

- How to use MIDI and audio activity meters

- How to record from single and multiple MIDI sources

- How to use Cubase 6's virtual MIDI keyboard

Record Modes

The Record mode section of the Transport panel enables you to set the record modes used by both Linear (normal) and Cycle recording. You display the Transport panel by pressing F2, or by selecting Transport > Transport Panel.

Linear Record Mode

When you're recording in Linear mode, you have three options: New Parts (Normal), Merge, and Replace. All three options determine how Cubase will handle overlapping recorded events.

- **New Parts** record mode means that when you record MIDI events over existing MIDI parts, Cubase will create a new part, which will overlap the existing MIDI part without changing the previous content or location of these parts.

- **Merge** record mode means that when you record MIDI events over existing MIDI parts, Cubase will merge the new content and the existing content into a new merged part, essentially playing all the notes from all takes.

- **Replace** record mode will remove any existing event or part over the period overlapping with a new recording on a specific track. This would have the same result as a typical punch-in/punch-out operation on a standard analog multi-track recorder.

Change the MIDI Linear record mode on the Transport panel:

1. Click the MIDI Record Mode drop-down section of the Transport panel, shown in Figure 11.1. This displays the Record Mode pane.

2. Select the desired mode in the MIDI Record Mode section of the pane—New Parts, Merge, or Replace.

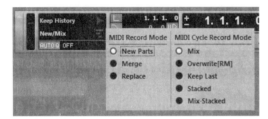

Figure 11.1 Record mode options on the Transport panel.

Cycle Record Mode

When recording MIDI in Cycle mode, you have five options available. These modes determine how MIDI will be recorded during a cycle (looped) recording.

When you are in Cycle mode, Cubase continuously plays the content found between the left and right locators. Each time Cubase starts again at the left locator, it is called a *lap*. How the events are handled during a recorded lap depends on the currently active Cycle record mode. The following MIDI cycle record modes are available:

- **Mix.** Each time a lap is completed, the MIDI events recorded in the next lap are mixed with the events from the previously recorded lap. This is the perfect mode to build up a rhythm track, adding each musical part over the previously recorded one. All events are recorded inside a single part.

- **Overwrite.** Each time a lap is completed, the MIDI events recorded in the next lap will overwrite (replace) the events that were previously recorded. Use this when you are trying to get the perfect take in one shot. Just be sure to stop recording before the next lap begins, or your last take will be overwritten.

- **Keep Last.** This mode keeps whatever was recorded in the last *complete* lap. So if you start playing a lap but stop before it's done, it will not keep that lap. However, if you complete a lap and stop halfway during the next lap, the last completed lap will be the one kept, as with the Overwrite option. This is a good mode to use when you want to record different takes until you get the perfect one.

■ **Stacked.** This is a great way to use cycle recording when you are not as proficient as you would like to be with your playing skills. Every time you complete a lap, an event is created and Cubase continues recording, creating a new event on the same track, lap after lap, stacking up events. Once events are stacked, you will only hear the last one recorded, but you can use the best moments of each take to compile an edited version of the part you were trying to record.

■ **Mix-Stacked.** This is similar to Stacked mode in that events are created for each lap completed. The difference with Mix-Stacked mode is that all the takes (laps) remain audible, without automatically muting previous laps as in normal Stacked mode.

Change the MIDI Cycle record mode on the Transport panel:

1. Click the MIDI Record Mode section on the Transport panel to display the Record Mode pane.

2. Select the desired mode from the MIDI Cycle Record Mode—Mix, Overwrite, Keep Last, Stacked, or Mix-Stacked.

Auto-Quantize

Below the Linear and Cycle record modes on the Transport panel, you will find the Auto-Quantize toggle button (AUTO Q). When this option is enabled (the button is lit, and the text next to the button reads "ON"), new MIDI recordings will automatically snap to the current grid and quantize values without additional steps.

Quantizing: Quantizing is an important technique when recording and editing MIDI events. Learn more in Chapter 26, "Quantizing Events."

Left and Right Locators

The left and right locators are used to identify positions in the project timeline, which are used as boundary markers for cycle recording and as punch-in/punch-out markers during recording when these options are enabled. Locators are also used to define a cycle area during playback, and they play an important role in exporting audio mixdowns and many project-editing operations.

Locators appear in most content editing windows inside Cubase that display a Ruler bar—the Project window, and the Key, Drum, Sample, and Audio Part Editors. However, it's the Project window locators, shown in Figure 11.2, that are important to this chapter's MIDI recording topic.

Figure 11.2   Locators in the Project window's toolbar.

Display locators' positions:

- In the toolbar: Right-click (PC)/Control-click (Mac) over an empty area of the toolbar and check the Locators option in the context menu.

- In the Transport panel: Right-click (PC)/Control-click (Mac) over the Transport panel and check the Locators option in the context menu.

You can quickly move the project cursor to the position of the left or right locator by clicking on the L or R button found at the left of the locator position fields in the Transport panel, as shown in Figure 11.3. Note that you can achieve the same thing by pressing 1 (for left) or 2 (for right) on the numeric keypad.

Figure 11.3   Move the cursor to the left or right locator via the L and R buttons on the Transport panel.

Change locators' positions:

- Move the cursor over the Left or Right locator handle in the timeline ruler. When the cursor changes into a hand, drag to the desired location.

- Position the cursor in the ruler where you want the left locator, and then Ctrl-click (PC)/⌘-click (Mac).

- Position the cursor where you want the right locator, and then Alt-click (PC)/Option-click (Mac).

- Click on a value in the Left or Right Locator section of the Transport panel and enter a new position for it by using your keyboard.

MIDI and Audio Activity Indicators

The MIDI activity indicator (see Figure 11.4) displays incoming (red) or outgoing (green) MIDI activity. Right next to it, the audio activity indicator displays incoming and outgoing audio (green for both) from and to external devices, as well as clips when they occur. A clip occurs when the digital signal is louder than the 0 dB Full Scale (or 0 dBFS) on a digital audio system. If you're not hearing anything (MIDI or audio), try taking a look at these activity meters first. If you see activity here, the problem might be outside of Cubase. If you don't see activity here when you should, it's possible that Cubase is not receiving or transmitting MIDI or audio properly. Note that MIDI or audio metronome activity will not be displayed in these activity output meters.

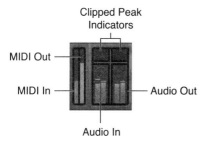

Figure 11.4 The MIDI and audio activity monitors on the Transport panel.

MIDI Activity Troubleshooting Tips: If you are not seeing any MIDI activity when sending messages from an external controller, be sure the selected MIDI track's MIDI In port is configured properly.

MIDI events sent to a VST instrument will not show up in the MIDI activity output monitors. However, if you are not seeing any MIDI activity when playing recorded MIDI events that are supposed to go to an external device, chances are this is caused by one of the following reasons:

- The tracks in your project contain no MIDI events.

- You have not set the track(s) containing MIDI events to play out through a physical MIDI port such as your MIDI interface.

For example, if your external instruments are not receiving MIDI data, try loading a virtual instrument (VST instrument) and routing your MIDI track to that VSTi's MIDI input. If you do hear the MIDI data playing through the VSTi, try reassigning the previous MIDI output port to this track again. If you still don't hear MIDI coming from your external instrument, your problem is probably somewhere else.

- Be sure your MIDI connectors and cables are connected properly. If they are, try switching them around to see whether one of them is faulty.

- Are the MIDI ports you're trying to use properly configured in the Device Setup dialog box?

- Is your MIDI interface installed properly?

- Is the MIDI Thru active in Cubase? To check this out, look in the MIDI tab of the Preferences dialog box.

Recording MIDI

When you record a MIDI performance, you create a unique MIDI event. That event can later be edited to change the duration or pitch of the notes played, as well as to process or edit the sound generated by the instrument playing the performance. It offers a very powerful creative tool.

Before first recording MIDI, select File > Preferences to open the Preferences dialog box, then go to the MIDI tab and make sure the MIDI Thru Active option is selected. Then, as you play into a MIDI track, the MIDI Thru function re-sends the MIDI information Cubase receives through that track's MIDI output destination.

Record MIDI events on one or multiple tracks:

1. Activate the Record Enable button on the MIDI track you want to use to record incoming MIDI events.

2. In the Transport panel, set the appropriate Record mode for either Linear (New Parts, Merge, or Replace) or Cycle (Mix, Overwrite, Keep Last, Stacked, or Mix-Stacked) recording.

3. Position your left and right locators appropriately. For example, if you want to record from Bar 5 Beat 1 to Bar 9 Beat 1, set the left and right locators to Bar 5 and Bar 9, respectively.

4. Activate the metronome click on the Transport panel to hear a click while recording.

5. Click the Record button on the Transport panel and start playing your MIDI instrument. If you've enabled the metronome click, the precount value you've entered in the Metronome Setting dialog box determines how many bars of the metronome click sound you will hear before the cursor starts moving forward in the project timeline.

6. When you're finished recording, click the Stop button on the Transport panel or press the spacebar on your computer keyboard. If the Punch-Out button was enabled, Cubase should stop automatically when it reaches that location.

Recording Multiple MIDI Channels Simultaneously: When transferring a MIDI sequence from a hardware sequencer to Cubase, or when several MIDI controllers need to be recorded simultaneously, you will need to take additional measures to record MIDI events.

You can record all MIDI events on the same track and split up (dissolve) the events by channel later by setting the track's MIDI output channel to Any. This enables the incoming events to be redistributed to the output port without re-channeling the events to a single, common MIDI channel. You'll find out more about dissolving MIDI parts in Chapter 25, "Understanding MIDI Menu Options."

If you have a multiport MIDI interface, you can record MIDI events on separate tracks—one per channel, for example. To do this, simply assign each track to a different input port.

Now that you've just recorded events on a track or multiple enabled tracks, you might want to record over a portion of this recording to correct errors that would take too long to edit in the editor. Or, maybe you just feel like recording over a portion of the track. In the previous steps, you were using the left and right locators as a point of reference to both begin playback and recording, as well as to stop recording. You can also use the pre-roll value in the Transport panel to begin playback before you start recording and the post-roll value to have Cubase continue playing after you've stopped recording.

Recording Multiple Takes

As with recording digital audio tracks, you can record multiple takes of your MIDI tracks, and then use the take (or part of a take) that sounds the best for your final recording. As you learned in Chapter 9, "Overdubbing," this is most often accomplished using Cubase's Cycle recording mode.

Recording MIDI in Cycle Mode

When you work in Cycle mode, Cubase repeats a section of your song over and over again; you or the musician you're recording keeps playing through all these cycles, trying different approaches on each take. When you're finished, you can edit together portions of the different takes.

Activate and record in Cycle mode:

1. Click the Cycle button on the Transport panel.

2. Click the MIDI Record Mode section of the Transport panel and select Stacked.

Building a MIDI Track: Another use of cycle recording is to build a complex MIDI track from different performances. With this approach, each take is actually a different part of the finished track; for example, you might record a drum track in multiple takes, one for each component of the drum kit (bass drum, snare drum, cymbal, and so on).

To accomplish this, you'll want to use the Mix-Stacked mode, and then select the desired events across multiple takes.

3. Ctrl-click (PC)/⌘-click (Mac) on the point in the project timeline where you want the cycle to begin.

4. Alt-click (PC)/Option-click (Mac) on the point in the project timeline where you want to the cycle to end.

5. Click the Record button to begin recording. The recording runs through the selected portion of the project timeline and then automatically repeats, with no space between. The recording continues to repeat until you click the Stop button.

6. Click the Stop button to end the recording.

Working with MIDI Lanes

If you select Stacked or Mix-Stacked mode, each pass of a repeated section in a MIDI recording is recorded as a separate event on the selected track. The last-recorded take is active and on top.

To view all the takes you recorded, click the Show Lanes button in the Inspector for that track; all the recorded events for that track are now displayed, in separate lanes. Only the lane that is currently activated for playback is heard.

Assembling a Master MIDI Take

To assemble a master take of a multiple-pass MIDI recording, use the Range Selection tool. The process is similar to working with lanes in an audio recording.

Assemble a master MIDI take:

1. Click on the Range Selection tool.

2. Swipe the Range Selection tool to select a range on a specific take, then double-click that range to bring it to the front.

3. Select ranges, in order, from multiple lanes to assemble the master take, as shown in Figure 11.5. You can select multiple events that play simultaneously to build a complex MIDI track.

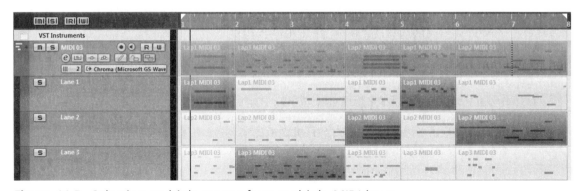

Figure 11.5 Selecting multiple ranges from multiple MIDI lanes.

4. If necessary, open your takes in one of Cubase's MIDI editors to perform fine adjustments, such as removing or editing notes at the beginning or end of an event.

5. When all ranges have been selected, select MIDI > Merge MIDI in Loop. When the MIDI Merge Options dialog box appears, select Erase Destination and click OK. This creates a single MIDI part that contains your "perfect" take.

Virtual MIDI Keyboard

Cubase 6 includes another way to record MIDI performances, via the Virtual MIDI Keyboard. This is a software-based musical keyboard that you can "play" with your mouse or computer keyboard.

To display the Virtual MIDI Keyboard, select Devices > Virtual Keyboard, or press Alt+K. The Virtual Keyboard displays as part of the Transport panel, as shown in Figure 11.6.

Figure 11.6 Cubase 6's Virtual MIDI Keyboard.

The Virtual Keyboard displays one octave at a time, from C to C. You play the keyboard by clicking the keys of the onscreen Virtual Keyboard with your mouse, or by pressing the corresponding keys on your computer keyboard—Q through I for the white keys, 2 through 7 for the black keys. To change octaves, drag the bar beneath the Virtual Keyboard to the right (higher) or left (lower).

By default, the Virtual Keyboard displays computer keyboard keys, with specific keys assigned to keys on the piano keyboard. You can shift to a piano keyboard display, shown in Figure 11.7, by pressing the Tab key. In this display mode, three octaves are displayed on screen.

Figure 11.7 The Virtual MIDI Keyboard in piano keyboard display mode.

Record MIDI events with the Virtual MIDI Keyboard:

1. Create an empty MIDI track and activate the Record Enable button for that track.

2. In the Transport panel, set the appropriate Record mode for either linear or cycle recording.

3. Position your left and right locators appropriately. For example, if you want to record from Bar 5 Beat 1 to Bar 9 Beat 1, set the left and right locators to Bar 5 and Bar 9, respectively.

4. Activate the metronome click on the Transport panel to hear a click while recording.

5. In the Inspector for this track, click the Output Routing field and select the VST or MIDI instrument you want to "play" the sounds for this track.

6. Also in the Inspector, click the Programs field and select the preset program you want to use for this instrument.

7. Click the Record button on the Transport panel and start playing the Virtual Keyboard, either by typing keys on your computer keyboard or by clicking keys on screen with your mouse.

8. When you're finished recording, click the Stop button on the Transport panel or press the spacebar on your computer keyboard.

12 Using ReWire

eWire is a software-based technology that lets you share application resources inside your computer—as long as those resources are ReWire-compatible. The ReWire technology was jointly developed by Propellerhead Software and Steinberg, so most products sold by either company are compatible with this technology. In addition, a large number of third-party developers have made their applications ReWire-compatible. This chapter looks at some setup tips when working with ReWire applications in a Cubase project.

Here's a summary of what you will learn in this chapter:

■ How to use Cubase as a ReWire host

■ How to set up a ReWire channel in a project

■ How to use ReWire and VSTi (VST instrument) channels in the Mixer

■ How to export ReWire tracks as audio files

ReWire Setup

ReWire's functionality is really quite simple and quite useful: It patches the outputs of one software application into the inputs of another software application and synchronizes their Transport controls. This has some similarities to using a VSTi, except that ReWire instruments or ReWire software applications are not running inside Cubase, as a VSTi is—it's a cross-application technology.

Active ReWire channels appear as additional channels in Cubase's Mixer. This enables all ReWire-compatible applications to share the same audio hardware, assigning each ReWire instrument a different output if you want and also providing a common Transport control and timing base; you can control playback for all applications from Cubase.

32-Bit Only: At present, ReWire is a 32-bit technology, which means it won't work with 64-bit versions of Cubase.

In other words, to use ReWire, you need to have ReWire-compatible applications installed on your system. Available ReWire applications appear at the bottom of Cubase's Devices menu once installed.

Prepare Cubase for ReWire applications:

1. Launch Cubase first. It is important that your other ReWire applications are launched *after* Cubase opens so that they will start up in ReWire Slave mode; otherwise, both applications run independently. This can create conflicts and might prevent you from using either application.

2. Select Devices > Device Setup > VST Audio System and make sure that the Release ASIO Driver in Background option is *not* selected.

3. Select the installed ReWire application from the Devices menu. The ReWire panel will now appear; what displays in this panel depends on which ReWire-compatible application you're using.

4. Click the Activate button to the left of the channels that you want to create inside Cubase's Mixer.

5. If you want to rename a channel, click in the Display As column and type the label you want to use.

6. Launch the ReWire application.

Each application can offer a large number of channels; for example, ReWire 2.0–compatible applications support up to 256 channels. For a given project, however, you will enable only the specific number of channels you want to stream between applications. That's because each active ReWire channel imposes an additional load on your system, and you want to keep the load to a minimum to improve system performance. Once a channel is enabled, a corresponding ReWire channel appears in Cubase's Mixer. You can always enable additional ReWire channels in your project later if needed.

The order in which you launch ReWire applications is important because the first ReWire application will be considered the ReWire *host*. Each subsequent ReWire application you launch will run in ReWire *slave* mode. The audio properties and tempo settings of slaved applications will conform to the host's properties and settings. If you change the tempo in the slave application, Cubase will turn its tempo track off to follow this new tempo. In other words, to keep any tempo changes accurate in both applications, it's better to use the tempo track in Cubase to change tempos.

At this point, the Transport bars in both applications are linked. This means that you can start and stop playback within any ReWire-compatible application, and the others will follow. If you record events, they are recorded in the application that is active—in other words, the recording takes place in the application where you clicked the Record button. So, recording in each application is independent, but playback follows.

If you use cycle playback or recording, all applications follow this loop. And, as the ReWire host, Cubase always controls the tempo setting when the Tempo track is active. If you change the tempo in Cubase's Tempo track, the other applications follow its lead. If you are not using the Tempo track, you can change the manual tempo setting in either application, and the playback reflects it. When you start playback at 100 BPM in Live and the Tempo track in Cubase is not enabled to control the project tempo, both applications play at 100 BPM.

All ReWire channels that are not muted when you export your mix-down using the File > Export > Audio mix-down option are included in the output file.

Sampling Rate and Pitch: Make sure both applications are set to the same sampling rate. When the rates don't match, the ReWired application might not play at the right pitch.

When the ReWired application uses MIDI to trigger software instruments, you may need to create a MIDI track in Cubase and select the ReWire-compatible MIDI output port as its output. This will send the MIDI events from this Cubase track to the ReWire application in order for it to generate the sounds that will appear in the ReWire audio channel you have configured inside Cubase for the output from that ReWire application. On the other hand, if the ReWire-compatible application is strictly audio-based, using audio loops or events on tracks of its own, simply activating the bus to which the audio is routed inside Cubase will do. For example, if you have audio tracks in a ReWire application that are coming out through its Main Mix bus, activating this bus inside Cubase will cause any audio routed to that application's Main Mix to be sent (rerouted) into the Cubase Mixer's ReWire channel.

VSTi and ReWire Channels

You saw in Chapter 10 that you can use a VST instrument either by loading it as you create an instrument track, or by loading the VSTi in the VST Instruments panel and then selecting this VSTi as the output destination for one or more MIDI tracks. With ReWire 2.0 applications, a MIDI track can be routed through a ReWired MIDI output port. This enables you to send MIDI events from Cubase to a software instrument loaded in the ReWired application. Once the ReWired instrument receives the signal, you then need to route the audio output back to Cubase by enabling that channel, as described earlier in this chapter.

For the most part, audio channels representing audio tracks or the audio output from a VSTi or ReWire instrument are fairly similar. There are, however, some notable differences:

■   You can't assign an audio input bus to an instrument, VSTi, or ReWire audio channel.

■   There are no Record Enable buttons on these audio channels. Instrument channels do have a Record Enable button that will record MIDI events, but not audio.

■   There is no Monitor button because there are no audio inputs to monitor. On instrument channels, the Monitor button lets you monitor or play MIDI events without having to record-enable the track. This is convenient when you simply want to play through the instrument while recording something else on another track.

■   Below the Bypass Send Effect button on VSTi and instrument tracks is the Edit VST Instrument button that opens the VSTi interface for changing settings in the instrument. In contrast, because ReWire instruments are not inside Cubase, you need to access their host application to make changes to their settings.

■   VSTi and ReWire channels have a separate button in the Mixer's Common panel on the left, allowing you to hide all instances of either type of channel from view.

■   In the Mixer, there are distinct background colors behind the volume faders on Instrument and VSTi channels, ReWire channels, and audio channels.

Exporting VSTi and ReWire Channels

Because VSTi and ReWire channels are audio channels within Cubase's Mixer, they will be included in the audio mix-down when the File > Export > Audio Mixdown function is used. Make sure these tracks are unmuted if you want to include them in the exported audio file for your mix-down.

VSTi and ReWire devices can eat up resources from your computer; exporting those tracks as audio files might also let you unload them from memory to add more real-time inserts or FX channels. If this is what you need to do, always save your project with a different name to keep access to the original MIDI-based tracks and synth settings in the project.

Export a VSTi or ReWire channel:

1.   Set the left and right locators at the start and end of the portion you want to export.

2.   Take note of the VSTi or ReWire channel you want to export and solo the MIDI track you want to export.

3. Monitor the instrument's audio channel in the Mixer, adjust any settings to avoid clipping, and optimize the sound.

4. Select File > Export > Audio Mixdown.

5. In the Export Audio Mixdown dialog box, enter a name for the file.

6. Select a path (destination folder) for the file or enable the Use Project Audio Folder option to save the file in that location.

7. Select the file format; WAV and AIFF are your best choices. Avoid lossy compression types, such as MP3, WMA, and OGG when exporting any audio that you want to use as part of a subsequent mixing or mastering operation in Cubase or some other audio program. Some file types offer additional attribute options when selected. Choose the desired attributes according to your requirements.

8. Choose the appropriate sample rate and bit depth settings for the exported file from the corresponding drop-down menus. When exporting audio to integrate it back into a project, be sure these settings correspond to the current project settings.

9. From the Channel Selections list, choose the VSTi or ReWire channel you want to export.

Real-Time Export: With some automated VST or ReWire instruments, you might need to export the information in real time to include all the parameters being automated in the export. Whether this is needed depends on the instrument itself. Please read the instrument's documentation to find out whether real-time export is required when exporting a MIDI track with parameter automation. If you did use any parameter automation for this VSTi, don't enable this option. In most instances, you *won't* need it, but if you run into problems, check the Realtime Export option in the Audio Engine Output section of the Export Audio Mixdown panel.

10. Enable the Pool and Audio Track options in the Import into Project section.

11. Enable the Close Dialog after Export option only if you don't intend to export another track.

12. Click on the Export button when you are finished.

Obviously, you should repeat these steps for each ReWire channel you need to export. When you are finished exporting channels, you can unload the ReWire application from your computer's memory. Delete all corresponding MIDI tracks, or even better, place them inside a folder track in case you want to try playing the same MIDI events through a different instrument later. You should then save this new copy of your project file with a different name. This keeps your original file intact in case you need to go back and re-edit the ReWire tracks; you can then use this "lighter" version of the project for the mixing process.

For instrument tracks you can use the Freeze Instrument Channel functionality, which offers a number of convenient resource optimization options. You will find more on the freeze options in Chapter 40, "Optimizing Your Project."

13 Using Insert Effects

In traditional recording, you apply signal processing—such as compression and equalization—via an insert effect. On a hardware mixing board, an *insert* is a point in the audio channel strip where the signal can leave the channel, pass through an external effect, and then be re-introduced into the signal path of the channel.

In Cubase, inserts play a very similar role. Most inserts are software-based effects inserted into the signal path, although you can also insert external hardware-based effects. Software-based effects—often called *plug-ins*—let you do things like apply dynamic compression, add reverb and echo, and even use various filters and modulators to alter recorded events in very distinctive ways—all of which can dramatically change or improve the quality of your final recording. Cubase includes a number of these plug-in effects as part of the Cubase package. Other plug-ins can be downloaded from the Internet or purchased from third parties.

Here's a summary of what you will learn in this chapter:

- How plug-in effects work

- The various plug-ins available with Cubase 6

- When and where to apply plug-in effects

- The signal flow of insert plug-in effects

- How to apply insert effects

- How to add inserts to Control Room studio and headphone channels

- How to add inserts to Control Room talkback and external input channels

- How to load insert plug-ins into monitor channels

How Plug-In Effects Work

In old-school tape-based recording, audio effects were added via outboard boxes that literally plugged into the recording console. With computer-based recording, the plug-ins are software programs or utilities that perform the same functions as the traditional outboard boxes.

Cubase follows this paradigm by offering a variety of plug-in effects, from simple reverb to complex filtering and modulation. Each plug-in effect you select is inserted into the audio signal path at a given point and effects the audio signal from that point onward. The effect is applied in real time, which means that the audio processing requires a fair amount of computing horsepower; some effects are more power-hungry than others, of course. But because the processing is in real time and is applied after the original audio signal enters the system, the original audio is not altered by the effect—only the resulting sound is changed.

Applying Effects

You can apply plug-in effects at five different points in the recording process:

- **Input insert effects.** These effects are added to the input bus as the recording is being made, so that the recorded track includes the effect processing.

- **Offline audio processing.** These effects are added directly to the recorded audio event—*not* to the entire track.

- **Insert effects.** These effects are inserted into the signal path just after the original channel input and before equalization and volume are applied. Insert effects are applied to the entire track, not just a single recorded event.

- **Send effects.** These effects are added to the end of the signal path as separate effects tracks; the final audio is routed to the effects track as the final step in the process.

- **Master insert effects.** These effects are inserted into the master output bus during the mastering process, after the individual tracks have been mixed to a stereo signal. These master effects are applied to the entire mix, not individual channels.

Audio Processing Effects: Offline audio processing effects (found on the Audio > Process menu) cannot be applied as insert, send, or master insert effects; these effects are only available for offline processing. For insert/send/master insert effects, the only effects you can use are plug-in effects. Learn more about audio processing in Chapter 20, "Using Audio Processing Options."

To simplify things, just remember that insert effects apply to your *inputs*, and send effects apply to your *outputs*. In addition, input insert effects are applied directly to a track when you're recording, and master insert effects are applied at the end of the process, to your entire recording.

Inserts versus Sends

This chapter focuses on the most-used type of effect, the insert effect. Let's say, for example, that you want to apply some distortion to a guitar track you've just recorded.

The audio from the event is routed through the selected plug-in, which adds a distortion effect to the signal. The now-distorted signal comes back into the channel and continues through the path, on to the output bus and ultimately to the monitor mix (or, when you're ready, the final mix). Note that the original recorded event remains unchanged in the track listing, altered not at all by the process; the effect is applied to the signal after the event is played.

Compare this type of insert effect to a send effect—for example, adding reverb to a vocal track. With a send effect, the audio stays in the signal path until it reaches the output bus, where it is sent to the selected plug-in. The processed signal is then available to be sent to the monitor mix or to the final mix-down.

When, then, should you use a particular type of effect? It all comes down to how much computer horsepower each operation takes—and what type of effect you're applying.

Let's start by making a distinction between real-time or "online" processing versus offline processing. Online effects—which include insert, send, and master effects—are calculated and processed by your computer in real time and require tons of processing power. If you apply too many online effects at the same time, your computer will slow down considerably, and might even freeze up. (Naturally, the newer and more powerful your computer, the less of a problem this is.)

In contrast, offline effects, which are applied directly to an audio event (and subsequently change the original event) are processed before you initiate playback or mixing, and thus use up none of your computer's precious processing power. If you need to reduce the load on your PC, you should choose offline effects over online ones whenever practical.

And, just to confuse things even more, insert effects (including input inserts and master inserts) can require more processing power than send effects. (This is why you can save processing power by using sends instead of inserts.)

Equally important, some types of effects are simply more effective when applied at specific places in the signal path. Here are some guidelines:

- Use *input insert effects* for adding compression when recording vocal tracks.

- Use regular *insert effects* for filters, choruses, phasers, noise gates, compression, and other dynamic effects.

- Use *send effects* for equalization, reverb, delays, and modulation effects.

- Use *master insert effects* for any effects you want to apply to your entire mix—typically compression, reverb, and equalization.

- Use *offline processing* for any of Cubase's audio processes (on the Audio > Process menu), as well as for those effects you want to apply to only a section of a track.

EQ Effects: Although Cubase offers a dedicated four-band parametric EQ section on each audio-related channel type, you might prefer loading a particular EQ plug-in into one of the track's insert slots because you prefer its sound and the parameters it offers. If this is the case, you would load such EQ and filter plug-ins as insert effects.

Send Effects: You can apply the same plug-ins either as insert or send effects. Learn more about send effects in Chapter 33, "Working with FX Channel Tracks."

Cubase's Audio Plug-In Effects

Cubase 6 includes a number of plug-in effects for audio recording. In addition, plug-ins can be purchased from a variety of third-party manufacturers. For now, however, this chapter focuses on those plug-ins that come in the Cubase 6 box.

Table 13.1 describes the audio effects shipping with Cubase 6—that is, those effects that can be applied to audio recordings.

Table 13.1 Cubase 6 Audio Plug-In Effects

Plug-In	Description
AmpSimulator	A distortion effect that emulates the sound of various guitar amp and speaker combinations.
Autopan	Modulates the right and left stereo positions.
Bitcrusher	Produces a noisy, distorted sound, like that in lower-bitrate recordings.
Chopper	Produces a combined tremolo and autopan effect.
Chorus	Adds short delays to the original signal and pitch modulates the delayed signals to create a "doubling" effect.
Cloner	"Fattens" a track by adding up to four detuned and delayed voices to the original audio.
Compressor	Compresses the dynamic range of the audio; makes softer sounds louder and louder sounds softer.
DaTube	Emulates the warm sound of a tube amplifier; typically applied to individual instruments.
DeEsser	A special type of compressor that reduces sibilance in vocal recordings.
Distortion	Adds a classic guitar/amp buzz-like distortion to a track.
DualFilter	Filters out specific frequencies while allowing others to pass through.

Table 13.1 *(Continued)*

Plug-In	Description
EnvelopeShaper	Cuts or boosts the gain of the attack and release phases of an audio track.
Expander	Reduces the dynamic range of a recording; also used to reduce noise in quiet passages.
Flanger	Provides classic stereo flange effects.
Gate	A traditional noise gate plug-in; silences audio levels below a set threshold level.
GEQ-10	A 10-band graphic equalizer.
GEQ-30	A 30-band graphic equalizer.
Grungelizer	Adds noise and static, similar to that found on a worn-out vinyl record.
Limiter	Limits the output level to make sure it never exceeds a set level.
Maximizer	Raises the level of audio material without inducing clipping.
Metalizer	Feeds the audio signal through a variable frequency filter, with feedback control.
MIDI Gate	An audio noise gate that works in conjunction with a MIDI track.
Mix6To2	For surround sound recordings, enables the mixing of up to six surround channels to a stereo output.
MixerDelay	New to Cubase 6, enables you to adjust and manipulate each individual channel in a surround track, group, or bus.
ModMachine	Combines various modulation effects, including delay modulation.
MonoDelay	Adds a simple mono delay effect.
MonoToStereo	Turns a mono signal into a pseudo-stereo signal.
MultibandCompressor	Professional-level four-band dynamic compressor.
MultiScope	Used for viewing the waveform, phase linearity, or frequency content of a signal.
Octaver	Generates two additional voices that track an octave above and below the pitch of the original.
Phaser	Produces the classic "swooshing" phasing sound.
PingPongDelay	A stereo delay that alternates between the left and right channels, for a "ping pong" effect.
Pitch Correct	Automatically detects, adjusts, and fixes off-pitch vocals and instruments in real time.
REVerence	Advanced reverb generator; enables you to apply specific room effects to a track.

Table 13.1 Cubase 6 Audio Plug-In Effects (*Continued*)

Plug-In	Description
Ringmodulator	Produces complex, bell-like enharmonic sounds by multiplying two audio signals.
RoomWorks	Professional-level reverb plug-in, used to create realistic room ambience and reverb effects in both stereo and surround formats.
RoomWorks SE	A "lite" version of the RoomWorks plug-in; less CPU-demanding than its older brother.
Rotary	Simulates the effect of a classic rotary speaker.
SMPTEGenerator	Not an actual audio effect, but rather a tool that generates SMPTE timecode to an audio output to synchronize other equipment with Cubase.
SoftClipper	Adds soft overdrive to a track.
StepFilter	Multimode filter that can create pulsating filter effects and patterns.
StereoDelay	A sophisticated stereo delay effect; uses a slight delay to expand the stereo effect.
StereoEnhancer	Expands the width of stereo signals.
StudioChorus	Two-stage chorus effect, used to "double" audio tracks.
StudioEQ	A high-quality four-band parametric stereo graphics equalizer.
TestGenerator	Generates an audio signal for testing purposes.
ToneBooster	A filter that enables you to increase the gain in a specific frequency range.
Tonic	Analog modeling filter, based on the design of the Monologue monophonic synthesizer.
Tranceformer	Produces a ring modulator effect.
Tremolo	Produces a vibrating tremolo effect via amplitude modulation.
Tuner	A simple guitar tuner.
UV22HR	Introduces background noise via dithering for mastering.
Vibrato	Produces a vibrato effect, via pitch modulation.
VintageCompressor	Old-school compressor effects.
VST Amp Rack	A powerful guitar amp simulator, new to Cubase 6, that offers a choice of various amplifiers, speaker cabinets, and stomp box effects.
VSTDynamics	An advanced dynamics processor, consisting of Gate, Compressor, and Limiter functions.
WahWah	A variable-slope bandpass filter for the classic guitar "wah wah" effect.

MIDI Effects: Cubase also includes a variety of plug-in effects for use with MIDI tracks. Learn more in Chapter 27, "Adding MIDI Track Effects."

Audio Track Inserts

In Cubase 6, you can apply up to eight insert effects per channel. The signal from an audio track is routed through each active insert effect, one after another—in other words, the output of one insert effect feeds the next one, and so on, from top to bottom in a kind of chain.

How Track Inserts Work

The first six effects slots are applied before the fader and the last two after the fader. As you can see in Figure 13.1, the signal enters the first six *pre*-fader inserts once it enters the channel and passes through the phase and trim control. The output level of the active effect in each insert slot determines the input level of the following insert in this chain; there is no control over the amount of output signal for the insert section as a whole. Some plug-ins, however, do offer their own output level control. After the signal passes by the access points for any sends sent to pre-fader (which are not affected by the track's main volume fader), EQ section, level, and mute controls, it enters the two *post*-fader inserts.

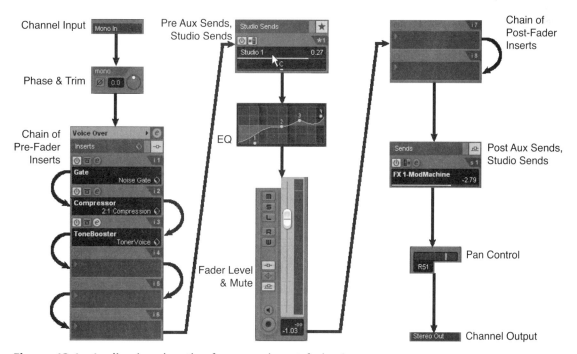

Figure 13.1 Audio signal path of pre- and post-fader inserts.

By the way, it's important to note that the order of insert effects matters. That is, inserts work in a chain, one after another. So if you apply a distortion effect before a compression effect, it's going to sound different than if you apply the compressor before the distortion—in that first instance, the compression is applied to the distorted sound, while in the second instance the distortion is applied to the compressed sound.

Because the first six insert slots are not affected by the track's main volume fader, this is the best place to apply a compressor and control the peaks of a signal. You can then use the fader to adjust a signal that has already been dynamically controlled, allowing for greater flexibility and presence when needed.

Using Inserts 7–8 for Post-Fader Processing: With insert slots 1-6, the signal passes through the effect before the volume control (pre-fader) and before any EQ is applied to the track. However, with inserts 7 and 8, the signal is sent to the insert *after* the track's EQ section and its main volume control.

This type of post-fader insert is best suited for effects that should be applied *after* the track's volume and EQ settings. A good example of this would be final dynamic processing such as limiters or compressors during the mastering process or dithering processes. These would typically be applied as inserts 7 and 8 on the output bus for your mix.

Insert Effect Controls

As shown in Figure 13.2, each insert effect slot has six controls:

- **Activate/Deactivate Insert button.** The plug-in stops processing the signal when the inserts are turned off, but it retains all of its current settings.

- **Bypass button.** Cubase continues to process the signal as it passes through the plug-in, but the channel's signal bypasses the plug-in's output.

- **Open/Close Editor button.** This button will open the control panel for that slot's active insert plug-in.

- **Plug-in effect selection field.** This field lets you choose from a list of installed plug-ins.

- **Preset selection field.** This field displays the selected preset or lets you access to Cubase's SoundFrame preset management system.

- **Cube-shaped preset management button.** This button lets you load or store saved plug-in presets.

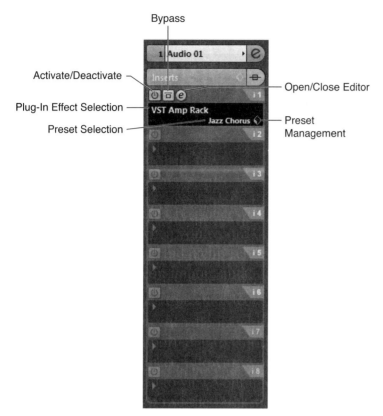

Figure 13.2 Insert slot controls.

You also find a number of controls in the Inserts section of the Inspector. These controls affect all inserts within it:

- The *Bypass Inserts button* bypasses the entire Inserts section on this track. As with the Active/Deactivate button for each insert slot, this can be useful for comparing your track (with or without effects), without having to alter each individual effect. When the Inserts section is bypassed, a yellow rectangle appears at the location of the Bypass Inserts button.

- The *Inserts title bar* maximizes or minimizes this section of the Inspector, whereas the Show Active Inserts indicator to the right of the title bar displays whether any inserts are currently active in this track. The default project color means that there are no active inserts on this track (even though some may be selected for the slot but not currently active), blue means there are active inserts, and yellow means there are inserts that are not currently active.

> **Switching In and Out:** One of the most useful things about insert and send effects is that you can easily switch the effect in and out as the effects are processed in real time. Initiate playback with the effect switched off, and then switch it on so you can hear the effect of the effect—and make any adjustments to the effect as necessary.

Applying Insert Effects

As discussed previously, Cubase lets you apply insert effects either as traditional inserts or as input insert effects. Use input inserts to apply the effect as the track is being recorded.

In other words, input insert effects are added to the beginning of the signal path as a recording is being made. This means that the processed sound is recorded to disk; once added, you can't remove an input insert effect.

Apply input insert effects while recording:

1. In the Mixer, click the Edit button for the input bus (*not* the selected track) you're using to record, as shown in Figure 13.3.

2. This displays the VST Input Channel Settings dialog box, shown in Figure 13.4.

3. Click the first Insert Effects slot to display the list of available effects.

4. Select an effect from the list.

5. The control panel for that effect now appears in a separate window. Configure the effect as necessary, and then close the window. (You can reopen the effect control panel at any time by clicking the Edit button in the insert effects slot.)

6. To activate the insert effect, make sure the Inserts State button is clicked on (displays blue).

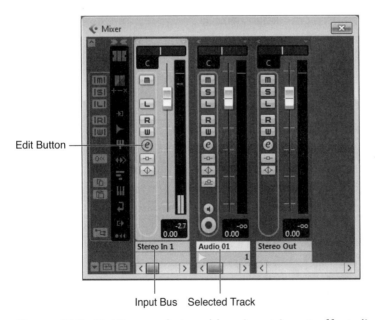

Figure 13.3 Getting ready to add an input insert effect directly to the input bus.

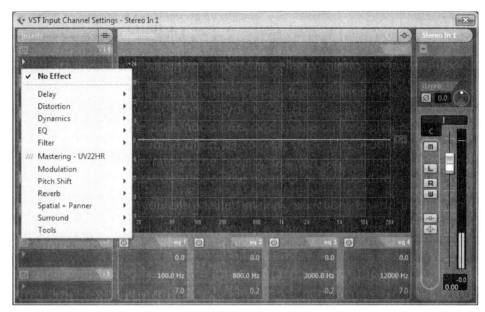

Figure 13.4 Adding an input insert effect.

In contrast, regular insert effects are added to the signal path just after the original channel input, which means that the audio is routed through the effect—affecting everything that comes after that point in the process. Inserts require the most processing power of any type of audio processing or effect.

Apply insert effects after recording:

1.   In the Project window's Track List, select the track to which you want to apply the effect.

2.   In the track Inspector, click the Inserts control. This expands the Inserts panel to show slots for eight insert effects.

3.   Click the Effects control in the first insert effects slot to display the list of available effects.

4.   Select an effect from the list.

5.   The control panel for that effect now appears in a separate window. Configure the effect as necessary, and then close the window. (You can reopen the effect control panel at any time by clicking the Edit button in the insert effects slot.)

6.   To activate the insert effect, make sure the Inserts State button is clicked on (displays blue).

Processing Power

When working on a mix, it is important to understand that the more effects you have running in real time (online, as opposed to offline), the more processing power is required from your computer. Each instance of an effect loaded into an insert effect slot on an individual channel uses the same processing power and memory as it does if it were loaded into an insert slot on a group or FX channel and used as the common destination for multiple sends from *multiple* source tracks.

With this in mind, it is highly recommended that you use the send effects (through FX channels) rather than using the inserts, if you're going to apply the same effect with the same settings to various tracks (typical with delay and reverb effects, for example). If you need to apply the same dynamic process on several channels, route the output from all these channels to the same group channel by setting these channels' output to an available group channel (or create one if necessary) and add an insert effect to that group channel instead. By doing so, all channels routed to this group channel will be processed through the same plug-in with the same setting, and you will use fewer computer resources, which will allow you to save these resources for when you really need them.

To monitor how your computer is doing in terms of system resources, you can take a look at the VST Performance window (Devices > VST Performance, or F12) or the Transport panel. The VST Performance window provides a tool for monitoring system performance so that, if necessary, you can make changes to your project before your computer starts to become overloaded.

And when you're finished tweaking the inserts on a track, you can always use the Freeze command to free up some resources by temporarily freezing these settings in place. To find out more on how to use the Freeze command on audio channels, take a look at Chapter 40, "Optimizing Your Project."

Inserts on Control Room Connections

Cubase's Control Room Mixer (CRM) provides additional monitoring controls, most of which also support the addition of processing through the use of insert plug-in effects. For example, you can add a limiter plug-in effect to a talkback, studio, or headphones channel in order to prevent any strong peaks from damaging monitoring equipment (or the ears of the musicians themselves!).

Add inserts to Control Room studio and headphones channels:

1. In the Control Room Mixer, expand the extended view.

2. If the meters are currently displayed, click the Show Meters/Inserts button to switch to Inserts view, as shown in Figure 13.5.

Click to Add Insert Effect

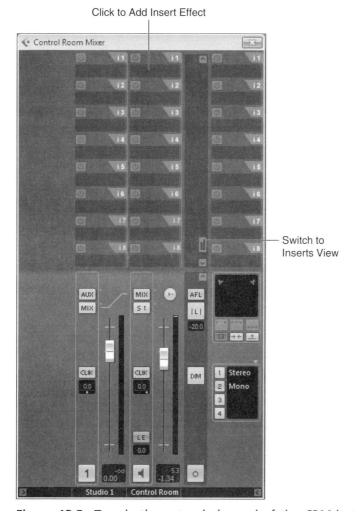

Switch to
Inserts View

Figure 13.5 Toggle the extended panel of the CRM between inserts and meters.

3. Click the first insert selection field in either the Studio 1 or Phones channel and select the insert you want to enable.

4. The control panel for this plug-in opens by default, so you can choose a preset from its preset menu and adjust its settings as needed.

5. Close the plug-in's control panel when you are finished.

Add inserts to Control Room talkback and external input channels:

1. Click on the Show Left Strip button at the bottom-left corner of the CRM to display these channels.

2. To view the talkback channel settings and its inserts in the extended panel, click on the Talk button of the CRM.

3. Set up the inserts as discussed earlier in this chapter.

4. To switch back to the external inputs, deactivate the Talk button.

Loading Insert Plug-Ins into Monitor Channels: Click on the Show Right Strip button (a small arrow in the lower-right corner) to display the Monitor section, and then repeat the same steps found here to load inserts in the monitor channels of the CRM.

14 Using the Pool

The Pool holds references to all audio and video clips used in a project. For example, when you record onto an audio track, an event is created in the Project window, and a clip representing the audio file on disk appears in the Pool. In addition, when you import an audio file, an audio clip representing this file appears in the Pool.

Each project has its own Pool, which optionally can be saved separately so that its contents can be imported into another project. You also can open more than one Pool in a single project, allowing you to share Pool resources between projects. The Pool also enables you to view your audio clip references (called *events*) and corresponding regions. You can use the Pool to monitor, update, and manage these references.

Here's a summary of what you will learn in this chapter:

- How to access and use the Pool

- How to use the audio event preview functions in the Pool

- How to find audio files using the Pool's Search functionality

- How to recover missing audio files with the Pool

- How to optimize the disk space used by the project's audio assets

- How to archive and export Pools from a project

- How the Pool can interact with a project

- How to use offline processes in the Pool

Understanding the Pool

You open the Pool for your current project by selecting Media > Open Pool Window, clicking the Open Pool button on the Project window's toolbar, or by using the keyboard shortcut Ctrl+P (PC)/⌘+P (Mac). As you can see in Figure 14.1, the Media column shows three default folders in the Pool: Audio, Video, and Trash. You can create any number of additional subfolders within these folders as you see fit, but you can't rename or delete these default folders.

157

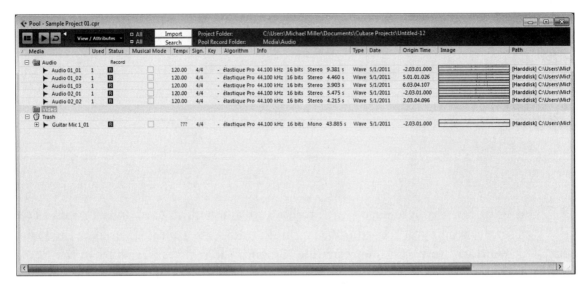

Figure 14.1 The Pool window contains three default folders.

Enable the Show Info button (the first button on the left in Figure 14.1) to reveal the Information bar at the bottom of the Pool to view the current status information for your Pool, the number of files it contains, how many are currently used in this project, the total size of the Pool, and how many of the media files that it references reside outside the project's folder.

The next two buttons in the toolbar are used to monitor a selected event or region in the Media column below. The Play button starts/stops playback of the selected file. The Loop button next to it loops the playback, and the small fader adjusts the preview volume. This volume is linked to the main stereo output when the Control Room features are disabled or to the main Control Room monitors when this latter feature is enabled. To stop the playback, click the Play button again.

The View/Attributes field customizes the Pool columns displayed below it. There is a total of 12 information columns available. To add an attribute to the columns displayed in the Pool, check that attribute in the View drop-down menu. Selecting the Hide All option hides every column to the right of the Media column.

Use the plus (+) All or minus (−) All button next to the View field to expand/collapse the tree found under the Media column. The Import button lets you import supported media files to the project's Pool. Cubase supports most audio file formats, as well as video files in AVI, QuickTime, WMV (Windows only), DV (Mac OS X only), and MPEG 1 and 2 formats.

Import media files into the Pool:

1. Click the Import button in the Pool. This displays the Import Medium window.

2. Browse your hard disk to find and select the file you want to import.

3. After a file is selected, preview it by using the Play button found below the File Display area in the Import Options dialog box.

4. Click the Open button to import the selected file to the current Pool.

5. When the file you want to import is not currently inside the Audio folder of your project, Cubase prompts you to select different import options. When the imported file does not correspond to the current project sample rate and bit depth, Cubase offers to convert these files. Audio files must have the same sample rate as the project, but can have different word lengths (also known as bit depths, or the number of bits used for each sample).

6. Click OK when you are finished making selections to add the files to the Pool.

The Search button, found below the Import button, opens the Search panel at the bottom of the Pool, shown in Figure 14.2. The search parameters are similar to any search tool on your computer. For example, enter keywords or use wildcard characters to find multiple files whose names contain specific strings of characters.

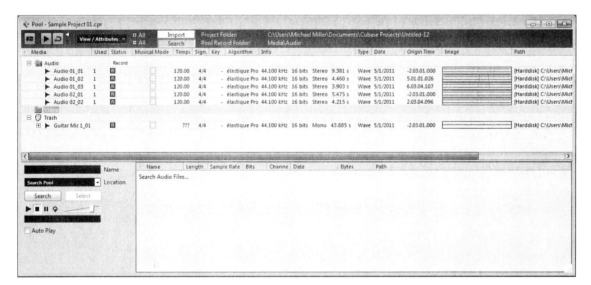

Figure 14.2 The Search panel found in the Pool when the Search function is activated.

Search for files to import:

1. Click the Search button in the Pool's toolbar.

2. In the Name field of the Search panel, type the name of the file you want to find. You can use wildcard characters to widen your search criteria.

3. In the Location field, select the drive or drives you want to look in or select a specific path to look in at the bottom of the drop-down menu.

4. Click the Search button. The search results will appear in the list to the right.

5. Enable the Auto Play check box if you want to automatically preview the files found by the search. To preview a file, select it in the list. If the Auto Play option is not activated, you can click the Play button below the Search button in this panel. You can also adjust the level of the preview by using the Preview Level fader.

6. To import the selected file or files, click the Import button.

7. Select the appropriate import options from the dialog box and click OK to import the files into the Pool.

To the right of the Import and Search buttons at the top of the Pool window, you can see the project folder's path and its associated Pool Record folder. By default, the Pool Record folder is found inside the project folder and is called Audio; it can easily be backed up later with the rest of the project.

Directly below the toolbar are the column headers for each column in the Pool. Click on a header to sort the Pool's contents according to the information in this column if necessary. Columns used to sort information have a little arrow pointing up or down next to the column's header that indicates ascending or descending order. You also can drag the column headers horizontally to change the columns' order. The header is inserted to the right of the column found on the left edge of the header's border when dragged.

You perform most Pool-related operations not from the Pool window itself, but from Cubase's Media menu. You can also access the options from this menu by right-clicking (PC)/Control-clicking (Mac) anywhere in the Pool window to display the context menu.

Understanding the Information

The Media column displays the names and types of media used in the project, as well as any folders that you might have created inside the Pool to organize your media files. There are three different icons displayed next to the name (see Figure 14.3), representing an event object, a region object, and a sliced event object. Region objects are positioned under the event object to which they refer. You can click on the plus sign to expand an event object to reveal its defined regions.

Folder   Record   Event   Region   Sliced Event
          Folder   Object   Object   Object

Figure 14.3 Icons associated with different objects in the Pool window.

Rename objects in the Pool:

1.   Select the object you want to rename. A light blue box will appear around it.

2.   Click again to make the blue box change into a frame.

3.   Type the new name for the object.

The Used column displays the number of times the object in the row appears in the project. In other words, it displays how many times you've used it. Objects that aren't used anywhere in the project have no value in this column. Used sliced objects are incremented by the number of slices found in the object every time you repeat, copy, or duplicate the corresponding part in the Project window. For example, a drum loop divided into eight slices will display 16 in the Used column if this object is used twice in a project (two parts), even if these are shared copies of the same object.

The Status column offers information on the status of the objects inside your Pool. Table 14.1 describes each icon's meaning in this column.

The Musical Mode column identifies samples that contain musical loops that have been detected when the file was imported or that you have identified in the Sample Editor by enabling the Musical Mode button. Clips that are in Musical mode will be time-stretched when the tempo of a project changes, without altering the pitch of the sample. A check in the Musical Mode column also will appear when you import ACID wave files, and Cubase will automatically adjust the tempo of the file to its current project tempo when you add the file into the project. The Tempo and Signature columns are also associated with the Musical mode. You can toggle the Musical mode on and off for a sample by adding or removing a check mark in the option box.

The Info column displays one of two things—either the event's file format and length details or a region's start and end locations.

The Image column displays a graphical representation of the event or the region within the event's boundaries. You will notice that the contents of all the events are displayed within rectangles corresponding to the current width of the Image column; however, regions are represented as a portion of this length. You can quickly preview any portion of an object's content by clicking on its image representation.

Preview an audio object using the Image column in the Pool window:

1.   To begin playback, click anywhere in the image of the chosen event. Playback occurs from the clicked point until the end of the object or until you stop the playback. For more precision, drag the right edge of the Image column header to increase its width.

2.   To skip to another portion of the same object, click approximately where you want to hear in the display before the preview ends.

3.   To stop the playback, click "off" the Play Preview button in the toolbar.

Table 14.1 Understanding the Status Column's Icons

Icon	Its Meaning
Record	Represents the content found in the Pool's Record folder; found next to the Audio folder. If you create a folder in the Pool, you can click in the Status column next to this folder to make this the new Record folder. Subsequent recordings appear under this folder. This does not create a new folder on your hard disk, but it helps you manage the appearance of your files in the Pool. For example, you could create a folder for a vocal session called Vocals. When you click in the Status column next to this folder, the record icon moves next to it, and all recordings made from this point on appear in this Pool folder.
R	Represents events that have been recorded since the last time you opened the project, making it easy to find newly recorded material.
X	Represents events that are not located in the current Pool Record folder. These events might have been imported from another location on your hard disk. This occurs if you don't select the Copy to Project Folder option when importing them. In other words, if you were to back up your project's folders, these files would not be included unless you use the Prepare Archive function described later.
(waveform icon)	Represents events that have been processed offline. In other words, they consist of both references to the original clip and other portions that have been processed and saved in the Edits subfolder within your project's folder.
?	Represents files that have not been found when loading the project. You can use the Find Missing File function to scan these missing files. This is explained later in this chapter.
reconstructible	Represents files that have been processed in some way by using offline processes or effects and for which some of the processed portions have been lost or misplaced. Cubase displays this indication in the Status column when it can reconstruct the missing portions.

Using the Pool Functions

Generally speaking, the Pool is not something you worry about or use the most at the beginning of a project unless you begin the project by importing a whole bunch of audio files. When your project is taking shape, you will probably also want to organize your Pool to quickly find what you need, so managing content should be something to keep in mind here.

We've already discussed certain managing functions related to the Pool through the creation of folders in which to put additional media objects, or through the renaming of existing objects. Let's take a look at other typical Pool functions, such as knowing what to do when an audio file goes missing, or when the Pool starts getting messy and locating the files you need gets hard. Archiving a Pool for backup is also something to keep in mind to avoid losing precious work later.

Dealing with Missing Files

Not that you try to make mistakes, but it happens; just about every recordist has, at one time or another, accidentally deleted important audio files. When a mistake like this happens, Cubase might not be able to find files previously used in this project—especially if you forget to update your Pool before saving it. The file references in Cubase are now pointing to the wrong place. Whatever the reason may be for Cubase not finding missing files, when references to files need to be reestablished, use the Find Missing Files option from the Media menu. Missing files are identified with a question mark in the Status column.

Find missing files in the Pool:

1. Select Media > Find Missing Files. The Resolve Missing Files dialog box will appear.

2a. To locate the files, click the Locate button.

    OR

2b. To let Cubase look for the missing files, click the Search button, and then the Folder button and choose the desired folder.

3. Depending on the option selected in Step 2, you are offered different solutions or results. However, if you have chosen the Search option, a new dialog box will appear in which you can change the name of the file you are looking for. Use this option when you remember renaming the file in the operating system after it was last saved with the Cubase project. Enter the new name in the appropriate field, and then click the Start button to begin the search process.

4. If the search successfully finds the missing files, select the file you want from the list displayed and click the Accept button. This updates the link to the file in your Pool to the new file.

5. If you don't want to do this every time, save your project at this point.

In the event that a file is still missing, even after a search (or you don't want Cubase to keep referring to a file because you've erased it anyway), you can use the Remove Missing Files option from the Media menu. This affects any object in the Pool with a question mark in the Status column.

Optimizing the Pool

After five or six recording and editing sessions, or a long import session, hundreds of audio files can start piling up in the Pool. Optimizing the Pool lets you keep it organized so that files are easy to access. That's when you can create folders, drag and drop objects inside these folders, and organize your project's assets. When you delete events or regions from the Pool, they often end up in the Trash folder. This means that the files are still using space on your computer. Use the Empty Trash option in the Media menu to free up some of that media drive real estate. Cubase prompts you once again to make sure you really want to erase the files from the hard disk or only remove them from the Pool. If you choose to erase the files, you cannot get them back because this function can't be undone. This is one of the only ways that you can erase audio clips from your drive within Cubase.

Besides the trash you've collected, there might be some files that were used at the beginning of your project, but aren't being used any longer. If you don't need them, you can use the Remove Unused Media option in the Media menu. This time, you are prompted to choose whether you want to remove these files from the Pool completely (although the source files will still remain on your media drive) or just send them to the Trash folder of the Pool. Removing files from the Pool when you are done with them doesn't erase them from your computer's hard drive. It is, therefore, recommended that you always use the Trash folder as a transitional stage when optimizing your Pool. When you are finished, the Media > Empty Trash command gives you the option to actually erase the source files for items in the Pool's Trash folder, which will free up space on your hard drive.

Deleting Files: Be careful when deleting Cubase-related files. Unless you've backed up these files, when you delete them they're permanently gone—they cannot be recovered if you later change your mind.

Recording long segments often includes useless audio that takes up extra space on your hard drive. Creating regions, resizing, or splitting events in the Project window to hide unneeded portions does not remove these portions from the source file on your hard drive. Using the Minimize File option in the Media menu creates new copies of the selected files in the project, effectively removing any portions of the original file on your hard drive that aren't used in the current project. It also initializes the offline process history for this file. However, bear in mind that the Minimize File command doesn't take into account how the affected files may be used in *other* Cubase projects! Before using this option, it might be advisable to consider another option available in Cubase that also enables you to minimize the file sizes of all audio clips for your project.

Use the Save Project to New Folder option in the File menu to save all the files referenced in a project, as well as the project file itself, to a new folder, minimizing the space used by the project. However, by doing this, you still have the original content in the original folder where you began the project. If you want to revert to this project at a later date, the files will still be there.

Minimize file sizes in your project:

1. Select the files you want to minimize in the Pool window.

2. Select Media > Minimize File.

3. When completed, Cubase prompts to save the project so that the new file references take effect; click the Save button.

Archiving and Exporting a Pool

When you want to save a backup of your project or use it in another studio, it's important to have access to all the files that are used by the project. Saving the project using the Save command updates the project file, but it doesn't copy any files that reside outside the project folder. Use the Prepare Archive option in the Media menu or in the Pool's context menu to copy all the audio clips used in your project to the audio project folder. Cubase automatically copies the content of the Edit folder into a backup folder, along with all files used by the project. After this operation is completed, simply copy the resultant project file, its Audio folder, and any video file referenced in the project to a backup CD or DVD, for example.

Prepare a project for backup:

1. Select Media > Remove Unused Media.

2. Click the Trash button when you are prompted to choose between trashing and removing from the Pool.

3. Select Media > Empty Trash.

4. Click the Erase button when you are prompted once again to remove whatever files are not used in the project and erase them from the drive.

5. Select Media > Prepare Archive.

6. Because this is a backup, you can opt to freeze the edits or not. If you choose not to, be sure to also include the Edit subfolder of the project folder when you copy it to the backup medium.

7. Save the project file.

8. When you are ready to back up your files, be sure to include the project file, its Audio subfolder, and the video files you might have used with the project on the backup medium.

If you are in the final stages of a project and you want to save a final version of the project files, repeat the previous steps with the addition of a couple more steps to save only the necessary material. Before heading on to Step 3 from the previous list, you can use Media > Conform Files option to change all audio files in your project. This converts all your files to the currently selected sample rate and word length (bit depth) for your project. You can then use the Minimize Files option, as described previously, to reduce each file to only its portions that are actually used in the project. Then proceed to Step 7 and use the File > Save Project to New Folder option instead.

Exporting a Pool also makes it easy to store drum loops and sound effects that have been edited and need to be shared between project files. Whenever you want to use these sounds later on, all you need to do is import that Pool into your current project.

Export a Pool:

1. Prepare the Pool by making sure all your files conform to the project's format, removing or searching for missing links, and emptying the Pool's Trash folder.

2. Select Media > Export Pool.

3. Type a name for the Pool.

4. Click the Save button.

To import the saved Pool inside another project, select Media > Import Pool.

Pool Interaction

Now that you know how to files get into the Pool and sort them once they are in it, let's look at getting the content from the Pool into the project. The quickest and easiest way is to drag events from the Pool to the Project window. When you drag an object from the Pool into the Project window, the actual location of this object depends on two variables:

■ The snap and quantize grid settings.

■ The position of the snap point inside the audio event or region. Because the snap point can be anywhere within the event, when the Snap button is enabled, it's the snap point itself that adjusts to the closest grid line in the Project window.

The location displayed above the cursor as you move the selected object over a track indicates the snap or start position where this object will be inserted, depending on the two variables mentioned. When the blue line next to the cursor and location display the desired location, drop the object into place.

Dragging Events into a Project: Dragging an object from the Pool to the empty area below the last track in the Project window automatically creates a new audio track matching the sample's configuration. For example, dragging a mono event creates a mono track, dragging a stereo event creates a stereo track, and so on.

Applying Offline Processes in the Pool

When you apply any type of offline process (from the Audio > Process or Audio > Plug-Ins menu) to an object inside the Pool, this processing affects the entire object. For example, if you apply a delay effect to a region, the whole region is affected. To process only a portion of a region, use these processes from the Sample Editor's context menu instead. Offline processes in the Pool window can be viewed in the Offline Process History panel found in the Audio menu, as can processes applied in the Project window or Sample Editor.

Offline Processes: Learn more about offline audio processing in Chapter 20, "Using Audio Processing Options."

Apply an offline process to an object from the Pool window:

1. Select the object in the Media column.
2. From the Audio menu, select the process you want to apply.
3. Make the appropriate setting in the process's dialog box.
4. Click the Process button.

Navigation

15 Navigating the Project Window

J ust about everything you do in Cubase happens in the Project window, which contains a variety of tracks that serve as containers for different media types, such as audio and MIDI events, automation, effects, and VST instruments. You can create a project from a preset template that includes the appropriate types of tracks, or add new tracks to an empty project.

This chapter discusses the different areas found in the Project window and how you can work with the information and tools these areas provide. After all, most of your editing and production time will be spent in the Project window; you need to know what's what, as well as where and what it all does.

Here's a summary of what you will learn in this chapter:

- How to recognize the Project window areas

- What tools are available on the toolbar

- How to use the Inspector and Track List

- What different types of tracks are available

- How to add tracks to a project

Project Window Areas

The Project window is your main working area; it displays all the tracks and events for your project. More than one project can be open simultaneously, but only one can be active at any time. When you make a different Project window active (by clicking within it or selecting it from the Window menu, and then clicking its Activate Project button at the left end of the Project window toolbar), all other project-related windows also update their content to display the settings of this active Project window. The Project window is essentially divided into a dozen main areas, each one of which provides some kind of control, function, or access to information within a project.

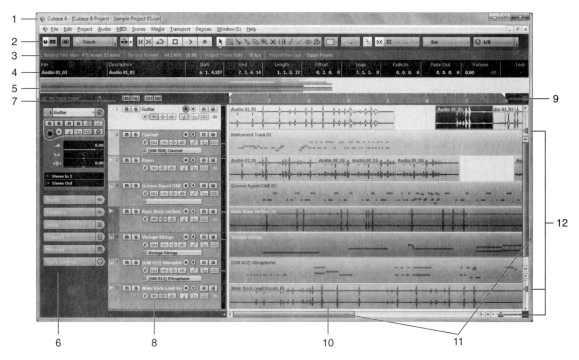

Figure 15.1 The Project window's main areas.

Here's a list of the areas identified in Figure 15.1, to serve as a quick reference to all the components included in the Project window.

1. **Title bar.** Displays the current project's title.

2. **Toolbar.** Displays commonly used tools and can be customized by right-clicking on it (or Control-clicking on a Mac) and selecting the tools you want to see or unselecting those you don't use.

3. **Status line.** (This is optional.) Displays information about the status of the project, including recorded time, record format, bit rate, and so forth.

4. **Information line.** (Optional.) Displays information on selected events in the event display area (see number 10).

5. **Overview line.** (Optional.) Displays an overview of the current project—that is, the portion of this project currently displayed in the window. This bar also serves as a navigational tool; you can quickly zoom to a specific section or move your point of view by using this area.

6. **Inspector.** Displays a series of settings for a selected track. The settings in the Inspector are different for each type of track.

7. **Track List Header bar.** Controls global track states as well as Track List (see number 8) display settings.

8. **Track List.** Displays controls for all the tracks in a project. Tracks are stacked as rows in a column, and you can rearrange them by dragging up or down the list with your mouse.

9. **Project Ruler.** Displays the main timeline for a project, as well as the left and right locators. You can't hide the ruler, but you can change its format or use it to move your cursor in the timeline.

10. **Event Display.** The main work area where all events and automation are represented. The Event Display area lets you move and edit events, such as MIDI, audio, and automation recordings. Most edits can be done within this area, whereas others are done in separate editing windows.

11. **Scroll bars.** Let you navigate within the project's timeline (horizontal) or tracks (vertical).

12. **Zoom controls.** Give you control over the time zoom level (horizontal zoom control), the track height (middle vertical zoom control), and the vertical scale of the audio and MIDI content displayed within the rectangles that represent events and parts on tracks (upper vertical zoom control).

When more than one project is open within Cubase, a blue rectangular button found in the upper-left corner of the Project window indicates the active project. Clicking the Activate Project button will make the top window active and automatically deactivate the background window. You can have many projects opened simultaneously, but only one can be active at a time.

Toolbar

The toolbar contains a variety of controls and tools for working with a Cubase project. We'll examine each part of the toolbar separately.

Default Toolbar: The buttons and controls discussed in this chapter are for the default toolbar in Cubase 6. Since you can customize the toolbar to include only those controls you want, your toolbar may look different.

Activate Project

This is the first button on the left side of the toolbar, as shown in Figure 15.2. As the name implies, clicking this button activates the current project. This is mostly used when you have more than one project open in Cubase.

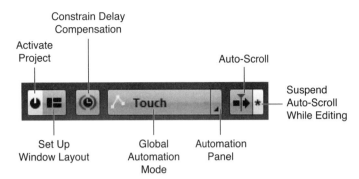

Figure 15.2 From left to right: Activate Project, Set Up Window Layout, and Constrain Delay Compensation buttons, along with the Global Automation Mode and Auto-Scroll controls.

Set Up Window Layout

This is the second button on the left in Figure 15.2. Click this button to display a panel that lets you show or hide specific Project window elements—Status Line, Info Line, Overview Line, and the Inspector. (The Inspector is the only one of these elements displayed by default.)

Constrain Delay Compensation

Use the Constrain Delay Compensation button (the third button on the left in Figure 15.2) if you encounter sync or latency issues when recording live audio through Cubase or playing VST instruments. If what you play syncs perfectly with your previously recorded tracks, leave this button deactivated; Cubase will automatically compensate for audio hardware and effect processing latency during playback or recording to maintain more coherent time alignment between your tracks.

Delay Compensation Threshold: The Constrain Delay Compensation button works with the Delay Compensation Threshold setting found in the VST page of the Preferences dialog box. When this button in the Project window toolbar is active, any plug-in that has a delay longer than the Threshold value either will be turned off or will have its default automatic delay compensation disregarded temporarily. If you do activate the button to solve latency issues during live play-back of VST instruments or recordings of digital audio tracks, remember to turn it off when you are finished.

Global Automation Mode

Click the Global Automation Mode button (fourth on the left in Figure 15.2) to select between three automation modes: Touch, Auto-Latch, and Cross-Over. Click the down-arrow next to this button to display the Automation Panel, shown in Figure 15.3. This is a floating panel that provides access to all of Cubase's automation options. Learn more about these automation options in Chapter 36, "Writing and Reading Automation."

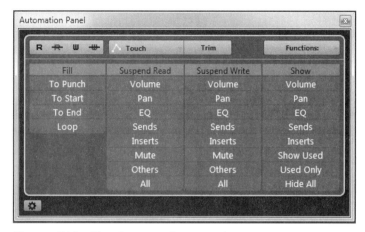

Figure 15.3 The Automation Panel.

Auto-Scroll

The final button in Figure 15.2 is the Auto-Scroll button. When the button is depressed (active), the tracks in the Project window follow the position of the project cursor in time as the project moves forward during playback; the display refreshes every time the project cursor moves past the right edge of the window. To turn Auto-Scroll off while making edits in the Project window, click the smaller Suspend Auto-Scroll While Editing button.

Transport Controls

Cubase 6 offers two sets of Transport controls. One set of Transport controls exists in the Project window toolbar, as shown in Figure 15.4. The other, more complete set is in the Transport panel, which we'll discuss later in this chapter. (The toolbar Transport controls lack the rewind and fast forward buttons found on the Transport panel.)

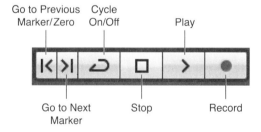

Figure 15.4 The Transport control buttons in the Project window toolbar.

The Transport controls in the toolbar include the following, from left to right:

- Go to Previous Marker/Zero

- Go to Next Marker/Project End

- Cycle

- Stop

- Play

- Record

Tools

In the middle of the Project window toolbar is a series of Tool buttons, as shown in Figure 15.5. You can also display a pop-up version of these tools by right-clicking (PC)/ Control-clicking (Mac) anywhere inside the Project window. From left to right, these tools include the following:

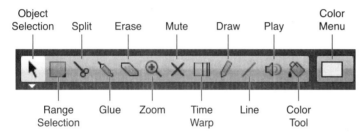

Figure 15.5 The Tool buttons on the toolbar.

- **Object Selection.** This "arrow" tool is probably the most-used tool on the toolbar. You use this tool to select events or parts by clicking on these event or by dragging a box over several events or parts. You can also use this tool to resize events by dragging the end of the event; learn more in Chapter 28, "Arranging in the Project Window."

- **Range Selection.** Make a selection of events over several tracks with this tool by dragging the mouse over the desired content. You can also select a specific portion within an event or part with the Range Selection tool. Once it is selected, you can apply different range-specific editing processes, such as delete, cut, insert, or crop to the selected range. These editing functions are also discussed in Chapter 28.

- **Split.** Clicking events or parts anywhere in the Event Display area separates them into two segments, with the exact point of the split depending on the currently active Snap mode and grid settings.

- **Glue.** Joins events or parts to the next event or part in the same track, creating either a continuous event (if you use Glue after splitting an event in two) or a continuous part containing two or more events (if you Glue either two nonconsecutive events or two parts together).

- **Erase.** Clicking with this tool deletes events/parts from a track.

- **Zoom.** Zoom in to your project by dragging a box around the area you want to view more closely, or click to zoom in one step closer. Hold the Alt (PC)/Option (Mac) key while clicking (double-clicking will have the same effect) to zoom out a step.

- **Mute.** Silences individual events or parts. This is an alternative to erasing them because muted events are not heard during playback; however, they can be "unmuted" later. This is different from the Track Mute button, which mutes *all* events on the track.

- **Time Warp.** Provides a way to insert tempo changes for musical events to match up with video sequences or tempo changes in a live recording. More on this in Chapter 30, "Working with Tempo."

- **Draw.** This "pencil" tool can be used to create an empty part on a track, a series of envelope points for a volume curve associated with an individual event, or a series of automation points in any of the automation subtracks for tracks in the Project window.

- **Line.** Adds automation points in any automation subtrack. As with the selection tools, a pop-up selector for the Line tool offers different operation modes. The Parabola, Sine, Triangle, and Square modes allow you to create different automation shapes, creating automation points that recreate the shape of the selected mode. For example, using the Line tool in Sine mode lets you create a panning automation shaped like a sine wave. These editing modes of the Line tool will also be discussed in Chapters 23, "Using the Key Editor and Note Expression," and 36.

- **Play.** In the Play mode of this tool, you use the "speaker" icon of the Play tool to monitor a specific audio or MIDI event/part from the point where you click until the moment you release the mouse. In Scrub mode, you can drag your mouse back and forth over an event/part to monitor its contents. The direction and speed of scrubbed playback is proportional to the movement of your mouse as you click and drag with this tool.

- **Color tool.** Click this button to activate the Color or "paint" tool. You can then click an element in the Project window to "paint" it with the currently selected color in the Color menu (next).

- **Color menu.** Click this button to display a drop-down menu of available colors. Click a color to then "paint" the color using the Color tool.

Project Root Key

To change the key signature of all the events in your project, use the Project Root Key button, the first button shown in Figure 15.6. Click this button to display a pull-down

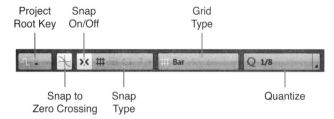

Figure 15.6 The Project Root Key, Snap, Grid, and Quantize buttons.

menu of key signatures; select the desired key signature from the list, and your project will be transposed to the new key.

Snap to Zero Crossing

This button is the second on the left in Figure 15.6. When you activate this button, splitting and sizing of audio events are done at zero crossings—that is, places in the audio where the amplitude (volume level) is zero. This helps avoid pops and clicks at editing points.

Snap On/Off and Snap Type

This is a connected group of snap controls on the toolbar, as shown in Figure 15.6. These controls help you determine the accuracy of these movements by snapping events to the time increments on a grid, other events, the cursor, or any combination of these items.

The Snap On/Off button enables/disables the Snap Type button to the right. When enabled, movement of events/ parts is restricted by the selected Snap mode—by default, a grid—selected by the Snap Type button. Cubase offers eight Snap modes from which to choose, which you access from a drop-down menu that appears when you click the Snap Type button:

■ **Grid.** When Grid is selected in Snap mode, snap positions are set to an invisible grid of either bars or beats, selected by the Grid Type button to the right.

■ **Grid Relative.** With this snap type, events and parts are not precisely "magnetic" to the grid. Rather, the grid determines the step size for moving events, and a moved event keeps its original position relative to the grid.

■ **Events.** The start and end of parts or events, as well as markers on marker tracks, become "magnetized." So when you move a part, it will snap to the previous or next event as you move closer to it.

■ **Shuffle.** This moves events/parts that are adjacent to other events/parts by switching places with them. Shuffle mode is also very useful for editing voice-over narrations, since when you cut out any portion of the track's content, such as a false start by the narrator, the following material in the track will move up earlier in the timeline to close that gap.

- **Magnetic Cursor.** The project cursor becomes magnetic. Moving an event/part close to it will cause it to snap to the cursor's position.

- **Grid + Cursor.** A combination of the Grid and Magnetic Cursor modes.

- **Events + Cursor.** A combination of the Events and Magnetic Cursor modes.

- **Events + Grid + Cursor.** A combination of the Events, Grid, and Magnetic Cursor modes.

Grid Type

This button lets you select which type of grid is used when you activate one of the Grid Snap modes. You can choose from the following:

- **Bar.** The grid is based on the bars (measures) of the project.

- **Beat.** The grid is based on the individual beats within each bar.

- **Use Quantize.** The grid is customized to the value set with the Quantize control, discussed next.

Quantize

The final button on the default toolbar is the Quantize control. This lets you set the Grid Snap value to any specific note value within your project. That is, quantize values divide each bar in fractions equivalent to a note value. For example, a 1/4 quantize value indicates that there will be a grid line at every quarter note.

There are three groups of quantize value fractions: normal, triplet, and dotted. Here's how they work:

- **Normal.** The normal fractions (1/2, 1/4, 1/8, 1/16, and so on) represent note values that can be divided by two. For example, there can be four quarter notes in each 4/4 bar, eight eighth notes per 4/4 bar, and 16 sixteenth notes per 4/4 bar.

- **Triplet.** Triplet notes are divisible by three and place three notes in the place of two. For example, a 1/4 triplet value means that you can have up to six quarter-note triplets per 4/4 bar, a 1/8 triplet value means 12 eighth notes per 4/4 bar, and so on. In other words, for every two notes in normal quantize value, you have three notes in triplet quantize value.

- **Dotted.** A dotted quantize value represents one and a half normal quantize value. For example, three quarter notes are equal to two dotted quarter notes, or three eighth notes are equivalent to a single dotted quarter note.

The Inspector

The Inspector is the area below the toolbar to the left of the recorded tracks in the Project window. It's visible by default, but it can be hidden if you need more screen real estate.

You use the Inspector to view or edit certain details pertaining to a selected track. The information displayed in the Inspector is always relevant to the selected type of track, and is organized on multiple tabs. For example, an audio track Inspector, like the one in Figure 15.7, has tabs for Inserts, Equalizers, Sends, Channel, Notepad, and Quick Controls. A MIDI track Inspector, like the one in Figure 15.8, has tabs for Expression Map, Note Expression, MIDI Inserts, MIDI Fader, Notepad, and Quick Controls. Click a tab to expand that section and access the available settings.

Figure 15.7 The default Inspector for an audio track.

Figure 15.8 The default Inspector for a MIDI track.

Color Coding: To change the color of a given track, click the arrow in the Track Settings section of the Inspector (next to the track's name) and select a new color from the color bar. Associating a color with a track makes it easy to color-code tracks and organize them when the project becomes bigger.

For track types that support insert and send effects, the symbol next to the corresponding section's title bar will be colored when any insert effect or send is active in that section. A similar color indicator appears on the EQ tab of any track that contains an active EQ setting. (An active EQ is displayed as green.)

By default, when you click on one tab to expand that section of the Inspector, any other expanded section automatically folds up. When a section is folded, all the settings you have made in that section remain intact, and bypass and assignment indicators remain visible.

Viewing Multiple Sections of the Inspector Simultaneously: To maximize more than one section of the Inspector area at once, hold down the Ctrl (PC)/⌘ (Mac) key as you click the tab for an additional section. You also can minimize all currently open panels at once by holding down the Alt (PC)/Option (Mac) key while clicking on any tab. Inversely, you can maximize all the sections at once by using the same key combination.

The Track List

The Track List area in the Project window, shown in Figure 15.9, enables you to view all tracks at once, enable multiple tracks for recording, and organize your material by type of content. Changes made in the Track List are also reflected in the Inspector and the Mixer.

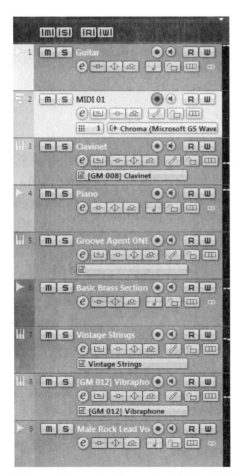

Figure 15.9 Audio and MIDI tracks in the Track List area.

All events inside a track appear to the right of the track's position in the Track List. The content of each track in the Track List differs according to the type of track. You can resize each individual track vertically to make it easier to view the contents of recorded events, as well as reorder the tracks by clicking and dragging them into new positions.

Resize an individual track's height:

1. Bring your cursor over the lower edge of the track you want to resize.

2. When your cursor changes into a double-headed arrow, drag your mouse up to reduce the track's size or down to increase its size.

Resizing the Track List: You also can resize the width of the entire Track List by dragging the right edge of the Track List area left or right. To adjust the *height* of all tracks simultaneously, hold down the Ctrl (PC)/⌘ (Mac) key as you drag the lower border of any track.

Recorded automation associated with tracks—such as volume or pan, for example—is saved in automation subtracks, called "lanes," and moves along with the track whenever you move it inside a project. Each automation parameter can be viewed in its own automation lane. For example, if you automate the Gain, Frequency, and Q-Factor on one band of the StudioEQ plug-in, you would have three automation lanes associated with the audio track where this insert resides.

To view an automation lane, right-click the associated audio or MIDI track and select Show Used Automation from the context menu; alternately, you can click the down arrow that appears in the bottom-left corner of the desired track. If you want the used automation visible for all tracks, select the Show Used Automation for All Tracks option instead.

There are two fields in each automation lane. The first field indicates the automation parameter displayed in that lane. The second field represents the value of the automation parameter at the current cursor location. You also can change the automation parameter displayed in the current lane without affecting any recorded automation if you want.

Transport Panel

The Transport panel, shown in Figure 15.10, is a floating panel that duplicates and supplements the toolbar's Transport controls. You display the Transport panel by selecting Transport > Transport Panel, or by pressing F2 on your computer keyboard. We'll discuss the Transport panel in more detail in Chapter 16, "Mastering Project Navigation."

Figure 15.10 Cubase 6's Transport panel.

Context Menus: In the Project window, as in many other windows in Cubase, you will find that right-clicking (Control-clicking for Mac users) in different regions will reveal a menu with a number of options related to the area in which you click. In many cases, these context menus allow you to choose options that are also available in the menu or toolbar of the Project window. However, having these options readily available in your workspace makes it easy to stay focused on a specific area and apply changes to events without having to move your mouse across the screen all the time. You will learn more about these context menus as you learn how to edit events and work with a project.

Track Classes

There are several types of tracks in a Cubase project; these types are sometimes called *classes*. In Cubase 6, these track classes include the following:

- **Audio** tracks are used for audio events and automation. You can have an unlimited number of audio tracks per project (in theory).

- **MIDI** tracks are used for MIDI events and automation. They are also unlimited in Cubase 6.

- **Instrument** tracks provide a fast and convenient way to use VST instrument plug-ins in a combined MIDI/audio channel/track.

- **Arranger** tracks (called Play Order tracks in older versions of Cubase) enable you to work with sections of your project in a non-linear fashion. Within this track you create arranger events of any length; they don't have to correspond to existing audio or MIDI events. You can then rearrange the arranger events to reorganize the sections of your recording. For example, you might create arranger events for each verse and chorus of a song, and then rearrange the events to change the order of verses and choruses. You can create one Arranger track per project.

- **FX Channel** tracks are used for audio plug-in effects. You can route audio to FX Channel tracks by using sends from various other audio-related track types, in order to process their signal in real time with insert effects you have placed on the FX Channel track. You can create up to 64 FX channels in Cubase 6.

- **Folder** tracks are used to group together other tracks in the Project window, making it easier to work on projects with a great number of tracks. For example, use folder tracks to group different takes of a solo or multiple drum tracks. Some folder tracks are created automatically. For example, a VST instruments folder track contains all VST instruments that you add to the project.

■ **Group Channel** tracks are used to combine the signal from various tracks into a single channel. Use Group Channel tracks to create submixes where a common set of controls or insert points for effects for all the channels assigned to this group are needed. For example, you can have the track outputs for various backup singers assigned to the same Group Channel fader in the Mixer, where perhaps a compressor plug-in has been inserted. When you want the level of the background vocals to go down, reduce the level of this group channel, rather than reducing the levels of individual tracks. You can create up to 256 group channels in Cubase 6.

■ **Marker** tracks are used to easily manage markers in a project. You can create only one marker track per project.

■ **Ruler** tracks are used to view the time displayed in a project's timeline. Create additional ruler tracks when you need to view alternate time references, such as timecode, seconds, and bars and beats simultaneously with the main ruler in the Project window.

■ **Signature** tracks enable you to view and edit key signature data in your project. There is one signature track per project.

■ **Tempo** tracks enable you to view and edit the tempo of your project. There is one tempo track per project.

■ **Transpose** tracks enable you to transpose sections of your project into a different key. There is one transpose track per project.

■ **Video** tracks are used to synchronize your music to a digital video file whenever this is needed.

Adding Tracks

When you start with an empty project, you have to add tracks for each instrument you record. New tracks are also added for automation and certain types of effects.

Add a track to your project:

1. Click Project > Add Track on the menu bar, and then select the type of track you want to add. Alternately, you can right-click (PC)/Control-click (Mac) anywhere in the Track List and select the type of track you want to add.

2. When the Add Audio Track dialog box appears, as shown in Figure 15.11, select how many instances of that type of track you want to add by changing the number in the Count field.

Figure 15.11 The Add Audio Track dialog box.

3. Some types of tracks have a mono or stereo option; select the appropriate option for your new track, if available.

4. Many types of tracks let you choose from a variety of preset configurations. If you want to use a track preset, click the Browse button and choose from the available presets.

5. Click OK to create the new track(s).

16 Mastering Project Navigation

The Project window represents the main view of a project; it is where most of the editing takes place—or at least where it all begins. Navigating from one part of the project to the other or focusing your attention on the first four bars of a chorus and then on the last eight bars of the second verse is something you will need to do quite frequently. Although repeatedly pressing the G key command to zoom out or the H key command to zoom in will work in some instances, there are more effective and elegant ways to move around in the project, which don't involve increasing your chances of getting carpal tunnel syndrome!

Here's a summary of what you will learn in this chapter:

- How to navigate using the Overview line

- Where to find different navigation menus in the Project window

- What the basics of the Project window's context menus are

- How to zoom in to your work using the appropriate tool

- How to change the time format of the Transport panel

- How to use the jog, nudge, and shuttle features of the Transport panel

- How to identify the tools and functions available in the Transport panel

Changing Your Focus

Moving around in a project, finding what you want to edit, focusing on the task at hand, and then looking at the project in a more global perspective are as much a part of your work as is editing audio and MIDI events. Changing your display and opening and closing windows is unfortunately part of the computer-based musician's reality, even if you use a large widescreen monitor—or even multiple monitors.

With so many items appearing onscreen and with screen space at a premium, it's important to know how best to get around the Cubase interface. Fortunately, Cubase offers many options in this respect, allowing you to get to what you need in different ways. The idea is not necessarily to use all the techniques presented here, but rather to find out what is possible and to use a working method that makes it easy for you to quickly perform necessary tasks.

Using the Overview Line

Although the Event Display area in the Project window can display a project from start to finish, you will quite often need to zoom in closer to gain greater accuracy for the task at hand, or to focus your attention on the section you're currently editing. Cubase's Overview line provides a way to always keep an eye on the entire project and the relation of the current Event Display within the project; this works no matter what your Project window's zoom level.

Unfortunately, the Overview line is not displayed by default. To display the Overview, click the Set Up Window Layout button on the toolbar, and check the Overview Line box.

The Overview line now appears below the standard toolbar, as shown in Figure 16.1. The amount of the project, in terms of time, displayed in this Overview depends on the project's Length value, which you can change in the Project Setup dialog box. Inside the Overview area is a shaded box called the *track view rectangle,* which varies both in size and placement. It essentially reflects the portion of the project that is currently visible in the Event Display area of the Project window. You can use this box to navigate throughout your project.

Figure 16.1 The Project Overview line.

Navigate using the track view rectangle:

1. Draw a shaded box in the Overview line to indicate the portion of the project's timeline you want to display in the Event Display portion of the Project window. Draw the shaded box by clicking and dragging your mouse either right to left or left to right. The size of the rectangle determines the amount of time displayed in the Event Display area.

2. To scroll back and forth in time throughout your project, drag the shaded box right or left in the Overview line.

3. To change the amount of your project that's visible in the Event Display area, resize the shaded box by clicking and dragging either end of the shaded box.

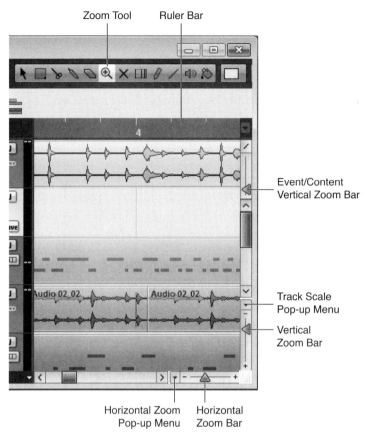

Figure 16.2   The various zoom controls.

Using the Zoom Tools

Cubase provides other tools you can use to control the content displayed on your screen. Here's a look at these options, as shown in Figure 16.2.

Zoom in to your work using the appropriate tool:

- **Zoom tool.** With this tool selected, you can use its "magnifying glass" cursor to zoom in on an area by drawing a rectangle around it. Hold down the Ctrl (PC)/⌘ (Mac) key while using the Zoom tool to zoom vertically and horizontally at the same time.

- **Ruler bar.** This enables you to zoom in or out by clicking and dragging your mouse. Click in the lower half of the Ruler bar and drag your mouse downward to zoom in or drag your mouse upward to zoom out. Drag your mouse to the left to move back in time or the right to move forward in time. Your zoom always centers on the position of your mouse in the ruler.

- **Event and Content Vertical Zoom bar.** This enables you to scale the vertical axis of the content within events or parts. Drag the handle up to enlarge the events within the event or part's vertical boundary, or drag the handle down to reduce the vertical scale of this content.

■ **Track Scale pop-up menu.** This menu at the lower-right edge of the Project window sets the track height to a preset list of values or lets you enter how wide you want the tracks to be. Selecting the Zoom Tracks N Rows or Zoom N Tracks option brings up a dialog box in which you can type in the number of tracks you want to fit in your Event Display area. This menu is available by clicking on the down arrow found between the vertical scroll bar and the Vertical Zoom bar.

■ **Vertical Zoom bar.** This zooms in (move downward) or out (move upward) vertically, affecting the height of tracks in your Event Display area. You can either drag the handle in the Zoom bar to get the desired height for each track or click on the arrows above and below to increase or decrease by one row at a time.

■ **Horizontal Zoom bar.** This adjusts the portion of time displayed in the window. You can zoom in (move to the right) or out (move to the left) horizontally. You can either drag the handle in the Zoom bar to get the desired time frame inside the Event Display area or click the left or right arrow to increase or decrease by the time frame one step at a time.

■ **Horizontal Zoom pop-up menu.** This enables you to select a preset amount of time, the space between the left and right locators, or any cycle marker and zoom in on it. You can also save a zoom level as a preset that you can recall later. For example, you can create two states—one for a larger perspective and another for a more detailed look at events or parts on your timeline. Then you can use this menu to toggle between the two (or more) zoom settings. Use the Add option to save the current zoom state to memory and the Organize option to manage the items available in this menu. This menu is available by clicking on the down arrow found between the horizontal scroll bar and the Horizontal Zoom bar.

In addition, you can select Edit > Zoom to display a submenu with a variety of zooming options.

The Transport Panel

As first discussed in Chapter 15, "Navigating the Project Window," the Transport panel is a multitask floating panel, several areas of which are important to project navigation. To hide or display the Transport panel, select Transport > Transport Panel, or press F2 on your computer keyboard. To display various areas of the Transport panel, right-click (PC)/Control-click (Mac) on the panel itself and check those sections you want to display; uncheck those sections you want to hide.

Main Transport

In the middle of the Transport panel are the main Transport controls (Stop, Play, Record, and so on). Above these controls are the primary (left) and secondary (right) time displays, shown in Figure 16.3. These displays show the current location of the cursor in two customizable formats. Between the two formats is a toggle button, which allows you to switch the position of the two currently displayed formats.

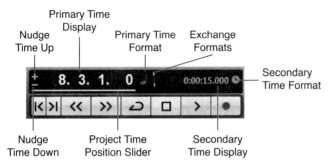

Figure 16.3 The primary and secondary time displays in the Transport panel.

Changing the format of the primary time display also changes the time format in the project's ruler—although afterward you can also set the ruler's time format independently without affecting this primary time display in the Transport. The secondary time format on the right does not have the same effect; it is there only to provide information about time and position in an alternate format.

The small plus and minus signs on the left of the time display allow you to nudge the position of the project cursor one unit at a time. Below the time display is a project cursor overview display (blue line), which enables you to monitor the location of the project cursor as your project moves along. You can click within the line to drag its cursor to any location you desire in the project's timeline, or simply click once anywhere in the line to make your project cursor jump to that location immediately.

Change the time format from the Transport panel:

1. Click on the time format icon (refer to Figure 16.3) to the right of the primary or secondary time display in the Transport panel to reveal a display format drop-down menu.

2. Select the desired time display format.

Shuttle, Jog, and Nudge

Cubase 6's Shuttle, Jog, and Nudge wheels, shown in Figure 16.4, are useful editing tools that quickly move the cursor within a project while you are listening to the audio/MIDI. These controls are not displayed by default; make them visible by right-clicking (PC)/Control-clicking (Mac) the Transport panel and selecting Jog/Scrub from the pop-up menu.

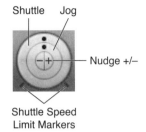

Figure 16.4 The Shuttle, Jog, and Nudge functions on the Transport panel.

Here's an overview of these functions:

■ **Shuttle wheel (outside ring).** Moving the ring to the right or the left causes the cursor to move forward or backward in time. The farther away from the center position you move the wheel, the faster the playback is. The maximum shuttle speed is indicated by the small markings on the lower half of the shuttle, on each side of the ring itself (see Figure 16.4). You can operate the Shuttle wheel by clicking on the ring and moving your mouse to the left or right.

■ **Jog wheel (middle ring).** By holding down the mouse button over the Jog wheel and moving it toward the right or left in a circular motion, the project cursor moves forward or back in time. Unlike the Shuttle wheel, you can turn the Jog wheel as much as you want. This is a great tool to look for specific cues in a project, because you will hear your events under the playback cursor playing back at a speed and direction that's relative to how fast you rotate the Jog wheel. (This technique is known as *scrubbing*.) Typically, you would use the Jog wheel when you are looking for something, going slowly over events. When you stop moving the mouse, playback stops.

■ **Nudge Frame buttons (inside the Jog wheel).** These two buttons move your project one frame ahead (plus sign) or one frame behind (minus sign), no matter what your time display may be. The number of frames per second, however, is determined by your settings for this project in the Project Setup dialog box. Obviously, if you don't work with video, nudging the project cursor by a frame at a time may not be especially useful to you if you customarily deal with bars and beats.

17 Navigating MIDI Tracks

In a Cubase project, MIDI tracks hold any type of MIDI event—from MIDI note events to controllers, such as velocity, modulation wheel, pitch bend, and so on. MIDI tracks also contain MIDI automation information for parameters such as pan, volume, or MIDI plug-in and send effects that might be assigned to a track. MIDI tracks can also contain MIDI filters and effects, such as MIDI compression. All recorded MIDI events are saved as part of the Cubase project file itself.

Here's a summary of what you will learn in this chapter:

- How to set your MIDI input port

- How to recognize the different functions associated with MIDI tracks

- How to recognize the different functions associated with MIDI channels

- How to change and access the MIDI Channel Settings panel

- How to convert MIDI into audio tracks for your final mix-down

MIDI Events in Cubase

When you record MIDI events, such as musical performances, through your MIDI controller, these events are stored in a MIDI part, which appears on the MIDI track's Event Display area in Cubase's Project window. You can have many parts containing MIDI events on your track, and parts can overlap each other on the track. Parts that are underneath other parts on the same MIDI track will still be active, and events inside them will still be heard when you play the track.

You can compare a part to a container for MIDI events. In the case of MIDI, these containers can be stacked one on top of the other, playing either different drum instruments, different channels (if the MIDI track is set to play "any" MIDI channels, rather than just a specific one), or simply as part of your working process.

In the example in Figure 17.1, there are three different parts playing at the same time on the same track, creating a rhythmic pattern. These three parts could be playing events for different MIDI channels. However, you should know that when parts are stacked one on top of the other in a MIDI track, the only visible part is the one on top of the

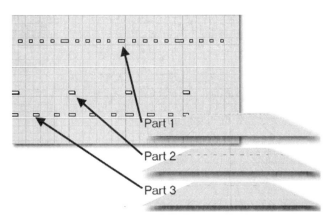

Figure 17.1 Overlapping MIDI parts on a MIDI track.

others. If all the parts are of equal length, this might lead to confusion because you will hear the parts playing, but you won't see them unless you select all the parts by dragging the Selection tool around the visible part and then opening your selection in the MIDI (Key or Drum) Editor.

Setting Up a MIDI Track

To create a new MIDI track, select Project > Add Track > MIDI. Alternatively, you can right-click (PC)/Control-click (Mac) in the same area and select Add MIDI Track.

To use a MIDI track, you must choose a MIDI input port and a MIDI output port for that track. The MIDI input port receives incoming MIDI events on the track and should reflect the MIDI input device you're using. For example, if a MIDI keyboard or other controller is hooked up to your MIDI input port A, you set your MIDI track to input port A to record events from your keyboard/controller. (You could also select All MIDI Inputs, which would send *all* incoming MIDI ports to the selected track.)

Set your MIDI input port for an external MIDI instrument:

1.   Be sure the MIDI Thru is active in the File (PC)/Cubase (Mac) > Preferences > MIDI option.

2.   Select the MIDI track you want to set up for input.

3.   Open the Track Settings section in the Inspector, shown in Figure 17.2, by clicking the track name at the top of the Inspector.

4.   Click in the MIDI Input field to reveal a pop-up menu showing the available MIDI input ports.

5.   Select the appropriate port.

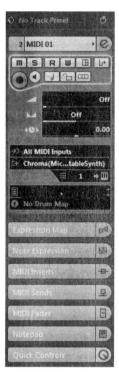

Figure 17.2 The basic track settings for a MIDI track in the Inspector area.

Figure 17.3 provides a look at each element found in the Track Settings section of the Inspector and in the Track List. Here are a few of the tasks you can perform in these areas:

- Double-click on the track name to edit it, or click on it to reveal/hide the Track Settings section.

- Click the right arrow next to the track name to assign a color to all events in a track.

- Click the Input Transformer button if you want to transform MIDI messages between the MIDI input and the track itself (thereby affecting what actually gets recorded). For example, you can use this function to filter channels in the MIDI input port, allowing only the desired input channels to be recorded for this track.

- Click the Record Enable button to arm this track for recording. When you press the Record button on the Transport panel, incoming MIDI events will be recorded on this track.

- Enable the monitor to hear incoming MIDI messages played through this track even when its Record Enable button is not active.

- Use the Timebase button to switch the track's time references for the events it contains between linear and musical timebase. When a track is displayed in musical timebase, changing the tempo of the song readjusts the events in the part according

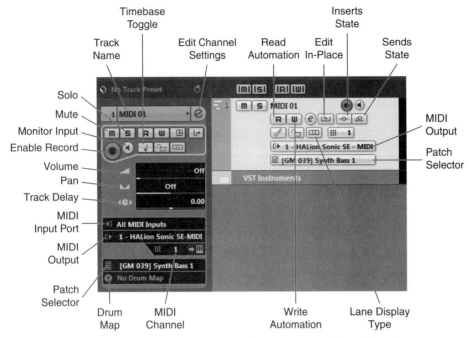

Figure 17.3 The MIDI track controls and parameters found in the Inspector and Track Settings area.

to the new tempo setting. When a track is displayed in linear time, changing the tempo of the song does not affect the start position of the parts it contains.

- Lock your track from editing using the Lock button.

- Click the Show Lanes button to enable a display mode where overlapping parts appear on several lanes inside the MIDI track.

- The Edit In-Place button expands the track to display a piano-roll style MIDI editor within the track that is very similar to the Key Editor for MIDI events. This function is called "in-place" because it allows users to edit MIDI events directly in the Project window. A keyboard is also displayed along its left side, as is the case in the Key Editor.

- The Track Volume and Track Pan controls transmit MIDI Control Change message numbers 7 and 10, and display the corresponding values for these controller types if any MIDI volume or pan automation is active for this track.

- The track delay slider adds a positive or negative delay in milliseconds to your track. Events in a track with a negative delay play earlier, whereas positive values make them occur later in time.

Track Delays: Track delays are typically used to adjust the timing of instruments that have some latency—for example, a keyboard that's a little slow on the attack. You can also use a track delay to "thicken" the sound of an instrument by creating a duplicate track and adding a slight delay.

- MIDI events coming through the MIDI Input Port selection field can be recorded onto the track and/or monitored through its assigned MIDI output port. Note that the main Track Settings controls don't allow you to select which MIDI input channel passes through a MIDI track, but usually this is not a problem. If you *do* need to select which channel comes in, try the presets available for the Input Transformer. MIDI events that have been recorded on a track play through the devices or software selected in its MIDI Output Port field. You can also use the output port to monitor incoming MIDI events through some other port.

- When a VSTi is assigned to the track, the Edit Instrument button opens the control panel for that VST Instrument, which allows you to edit its parameters and settings. (MIDI tracks assigned to a physical MIDI output, any other non-VSTi-compatible MIDI port, or a ReWire MIDI output will not display the Edit Instrument button.)

- The MIDI output channel sets the MIDI channel used by the MIDI output port to play MIDI events on this track.

- For any MIDI device that *hasn't* been configured through the MIDI Device Manager, the Bank Selector and Program Selector fields are used to send MIDI messages that change bank and program numbers according to your particular MIDI device's preset structure. Typically, programs are grouped in banks of 128 sounds each. (This is the maximum number of sounds MIDI can support.) To access sounds above this value, banks are created. You can access up to 128 banks of 128 programs using these settings.

- With some VSTi or MIDI devices that have been configured through the MIDI Device Manager panel, you can select the presets the instrument should play by name, using the Patch Selector drop-down menu. This menu then replaces the Bank and Program fields, and the names for the instrument's presets appear in the Patch Selector.

- If the preset represents a drum kit, the Drum Map drop-down menu will associate a drum map with the MIDI events on this track. This is useful when you record a drum part on this track. You can also use the Drum Map setting in the Track List area.

- The Inserts State button monitors the state of MIDI insert effects assigned to this track. The button is blue when any insert effect is assigned to the track, and a corresponding blue rectangular "active inserts" indicator appears in the title bar of the Inserts tab in the Inspector. Pressing this button in the Track List causes the MIDI to bypass all the inserts in this particular track, indicated by a yellow color on this button. There is also a dedicated bypass button for the Inserts section in the Inspector, just to the left of the active inserts indicator, which additionally turns yellow when a track's entire Insert section is muted via either of these methods.

When the Insert section (or a specific insert within it) is bypassed, the MIDI events do not pass through the current inserts, but settings of these inserts remain untouched.

- The Sends State button, found in both the MIDI Fader section and in the Track List, monitors the state of MIDI send effects assigned to this track. The button is blue when any send effect is assigned to the track, and a yellow rectangle appears in the title bar of the Sends tab in the Inspector. Pressing this button in the MIDI Fader section of the Inspector or in the Track List will prevent the MIDI on this track from going out through the MIDI send destinations, but the sends settings remain untouched.

- The track activity indicator at the right edge of the Track List monitors event activity on each track. In MIDI tracks, this may be any MIDI messages (note, controller, and SysEx if it is not filtered by Cubase).

Notepad

You can jot notes to yourself about any track by using that track's Notepad section. Use this feature if you need to exit quickly and you just want to keep some notes on the current state of your project, describe which devices, settings, and connections were used for this track, discuss whether it was changed from its original setup, enter names and phone numbers of your musicians or voice talent, and so on—anything you feel is worth writing down. The Notepad enables you to refresh your memory the next time you work on this project.

To enter a note in the Notepad, expand the Notebook section of a given track's Inspector, and then type your notes into the text field area. Any changes you make will be saved as part of the project file.

Quick Controls

Cubase lets you set up direct control of up to eight different MIDI parameters via the Quick Controls tab in the Inspector. Use the Quick Controls area as a track control center, with the most important controls assembled in one place. (Figure 17.4 shows a typical Quick Controls section, set up with a variety of controls.)

To set up the Quick Controls area, expand the Quick Controls tab and click in the first empty field. This displays a pop-up menu of control choices; double-click the control you want to appear in this slot.

Using the Quick Controls is relatively easy. If a slot controls a variable parameter, such as volume or pan, use your mouse to drag the colored bar at the bottom of the slot left or right and thus adjust the parameter. If a slot controls an on/off parameter, as with enabling insert effects, drag the colored bar all the way to the right to turn on the effect, or all the way to the left to turn it off.

Figure 17.4 A configured Quick Controls area; drag the colored bar to adjust the control in a given slot.

MIDI Fader

The MIDI Fader section of the Inspector (see Figure 17.5) offers many of the same options as you find in the MIDI Settings section of the Inspector area, as well as in the Track List area for a MIDI track. It also mirrors the information you find in the Mixer panel for this specific track class, as well as most of the buttons that you have seen earlier in the Track List and Track Settings sections of the Inspector area. You can use this section to set the pan and volume levels of the device or VSTi assigned as the output destination for this track. You also can use this section to change or monitor which insert or send effects are active.

Figure 17.5 The MIDI Fader section in the Inspector area.

A MIDI channel is added to the Mixer window each time you create a MIDI track in the Project window. Although VST instrument tracks display MIDI settings in the Inspector, their corresponding channel in the Mixer displays the audio output of the VST instrument, rather than the MIDI controls found in on a normal MIDI track—you can choose to view the MIDI inserts for an Instrument channel in the Mixer window. A MIDI channel in the Mixer window displays an exact replica of the MIDI Channel section in the Inspector for a MIDI track with the exception of the View Options menu. The function of each control found in Figure 17.6 is described in the following list:

- **MIDI Input and Output Port selection fields.** These allow you to choose the source and destination of MIDI events for this channel.

- **MIDI Channel selection field.** This allows you to choose the destination channel for your MIDI events.

- **Edit Instrument button.** This opens the control panel for the VSTi and makes it possible to perform parameter changes to the instrument or loads and changes presets in the VSTi.

- **Input Transformer button.** This allows you to access the Input Transformer panel for the selected track.

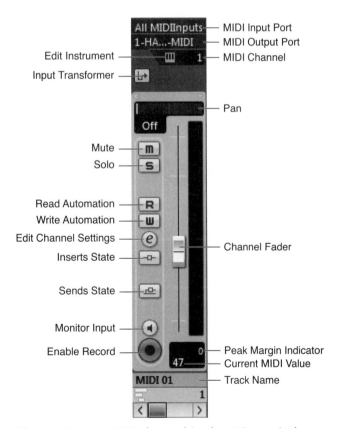

Figure 17.6 A MIDI channel in the Mixer window.

■ **Pan control and display.** This displays a numeric and graphic representation of the Pan setting for this MIDI channel. Ctrl-clicking (PC)/⌘-clicking (Mac) brings the pan back to its center position, which is represented by a C in the numeric display. On MIDI tracks, the Pan control actually corresponds to MIDI Controller #10.

■ **Channel setting option buttons.** This is a group of buttons, identical to those found in the MIDI Channel section in the track's Inspector area; whatever settings you made in the Inspector are displayed here and vice versa. These buttons include Mute, Solo, Read, Write, Open Channel Editor Panel, Insert Bypass, Send Effect Bypass, Monitor (switches the track to input monitor mode), and Record Enable.

■ **Channel fader.** This controls MIDI Controller #7 (Volume), which can only be an integer value between 0 and 127. You should also be aware that the fader's default position is set at 100; holding down the Ctrl (PC)/⌘ (Mac) key as you click on the fader's handle brings it back to this value. You also can hold down the Shift key while moving your fader for a finer level of precision. The level display on the right of a MIDI channel's fader, unlike the audio channels, does not represent the output level of the instrument. This level cannot be monitored because the sound of the MIDI instrument a MIDI channel is destined for is not monitored through the MIDI channel itself. In fact, this meter represents the velocity value of Note On and Note Off messages. Changing the volume level with the fader to the right does not, therefore, affect the level displayed in this bar, and no digital clipping can occur because of high velocities being monitored by this display.

■ **Current MIDI value and Peak Margin Indicator.** Both fields display MIDI values. The first represents the current position of the MIDI volume fader, and the second represents the highest MIDI Note On velocity value.

MIDI Channel Settings

The MIDI Channel Settings panel offers a convenient way to edit all MIDI channel settings for a selected MIDI channel in a single window. You can access a Channel Settings panel through the Edit MIDI Channel Settings button in the Inspector's Channel section, the Track List area, or in the Mixer window.

As you can see in Figure 17.7, the MIDI Channel Settings panel presents three distinct areas. Here they are, from left to right:

■ The MIDI Inserts panel displays the current inserts settings for this channel. As with the MIDI channel settings, any changes you make here or in any other window in the project update this channel's settings in all windows.

■ The MIDI Sends panel, as with the inserts, displays the current settings for this channel.

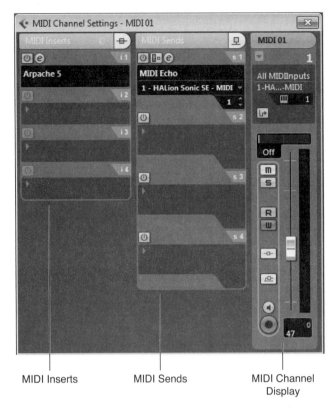

MIDI Inserts   MIDI Sends   MIDI Channel
                                               Display

Figure 17.7 The MIDI Channel Settings panel.

- The MIDI Channel display offers settings identical to the ones found in the Mixer or Channel section of the Inspector in the Project window. Any changes you make here or anywhere else are reflected in all parts of the project.

You can change the channel currently displayed in the MIDI (or audio) Channel Settings panel by accessing the drop-down menu in the upper-right corner of this panel. This makes it easy to navigate or change the settings for different channels without changing your view.

You also customize this panel by right-clicking (PC)/Control-clicking (Mac) in an empty area of the panel and selecting Customize View > Setup from the context menu. The resulting Setup dialog box, shown in Figure 17.8, lets you hide or display panels and re-sort the order in which they appear. Clicking on the Save Preset button (a small disk icon) allows you to save the current view and name it accordingly.

Once you've saved a customized view of the Channel Settings panel, it will appear as a selection in the context menu when you right-click (PC)/Control-click (Mac) in the panel. To switch between different views, simply select the appropriate preset from the context menu.

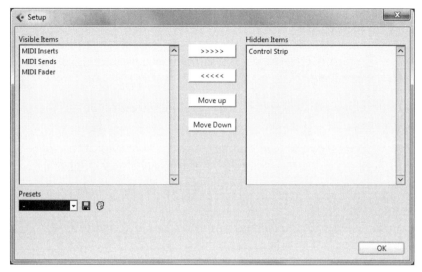

Figure 17.8 Customizing the Channel Settings panel.

Converting MIDI to Audio Track

MIDI provides a great way to lay down ideas and record music using synthesizers, samplers, and drum machines, among other things. However, distributing your work on a CD or through the Internet using MIDI files is not a practical solution. That's because all a MIDI track records is MIDI instructions, which don't copy directly to a digital file or CD.

If you want to include MIDI tracks in you final recording, you first have to convert those tracks to VST instrument or standard audio tracks. This MIDI-to-audio conversion process typically takes place before you begin the final mix-down and mastering for your project, although it can occur at any point when you're done working with a given MIDI track.

VST Instrument Tracks: Unlike pure MIDI tracks, VSTi tracks *do* copy directly to audio files during the mix-down process and don't have to be manually converted. (This is one more good reason to use VST instruments in your projects.)

Before you can convert the audio output from an external MIDI instrument into an audio track, it's important to set up the connections properly in the VST Connections panel, as described in Chapter 4, "Monitoring and Connecting Audio." An external instrument connection ensures that MIDI events are sent to the external MIDI device and that its audio outputs are routed back to the project through instrument tracks. This is definitely the best way to set up your external MIDI keyboards and sound modules in Cubase.

Convert a MIDI track into an audio track:

1. Turn off the MIDI metronome, especially if the same device you are using to record generates that sound.

2. In the Project window, select Project > Add Track > Audio to create a new audio track.

3. When the Add Audio Track dialog box appears, select either Mono (to record a mono MIDI track) or Stereo (to record a stereo MIDI track), and then click OK.

4. In the Track List, go to the MIDI track you want to convert and click "on" the Solo button. Make sure that the Record and Monitor buttons for this track are clicked "off."

5. Make sure that the output for the MIDI track is routed to the correct MIDI instrument/synthesizer.

6. In the new audio track, click "on" the Record Enable and Monitor buttons.

7. In the Transport panel, click the Play button and then move to the Mixer and adjust the level sliders for the new audio track to avoid clipping.

8. When you have the levels properly set, go to the ruler and position the cursor at the beginning of the MIDI track you want to convert.

9. In the Transport panel, click the Record button.

10. When the entire MIDI track has played through, click the Stop button.

What you now have is an audio track that mirrors your original MIDI track, with the selected MIDI instrument playing. From this point on in the mixing process, you should mute the original MIDI track (by clicking that track's Mute button in the Track List) and perform all future mixing, EQ, and effects processing on the new audio track.

Tweaking the Track: You'll probably want to take another listen to your mix after you've converted MIDI tracks to audio tracks. That's because the conversion from MIDI to audio isn't always perfect; sometimes volume levels get changed, or sonic characteristics get subtly altered. Fortunately, you can go back and tweak the volume levels for the newly created audio tracks, as well as apply any audio effects and EQ you might like.

18 Navigating Audio Tracks

In a Cubase project, audio tracks can contain any type of audio events—from live audio recordings to looped samples, from rendered effect tracks to duplicated and processed audio tracks. Audio tracks can be automated and routed to various audio outputs, including studio sends and group channels. Each audio track in Cubase has its own dedicated four-band parametric equalizer section and can have up to eight inserts and eight sends for effects processing.

Many of the controls found in audio tracks are similar to the ones discussed for MIDI tracks in the previous chapter and will behave in a way that should start to feel familiar to you by now. Also, audio, instrument, input, output, FX channel, and group tracks share many of the same basic controls.

Here's a summary of what you will learn in this chapter:

- How to display and change audio track settings through the Inspector sections

- How to set up the Auto Fade options associated with audio tracks

- How to configure the input and output busses of an audio track

- How to use and customize the Channel Settings panel

- How to work with overlapping audio events

Setting Up an Audio Track

Because audio tracks are very common to Cubase projects, they can be created in a number of ways and in various windows inside Cubase. For example, you can add an audio track through the Track List area's context menu, in the Mixer window's context menu, or by dragging an audio clip from the Pool or desktop to the empty area below the last track in the Project window's Track List. The most common method, however, involves selecting Project > Add Track > Audio. This displays the Add Audio Track dialog box, where you can select a preset configuration for your new track.

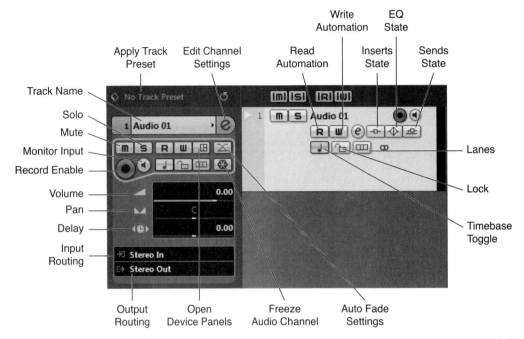

Figure 18.1 Controls and parameters for audio-related tracks in the Inspector and the Track List.

Controls and Parameters

Once an audio track is created, its settings are available in the Inspector. Some of these settings are also mirrored in the Mixer window, through the channels strip for that track.

As you can see in Figure 18.1, the Audio Track Settings in the Inspector (on the left) and the Track List controls offer many of the same functionalities. Many of these functions are similar to those available on MIDI tracks, with a few new functions available:

- Double-click on the track name to edit it, or click on it to reveal/hide the Track Settings section.

- Click the right-arrow next to the track name to assign a color to all events in a track.

- Click the Record Enable button to arm this track for recording.

- Enable the monitor to listen to the incoming audio even when the Record Enable button is not active.

- Use the Timebase button to switch the track's time references for the events it contains between linear and musical timebase.

- Lock your track from editing using the Lock button.

- The Lanes button lets you display (or not display) individual lanes for overlapping events within the track.

- The Freeze Audio Channel button "freezes" the track to help reduce the CPU load imposed by using real-time plug-in effects as inserts. Learn more in Chapter 40, "Optimizing Your Project."

- The Volume and Pan sliders control the track's volume level and left-to-right position within the stereo space.

- The Delay slider adds a positive or negative delay in milliseconds to your track. Use this control to adjust for tracks that do not properly sync up to other tracks or to create a "fattening" duplicate track with a slight delay.

- The Input Routing field lets you select the audio source for this track. This setting is particularly important when you are recording multiple audio sources, because it determines which track will record each input signal on your audio interface. The input busses available in this menu are those created previously in the VST Connections window.

- The Output Routing field lets you select where the signal gets routed at the output of each track. Audio tracks can be routed either to output busses created in the VST Connections panel or to group channels. If your project contains any group channels, a horizontal line in this pop-up menu will separate the output busses from the group channel assignments.

- Clicking the Edit Channel Settings button opens the Channel Settings panel, which displays key audio channel controls all in one location, including inserts, sends, and equalization.

- Click the Open Device Panels button to see a tree structure view of all inputs, sends, EQ, and the like.

- The Inserts State button monitors the state of insert effects assigned to this track. Clicking this button causes all inserts for this track to be bypassed, as indicated by a yellow color on this button.

- The EQ State button determines the status of equalization for this track. Click the button green to activate EQ settings; click it yellow to bypass all EQ settings.

- The Sends State button functions in much the same fashion as the Inserts State button, except for sends effects.

- Clicking the Auto Fade Settings button opens the Auto Fades dialog box, shown in Figure 18.2. Here you can create short 1- to 500-millisecond fades at the start and end of an event, typically used to reduce the possibility of clicks—an audio glitch that occurs when an audio event ends or begins at a point where the audio waveform is not at a zero crossing (silence on the amplitude scale). When the Auto Fade In, Auto Fade Out, or Auto Crossfades option is enabled for an audio track, Cubase automatically applies the corresponding fade at the beginning or end of

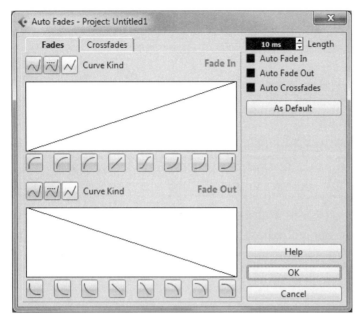

Figure 18.2 The Auto Fades dialog box.

each event in real time. The dialog box also lets you choose the type of fade curve to apply. To use the dialog box's settings across all audio tracks, click on the As Default button. Note that Auto Fade lengths can't exceed 500 ms (half a second)

Applying Auto Fade Settings: The Auto Fade settings can be customized for each track, or you can apply a single setting to the entire project through the Project > Auto Fade Settings menu.

Inspector Sections

By default, the Inspector displays the audio settings at the top, followed by the Inserts, Equalizers, Sends, Channel, Notepad, and Quick Controls sections. You can customize which sections the Inspector displays by right-clicking (PC)/Control-clicking (Mac) over a section's header. A context menu will reveal a number of additional sections, including an EQ curve display, studio sends (which can be used to route the track to a headphone mix, for example), a graphic surround pan display, and a customizable user panel. All these sections share a few functionalities:

- Click on the section header to expand the section and reveal its controls, hiding all others.

- Hold the Ctrl key (PC)/⌘ key (Mac) while clicking on a header to expand the section's controls without collapsing any other Inspector sections that are already open. For example, this will be particularly useful for keeping both the Equalizers and Equalizer Curve sections of the Inspector, discussed later in this chapter, open simultaneously.

■ The Inserts, Equalizers, Sends, and Studio Sends sections offer a bypass button. This control lets you bypass these entire sections with a single click. The Track List, the Channel section of the Inspector, and the Mixer window also offer Inserts, EQ, and Sends State buttons that perform a similar function for bypassing these entire sections on a channel. Whenever the bypass function is enabled, this button in the Inspector turns yellow. An indicator at the right end of these same sections of the Inspector also shows whether any insert, equalizer band, or send is currently active within them.

■ The Inserts and Equalizers sections offer a Preset Management button that lets you load, save, or manage presets for these sections.

For more information on the Inserts section, please take a look at Chapter 13, "Using Insert Effects."

The Channel Section

The Inspector's Channel section, shown in Figure 18.3, offers controls over the track's audio signal path. Many of these controls are mirrored in the Track List area and the Mixer.

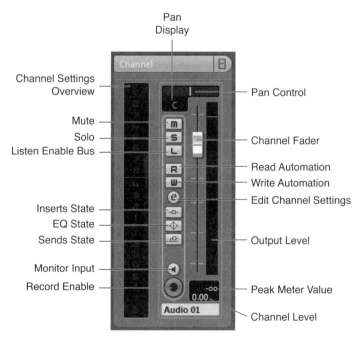

Figure 18.3 The Channel section of the Inspector.

Channel Section Controls

Among the controls found in the Channel section of the Inspector are the Mute, Solo, Listen Enable bus, Read/Write Automation, Edit Channel Settings, Inserts State, EQ State, Sends State, Monitor Input, and Record Enabled buttons. Remember that when the Monitor button is enabled, the level indicator to the right of the channel fader becomes a pre-fader input level meter; changing the level of this fader will not have any effect on the input level.

The settings overview panel on the left of the Channel section displays active settings found in the channel. The eight numbers on the top correspond to the eight channel inserts (the last two of which are post-fader), the following four numbers correspond to the four EQ bands, and the last eight numbers correspond to the eight channel sends (each of which can be switched between pre- and post-fader modes). Clicking on any of the numbers currently illuminated will disable the corresponding setting.

The channel fader controls the output level of this channel. As with many other controls in Cubase, to return the fader to its default 0 dB position, hold the Ctrl (PC)/⌘ (Mac) key down as you click on it. If you want to move the fader by smaller, more precise increments, hold down the Shift key as you click and drag. This is useful when you want to create slow and precise fade effects with automation. The Channel Level numeric display below the fader tells you the position value (in dB) of this channel's fader. If you have a scroll wheel on your mouse, you can also adjust the selected channel's fader level by moving the wheel up or down.

Directly below the output level for the channel, the Peak Meter Value indicator represents the distance between the highest audio peak in this track and the maximum digital audio level. This value resets itself as soon as you move the channel's fader or if you click inside the field. It's important to keep an eye on this margin because you don't want the audio on this track to go above 0 dB, but you don't want it to always stay very low when recording either. Ultimately, the Peak Meter Value indicator should remain between −12 dB and 0 dB when recording.

Channel Settings Panel

The Audio Channel Settings panel, shown in Figure 18.4, appears when you press the Edit Channel Settings button for any audio-related track in the Inspector, Track List, or Mixer window. This window shows all of that track's audio parameters, making it easy to perform detailed settings.

By default, the Channel Settings panel displays four key sections—Inserts, Equalizers, Sends, and Faders. However, you can customize its contents to display up to 11 types of settings. Just right-click (PC)/Control-click (Mac) anywhere inside the window and select Customize View from the context menu. From the resulting submenu, check those sections you want to display.

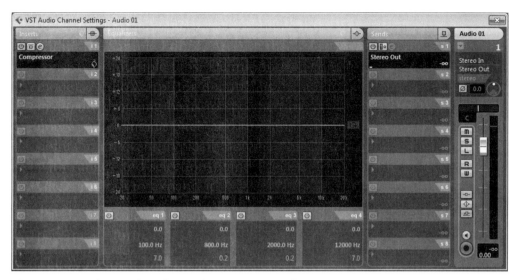

Figure 18.4   The Audio Channel Settings panel.

Saving Views: To save a custom view in the Channel Settings panel, right-click (PC)/Control-click (Mac) within the window and select Customize View > Setup. In the resulting Setup dialog box, modify the Customize View window's display and then click the Save button.

Overlapping Audio Events

When you record audio on a track, an audio event is created in your project. You can record multiple events on a track, as shown in Figure 18.5, and then move events along the project's timeline.

Figure 18.5   Multiple events recorded on an audio track.

Know, however, that each audio track can play only one audio event at a time. This is fine if the multiple events follow each other successively, but if audio events overlap each other, you only hear the topmost event at any given position.

Changing the order of these events offers a way to control which event plays back on the track, as shown in Figure 18.6. In the overlapping events found in the upper portion of this figure, Event A is in front (on top) and Event B is in back (behind). As a result, the track plays Event A until its end, and then plays Event B. The same events overlap

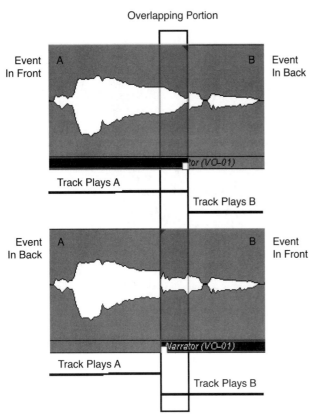

Figure 18.6 Changing the order of overlapping events on an audio track.

in the lower portion of the figure, but this time, Event A is the one behind, while Event B is in front. You can change the order of these events by selecting the event you want to place in front, and then selecting Edit > Move To > Front.

Editing

19 Using the Sample Editor

The raw audio you record with Cubase is contained in a series of audio events. Each event is actually a digital waveform that represents the analog waveform of the original instrument or vocal. To trained eyes, that waveform maps out everything you need to know about the recorded sound—pitch, amplitude, and duration.

To edit these audio events, Cubase provides two primary audio editing environments (the Sample and Audio Part Editors) and a number of audio asset management windows (the Pool and the MediaBay, SoundFrame, and Loop Browsers). You can also, of course, perform some editing directly from the Project window.

All that said, this chapter focuses on the Sample Editor, which lets you edit recorded or imported audio, create regions and slices, and add special tempo markers to time-stretch audio events in real time. This type of audio warping makes it possible to match the tempo of an audio event, such as a loop, to the project tempo without affecting its pitch; it also automatically adjusts the tempo of the audio event whenever the project tempo is changed, making audio events almost as flexible as MIDI events when it comes to altering project tempos.

Here's a summary of what you will learn in this chapter:

- How to edit the boundaries of objects (events or regions) in the Sample Editor

- How to cut, copy, or paste audio inside an event

- How to insert or remove silence inside an event

- How to delete individual notes

- How to create and edit regions inside the Sample Editor

- How to edit a snap point's position

Sample Editor Areas

When you want to directly edit the audio waveforms you've recorded or imported, you use Cubase's Sample Editor. The Sample Editor edits the contents of one audio event at a time in a nondestructive environment. You can create regions within an event, add effects, or edit an event by using offline processes and effects.

To open the Sample Editor for an audio event, as shown in Figure 19.1, simply double-click that event. You can have more than one Sample Editor window open at the same time, to edit multiple audio events.

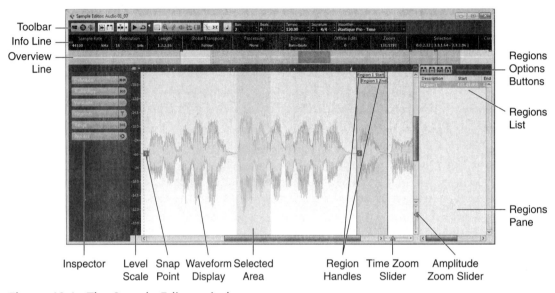

Figure 19.1 The Sample Editor window.

Audio Editing: The Sample Editor edits only audio events, not MIDI events. Since MIDI events are actually sets of digital instructions, they have no wave-forms to edit.

Main Areas

The main area of the Sample Editor consists of the Waveform Display. The Editor window also displays a number of bars similar to the other editors—a toolbar, which includes various audio-specific tools, the Overview line that provides a wave-form overview of the entire event, the Info line, the ruler for the horizontal time scale, and the vertical Level Scale that depicts amplitude. The following list describes the key areas of the Sample Editor window.

■ The Info line (status) area displays information about the sample being edited.

■ The Overview line presents a thumbnail display that can be used to zoom and navigate within the audio event. The currently displayed area in the Overview area is displayed inside a box that can be used to resize or move the portion of this audio event or clip that is shown below in this editor's Waveform Display.

■ The Sample Editor Inspector contains all the tools and functions you need to work within the Sample Editor. As with the Track Inspector, the Sample Editor Inspector consists of multiple tabs: Definition (for adjusting the audio grid and musical mode); AudioWarp (for quantizing the audio, applying a swing setting, and manually dragging beats to specific time positions); VariAudio (for editing single notes and changing pitch and timing); Hitpoints (for marking and editing specific points in an event, typically for the "hits" in a drum track); Range (for working with ranges and selections); and Process (for applying processes and plug-ins). Click any tab to expand it.

■ The Level Scale represents amplitude, which can be switched between decibel and percentage formats.

■ The Waveform Display area, which you can then edit.

■ The selected portion inside the Waveform Display area.

■ The snap point of the object (event or region).

■ Region handles that identify the start and end of a region inside an audio event.

■ The Time Zoom slider.

■ The Amplitude Zoom slider.

■ The Regions pane, which includes a list of named regions within the event and buttons to create and edit regions.

Editing Waveforms: If you zoom in all the way on a waveform in the Sample Editor, you'll see the individual points that make up the wave. You can then use Cubase's Draw tool to alter the shape of the waveform, thus changing the sound of the recorded note or pitch. Beware—this is a very powerful way to edit. Small changes can have a big effect!

Toolbar

Figure 19.2 displays the first few tools found in the Sample Editor's toolbar. The first button lets you configure the contents of the Sample Editor window, while the next two buttons toggle the solo editor and acoustic pitch feedback.

Next is the Show Audio Event button, which toggles on or off the start and end points of the audio event being edited. Next to that is the Show Regions button, which toggles on or off the Regions pane, shown in Figure 19.3. This area displays information on regions currently associated with an audio clip or event, as well as allows you to create, remove, rename, select, edit, or preview regions; it also displays region handles, if there are any. This Regions List (on the bottom part of the pane) enables you to create a

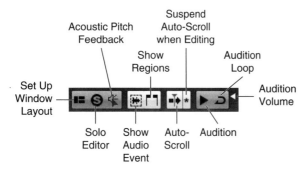

Figure 19.2 The main audio editing tools of the Sample Editor.

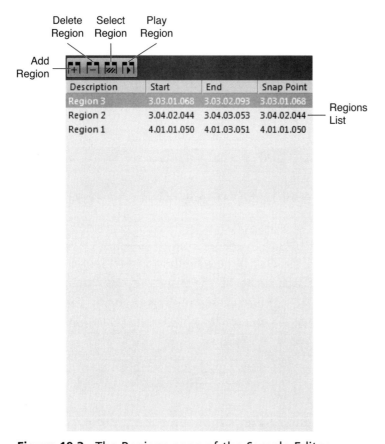

Figure 19.3 The Regions pane of the Sample Editor.

region from a selection in the Waveform Display area, remove an existing region, select the highlighted region in the Waveform Display area, and play the highlighted region. Unless you have recorded audio in Cycle mode with the Create Regions option enabled, events do not normally contain any regions when they are recorded or imported. It is through editing options or preference settings that regions are created, or, as you'll see later in this chapter, through the buttons above the Regions List.

Next is the Auto-Scroll button, which turns on or off automatic scrolling through the event; click the arrow next to the Auto-Scroll button to suspend Auto-Scroll when editing. This is followed by the Audition and Audition Loop buttons, which have the same properties as in the Pool window. The Audition Volume arrow next to the Audition Loop tool displays a fader that enables you to control the preview level when you are playing an event inside the Sample Editor. (This preview level does not affect the level of the event in the Project window.)

Figure 19.4 shows the next group of buttons in the toolbar. These buttons perform distinct editing operations, such as selecting a range, zooming in or out, editing the waveform, performing audio playback, scrubbing, and time warping. We'll discuss these tools later, when we examine the operations available in this window.

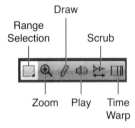

Figure 19.4 Editing buttons in the Sample Editor.

Figure 19.5 starts with two "snap" buttons, Snap to Zero Crossing and Snap On/Off. Clicking "on" the Snap On/Off button enables you to find exact positions when editing. Clicking "on" the Snap to Zero Crossing button forces any selection you make to move to the nearest zero crossing. Enabling this function is a useful way of being sure that regions you create or process will not begin or end at a position within the audio not corresponding to zero percent amplitude (silence). This helps in preventing clicks, pops, and other audio glitches from occurring due to sudden jumps in audio amplitudes at the beginning or end of a region.

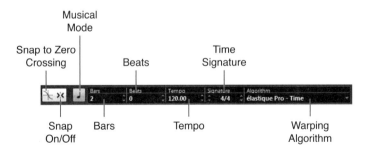

Figure 19.5 Snap and Musical mode controls.

Next to the Snap buttons is a button that toggles on/off Cubase's Musical mode, which matches playback to the selected bars and beats. The balance of the toolbar contains controls related to Musical mode: Bars, Beats, Tempo, Time Signature, and Warping Algorithm. We'll discuss these later in this chapter.

Thumbnail and Waveform Displays

Below the toolbar is the Overview line that provides a thumbnail view of the current event loaded in the Sample Editor. You can have only one event loaded in this editor at a time, so this overview displays only one event or several regions defined within this event.

The visual representation of the audio sample appears in the Waveform Display area. Cubase can display mono, stereo, and surround formats with up to six channels. The waveforms are displayed around a zero axis at the center of each waveform, which is also indicated in the vertical Level Scale along the left side of the Waveform Display. You can customize the elements displayed in this area by right-clicking (PC)/Control-clicking (Mac) in the Sample Editor, selecting the Elements option at the bottom of the context menu, and selecting or deselecting elements found in this submenu. You can change the Level Scale from decibel (dB) to percentage display by clicking the down arrow at the top of the Level Scale.

Basic Editing Functions

If you want to edit, cut, copy, and paste entire events, you can do so from Cubase's main Project window; we discuss this in Chapter 28, "Arranging in the Project Window." To cut, copy, and paste audio data *within* an audio event, however, you use the editing functions in the Sample Editor.

Trimming Start and End Points

One of the most common editing functions is to trim the beginning or ending of a clip. This is typically done when you start recording before a musician starts playing; you can trim the non-playing part of the event.

Edit the start and end of an event in the Sample Editor:

1. In the Sample Editor's toolbar, enable the Show Audio Event button.

2. Next, select the Range Selection tool in the toolbar.

3. Click the marker for the start point of the event and drag it to the desired new location. (Note that you can't extend these markers beyond the limit of the audio clip to which the event refers.)

4. Click the marker for the end point of the event and drag it to the desired new location.

The event is now shortened per your edit—both in the Sample Editor and for the event as it appears in the Project window.

Cutting and Pasting

You can also cut and paste any section of an event elsewhere within the same event. These basic editing functions are similar to those in any other type of application, just applied to the audio waveform in the Sample Editor window.

For our purposes, cutting and pasting audio can be summed up in four steps:

1. Use the Range Selection tool to select the desired audio.

2. Apply the desired function, such as Cut or Copy, from Cubase's main Edit menu.

3. Position the cursor where you want to paste the audio.

4. Use the Paste command in the Edit menu.

Inserting Silence

You also can insert silence within an existing audio clip. This is useful when you want to add pauses between specific audio content.

Know, however, that inserting silence doesn't erase any of the existing event; when you insert an area of silence, it moves the rest of the audio clip (the bit to the right of the inserted silence) farther to the right. For example, if you insert a second of silence, it just makes the event one second longer.

Add silence in an audio event:

1. With the Range Selection tool selected, drag a selection box over the area where you want to add silence.

2. Select Edit > Range > Insert Silence. [This is also available in the editor's context menu or by pressing Ctrl+Shift+E (PC)/⌘+Shift+E (Mac).]

Erasing Individual Notes

Want to delete a bad note? You can do it from the Sample Editor—although you don't want to use the Delete function found in the Edit menu. That's because when you use the Delete function, you delete not only that part of the waveform you selected, but also that part of the timeline. That is, cutting a note makes the measure (and thus the entire song) shorter by the length of that note.

You also don't want to use the Insert Silence function, found in the Edit > Range menu. Inserting silence in this manner doesn't actually erase any of the existing event; it literally inserts a new range without any recorded audio, moving the rest of the audio clip (the bit to the right of the inserted silence) farther to the right. For example, if you insert a second of silence, it just makes the event one second longer.

Instead, you want to select the note you want to erase, and then use Cubase's Silence audio process. This effectively mutes the selected region of the audio event, removing the undesired note.

Erase an individual note:

1. Select the Range Selection tool in the toolbar.

2. Click and drag the cursor across the area you want to delete; make sure you select the entire duration of the note, as shown in Figure 19.6.

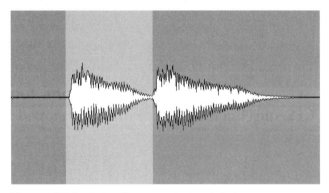

Figure 19.6 Selecting a note to delete.

3. Select Audio > Process > Silence.

The audio is now removed from the selected region.

Select the Entire Note: When you delete a note, make sure you select the entire note—including the full decay. Deleting or replacing just the thick attack portion of the waveform will leave the note's sustain or resonance in the event, which will not sound right. (Imagine hearing the sustain of a cymbal hit without hearing the hit itself.) You want to delete the entire note from start to finish—which is easier done with a large zoom into the editor.

Musical Mode

You also can use the Sample Editor to define loop properties needed for Musical mode samples. Once Musical mode is enabled on a sample, its tempo becomes locked to the project's tempo setting. Cubase automatically time-stretches the loop to reflect any tempo changes that occur in real time. This type of feature is now commonly used in many loop-based composition tools, and using it in Cubase is pretty straightforward.

I will further discuss how to use Musical mode in this fashion to quantize audio, tighten up the timing of a rhythmic part using AudioWarp tabs, and match an audio file's fluctuating tempo with the project's fixed tempo in Chapter 20, "Using Audio Processing Options." Turn there for more information.

Working with Regions

Regions enable you to define portions within an audio event that you can reuse several times in a project. For example, you could create regions from a 16-bar groove played by a drummer, naming each region appropriately: intro, beat, break, fill, and ending. You can then drag the regions from the Regions List in the Sample Editor into the Project window, just as you do when dragging objects from the Pool into the Project window.

Create a new region:

1. Enable the Show Regions button to display the Regions pane.

2. Use the Range Selection tool to click and drag over the area in the Sample Editor you want to include in the new region. At this point, you don't need to be precise.

3. When you have a good idea of the range, right-click (PC)/Control-click (Mac) and select Zoom > Zoom to Selection to view your selection close up.

4. Edit the start or end of the selection as needed by dragging its edges. When the cursor becomes a double-headed arrow (which occurs when the cursor crosses one of the selection's edges), you can modify the selection without losing it.

5. Enable the Audition Loop button and click the Audition icon (the "play" button) in the Sample Editor toolbar to hear the selection. Make any necessary modifications to your selection.

6. When you are satisfied with the selection, click the Add button in the Regions pane.

7. Type a name in the Name field for your new selection.

Using the Snap to Zero Option: Keep the Snap to Zero Crossing button enabled to make sure the amplitude of the audio signal is at its lowest possible value (zero percent or minus infinity when displayed in dB) at the start and end points of the selections you make in the Waveform Display. This technique reduces the chances that glitches might occur during playback due to an abrupt change in amplitude. When the button is enabled, you will notice that the precise start and end points of your selection might skip over areas in the Waveform Display because Cubase cannot find a proper zero crossing in that portion of the audio.

Modify an existing region:

1. In the Regions List, select the region you want to edit.

2. Click the Select button. The region's start and end handles will appear.

3. Right-click (PC)/Control-click (Mac) and select Zoom > Zoom Selection to center the selection in the display area.

4. With the Range Selection tool, drag the region's start or end handle to the new desired location.

You can also change the current region's start and end locations numerically by changing the values manually in the Start and End columns of the Regions List.

For more precise range selection, use the controls in the Range tab of the Sample Editor Inspector, shown in Figure 19.7. You can enter precise start and end times, or pull down the Select menu to select specific areas. Pull down the Zoom menu to select zoom levels.

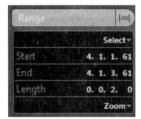

Figure 19.7 The Range tab in the Sample Editor Inspector.

Snap Point

Because audio events or regions don't necessarily begin at a specific quantize value, you can change the location of the sensitive area or "hook" within them that will used for snapping them to the increments of the current quantize grid. This is called the *snap point*, and here in the Sample Editor it is displayed as a dotted vertical line, with an S in a box at the center of this line, as shown in Figure 19.8.

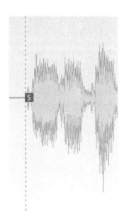

Figure 19.8 The snap point in an audio event.

By default, the snap point is located at the very beginning of an event. This is not necessarily where the first beat is, however. You can therefore drag the snap point anywhere within the event, to the first beat or another important point in the event.

As you drag the event within a track in the Project window or a lane in the Sample Editor, the object snaps to the grid based on the location of this snap point, rather than the actual start position of the event that contains it. By default, snap points are placed at the event start point of audio events and regions.

Edit the snap point's position:

1. Open the event or region in the Sample Editor.

2. Zoom to view the current snap point and the place where you want to reposition it.

3. For more precision, you can use Audition button to find the exact place where the snap point should go.

4. Click and drag the S (in the box on the snap point line) and move it to the appropriate location.

20 Using Audio Processing Options

This chapter takes a look at Cubase's online and offline audio processing options. Offline and online processes offer identical parameters and results; however, offline processes are rendered to a temporary file. Cubase then reads this temporary file instead of calculating the effect each time. This technique lessens the load on the computer's resources.

Here's a summary of what you will learn in this chapter:

- How to use audio processes found in the Audio menu

- How to use the recovery tools found in the Offline Process History panel

- How to shift tempo and pitch in Musical mode

Audio Processing Options

Audio processing can be applied to audio in two ways: You can apply effects in real time that affect the entire track (known as *online processing*), or you can apply processing that alters the content of the audio events played back by Cubase (known as *offline processing*). With online processing, you can change an effect's parameters in real time. With offline processing, effects are calculated beforehand and fixed to the selected audio event.

The end result of both types of processing is the same in terms of sonic qualities, but the impact on your system's performance is significantly different. Online processing can slow down system performance, whereas offline processing doesn't affect system performance at all.

Online vs. Offline Processing

When you apply an *online* effect to a track, the audio passing through an insert, send, or main bus effect is processed by your computer in real time. The effect itself is not saved to an audio file, although the effect's parameters are saved as part of your project. Every time you play the project, the computer has to process all the active effects, which is why you can change parameters easily. On the other hand, this type of real-time effects processing can add a serious load on your computer, slowing performance down to a grind when your real-time processing needs exceed the computer's capabilities.

In contrast, an *offline* effect does not use up the computer's CPU time each time the file plays. Processing audio offline offers a less CPU-intensive method of processing audio because the CPU doesn't have to process the audio every time you press Play.

When you process audio files offline, you replace the affected portion of an audio event with the processed version. This alteration, saved as part of the project file, creates the effects without changing the original audio file's content. It also doesn't require any processing time during playback, because the files are simply read from the media drive.

The disadvantage of offline processing is that you cannot automate the application of effects by using automation in real time. There are many instances, however, in which automation is not needed. When you want to add an effect to a portion of an audio clip, event, region, or slice, processing this portion and writing the effect to a file might be more effective than using real-time effects—not to mention it would reduce the load imposed on your computer. Pitch-shifting and time-stretching operations are notoriously heavy consumers of computer resources, so using them in offline processes is highly recommended, especially on slower computers or for large process-intensive projects.

You apply real-time online effects and processes through the insert effects and FX channels (a special type of audio track intended as a send destination, where you have enabled one or more insert effects). You apply offline processes and plug-in effects through the Plug-Ins or Process submenu found in the Audio menu, or through the same submenus in the Project window's context menu.

Using Audio Processes and Effects

In audio terminology, any effect applied to an audio signal is referred to as *audio processing*. However, in Cubase, the commands found in the Audio > Process submenu relate to more basic audio transformations, such as changing gain or pitch.

Audio effects, such as reverb, chorus, and delay, are found under the Audio > Plug-ins submenu; this submenu effectively mirrors the offline processing options available using VST plug-in effects. Although I can't go into all these options (which are useful for applying layers of special effects on specific audio selections within a track, for example), bear in mind that many of the same basic dialog box options apply.

Exclusive Audio Processes: Cubase 6 includes some audio processes that are unique to offline processing, in that they can't be applied to all the events in the signal path. For example, Cubase lets you reverse an event—that is, play it backward. You can't reverse an entire track in real time because Cubase can't know what to start with until it comes to the end. Cubase can, however, reverse a selected event by processing it offline, before initiating playback.

You can apply processing to an entire audio event or region in the Project window or just to a portion selected within it using the Range Selection tool. You can also apply processing on individual audio events seen within the Audio Part Editor. Selecting an event or region in the Pool applies the processing to the entire selected object. Finally, you can apply a process specifically to a selected portion of an event or region in the Sample Editor. In all these situations offline processing can be applied either via the Audio > Process submenu or via the Process submenu of that window's context menu.

Apply an audio process:

1. From the Project window, select the event you want to process, or use the Range Selection tool to select a range across one or more events.

2. Select Audio > Process.

3. From the Process submenu, select the process you want to apply to the selection.

4. The control panel for the selected process now appears. Each process has its own particular controls and settings; select a preset or adjust the controls to achieve the sound you desire.

Applying an offline effect is similar to applying an audio process. Remember, offline effects are identical to the online plug-in effects discussed in Chapter 13, "Using Insert Effects;" they're just applied offline, rather than in real time.

Apply an offline audio effect:

1. From the Project window, select the event to which you want to apply the effect, or use the Range Selection tool to select a range across one or more events.

2. Select Audio > Plug-Ins.

3. From the Plug-Ins submenu, select the type of effect you want to apply, and then select the specific plug-in.

4. The control panel for the selected plug-in now appears. Each effect has its own particular controls and settings; select the desired preset or adjust the controls to achieve the effect you desire.

Because some objects may be shared (used more than one time in the project's timeline), when applying a process or effect, Cubase asks whether you want to create a new version or change all the instances of this object throughout the project's timeline. If you opt to create a new version, the selected object is the only one affected by this process, and the processed version of the object replaces that instance of the original content in the Project window (but not on your media drive; the results of online processing are always stored in your project's Edits subfolder). If you want all the shared instances of this object (event or region) to change, you can select the Continue button. This replaces the currently selected object rather than creating a new version, which causes all shared occurrences to change as well in the project.

Cubase 6 Offline Processes

Cubase 6 offers 15 offline audio processes. These processes are described in Table 20.1. I'll discuss the parameters for the most popular of these processes in the following sections.

Table 20.1 Cubase 6 Audio Processes

Process	Location	Description
Envelope	Audio > Process > Envelope	Applies a volume curve for a given event, which can be used to limit the upper and lower volume levels.
Fade In	Audio > Process > Fade In	Gradually fades in the volume.
Fade Out	Audio > Process > Fade Out	Gradually fades out the volume.
Gain	Audio > Process > Gain	Increases or decreases the overall volume level of the event. Typically used to increase the volume level (add gain) to an event recorded at too low a level.
Merge Clipboard	Audio > Process > Merge Clipboard	Mixes the audio in Cubase's clipboard into the selected event.
Noise Gate	Audio > Process > Noise Gate	Silences any audio that occurs below a selected threshold level; typically used to remove background noise from areas of a recording that should be silent.
Normalize	Audio > Process > Normalize	Specifies a desired maximum audio level and raises other levels accordingly; typically used to increase the level of audio recorded at too low an input level.
Phase Reverse	Audio > Process > Phase Reverse	Reverses the phase of the selected event, turning the waveform "upside down."
Pitch Shift	Audio > Process > Pitch Shift	Shifts the pitch of the selected event up or down by a specified number of half-tones, without altering the tempo or length of the event.
Remove DC Offset	Audio > Process > Remove DC Offset	Removes a large direct current (DC) component in the audio signal.
Resample	Audio > Process > Resample	Resamples the event at a lower or higher sampling rate.
Reverse	Audio > Process > Reverse	Reverses the selected event, essentially playing it backwards.

Table 20.1 *(Continued)*

Process	Location	Description
Silence	Audio > Process > Silence	Replaces the selection with silence.
Stereo Flip	Audio > Process > Stereo Flip	Flips the right and left channels in a stereo recording.
Time Stretch	Audio > Process > Time Stretch	Changes the length or tempo of a recording, without altering the pitch.

Envelope

The Envelope process lets you apply a volume envelope to the selected audio event, effectively limiting the upper and lower volume levels of the event. As you can see in Figure 20.1, you can choose from three envelope curves or apply a preset envelope.

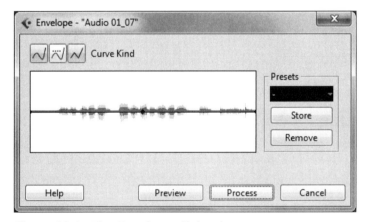

Figure 20.1 The Envelope dialog box.

Fade In and Fade Out

When you want to add a soft attack to a new event, use Cubase's Fade In process, shown in Figure 20.2. Likewise, you can create smooth fade outs by using the Fade Out process. They both work in a similar fashion, applying a specific type of fade curve to the beginning or end of the audio event.

> **Selecting a Fade Region:** The Fade In/Out processes apply to the entire area selected. So if you select an event, the fade in (for example) will start at the beginning of the selection and reach full volume at the end of the selection. For this reason, you want to select a region within an event for the fade to take place.

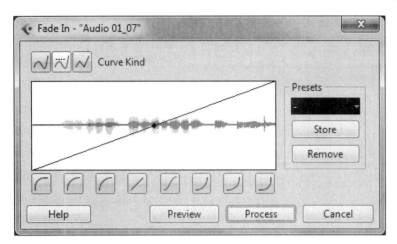

Figure 20.2   The Fade In dialog box.

Gain

The Gain dialog box, shown in Figure 20.3, lets you increase the gain, or volume level, of a recorded signal. Moving the slider to the right adds gain, whereas moving the slider to the left reduces it. You also can enter the desired amount of change in the Gain field by typing in the appropriate value. When you click the Preview button, Cubase indicates whether this gain change causes the object to clip (digital distortion caused by the amount of gain change exceeding the maximum permitted level).

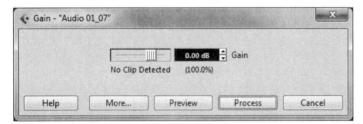

Figure 20.3   The Gain dialog box.

Noise Levels: When you increase the gain for an event, you also increase the noise level. For this reason, use the Gain control sparingly, and be prepared to live with an increased level of background noise.

Merge Clipboard

The Merge Clipboard process merges audio content that has been previously copied to the clipboard into the currently selected object. This process enables you to specify a mix ratio between the audio selected for processing and the audio on the clipboard through a percentage slider. On the left side, you can see the proportion of the original (selected) object, and on the right side, you can see the proportion of the audio previously copied in the clipboard.

Noise Gate

When you make a noisy recording, much of the noise is hidden by the recorded sound itself. That is to say, when an instrument is playing, the listener hears the instrument, not the background noise. However, when the instrument stops playing (or the vocalist stops singing), that background noise is no longer masked. The listener hears the noise clearly and distinctly, and that isn't good.

This is why audio engineers invented noise gates. A *noise gate* is a device or process that identifies passages that should be silent and automatically erases all noise and hiss from those passages. The process works by setting a volume threshold; all signals below that threshold are muted.

The Noise Gate dialog box (see Figure 20.4), then, lets you silence any portions of an audio signal that are below the specified Threshold level. Imagine a gate that opens when a signal is strong enough (above threshold) and closes when it isn't (below threshold). You can use this to silence portions of an audio signal during relatively silent passages. For example, you can use a noise gate to remove a guitar amplifier's humming noise from your recording during passages where the guitar player is not actually playing any notes. A noise gate does not remove this noise when the guitarist is playing because the signal will most likely be loud enough to pass the threshold, but the noise at that point should be less noticeable because it is masked by the guitar sound. If the noise level is too loud even when the guitarist is playing, you should consider using a noise reduction plug-in or rerecording this part.

Figure 20.4 The Noise Gate dialog box.

The Attack Time controls how long it takes for the gate to open, letting the sound through, and the Release Time controls how long it takes to close after the signal goes below the threshold level. The Minimum Opening Time defines the minimum amount of time the signal has to be over the threshold before the gate can close again; this can be useful if you discover after using this dialog box's Preview button that many brief transients in the selected audio are causing the gate to "flutter" open and closed.

Normalize

Normalizing an audio signal affects its overall amplitude level by adjusting its highest peak to the value set in the Normalize process dialog box (see Figure 20.5). It is similar to the Gain process in the sense that it acts on the level of the signal, but instead of calculating the level generally, it brings these levels up in proportion to the highest peak found in the signal, making sure that there is no clipping in the signal as a result of the level change. You can set the level value you want to assign to the highest peak level in this object by adjusting the slider or entering a value in the Maximum field.

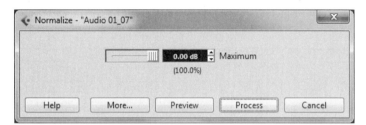

Figure 20.5 The Normalize dialog box.

Phase Reverse

Reversing phase, or polarity, does not change the shape of a sound file, but it changes the direction this shape takes. For example, the slopes going up will now go down, and vice versa. In practice, this function is only rarely required, since each channel in Cubase has an Input Phase button (in the Mixer or VST Audio Channel Settings window), which is generally a more efficient way to accomplish such a fix.

When you mix different sound files that contain the same audio content captured by microphones at different distances, phase cancellation can occur. The most common examples are probably snares being captured from above and below or guitar amps from the front and back. This can sometimes produce a hollow sound as different frequencies in its harmonic spectrum are reinforced or cancelled out, known as *comb filtering*. Inverting the waveform on one of the files can prevent this phase cancellation from occurring. In other words, if the phase of the current audio file does not sound correct, changing its polarity via this Phase Reverse process might fix the problem.

If you can barely hear the signal, you might have phase cancellation occurring. In Cubase, you can reverse the polarity of both channels in a stereo file or only one or the other. You should preview the result before applying this process.

Pitch Shift

Imagine that you've recorded a backing track for a vocalist to sing to. The singer arrives, but says, "This is a little outside my range. Can you lower the key a half-step?" What do you do?

In the old days, the only way to change pitch was to speed up or slow down the tape, which also affected tempo. Fortunately, computer technology enables more sophisticated changes, which in this case means changing the pitch without changing the tempo.

Cubase's Pitch Shift process can either change the pitch of the selection by a fixed amount throughout its duration, or vary the amount of pitch change over time by using an envelope that determines how and when the pitch is shifted upward or downward.

At the top of the Transpose tab in the Pitch Shift dialog box (see Figure 20.6) is a keyboard layout that can help you set the relationship between the pitch of the original audio content and the pitch-shifted version. In this example, the fundamental pitch or "root note" of the original content is D3, so this note is selected as the pitch-shift base area and appears red on the keyboard display. Clicking another note changes the pitch-shift settings automatically to match the value needed to get this pitch. In this case, B2 is pressed and displayed in blue on the keyboard. If you want to create a chord effect, creating several pitch shifts simultaneously, you can enable the Multi Shift check box, which adds other notes to the process. Remember that if you also want the root note to be included in the multi-shifted signal, it must also be selected (highlighted in blue). You can use the Listen Key (or the Listen Chord button, if Multi Shift is selected) to hear the notes you selected.

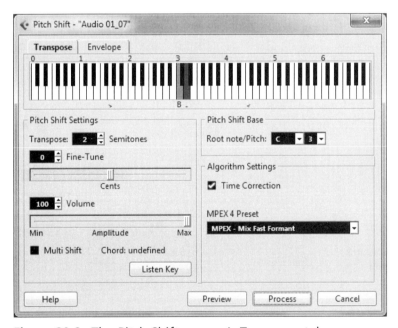

Figure 20.6 The Pitch Shift process's Transpose tab.

Keeping the Time Correction option enabled changes the pitch without altering the duration of the shifted content. If this option is disabled, events shifted upward play faster, and events shifted downward play slower. Finally, the MPEX 4 Preset list lets you select from a variety of algorithms for implementing the pitch shift.

Clicking the Envelope tab at the top of the dialog box reveals the envelope settings for this process. Using an envelope rather than a keyboard changes how the affected audio selection is shifted over time. The settings in this tab are similar to those on the Transpose tab.

Apply a pitch shift to a selected object:

1. Select the desired object.

2. Select the Pitch Shift process from the Process option in the Audio menu.

3. Make the appropriate adjustments in the Pitch Shift dialog box. To preview the result, click the Preview button.

4. When you are satisfied with the settings, click the Process button.

Stereo Flip

The Stereo Flip process can only be applied on stereo audio objects because it manipulates the stereo channels of the selected audio clip or event (including regions or other selections within an audio event). You have four modes available in this process, which appear in the Mode field. For example, you can merge both channels to create a mono file, or subtract the left channel from the right channel to remove the lead vocal. (In this regard, items that are equally present in both channels, like a lead vocal, will be cancelled out.) Note that if you want to apply the basic mode here, Flip Left-Right, to an entire *track* rather than just a specific audio event or other selection, this is more efficiently accomplished by simply enabling the Dual Combined Panner view and dragging the left and right channel panners to their opposite sides.

Time Stretch

When you're doing television or movie work, you often have to work within very rigid time constraints. Imagine that you've recorded a theme song for a movie or television show. The song clocks in at exactly 63 seconds in length, but the producer comes to you and says that the closing credits are only 60 seconds long. Somehow, you have to make that 63-second recording fit into a 60-second slot—without affecting the pitch.

Here's another fun situation. Imagine you've recorded a dance track at 120 beats per minute. But the track just before this one is at 110 bpm, and your producer wants the two tracks to merge seamlessly into another. That means slowing down the tempo of your song, without changing the pitch of the recording.

In the old days, your only solutions to these problems involved speeding up or slowing down the tape, which also affected the pitch of the original recording. With Cubase 6, these challenges can be solved using Cubase's Time Stretch process—without affecting the underlying pitch.

As you can see in Figure 20.7, you can change the selection's tempo (in beats per minute) or length. You'll probably have to do a little math beforehand, but the results are impressive.

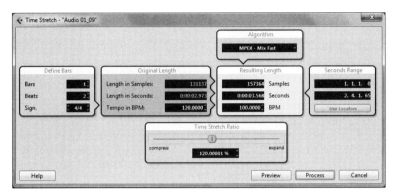

Figure 20.7 The Time Stretch dialog box.

Small Changes: Stretching or shrinking a recording by too large an amount can adversely affect the quality of the recording. It's best to make changes in small percentages, no more than 10%–20% of the original recording.

DC Offset, Reverse, and Silence

These three processes offer very different results; however, they do not offer any settings for you to configure. DC offset is a bad thing, reducing headroom and introducing random pops and clicks; Cubase's DC Offset process removes any audio signal offset of this type. The Reverse process simply reverses the audio, making it sound as if it is playing backward. The Silence process brings all the samples in a selection to a zero value, creating an absolute digital silence.

Managing Offline Process History

When you apply an offline process or plug-in to an audio event or selection, an entry is made in that event's Offline Process History. Remember that offline processes mean that the effect is not calculated during playback (online), but on a "one-shot" basis that actually creates new audio data to contain the result (offline). Each process is displayed on its own row in the Offline Process History dialog box, shown in Figure 20.8. You can decide to modify the settings of any process that appears here, even if there are subsequent offline processes in this list.

For example, you can select a previously rendered Normalize process and change the peak value. If a process has no parameters to modify (for example, the Reverse process), clicking the Modify button simply displays a warning telling you this process cannot be modified.

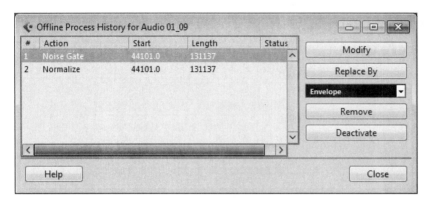

Figure 20.8 The Offline Process History dialog box.

You also can replace one previous offline process with another. For instance, you could select the Reverse process and select another process in the drop-down menu below the Replace By button. The new process's dialog box will appear. Once replaced, the old process is removed from the list, and the new process takes its place.

Finally, you can remove a process from the list entirely by selecting it and clicking the Remove button, no matter where it is in this list, as long as you haven't applied any resampling or time-stretching processes, which affect the overall number of samples (and ultimately this event's position in the project).

Modify, replace, or remove an action from the Offline Process History:

1. Select the event containing offline processes you want to modify.

2. Select Audio > Offline Process History option.

3. Select the process you want to modify (Step 4a), replace (Step 4b), or remove (Step 4c).

4a. Click the Modify button and edit the parameters inside the process's dialog box, and then click the Process button to update the Offline Process History dialog box.

    OR

4b. Select the new process you want to use instead of the currently selected one in the drop-down menu below the Replace By button, and then click the Replace By button. Make the necessary adjustments in the process's dialog box, and then click Process to update the Offline Process History dialog box.

    OR

4c. Click the Remove button to remove this process from the list.

5. When you have completed modifying, replacing, or removing the processes, click the Close button.

Changing Tempo and Pitch with AudioWarp

As you just learned, you can change the tempo and pitch of an event or selection by using offline audio processing. You can also make these changes using Cubase's Audio-Warp function in Musical mode.

When you use the Musical mode approach, the tempo and pitch-shifting are performed in real time and affect the timing of audio events as they are played back within tracks. They also make some significant demands on your CPU's processing power. You apply these processes to an individual event via the Sample Editor; to this end, all the operations described in the following sections assume that you have already opened the audio event in the Sample Editor.

To employ these AudioWarp effects, you first must enable Musical mode for the selected audio event. This mode works best with "loopable" audio events, or at least events that start and end on a beat.

Time-Stretching

The AudioWarp features in Cubase let you match a time-based sample to a tempo-based grid. As a result, you can get a drum loop to match the tempo changes in a project, correct timing errors in an audio recording, or tighten the kick of a drum by shifting it closer to the project's feel—all without editing the original media file on the drive.

Enabling Musical mode for an audio event lets Cubase adjust an audio loop's tempo to the project's tempo in real time, without affecting the pitch. Whenever the tempo in the project is different than the tempo displayed next to a Musical mode–enabled event, this audio is automatically time-stretched to match the current project's tempo.

Change tempo via AudioWarp:

1. From the Project window, double-click the audio event you want to edit to open the Sample Editor.

2. As shown in Figure 20.9, enter the appropriate number of bars and beats (if necessary) in the corresponding fields of the Sample Editor's toolbar. Cubase will automatically display the audio tempo for this event.

Figure 20.9 Musical mode options in the Sample Editor.

3. Enable the Musical Mode button on the Sample Editor toolbar.

4. Click the Algorithm field and select the most appropriate time-stretching algorithm for this audio content. You can choose from seven standard algorithms (Drums, Plucked, Pads, Vocals, Mix, Custom, and Solo) or

nine more sophisticated élastique algorithms (Pro-Time, Pro-Pitch, Pro-Tape, Pro-Formant Time, Pro-Formant Pitch, Pro-Formant Tape, Efficient-Time, Efficient-Pitch, and Efficient-Tape). The standard algorithms are the most efficient for real-time processing; the élastique algorithms, while less efficient, often produce better-sounding results.

You can also customize the warp settings if you wish. Choose the Standard Custom option in the Algorithm control to open the Advanced Warp Settings dialog box; enter your desired settings, then click OK.

Best Results: For best results when working with drum or rhythmic loops, choose the élastique Pro-Time algorithm. This algorithm delivers the best audio quality, with timing accuracy favored over pitch accuracy.

You can also manually position the musical bars/beats gridline over the audio event, as long as the beat does not change tempo over the course of the event. Open the Definition tab in the Sample Editor Inspector and click the Manual Adjust button. You can then use your mouse to drag the first bar marker in the waveform display to correspond to the first downbeat in your sample. The remaining gridlines should adjust themselves accordingly. Even better, go to the Sample Editor Inspector's Definition tab and try the Auto Adjust control. In many cases, this will automatically fit the gridline to your existing beats.

Importing ACID Loops: Whenever audio loops containing ACID properties or any other commercially available loops with embedded tempo and pitch information in them are imported into a project, Cubase automatically enables Musical mode for these audio clips in the Pool and sets the tempo according to these properties. As a result, the events within these loops always follow the project's tempo when placed on an audio track.

Pitch Shifting

You can also pitch-shift events when they are in Musical mode to match the key signature and the tempo of your project. For example, you can create new harmonic variations by using a rhythm guitar loop and transpose different occurrences of the same event.

Transpose Musical mode events in a project:

1. Select the Musical mode–enabled audio event in the Project window that you want to transpose.

2. Make the Info line visible in the Project window (if it is not already visible) and click in the Transpose field. Each value in the Transpose field represents one semitone.

3. Use the mouse scroll wheel (or up and down arrows on your computer keyboard) to increase or decrease the value, or type in the desired value for this parameter.

Only the selected audio event is transposed by this setting in the Project window. Its tempo remains the same due to the tempo already defined for this event, whereas the Warp Setting preset field determines how time-stretching is applied in real time to this event during playback.

21 Editing Vocals

Recording, editing, and mixing vocal tracks is subtly different from instrumental tracks. There are distinct approaches and challenges involved with recording vocals; you must master these challenges to create a great-sounding vocal recording.

There are a variety of tools in Cubase that you can use when working with vocal tracks. Chief among these are a variety of plug-in effects that can make a mediocre vocal track sound good, and a good one sound great. Cubase 6 even includes the ability to correct the pitch of a vocal track—ideal for those times when the vocalist sings just a little flat or sharp.

Here's a summary of what you will learn in this chapter:

- How to best record a vocal track
- How to employ the Compressor plug-in
- How to reduce sibilance with the DeEsser plug-in
- How to reduce noise between notes with the Gate plug-in
- How to add presence with Cubase's reverb plug-ins
- How to fix pitch problems with the Pitch Correct plug-in
- How to use the VariAudio feature to change vocal pitch and timing

Recording Vocals

Let's start at the beginning—with the recording process. As you'll soon see, recording vocals isn't quite the same as recording most acoustic instruments.

The Recording Space

First, you probably don't want to record your vocals out in the middle of everything else, which can be a challenge when you're working in a home studio. Many vocalists prefer a little privacy when they're singing, which you can achieve by sectioning off your main recording space with baffles, or by putting the singer in a separate room or vocal booth; this type of physical separation is also great for improving sound isolation in your recording.

Some engineers prefer a vocal space to have some degree of reverberation. Toward this way of thinking, it's better to record vocals with a little natural reverb than to lay down totally dry tracks; the sound of a "live" room adds presence to the vocals, filling them out. (This is why you like the sound of your voice singing in a shower stall or stairwell; a full voice sounds better than a thin one.)

If you're going for a sound with natural reverb, don't rule out recording your vocals in a stairwell, garage, or bathroom. That's because these areas have a very "live" sound with lots of reflections and reverberation from all the hard surfaces. You want some of that reverberation to make its way back to the microphone to mix with the vocalist's natural singing voice.

Other engineers prefer to minimize the effect of the room on the vocal tracks. This means recording in a relatively dry room, without any natural reverberation or reflections. Reverb and other effects can then be added later in the mixing process.

To record this type of neutral vocal track, position the microphone in the middle of the room, away from any reflecting walls or surfaces. You may also need to use some acoustical foam, screens, or room dividers to soak up any stray reflections.

Vocal Microphones

As to what type of microphone to use, know that the quality of the microphone affects vocal tracks more than any other type of track. A vocal track made with a low-quality microphone is going to sound mediocre, no matter how much post-recording processing you apply within Cubase; to create a high-quality vocal recording, you have to start with a high-quality mic.

For vocal recording, the best results come from a large diaphragm condenser mic with a cardioid pattern. These are not inexpensive mics; expect to spend between $500 and $1,000 on a quality unit.

A condenser mic is powered by an outboard power source (sometimes called *phantom power*), and it is more sensitive than a lower-priced dynamic mic. Within the family of condenser mics, those with larger diaphragms are more sensitive (and more expensive) than those with smaller diaphragms, hence the higher cost for a quality vocal mic.

Microphone Placement

When recording, place the mic in front of the vocalist on a sturdy stand. You don't want the singer to hold the microphone when recording; you also don't want to tempt the singer to grab the mic stand as she would during a live performance. (Any movement of the mic or the stand will be heard on the recording—not ideal.) The best approach is to use a tall boom stand that lets you hang the mic down in front of the singer. And always use a windscreen or pop filter to reduce sibilance.

Equalization

You also need to consider adding both audio effects (discussed next) and equalization to the vocal track. While these are typically added post-recording, some engineers prefer to add effects during the recording process; it's a personal choice.

When it comes to equalizing vocal tracks, less is more. EQ should be used only if the voice has some specific defects you need to fix, or if you're trying to achieve a particular effect, or if the vocals are getting buried in the mix. That said, the topic of equalization is important enough to warrant its own chapter; turn to Chapter 34, "Adding Equalization," to learn more.

Using Popular Plug-Ins

A vocal track can be both subtly and significantly altered by applying one of several Cubase plug-in effects. These plug-ins help remove hiss and sibilance from vocals, as well as add a bit of presence to the sound.

Compressor

When it comes to the recording process, know that vocalists can sometimes be maddeningly inconsistent, not only in their pitch and vocal inflections but also in how they approach the microphone. Don't be surprised to see the vocalist backing up and leaning forward throughout the recording, which plays havoc with your input levels. If she's too close to the mic, the meters go into the red; if she's too far away, the meters might not move at all. Short of nailing the vocalist in place precisely six inches away from the mic (a near-perfect distance), how do you cope with this?

One solution, of course, is to work the sliders constantly throughout the recording. This requires a lot of skill and no little amount of effort, but a talented engineer can make it work. A better solution, however, is to use Cubase's Compressor plug-in as an input insert effect. This plug-in automatically lowers the volume when the input exceeds a certain threshold, thus guarding against level peaks when the vocalist leans too far forward or pumps up the volume. The Compressor can also be set to boost low volume levels, thus evening out any dynamic flux.

Of course, you can also use the Compressor after-the-fact as a standard insert effect, but it's nice to have a trouble-free track to work with during the mixing process. When using the Compressor as an input insert effect, the signal input from the microphone is routed through the plug-in, which applies the compression effect, and then is sent back through the input bus as normal. The signal recorded on disc includes the effect processing.

Apply compression to a vocal track:

1. In the Mixer, click the Edit button for the input bus (*not* the selected track) you're using to record.

2. This displays the VST Input Channel Settings dialog box, shown in Figure 21.1.

3. Click the first Effects slot to display the list of available effects.

4. Select Dynamics > Compressor from the list.

5. The Compressor control panel for that effect now appears in a separate window. Configure the effect as necessary, and then close the window. (You can reopen the Compressor control panel at any time by clicking the Edit button in the insert effects slot.)

6. To activate the Compressor, make sure the Inserts State button is clicked on (displays blue).

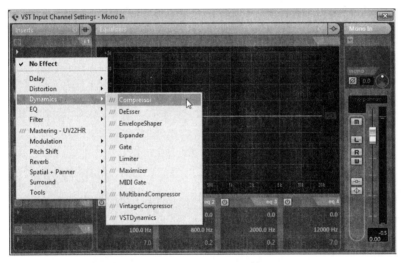

Figure 21.1 Applying the Compressor effect.

When using the Compressor plug-in, shown in Figure 21.2, pay attention to the following controls:

■ Adjust the Threshold control to determine the level where the Compressor kicks in. (Signals above the threshold level are affected by the compression; signals below the threshold level are not processed.)

■ Adjust the Ratio control to determine the amount of gain reduction applied to signals over the threshold level.

■ Adjust the Make-Up control to compensate for any output volume loss caused by use of the Compressor.

Figure 21.2 The Compressor plug-in panel.

- Adjust the Attack control to determine how fast the Compressor will respond to signals above the threshold level.

- Click the Auto button under the Release control to let the Compressor automatically set the amount of time it takes for the volume to return to the original level when the signal falls below the threshold level. Alternately, adjust this control manually.

DeEsser

In addition to applying compression, many engineers feel that it's important to apply de-essing to vocal tracks. De-essing reduces sibilance—those hard, spitty Ss, Zs, and CHs. When you use a de-esser, you can then add back upper mids and highs in the EQ process, which helps to push the vocals above the other tracks in the mix.

In Cubase 6, you typically apply the DeEsser plug-in as a traditional insert effect, after the vocal track has been recorded.

Apply the DeEsser effect:

1. In the Project window's Track List, select the track to which you want to apply the effect.

2. In the track Inspector, open the Inserts control.

3. Click the Effects control in the first insert effects slot and select Dynamics > DeEsser.

4. The control panel for the DeEsser plug-in now opens.

As you can see in Figure 21.3, there are only a few controls for the DeEsser plug-in:

- The Reduction control affects the intensity of the de-essing effect. In most instances, a value between 4 and 7 works best.

Figure 21.3 The DeEsser plug-in panel.

- Adjust the Release control to set the amount of time it takes for the effect to return to zero (once the signal drops below the threshold value).

- Activate the Auto Threshold control to automatically set a threshold for the incoming signal.

Gate

A noise gate is a plug-in effect that silences a track when the volume falls below a specified level. As soon as the signal level exceeds the set threshold, the gate opens to let the signal through. This is a great way to remove hiss or noise from a vocal track when the vocalist is silent. (The thinking is that the hiss is somewhat hidden when the vocalist is singing, but very audible when the instrument is silent.) It's also used to remove breathing noises on the vocal track.

Cubase 6's Gate plug-in, shown in Figure 21.4, should be applied as a traditional insert effect, after the vocal track has been recorded. You can then adjust the following parameters:

Figure 21.4 The Gate plug-in control panel.

■ Adjust the Threshold control to the signal level below which you want silence.

■ Adjust the Attack control to determine the time it takes for the gate to remain open after being triggered.

■ Adjust the Hold control to determine how long the noise gate stays open after the signal drops below the threshold level.

■ Adjust the Release control to set the amount of time it takes for the noise gate to close (after the set hold time).

Reverb

Unless you record your vocal in a "live" room with lots of hard, reflective surfaces, you'll want to add some presence to the dry sound by using one of Cubase's reverb plug-ins. Cubase offers three reverb plug-ins: REVerence, RoomWorks, and Room-Works SE. These plug-ins are discussed in more depth in Chapter 13, "Using Insert Effects."

You typically add reverb to a vocal track as a send effect. With a send effect, the audio stays in the signal path until it reaches the output bus, where it is sent to the selected plug-in. The processed signal is then available to be sent to the monitor mix or to the final mix-down.

Apply a reverb effect:

1. Select Project > Add Track > FX Channel.

2. When the Add FX Channel Track dialog box appears, as shown in Figure 21.5, pull down the Configuration list and select Stereo, and then pull down the Effect list, select Reverb, and then select the desired reverb effect. Click OK.

3. Cubase displays the new track in the Track List and opens the control panel for the reverb effect.

4. Select the vocal track and open the Sends section of the Inspector.

5. Click in the first Sends field and select the reverb effect you just added as an FX channel.

Figure 21.5 Adding a new FX channel for the reverb effect.

Pitch Correct

Cubase 6 includes the ability to change the pitch of vocal and instrumental tracks via the Pitch Correct plug-in. This is ideal for when a vocalist sings off-pitch; you can fix the recorded track without having to re-record it. Apply Pitch Correct as a traditional insert effect during the mixing process, after the vocal track has been recorded.

Vocoder Effects: You can also use the Pitch Correct plug-in creatively by using extreme values to create vocoder-like effects.

As you can see in Figure 21.6, you can adjust the following parameters:

Figure 21.6 The Pitch Correct plug-in control panel.

- Adjust the Correction Speed to determine the sensitivity of the analysis applied to the existing track.

- The Correction Tolerance determines the smoothness of the resulting pitch change. Higher values introduce a more artificial sound to the results, similar to vocoder effects.

- Adjust the Correction Transpose control to retune the pitch up or down by a set number of semitones.

- Set the Scale Source to Internal to set the target key for the fixed notes—Chromatic, Major, Minor, or Custom. (With the Custom option, you select the notes in the key from the keyboard in the panel.) Set the Scale Source to External-MIDI Scale or External-MIDI Note to play the target notes on an external MIDI keyboard.

- Use the Formant Shift control to change the natural characteristics of the source audio.

- Set the Formant Optimize control to favor male or female voices.

- Deactivate the Formant Preservation control to produce odd vocal effects. Higher values produce a Mickey Mouse–type sound; lower values produce a monster-like effect.

For minor pitch correction, set the Scale Source to Internal and Chromatic and let the plug-in do its thing; the underlying pitch will be shifted to the nearest chromatic note. To affect larger pitch changes, use the Transpose control to shift the pitch upward or downward through the scale.

Editing Vocals with VariAudio

For more dramatic editing of vocal pitch and timing, use Cubase 6's VariAudio feature. VariAudio enables editing of specific notes on any monophonic vocal event; the resulting modifications retain the sound characteristics of the original recording.

Vocals Only: VariAudio was developed specifically for monophonic vocal recordings. Although it can be used on monophonic instrumental recordings, the results may not be satisfactory.

VariAudio is accessed via a dedicated tab in the Inspector of the Sample Editor. You open the Sample Editor by double-clicking on any single audio event. It works by analyzing the vocal recording and organizing the recording into segments, as shown in Figure 21.7; in general, each segment represents an individual note sung or a part of that note. You can then change the pitch or timing of a note by moving its segment vertically (for pitch) or horizontally (for timing) in the Sample Editor window.

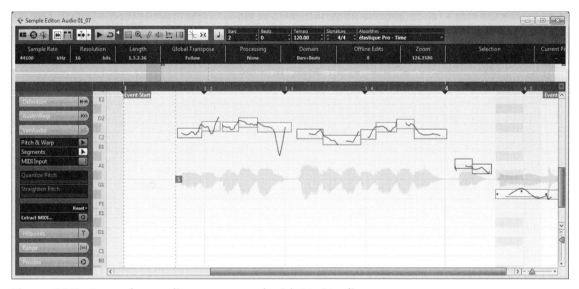

Figure 21.7 A vocal recording segmented with VariAudio.

Changing Pitch

VariAudio presents several ways to change the pitch of a vocal recording, all accessed via the Pitch & Warp control in the VariAudio tab of the Inspector.

Change the pitch of a note:

1.   From the VariAudio tab, click the Pitch & Warp button. VariAudio now analyzes and segments the audio event.

2.   Click the segment you want to change.

3.   Use the up arrow and down arrow keys to raise or lower the pitch of the note one semitone at a time. To move the pitch in smaller increments, hold down the Shift key while using the arrow keys.

You can also quantize the pitch of a note upward or downward to reduce the deviation from the nearest semitone position.

Quantize the pitch of a note:

1.   From the VariAudio tab, click the Pitch & Warp button.

2.   Click the segment or segments you want to quantize.

3.   In the Inspector, move the Pitch Quantize slider to the right.

Sometimes a singer will go flat or sharp at the end of a note. To "straighten" this type of fall or rise, use VariAudio's Straighten Pitch control.

Straighten the pitch of a note:

1.   From the VariAudio tab, click the Pitch & Warp button.

2.   Click the segment or segments you want to straighten.

3.   In the Inspector, move the Straighten Pitch slider to the right.

Changing Timing

VariAudio also lets you correct changes in timing—that is, when the vocalist sings off beat. You can use VariAudio to put individual notes on a specific beat, or even move them off beat for a syncopated effect.

Change the timing (position) of a note:

1.   From the VariAudio tab, click the Pitch & Warp button.

2.   Click and drag the left side of the selected segment to the left to move the note earlier or to the right to move the note later.

Change the length of a note:

1. From the VariAudio tab, click the Pitch & Warp button.

2. Click and drag the right side of the selected segment to the right to lengthen the note or to the left to shorten the note's duration.

Editing Notes

You can also use VariAudio to delete and move segments of a vocal event, via the Segments mode.

Deleting a note:

1. From the VariAudio tab, click the Segments button.

2. Click the note segment you want to delete.

3. Press the Delete key on your computer keyboard.

Move a note:

1. From the VariAudio tab, click the Segments button.

2. Click the top border of the segment you want to move, and then drag it left or right into a new position.

22 Editing MIDI Events with the In-Place Editor

Editing MIDI events is different from editing audio events for the sole reason that MIDI events contain digital instructions, not recorded audio. As such, you can edit these instructions using either the In-Place Editor or the Key Editor. In addition, Cubase 6 adds a new Note Expression feature that lets you draw controller values directly onto MIDI events.

Here's a summary of what you will learn in this chapter:

- How to select and edit MIDI events

- How to mute/unmute, merge, and resize one or more notes or controller events

- How to create notes using the Draw tool or insert events using the Line tool

- How to create a ramp of MIDI events using the Sine, Triangle, or Square tool

Using the In-Place Editor

You can edit MIDI events in either the In-Place Editor or the Key Editor; MIDI drum tracks are typically edited using the Drum Editor. Basic editing functions are similar between all of these MIDI editors. (Learn more about the Key Editor in Chapter 23; learn more about the Drum Editor in Chapter 24).

In this chapter, we'll use the In-Place Editor to discuss basic MIDI editing functions. To open the In-Place Editor, shown in Figure 22.1, click the Edit In-Place button found in the Track List area of the Project window.

Most of the In-Place Editor tools are available in the Project window's toolbar; select functions are also available from the context menu that appears when you right-click (PC)/Control-click (Mac) anywhere in the Event Display area. In addition, you can display a toolbar for the In-Place Editor window by clicking the small gray triangle in the upper-right corner of this MIDI track's Track List area.

Within the In-Place Editor window, individual notes (or *events*) are shown as "blocks." The pitch of the note is shown on the vertical axis; the timing of the note is represented on the horizontal axis. So, for example, a higher-pitched note appears higher in the window, whereas a longer note appears as a longer horizontal block.

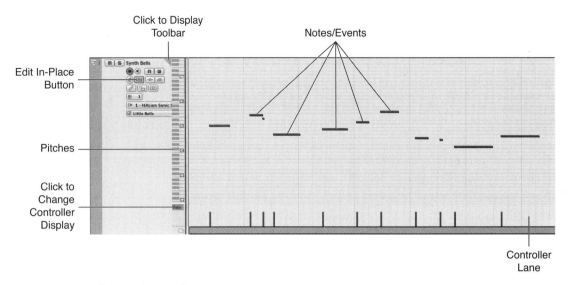

Figure 22.1 The In-Place Editor.

Editing MIDI events is not unlike editing text in a word processor. For example, if you want to copy, cut, or move a group of events, you need to select these events first, and then apply the desired operation to these selected events. That's when you use the Object Selection (arrow) tool.

Select MIDI/audio events:

- *Single event*: Just point and click on it.

- *Group of events*: Click and drag a selection box around these events.

- *Multiple nonconsecutive events*: Hold down the Shift key while selecting the additional events.

- *All the notes on the same pitch in a part*: Hold down the Ctrl (PC)/⌘ (Mac) key and click on the corresponding pitch in the Keyboard Display area to the left of the Event Display area.

Zooming

In all of Cubase's MIDI editors (except the List Editor), the zooming functions are similar to those found in the Project window, with the exception that you do not have a Presets menu next to the horizontal or vertical scroll bar. However, you do have access to the Zoom submenu options in the context menu or in the Zoom submenu of the Edit menu.

You also can use the Magnifying Glass tool on the toolbar to draw a selection box around the range you want to zoom into. Clicking inside the editor with the

Magnifying Glass tool zooms in one step at a time, and Ctrl-clicking (PC)/⌘-clicking (Mac) zooms out one step at a time. The data can be zoomed vertically and horizontally at the same time by holding down the Ctrl (PC)/⌘ (Mac) key while dragging the Zoom tool over the desired area.

Moving MIDI Events

After you select one or more MIDI events, you can apply the desired editing functions. Most editing consists of moving an event or note to a new pitch or beat.

Aligning Notes: If you want to keep the beginning of a group of notes aligned with a quantize grid, enable the Snap to Grid button and set the quantize grid to the appropriate value.

To move one event, you simply need to click and drag it to its new location. To move several events, select them as mentioned previously, and then click and drag one of the selected events to the new destination.

You can move both notes and Control Change values this way, provided that the appropriate Controller lane is visible; hold down the Alt (PC)/Option (Mac) key as you select and drag events in the Controller lane. If you move the velocity value of a note, you will also move the note.

To lock pitches in place as you move notes in time or to change the pitch without changing the timing, hold the Ctrl (PC)/⌘ (Mac) key down as you drag the notes. If you start moving the notes horizontally along the time axis, the pitch will be locked, and if you start moving the notes vertically along the pitch axis, their original time positions will be locked. You can also move selected notes by using the up and down keys on your keyboard or by using the Transpose Notes button on the toolbar.

Again, as with text in a word processor application, when you want to paste events to a new location, you need to select them, cut or copy to place these events into the clipboard, decide where you want to put them by placing your insertion point (in Cubase, this is the project cursor), and then apply the Paste command. As with the Project window, it is possible to hold the Alt (PC)/Option (Mac) key down as you drag selected events to copy rather than move them. You will see a small plus sign (+) appear next to the cursor as you move your mouse. If you hold down the same key (Alt or Option) as you drag parts or events horizontally by their bottom-right corner in the Project window, the pointer turns into a pencil, and the events will be copied instead of moved to the new time location.

Cubase offers additional functions that make editing MIDI easier. For example, you can use the Select options in the Edit > Select submenu to define what you want to select. Using this method, position the left and right locators across two bars, click in the Note Display area, and use the Select in Loop option. All the MIDI events (including both notes and controller events) between the locators will be selected; now click on a controller event and repeat these steps. You can copy these events, position the project cursor at another location, and then paste the events.

Muting Events

As an alternative to muting an entire track, you can also mute selected events (notes and controller events).

Mute/unmute one or several events:

- Select the events to mute with the Selection tool and press the Shift+M key command or select the Mute option from the Edit menu. Press Shift+U to unmute selected events.

- Or select the Mute tool in the Project window's toolbar and click the desired notes. Click once more on muted notes to unmute them.

- Or select the Mute tool and drag a selection box around the events you want to mute. All events within the box's range will be muted. Select muted notes in the same way to unmute them.

Splitting and Resizing Note Events

Splitting and resizing note events is handy when you need to modify the length of MIDI notes within a part or need to bring the end of a MIDI note inside the right boundary of a part. These operations also can be applied to a single note, a group of selected notes, or a range of notes in a MIDI editor.

Resize a note or a group of notes:

1. Select the note(s) using the Object Selection tool.

2. Bring the arrow over the start or end of the notes you want to resize. The arrow will turn into a double-headed arrow.

3. Click and drag the edge to the desired length. The precise increments as you resize will be determined by the quantize grid setting if it is enabled. Hold the Ctrl (PC)/⌘ (Mac) key while resizing to override this grid setting temporarily.

Using the Nudge Palette and Transpose Palette: When resizing a good number of events, use the Nudge Palette tools to resize selected events instead. The Nudge palette lets you precisely adjust durations and start times of events based on the

Snap settings. Select the events that need resizing, and use the appropriate Nudge tool to resize.

By default, the Nudge palette is not visible in the Project window's toolbar. To display it, right-click (PC)/Control-click (Mac) in the toolbar and check the Nudge Palette option.

The Transpose palette lets you shift the pitch of events by one half-step (semitone) or by one octave (12 semitones) at a time. To toggle any MIDI editor display on or off, right-click (PC)/Control-click (Mac) in the toolbar and select that option.

There are four ways you can split note events, and the quantize grid setting influences precisely where the split occurs in all methods:

- Use the Split (scissors) tool at the desired location on single or selected notes.

- Use the Split Loop function in the Edit menu or context menu, which splits selected notes at the current left and right locator positions.

- Use the Split at Cursor option in the Edit menu or the context menu to split all note events that cross the current position of the play cursor.

- Hold down the Alt (PC)/Option (Mac) key as you click notes with the Selection (arrow) tool to split them at the point where you clicked. If more than one event is selected, all events will be split.

Merging Note Events

The Glue tool is the counterpart to the Split tool. It joins the note you click with the following note of the same pitch or merges the selected event with the next one in time, as shown in Figure 22.2. Use it when you've split a note by mistake or when you need to join two or more notes into one.

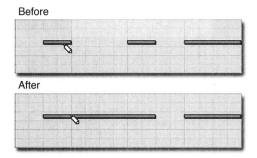

Figure 22.2 Gluing two events together.

Merge note events:

1. Select the Glue tool from the toolbar or in the context menu.

2. Click the first note you want to glue.

3. Click again to glue the current note to the next note of the same pitch.

Using the Draw Tool

Dragging a note with the Draw (arrow) tool determines the length of that note. You can also use the Line, Parabola, Sine, Triangle, Square, and Paint tools to add note events in the Event Display area.

Create notes using the Draw tool:

1. Set the quantize grid and length values appropriately. The length determines how long each note is, and the quantize grid determines the spacing between the notes.

2. Select the Draw tool from the toolbar, or right-click (PC)/Control-click (Mac) in the editor to select the Draw tool, or use the key command (by default, this is the number 8).

3. Adjust the Insert velocity setting in the toolbar to the desired value.

4. Click where you want to add a note. Each click adds a note with a length corresponding to the length value in the quantize length setting. Click and drag to draw longer notes instead.

Events are always created with the same MIDI channel as the part you are editing. After you have inserted notes using the Draw tool, you can modify their length by clicking on the existing note and dragging it farther to the right to lengthen the note or dragging it to the left to shorten the note. Remember that note lengths always snap to the next quantize grid value when Snap is enabled in the editor's toolbar.

The Draw tool can lengthen only the end point of an existing event. To modify the start point of a note, use the Selection tool, as described in earlier sections of this chapter.

Using the Line Tool

The Line tool, like the Draw tool, can be used to insert both note and controller events. The most common use for the Line tool is to edit Control Change information, creating MIDI ramps, such as pan effects or fade outs. Here's a look at these tools and their capabilities.

Double-click the Line tool to display other shapes to draw—Parabola, Sine, Triangle, and Square. Each of these shapes under the Line tool offers its own characteristics.

Moving the mouse up and down with the Paint tool adds notes on different pitches, whereas moving the mouse left and right adds them at different points in time. When dragging to create note events, the Paint tool is different from the Draw tool because it adds a note each time your cursor crosses a grid line. Both tools work the same when you are inserting Control Change events.

The Line tool draws a line across the Note Display area or the Controller Display area to create a series of events along the line. In the case of notes, these will be created at an interval, length, and velocity determined by the quantize setting. Figure 22.3 displays such lines: In the left half, note events are added, and in the right half, controller (Control Change) messages are added. In the case of controller events, you also can use the Line tool to edit existing controller messages to create a linear ramp.

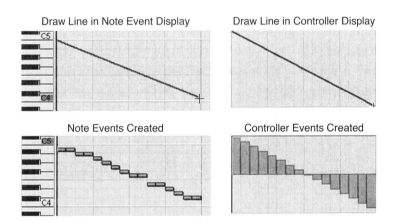

Figure 22.3 Adding note and controller events using the Line tool.

Insert events using the Line tool:

1. Set the quantize values appropriately. You also can leave the Snap off; however, a greater number of events will be generated, which can create a bottleneck in your MIDI stream if combined with other dense MIDI tracks.

2. Select the Line tool from the toolbar or the context menu.

3. Click where you want the line to begin. To move this point after clicking (but before releasing the mouse button to actually create the new events), hold Alt+Ctrl (PC)/Option+⌘ (Mac) keys down until you are satisfied with the start location.

4. Drag the mouse where you want the line to end, and release the mouse button to add the events.

The Parabola tool is similar to the Line tool except that it draws a parabolic ramp rather than a linear ramp (see Figure 22.4). Inserting events or modifying existing events using this tool is done in the same way as with the Line tool, with the following additional options:

■ While still dragging this tool (before releasing the mouse button to create the new events), press the Ctrl (PC)/⌘ (Mac) key to change the type of parabolic curve that will be created.

■ As with the Line tool, you can hold down the Alt+Ctrl (PC)/Option+⌘ (Mac) keys while still dragging to move your start point to a new location.

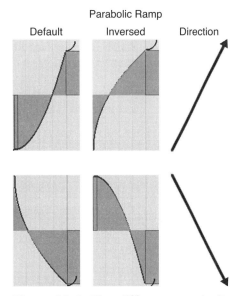

Figure 22.4 The different parabolic ramps available when using the Parabola tool.

The sine, triangle, and square ramps have similar options. However, as you drag to create these shapes, the farther you drag the mouse cursor away from the center point where you first clicked, the greater the amplitude of the shape will be. A small movement upward, for example, will create a small variation in note pitches or controller values. Dragging your mouse downward from the start point inverts the shape of the "waveform" you're using to draw.

Create a ramp using the Sine, Triangle, or Square tool:

1. Select the appropriate tool from the toolbar.

2. Set the quantize grid if you want to use this setting to control how many and where the events will be created. For a smoother curve or change, disable the Snap to Grid option.

3. Click where you want to start inserting the events and drag the mouse to the right.

    ■ To adjust the frequency of the shape you are drawing, hold down the Shift key as you move the mouse left or right to adjust its period to the desired length. When you are satisfied with the period of the waveform, release the Shift key and finish dragging the mouse to the desired end location for the entire shape.

    ■ Try holding down the Alt (PC)/Option (Mac) or Ctrl (PC)/⌘ (Mac) key down while dragging the mouse to obtain different behaviors. Experiment on an empty track with different grid settings or without the snap mode enabled.

    ■ Hold down both Alt+Ctrl (PC)/Option+⌘ (Mac) keys after you've started drawing the new shape (but before releasing the mouse button to create the new events) to drag the start point and entire shape to a new location.

4. Release the mouse button at the desired end location to insert events corresponding to the current shape setting.

23 Using the Key Editor and Note Expression

There are many ways to edit the MIDI events recorded inside individual MIDI parts. If all you want to do is select, move, copy, or erase note events and Control Change events within a MIDI part, you can use the In-Place Editor (refer to Chapter 22). On the other hand, if you want to edit several MIDI parts at once, you need to add events that cross the boundary between two MIDI parts. If you would like to move or copy parts while they are being edited, the Key Editor is a better and more robust choice.

Most of the basic editing techniques associated with the Key Editor are also available through the In-Place Editor in the Project window; however, the Key Editor offers several additional features, such as multi-event and multitrack MIDI editing, as well as the ability to edit multiple lanes of controller events simultaneously. In addition, the Key Editor offers Note Expression editing, which is Cubase 6's new way to edit MIDI controller data.

Here's a summary of what you will learn in this chapter:

- How to use the different tools in the Key Editor to edit MIDI events

- How to adjust the velocity of inserted events

- How to adjust the positioning of events using the Snap and Quantize features

- How to record MIDI events using step recording and real-time MIDI input

- How to create a playback loop within this MIDI editor, independently from the project's playback or locator positions

- How to add a Controller Lane to the Key Editor

- How to edit more than one event and track at a time

- How to view, record, and edit Note Expression data

Using the Key Editor

Like the In-Place Editor, Cubase's Key Editor uses a piano roll analogy, in which events appear as "blocks" within a strip moving from left to right as you play the events. The vertical axis represents the pitch, and the horizontal axis represents the timeline of the event being edited. The start of the MIDI part(s) currently being edited is always on the left of the piano roll, and the end of a part appears on the right of the piano roll.

You open the Key Editor, shown in Figure 23.1, by double-clicking on a MIDI event or by selecting the event and then selecting MIDI > Open Key Editor.

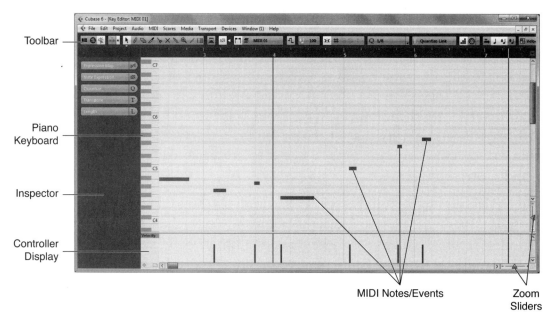

Figure 23.1 The MIDI Key Editor.

Solo Editor and Acoustic Feedback

Unlike the In-Place Editor, the Key Editor features its own dedicated toolbar. The first button, shown in Figure 23.2, lets you set up the layout of the Key Editor window. Next is the Solo Editor button, which mutes all MIDI parts not currently loaded in the Key Editor. The Acoustic Feedback button, next to that, plays notes when they are selected with the Selection tool or when you're moving a note in time or to different pitch values. This is basically the MIDI equivalent of the audio Audition (scrub) tool. Hold down the Ctrl (PC)/⌘ (Mac) key to hear all notes playing at the same time as the note you are selecting.

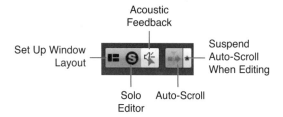

Figure 23.2 The first four buttons on the Key Editor toolbar.

The fourth button on the toolbar is the Auto-Scroll button, which toggles the Auto-Scroll function on or off. When enabled, the window follows the project playback cursor. When disabled, the contents of the window don't scroll. Alternatively, you can leave the button enabled but click the right-arrow next to the button; this suspends the Auto-Scroll function while you're editing.

Tool Buttons

Next is a series of 10 tools for applying various editing operations to MIDI events found in your editor (see Figure 23.3). These tools are similar to those found in the Project window, but they offer editor-specific characteristics.

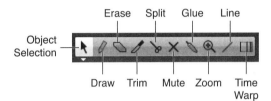

Figure 23.3 The Key Editor tools.

- **Object Selection.** This "arrow" tool serves to select and resize events. Use this tool to move, copy, and select a range of events or to change the start or end position of existing events in your editor.

- **Draw.** This "pencil" tool adds events by drawing them one by one inside the Key Editor or modifies existing note and controller events in a freehand style.

- **Erase.** This tool allows you to erase events by clicking on them. If multiple events were previously selected, they all can be erased by clicking on any one of them with this tool.

- **Trim.** This tool modifies the length of one or several events by trimming off the end (by default). If you hold down the Alt (PC)/Option (Mac) key before using this tool, the beginning of the note is trimmed instead.

- **Split.** This tool splits selected events at the split mark. Exactly where the split occurs is determined by the Snap and Grid modes.

- **Mute.** An alternative to the Erase tool, the Mute tool silences a note so that you don't hear it but does not erase it. This provides a way to mute certain events that you're not sure you want to get rid of but that you don't want to hear right now. Click and drag over a selection with the Mute tool to silence all events within the selection.

- **Glue.** This tool adheres two notes of the same pitch together. More specifically, when they are playing at the same pitch value, it glues the event that follows to the precedent event that you click on.

■ **Zoom.** This tool allows you to magnify your view of the content by dragging a box around it. You also can elect to click on a particular note to zoom in on it.

■ **Line.** This tool performs as a multifunction tool in two modes. The Line mode allows you to draw a series of events in the shape of the tool (you can switch between Line, Parabola, Sine, Triangle, and Square) or to draw controller information in one of these shapes as well. Paint, the last mode in the tool's pop-up selector, allows you to insert multiple notes by dragging the cursor across the note display area in a freehand style.

■ **Time Warp.** This tool creates tempo changes in the tempo track to match recorded musical events. Note that the Time Warp tool (available in the Project window, the Sample Editor, and the Audio Part Editor) plays a similar role in each—it's a tool that helps composers in the task of matching absolute, linear time (seconds, frames, and samples) with relative musical time (bars and beats). However, Time Warp is applied differently to MIDI than it is to audio. You will find more on this tool in Chapter 30, "Working with Tempo."

Auto Select Controllers

The Auto Select Controllers button, shown in Figure 23.4, is useful when you are editing or moving MIDI Control Change messages. When this button is enabled, selecting and moving note events also selects and moves any Control Change events with the identical start time.

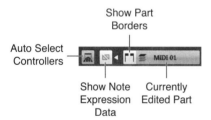

Figure 23.4 The Auto Select Controllers, Show Note Expression Data, Show Part Borders, and Currently Edited Part buttons.

Note Expression Data

Next to the Auto Select Controllers button is the Show Note Expression Data button. Note Expression is a new way of editing MIDI controller data; we'll discuss it in more detail later in this chapter.

Part Editing Options

The next two buttons shown in Figure 23.4 offer editing options related to editing multiple MIDI parts that have previously been selected in the Project window simultaneously inside the Key Editor.

Use the Show Part Borders button to display each MIDI part's border limits inside the Key Editor. When enabled, you will see a start and end handle for each MIDI part that is currently open in this MIDI editor. Clicking and dragging either one of these handles will modify the part's borders in the Project window as well.

The Currently Edited Part button is available for when you have opened several MIDI parts simultaneously in the Key Editor. Click this button and select the MIDI part from the Part List drop-down menu that you want to edit.

Indicate Transpositions and Insert Velocity

The Indicate Transpositions button, shown in Figure 23.5, helps you compare transposed notes with the originals. When you activate this control, the Key Editor shows the note pitch you hear after the transposition.

Indicate Transpositions   Insert Velocity

Figure 23.5 The Indicate Transpositions and Insert Velocity buttons.

Next to the Indicate Transpositions button is the Insert Velocity button. Click this button to specify a velocity value for any notes manually entered into the Key Editor. You can change this value in one of three ways:

■ Double-click the button and type in the desired value.

■ Click on the up or down arrow next to the current value to increase or decrease the value.

■ Click the button and select one of the preset values available in the drop-down menu.

Snap and Quantize

The Snap and Quantize options in the Key Editor are similar to the ones found in the Project window. Activate the Snap On/Off button (the first button on the left in Figure 23.6) to make the fields to the right of this button active. Click the Snap Type button to determine how the Snap and Quantize functions will work.

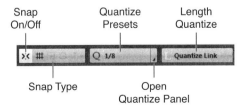

Snap On/Off   Quantize Presets   Length Quantize

Snap Type   Open Quantize Panel

Figure 23.6 Snap and Quantize controls.

The Quantize Presets button determines the grid's spacing and influences many operations inside the MIDI editors. For example, setting your grid to 1/32 note allows you to move, cut, and insert events at thirty-second-note intervals. In other words, the grid you select prevents you from moving, cutting, or inserting events at positions other than the one defined by the field.

The Length Quantize button determines the length of inserted events in the Key Editor. For example, if you set the length to 1/2, clicking in the display with the Draw tool will add a half-note to the part. When using the step-recording technique covered in detail later in this chapter with a Quantize value of 1/4 note and a Length Quantize value set to Quantize Link, all notes are inserted at quarter-note intervals and will be of quarter-note length. The Insert Velocity field, on the other hand, determines the velocity of Note On events that are added with the Draw tools.

Step Input and MIDI Edit Buttons

The next buttons on the toolbar, shown in Figure 23.7, help you configure how MIDI input is recorded.

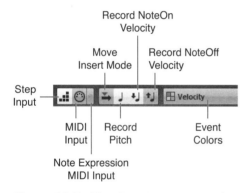

Figure 23.7 The Step Input controls.

The first of these buttons is the Step Input button. Step input is a boon for the rhythmically challenged—and for those less-than-proficient keyboard players who have great ideas but just need some help entering them into a sequencer. It's also great for creating rhythmically complex patterns, such as machine-like drum fills using sixty-fourth notes at 160 BPM, no matter what your skill level with the keyboard or other MIDI controller. Step input may also be useful for musicians who can't enter MIDI events in their computers using VSTi in real time because their sound card's latency is too high. No matter what the reason, step recording lets you enter notes or chords one by one without worrying about timing.

Table 23.1 describes the function associated with each of the Step Input buttons (also shown from left to right in Figure 23.7).

Table 23.1 Step Input Controls on the Editor's Toolbar

Button Name	Button Function
Step Input	Enables or disables the step input recording mode. Whenever this button is activated, the Auto-Scroll function is disabled.
MIDI Input	When this button is enabled, you can select a note and assign it a new pitch by playing a new note on your keyboard or other MIDI controller.
Note Expression MIDI Input	Same as the MIDI Input button, but with Note Expression data enabled.
Move Insert Mode	Adds the played event at the position corresponding to the next quantize value following the playback line, pushing any subsequent events to the next quantize value (when this option is enabled). When the Move Insert Point option is disabled, events added using Step Input mode are added at the current position of the Step Input cursor, leaving previously recorded content in place.
Record Pitch	Allows you to use your MIDI keyboard or other controller to reassign the pitches of existing events, advancing one note at a time through the existing MIDI note events in this editor as you play notes on your MIDI controller.
Record NoteOn Velocity	When enabled, the NoteOn velocity values of the notes you play in Step Input mode are recorded. When disabled, the velocity assigned to the note you record is fixed by the Velocity field in the toolbar. When Record NoteOn Velocity is enabled, pressing lightly on your keyboard adds notes with low velocity values, whereas pressing harder adds a higher velocity value to the notes recorded through the step recording method.
Record NoteOff Velocity	Records the NoteOff velocities entered in Step Input mode—otherwise set to a fixed value.

Finally, there's an Event Colors button at the very end of the toolbar. You use this button to change the color of specific events in the Key Editor window.

Key Editor Display Areas

The Key Editor offers two main display areas—one for MIDI note events and another for controller events. In the Note Display area, which is most of the top of the Key Editor window, a keyboard appears vertically along the left edge. The ruler spanning from left to right represents the time at which events occur. You can change how time is displayed by right-clicking (PC)/Control-clicking (Mac) in the ruler and selecting one of the many display formats available, or by selecting the desired format from the Ruler Format selection menu found at the right of the ruler itself.

Using the Ruler to Control Zoom: In the Key Editor (as well as in all the other windows), when you click in the lower half of the ruler and drag your mouse up or down, you zoom out or in, respectively, centering your display on the position where you clicked to start the zoom. Holding down your mouse and moving it left or right moves the window and the project cursor in time. When you release your mouse, the project cursor snaps to the closest quantize value (if the Snap is active).

The Controller Display area, shown in Figure 23.8, is a customizable portion of the window that displays one or more controller types, such as volume, pan, expression, pedal, pitch bends, and so on. Using multiple Controller Lanes gives you a better view of the MIDI messages associated with the part you are editing.

Figure 23.8 The Controller Display area of the Key Editor.

Add a Controller Lane to the Key Editor:

1. Right-click (PC)/Control-click (Mac) within the left side of the Controller Display area.

2. From the context menu, select the Create New Controller Lane option.

3. From the newly created lane, click the down-arrow next to the lane name and select the controller you want from the drop-down list. Controller types for which there are actually recorded events in the current part are identified by an asterisk (*) at the end of their names.

If the desired controller is not displayed in this list, select the Setup option at the bottom of the drop-down menu. This displays the MIDI Controller Setup dialog box, shown in Figure 23.9. There are two areas inside this dialog box: the Visible area and the Hidden area.

■ **To add a controller to the menu:** Select it from the Hidden area and click the triple-arrow button below the area.

■ **To remove a controller from the menu:** Select it from the Visible area and click the triple-arrow button below the area. Click OK when you are finished adding or

Figure 23.9 The MIDI Controller Setup dialog box.

removing controllers from the menu, and then select the new controller to add its corresponding lane.

- **To remove a Controller Lane:** Select the Remove This Lane option at the bottom of the same context menu you used to add a new lane.

Controller events seen in the Controller Display area are represented by blocks, whereas note velocity values are represented by lines and are aligned with their corresponding MIDI note events. Moving a note moves its associated velocity value, but it doesn't move any controller events unless the Auto Select Controllers button is enabled in the window's toolbar. The field below the controller's name represents the value of the controller if you were to add this value at the current cursor position. The Quantize value, when active, will affect the distance between each added or recorded controller event. For example, if a quantize grid is set to 1/2 note, controllers can be added at half-note intervals. To enter a greater number of controller events, disable the Snap mode or set the Quantize value to a smaller value. More controller events create smoother changes, but they also create greater numbers of MIDI events that can bog down the MIDI at the port's output. This is especially true when you are using lots of MIDI in your project.

Using Step Input

Step Input functions are available in the Key Editor's toolbar. When the Step Input mode is enabled, a new insert cursor (a vertical blue bar) appears in the note display area. Keep an eye on the location of this line; events that are inserted appear at the grid line immediately to the right of this insertion point. You can move this line by clicking inside the note display area at the location where you want to insert new events in Step Input mode.

Record MIDI in Step Input mode:

1. Enable the Step Input button in the toolbar, along with all the other Step Input controls except for the MIDI Connector button.

2. Enable the Snap button and select a Snap mode.

3. Set the Quantize Presets and Length Quantize values, which determine how far apart and how long the events will be.

4. Position the Step Input cursor at the point where you want to begin recording by clicking inside the note display area of the Key Editor.

5. If you do not want to use the NoteOn velocities you play as you step-enter these new MIDI note events, disable the Record NoteOn Velocity button and set the Insert Velocity field to the desired velocity.

6. Play a note or a chord on your keyboard or other MIDI controller. The notes you play determine the pitch and velocity (if that option is enabled) being recorded as you step-enter new notes, but the position in the timeline is determined by the insertion point and the Quantize Grid setting.

7. To move the Step Input cursor forward or backward, use the left or right arrow on your keyboard or click within the note display area. The insertion point where the notes will be added is displayed in the Time Value field in the toolbar of this editor.

8. To insert an event between two other events, activate the Insert Mode button in the toolbar of this MIDI editor, position your insert point (blue line) where you want to insert a note or a chord, and simply play the note or chord. To insert a note without moving the content found to the right of this location, disable the Insert Mode button on the toolbar.

9. When you are finished, don't forget to turn off the Step Input button; otherwise, Cubase will continue to insert events that you play on the keyboard in this part.

Editing Multiple Tracks

Editing several tracks together can be useful to compare events on different tracks in a single editing window. Fortunately, you can edit more than one MIDI track simultaneously by selecting parts on different tracks in the Project window and opening them in the Key Editor.

Edit more than one track at a time:

1. In the Project window, click the first part you want to edit in a track.

2. Shift-click the next part you want to edit in another track or, with the Object Selection tool, drag a selection box over the range of parts you want to edit simultaneously.

3. Press Ctrl+E (PC)/⌘+E (Mac) or select MIDI > Open Key Editor.

Editing Controller Data with Note Expression

Previously, we discussed how to edit MIDI controller data in the Key Editor's Controller Lane. Cubase 6 adds a new, more intuitive way to edit certain types of controller data for certain types of controllers. Note Expression, as this new functionality is called, lets you display and edit controller data directly on the associated MIDI events in the Key Editor display. By fine-tuning this articulation information, you can create remarkably real-sounding MIDI recordings.

With Note Expression enabled, a MIDI note and its associated controller data are treated as a unit. As you can see in Figure 23.10, you view Note Expression curves, each representing specific controller data (such as modulation, balance, and pitch bend) in the Key Editor on top of the corresponding MIDI note. When you move, copy, duplicate, quantize, or delete notes, all the associated controller data follows.

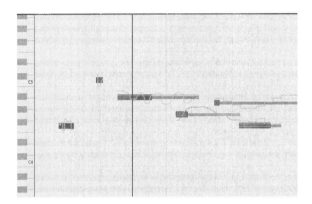

Figure 23.10 Viewing controller data as Note Expression curves in the Key Editor.

VSTi vs. MIDI Note Expression: Note Expression works best with VST3 controllers, such as HALion Sonic SE, as they provide articulation information for each individual note. With MIDI controllers (including older VST instruments), on the other hand, articulation information is applied to an entire channel. When using Note Expression with MIDI and older VST instruments, then, the articulation data on one note usually affects all the other notes playing on the same channel at the same time.

Activating Note Expression

To show Note Expression data in the Key Editor, click "on" the Show Note Expression Data button on the toolbar. This displays controller values, if any are recorded, on the individual MIDI notes.

You'll also want to get to know the elements of the Note Expression tab in the Key Editor Inspector. As you can see in Figure 23.11, the Note Expression tab includes the following parts:

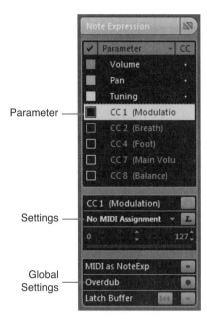

Parameter

Settings

Global
Settings

Figure 23.11 The Note Expression tab in the Key Editor Inspector.

- **Parameter.** This section lists available VST controllers (top) and MIDI controllers (bottom). Each controller is color coded; controller assignment, if any, is shown in the CC column.

- **Settings.** This section displays settings for the selected controller. These settings are specific to each controller type.

- **Global settings.** This section includes settings that apply to all controllers, such as Record MIDI Controller as Note Expression, Overdub Note Expression Data in Existing Notes, and Record Buffered Parameter Values as One-Shots to Notes.

Use the color-coding in the Inspector to identify specific controllers in the main display.

Mapping Controllers for Note Expression

Most external MIDI keyboards have no controls or faders to input the VST3 parameters used in Note Expression. Instead, you need to assign specific MIDI controllers (such as Pitchbend or Aftertouch) to each of the desired Note Expression parameters. You can map the same MIDI controller for different parameters, but only one controller can be active at a time.

When mapping controllers, know that the VST3 Tuning parameter is automatically assigned to the pitch bend wheel of your MIDI keyboard. All other parameters are assigned by default to the first MIDI controller (typically Modulation). You can, however, manually map parameters to controllers.

Manually map a MIDI controller to a Note Expression parameter:

1. In the Key Editor, open the Note Expression tab.

2. Select the parameter to map.

3. Click the MIDI Assignment control in the Settings section to display the drop-down menu, shown in Figure 23.12.

4. Select the MIDI controller to assign to the parameter.

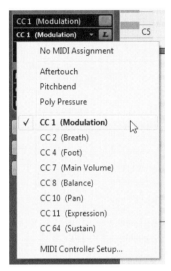

Figure 23.12   Mapping a Note Expression parameter to a MIDI controller.

Recording Note Expression Data

When recording new projects, you'll want to record Note Expression data along with your MIDI recordings. This is made easy by using the Note Expression tab in the Inspector in the Project window.

Record Note Expression data with MIDI notes:

1. Create a new instrument track in the Project window.

2. Open the Note Expression tab for this track.

3. Select a parameter from the list and map the parameter to a MIDI controller, as previously described.

4. Record the MIDI notes, along with the associated controller data.

Once you've recorded the MIDI data, you can open the Key Editor and activate the Show Note Expression Data button to view the recorded Note Expression data.

Editing Note Expression Data

You can edit Note Expression data for any MIDI note within the Key Editor. You can edit existing data or add new Note Expression data from scratch.

Edit Note Expression data:

1. In the Key Editor, double-click the MIDI note you want to edit. This opens the Note Expression Editor, shown in Figure 23.13. All parameters are displayed as curves on top of the MIDI note.

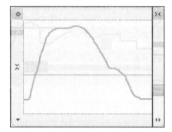

Figure 23.13 Editing parameters in the Note Expression Editor.

2. Select the parameter you wish to edit by clicking that curve in the editor. To add a new parameter to the note, select that parameter in the Note Expression tab of the Inspector.

3. Use the Draw or Line tool to enter or modify the selected curve.

Editing Note Expression data in this fashion enables you to create highly expressive MIDI recordings.

24 Editing MIDI Drum Tracks

The Key Editor is used to edit MIDI events that represent melodic instruments. Editing a MIDI drum part, however, is a slightly different beast—and requires a slightly different editor. To that end, Cubase includes a dedicated Drum Editor, just for editing MIDI drum parts.

Here's a summary of what you will learn in this chapter:

- Recognizing different areas of the Drum Editor

- How to edit drum parts

- How to load a drum map and assign it to a MIDI drum track

- How to create or customize a drum map

- How to quantize drum parts

Understanding the Drum Editor

What you read in Chapter 23 about the Key Editor applies for the most part to the Drum Editor, as well. The Drum Editor, however, is optimized for working with MIDI drum parts, where you're likely to have multiple parts of a drum set or percussion section playing simultaneously—but synced closely to the underlying beat.

You open the Drum Editor by selecting a MIDI event and then selecting MIDI > Open Drum Editor. As you can see in Figure 24.1, the Drum Editor looks a lot like the Key Editor. The big difference is that instead of pitches and a keyboard along the vertical axis, you have a list of drum sounds. In addition, each drum hit is indicated by a single diamond shape instead of a bar of specific length. (That's because drum hits are just that, hits; they don't have the sustain that you get when you hold a note on another instrument.)

As with the Key Editor, the Drum Editor is divided into task-specific areas. At the top of the window, of course, is the toolbar; with a few exceptions, the Drum Editor toolbar mirrors that of the Key Editor.

On the left side of the Drum Editor is the Drum Sound list; this replaces the keyboard display of the Key Editor. This list displays all the drum sounds in the current drum

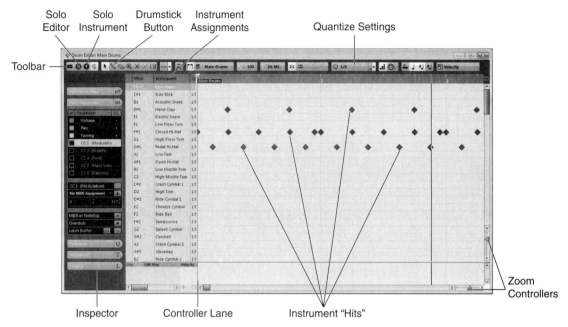

Figure 24.1 The Drum Editor.

map and details which sounds are associated with which notes. The number of columns displayed in the Drum Sound list depends on the drum map associated with the track.

If you drag the vertical divider line that separates the Drum Sound list from the note display area on the right, you will reveal some of the columns that might be hidden in the Drum Sound list. It can have up to nine columns, each representing a control parameter for an instrument. You can reorder these columns by dragging their headers, but I will list them here in their default order.

■ The first unnamed column lets you select and monitor the instrument associated with this pitch. Selecting an instrument reveals its NoteOn velocity in the Controller Lane.

■ The **Pitch** column represents the pitch associated with a particular instrument. This cannot be changed because most instruments are already preprogrammed to play a certain instrument on an assigned pitch value.

■ The **Instrument** column represents the name of the sound associated with this row's pitch. Each drum map has its own set of instruments. These can be renamed or dragged into any order that makes editing more convenient as you work.

■ The **Quantize** column represents the quantize value setting for each instrument. You can change this setting by clicking on the current value and selecting a new one. You also can change all the instruments' quantize value settings simultaneously by holding down the Ctrl (PC)/⌘ (Mac) key as you make your selection. The list that appears offers the same options as the Drum Editor's Quantize Grid drop-down menu.

- The **M** column controls whether an instrument is muted. To silence an instrument, click in its instrument row in the M column. To unmute that instrument, click in the M (or Mute) column next to that instrument once again.

- The **I-Note** column stands for the Input Note value or the note as recorded from the controller keyboard or drum machine, which I discuss when I cover the Drum Map feature in the next section. You can use the scroll wheel on your mouse to change this value (or the up/down arrow keys on a Mac), or you can simply click in the field and type in a new value.

- The **O-Note** column stands for Output Note and represents the note at which the sound you want to map will be played back. By default, the O-Note is the same as the I-Note, but the ability to remap each input note to a different output note is an essential aspect of using drum maps. Again, this is discussed in the next section. You can change the value in this column in the same ways as the I-Note column.

- The **Channel** column sets the MIDI channel assigned to the instrument in a specific row. Each row in the drum map can be routed out to a different MIDI channel. You can change the value in this column in the same ways as described for the I-Note and O-Note columns.

- The **Output** column allows assigning each instrument (row) in this drum map to a different MIDI output port. To change the output, click the appropriate row in the Output column and select a new MIDI output from this column's pop-up menu. Each note in a drum track could be assigned to a different instrument. For example, you could have the kick drum assigned to an external GM device, the snare to an LM-9 VST instrument, and so on.

Below the Drum Sound list, in the left corner, are the Map and Names fields. The Map field selects a map from the Drum Map list or sets up a new drum map if you haven't already done that. The Names field selects from a drop-down menu the names of instruments associated with different pitch values. So this field is grayed out when a drum map is selected.

To the right of the Drum Sound list is the note display area. The vertical axis represents different instruments or pitches, according to the information found in the drum sound list on the left and the timeline, which appears with smaller divisions per the current quantize settings. The blocks that represent MIDI note events in the Key Editor are replaced by diamonds here in the Drum Editor, each of which represents a NoteOn event. Notes are exactly aligned with the quantize grid when a vertical grid line crosses the diamond in its center.

Below the note display area are the Controller Lanes. Whereas the Key Editor displays the velocity of every note in this area, the Drum Editor only displays velocities for events in the currently selected instrument (row). For every other type of Control

Change message, the Drum Editor behaves the same way as the Key Editor described previously.

Editing Drum Parts

Editing a drum part is as simple as clicking, dragging, and dropping. For example:

- To change a particular hit from one beat to another, grab the note with your mouse and drag it to another location on the same horizontal line.

- To reassign a hit from one drum or instrument to another, grab the note with your mouse and drag it to another instrument line; make sure you keep the note at the same horizontal position.

- To delete a note, click the Erase button in the toolbar and then click the note.

- To add a new note, click the Drumstick button in the toolbar (see Figure 24.2) and then click where you want the note to be—both vertically (which drum/instrument) and horizontally (which part of the measure).

Figure 24.2 The Drumstick button in the Drum Editor's toolbar.

As you can see, the Drum Editor makes it fairly easy to make changes—big or small—to your MIDI drum tracks.

Solo Individual Drums: Click the Solo Instrument button to listen to a specific drum or percussion instrument and mute all other sounds (refer to Figure 24.1).

Working with Drum Maps

Depending on the manufacturer and model, MIDI instruments may use a wide variety of MIDI note values for similar drum sounds. For example, one device might use C1 and D1 for its basic kick and snare sounds, whereas another might use C1 and F1 for the same purpose. This is fine when you know which note is playing which sound. But what if you want to try a different drum set or drum machine? Do you need to rerecord all your beats because C1 is not the bass drum anymore? That's when drum mapping becomes very handy.

Understanding Drum Maps

A *drum map* is simply a map of all the available percussion sounds on a MIDI device. The individual drums, cymbals, and other sounds are mapped to specific keys on the MIDI keyboard. Play a key and you hear the drum sound mapped to that key.

Cubase comes with its own ready-made drum maps; check the installation disk or the Drum Maps folder on your computer to see what's available. Other drum maps can be downloaded from the Internet (try the forums at www.cubase.net), or you can create your own custom drum maps.

Only one drum map can be assigned to any specific MIDI track, but you can assign the same drum map to different MIDI tracks. For obvious reasons, if you use two tracks with the same MIDI output and MIDI channel, you can have only one drum map assigned to that MIDI device/VSTi plug-in.

Load a drum map and assign it to a drum track:

1.   In the basic track settings section of the Inspector for this MIDI track, click in the Drum Map field and select the Drum Map Setup option.

2.   When the Drum Map Setup window opens, as shown in Figure 24.3, click the Functions drop-down menu and select Load.

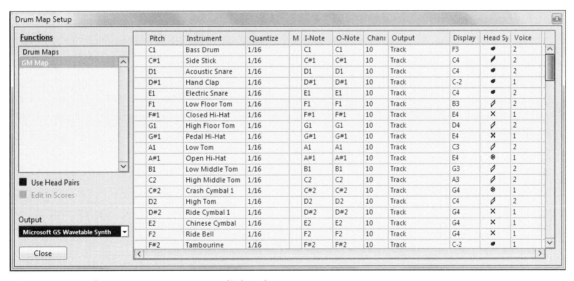

Figure 24.3   The Drum Map Setup dialog box.

3.   Browse to the folder containing the desired drum map file (*.drm), select it, and click the Open button.

4.   Select the newly loaded drum map from the Drum Map list and click Open.

5.   Back in the Drum Map Setup window, click the Output drop-down list and select the default MIDI port associated with this drum map.

6.   Click the Close button.

Remapping Drum Maps

A drum map is essentially a list of 128 sound names associated with a specific pitch, Note In event, and Note Out event. Each note in a drum map corresponds to a pitch value. Each pitch value (note number) can be associated with an instrument name, such as Kick Drum 1, Snare, Hi-Hat, and so forth. You can then assign the played note to that named instrument, which in turn is associated with a pitch, such as C1 (or note number 36).

As you read earlier in this chapter, the Drum Editor displays note input (I-Note) and output (O-Note) columns. These columns can remap recorded notes. By remapping the recorded kick-drum part from a C1 to a C3, for example, you can keep the recorded performance playing properly without permanently altering the MIDI events it contains.

Note In/Note Out: You can assign only one Note In instrument per note name or note number, but you can have more than one Note In assigned to the same Note Out.

Figure 24.4 shows how a typical remapping might work. The left side of the figure shows the original drum map as played on your MIDI keyboard. The right side of the figure shows the new drum map, with several sounds remapped to different notes.

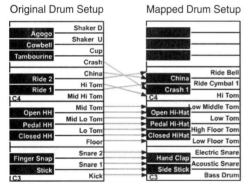

Figure 24.4   Remapping a drum map.

Create or customize a drum map:

1. Load the VSTi that will actually play the drum sounds or select the appropriate drum patch on the external MIDI device that is connected to the designated MIDI output port/channel.

2. In the basic track settings section of the Inspector for this MIDI track, click in the Drum Map field and select the Drum Map Setup option.

3. When the Drum Map Setup window opens, click the Functions drop-down menu and select New Map.

4. Rename the new map (currently labeled Empty Map).

5. Next to each pitch in the list of instruments, enter an appropriate instrument name.

6. Adjust the Quantize, I-Note, O-Note, Channel, and Output fields, if needed.

7. Repeat these steps for all the sounds available in your drum kit.

8. To save your changes, click the Functions drop-down menu and select Save.

Deleting Drum Maps: To remove an unneeded drum map, open the Drum Map Setup window, select the map, and then select Functions > Remove.

Quantizing MIDI Drum Parts

The Drum Editor window provides individual control over a set of parameters for up to 127 percussive instruments. One of these parameters is the quantize value, which can be set globally for the entire part or individually for each instrument assigned to a pitch in a drum patch. For example, set a different quantize value for the kick drum and the hi-hat when you step record.

The quantize value determines the spacing between each manually entered event. When the General Quantize button is disabled, the individual quantize settings take over. When the General Quantize button is enabled, the quantize value set in the toolbar dictates the quantize grid for each instrument in the part.

Setting an individual quantize value for each instrument in a drum track replaces the note lengths that will appear for this MIDI part in the Key Editor. Most percussive sounds need to have precise trigger timings rather than precision in their durations, so when using drum maps, you don't usually extend the length of MIDI note events. With the exception of some samplers, most instruments play drum sounds until the end, and the MIDI NoteOff event's position has little or no effect, no matter how long you hold the note. Unlike a guitar or keyboard note, the position of the attack, or NoteOn event, is more relevant in this case than the actual end of the event. As a direct result of this, there are no Split or Glue tools in the Drum Editor.

Quantizing Recorded Drum Tracks: Quantizing a drum track that is part of an audio recording is much different from quantizing a MIDI drum track. Learn more in Chapter 31, "Working with Beats and Loops."

25 Understanding MIDI Menu Options

Whichever editor you use to edit MIDI tracks, you eventually use the commands in Cubase's MIDI menu. You also use this menu to work with MIDI events in the Project window.

This MIDI menu is divided into five sections. The first section lists a number of commands that open different types of MIDI editing windows. In the second section are a number of quantizing options that can be used to modify the timing of MIDI events. The third section of the menu offers a number of specific MIDI editing features that aren't handled by the normal MIDI editors. The fourth section of the menu relates mostly to the Logical Editor functions, whereas the final section is basically a MIDI reset function. (This last function acts as a panic button on a MIDI patch bay, sending out All Notes Off and Reset Controllers messages on all MIDI output ports and channels; you can use this when you experience stuck notes after recording, playing, or editing a track.)

This chapter mainly discusses the commands found in the third section of the menu. Here's a summary of what you will learn in this chapter:

- How to transpose selected events using the MIDI Transpose command
- How to use the Merge MIDI in Loop command
- How to dissolve a MIDI part
- How to perform an O-Note (output note) conversion
- How to use a MIDI function

Using the MIDI Transpose Command

The Transpose Setup command in the MIDI menu opens the Transpose Setup dialog box, shown in Figure 25.1, and enables you to transpose the pitches of MIDI note events. There are three types of transpositions available. You can apply them individually or combine them if you want to experiment a little.

- Use the **Semitones** field if you simply want to shift the pitch of all currently selected MIDI events by the same amount. Unlike the Transpose field in the Inspector (which

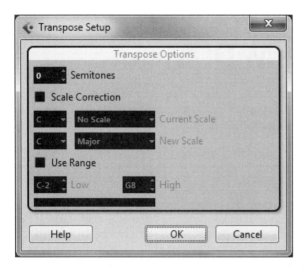

Figure 25.1 Cubase's MIDI Transpose Setup dialog box.

applies this transformation in real time), this command changes the MIDI note numbers of the events themselves.

- Use the **Scale Correction** fields to change the tonality of a line or harmonic part. Indicating the Root Note and Current Scale for the selected events tells Cubase how to interpret the source MIDI notes. Set the desired values for the Current Scale and New Scale fields, and Cubase will adjust the notes appropriately to match the nearest pitch in the destination scale. If a value has also been entered in the Semitones field, however, that pitch shift is applied *before* this scale correction step.

- Utilize the **Use Range** fields to force all affected notes (after transposition and scale correction are applied, if you have selected those options in this dialog box) to remain within a restricted range. All notes outside this range are octave-transposed to fit within the pitch limits set by the Low and High fields. For example, if the selected events contain a G6 (either in their untransposed state or as the result of operations in the first two fields of this dialog box), and your lower and upper barrier for the target pitch range are C2 and C5, that G6 would be transposed to C4, the nearest octave transposition for a G that will fall within the target range.

Transpose selected events using the MIDI Transpose command:

1.   Select one or more MIDI parts or specific events inside a MIDI part that you want to transpose.

2.   Select MIDI > Transpose Setup.

3.   In the Transpose Setup dialog box, set the desired options.

4.   Click OK to apply your changes.

Merge MIDI in Loop

Suppose you've applied different MIDI effects to a MIDI or instrument track as inserts or sends, and you've assigned different track parameter values to a MIDI part. When you are trying to edit certain details, you realize that the details you want to edit are transformed—or generated—in real time by the various settings you have assigned to this track.

If you want to create a new version of the MIDI track containing events that reflect the results of the all MIDI effects and parameters you've previously assigned, use the Merge MIDI in Loop option found in the MIDI menu. Here's how it works.

Let's say you've recorded a MIDI piano accompaniment and played certain chords. Afterward, you've applied the Track FX MIDI effect to adjust the notes in these chords to a different scale. When listening to your new chord coloring, you like the result, but you'd like to change a note in one of the chords so that it fits better with the rest of the arrangement. But because this is a real-time effect, you can't really change a note that you didn't play to begin with. That's when the Merge MIDI in Loop option comes in handy. The new merged track (containing the results of your real-time effects and parameters) can then be edited, and new track parameters or MIDI effects assigned to it. You will probably also want to merge all real-time MIDI effects and track parameters with recorded events before exporting MIDI parts to MIDI files to be used in another application.

Use the Merge MIDI in Loop option:

1. Start by identifying the MIDI events you want to merge. This can be a MIDI part on one track or several MIDI parts on several tracks assigned to various MIDI channels.

2. After you've identified what you want to merge, set the left and right locators to include this content.

3. Mute any other MIDI track you don't want to include in this process.

4. If you want to keep the original content intact, create a new MIDI track.

5. If you have chosen to create a new MIDI track for the merged destination, select it in the Track List area; otherwise, select the desired destination track (which might be the same track as the original content).

6. Select MIDI > Merge MIDI in Loop. The MIDI Merge Options dialog box will appear, as displayed in Figure 25.2.

7. Enable or disable any of these five options:
   - **Include Inserts.** This option converts any MIDI messages generated by MIDI insert effects into MIDI events in the new merged part, which can be edited further if necessary.

Figure 25.2 The MIDI Merge Options dialog box.

- **Include Sends**. This option converts any MIDI messages generated by MIDI send effects into MIDI events in the new merged part, which also can be edited further if necessary.

- **Erase Destination.** If you have selected a track that already contains MIDI events as the destination track for this command, check this option to erase that track's content. (If you do not check this option, the new MIDI part will appear on top of any overlapping MIDI parts that already exist on the destination track.)

- **Include Chase**. Check this option if you want to include control change values that are in effect prior to the selected range of events in the source track, such as program changes or pitch bend information.

- **Convert VST3**. This option converts all VST3 data within the selected area to MIDI data.

8. Click OK after setting your options.

Using the Dissolve Parts Function

Suppose you have a MIDI file that you want to import into Cubase. You do so by using the File > Import > MIDI File command, only to realize that this file contains only one track with all the different channel information and events on this single track. If that track contains multiple events, you might want to separate these events into separate tracks for easier editing. You can do this using Cubase's MIDI > Dissolve Part function.

Dissolve a MIDI part:

1. Select the MIDI part you want to dissolve.

2. Select MIDI > Dissolve Part.

3. Cubase now displays the Dissolve Part dialog box, shown in Figure 25.3. If the selected part contains MIDI events for more than one MIDI channel, Cubase offers you two choices: Separate Channels or Separate

Pitches. Select the appropriate option. On the other hand, if there are only MIDI events for one MIDI channel in the selected part, you can only separate pitches.

4.   Click OK to continue.

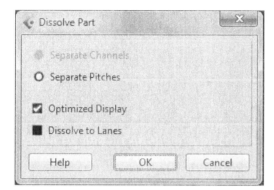

Figure 25.3 The Dissolve Part dialog box.

Note that the original track is automatically muted after being dissolved.

Using the O-Note Conversion Tool

The concept of the O-Note command is directly related to drum maps; this function becomes active only when a MIDI part associated with a drum-mapped MIDI track has been selected.

Drum maps use three specific note names to identify a drum instrument: the pitch, the I-Note (input note), and the O-Note (output note). The pitch is associated with a drum instrument and cannot be modified. So, a C1 can be associated with a kick drum, for example. The I-Note is the note you play on your MIDI controller to trigger a specific instrument. In practice, playing a C1 note should trigger a kick drum because that's what is loaded for this MIDI note number in the destination instrument. The O-Note is the note sent out by the drum map when that I-Note is received. In theory, the I-Note and the O-Note are usually the same.

Why all these note names? Well, sometimes you might want to reorganize which note triggers which instrument to lay out the drum kit more efficiently on your keyboard. This can make it easier, for example, to play a drum part on notes you are accustomed to using, even when the currently selected VSTi or external MIDI module uses some other mapping for its drum sounds. That's when you start playing with the drum mapping in Cubase, changing the I-Note and O-Note values.

As long as your MIDI part plays through this drum map within Cubase, you are fine, but if you want to convert this to a *non*-drum-mapped track to export your file as a MIDI file, you need to convert the drum map appropriately so that the MIDI note events in the result correspond to the output note currently being played by the drum map. To do this, you use the O-Note Conversion tool, which permanently converts the MIDI note number values according to whatever O-Note mapping is currently in effect. This allows you to play the part afterwards as a regular MIDI track (without any drum map) while still hearing the appropriate sounds played by the drum kit for which this MIDI track is intended.

Perform an O-Note conversion:

1. Select the MIDI part(s) with drum maps in effect that you want to convert.

2. From the MIDI menu, select the O-Note Conversion command.

3. A warning message might appear; click Yes if you want to proceed anyway or Cancel if you are not sure this is what you want to do.

Using MIDI Functions

The commands in the Functions submenu of the MIDI menu, such as Legato, Fixed Lengths, and Velocity, enable you to apply certain performance-based edits to a selected MIDI event. Most of these functions are self-explanatory; for example, the Delete Doubles function deletes any MIDI note that duplicates an existing note. Some of these functions display a dialog box, whereas others perform their task without needing additional input.

These MIDI functions play a similar role as the MIDI track parameters you assign in the Inspector. However, there are different reasons that would motivate you to use a MIDI function rather than an Inspector-based parameter.

For example, track parameters in the Inspector affect all events (parts) on a given track, whereas MIDI functions can be applied to selected parts in the Project window or selected events in any MIDI editor window. Another example is that the results of Inspector-based parameter settings do not show up in the MIDI editor (they're applied in real time), whereas MIDI functions actually change the appropriate value in the MIDI actual MIDI events, therefore making their results visible in the MIDI editor.

In other words, if you want to try things out before committing to them, use the real-time MIDI track parameters in the Inspector. But when you want to alter the track's MIDI events permanently, you are better off using the MIDI functions.

Use a MIDI function:

1. In the Project window, select the parts you want to edit or, if you don't want to affect all the events in the part, open the MIDI part in one of the MIDI editors and select the events you want to edit.

2. Select MIDI > Functions, and then select the MIDI function you want to apply.

3. Change any values needed in the dialog box if one shows up, and click OK to complete; otherwise, the function is automatically applied.

26 Quantizing Events

Quantizing rhythm makes events cling to a virtual grid. It's a way to make imprecise performances more precise. As you record MIDI or audio performances, notes might be recorded a little bit before or after a beat. Humans are not as steady and consistent as the timing in Cubase, nor would you want them to be when it comes to the music's feel.

Fortunately, you can *quantize* events and individual notes to "nudge" them this way or that on the time grid. For example, setting the quantize value to quarter notes (1/4) will make all recorded notes cling to quarter notes. Setting the quantize value to a lesser note value splits the grid into smaller, more precise subdivisions.

Cubase 6 lets you quantize both MIDI and audio events; we'll discuss both techniques in this chapter:

- Understanding different quantize methods

- How to save, rename, or delete a quantize setting to and from a preset list

- How to apply an automatic quantize value during the recording or editing process

- How to apply a quantize method to selected events

- How to undo quantization on selected events

- How to create a groove quantize preset based on selected MIDI events

- How to quantize audio events using hitpoints and audio warp

- How to quantize multiple audio events

Understanding and Configuring Quantize Methods

Cubase 6 offers two basic types of quantizing—over-quantizing and iterative quantizing.

Freezing Quantization: Quantizing MIDI events affects the way MIDI events are played back, but it does not alter the recorded material. It merely acts as an output filter, whereas the original position values are usually stored with the project

---

regardless of the Undo history list. If you desire, you can select Edit > Advanced Quantize > Freeze MIDI Quantize to permanently replace the original timing of the MIDI events with their quantized locations. After the quantization is frozen and the original timing is replaced, you can still re-quantize MIDI events to some other quantize groove or setting. The original position of frozen events is lost, however, being replaced by the quantized position of these events at the moment when the freeze command was applied.

Over-quantizing is Cubase's default method. It works by moving the start of an event to the closest time increment on the quantize grid.

Iterative quantizing (what Cubase dubs "iQ") is a looser version of the over-quantize method. It moves the start position of an event only a certain percentage of the distance toward the nearest increment on the quantize grid; this percentage is determined by the Iterative Strength field in the Quantize Panel window. Iterative quantizing uses the current location (this could be the quantized location) of the event rather than its original location (unquantized location). You can therefore quantize an event and then requantize it differently using the iterative quantize method.

Advanced Quantization: Cubase 6 offers two advanced MIDI quantization modes—Quantize MIDI Event Lengths and Quantize MIDI Event Ends. (There's also an AudioWarp Quantize option for audio events, which we'll discuss later in this chapter.) Choose these quantization modes by selecting Edit > Advanced Quantize.

Quantizing audio and MIDI events is similar, but with one key difference. With audio quantizing, the quantization affects only when selected events start. MIDI quantizing, on the other hand, can also affect the lengths of events, and when they end.

You configure quantization for an audio or MIDI part by selecting the part and then selecting Edit > Quantize Panel. (You can also open the Quantize Panel by clicking the down arrow next to the Quantize Presets button on the Project window toolbar.) The Quantize Panel window, shown in Figure 26.1, lets you customize the parameters of over-quantization to help make the quantized events sound more natural. You can also use this panel to select and configure iterative quantization.

Here are the controls available in the Quantize Panel:

- **Select Preset.** This lets you select from a variety of preset quantization values.
- **Quantize Grid.** This sets the quantize reference value for the grid. The values displayed in the grid pop-up menu represent note subdivisions from 1/1 to 1/64, in straight, triplet, and dotted note values.

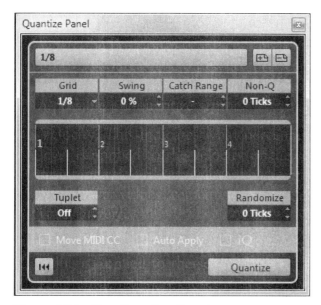

Figure 26.1 The Quantize Panel.

- **Swing Factor.** This shifts the position of a straight grid type to produce a swing or a shuffle feeling.

- **Quantize Catch Range.** This determines that only the area specified around the center of each increment on the grid is affected by quantizing. Each tick value represents 1/120 of a sixteenth note. This setting enables complex quantization tasks, such as quantizing only the heavy beats near each beat—and not the events in between.

- **Non-Quantize Range.** This is the mirror image of the Quantize Catch Range parameter, in that it establishes an area around the center of each increment on the grid, within which note events are *not* affected. In other words, any note already found within this range is left un-quantized, creating a more human-like (read "looser") feel to the quantization. In this case, quantization would be applied only to notes whose position is outside of the non-quantize area that surrounds each grid increment.

- **Grid Display.** Found in the center of the Quantize Panel, this shows the result of your settings in the Grid quantize area above. The entire display area represents a single 4/4 bar.

- **Tuplet.** This further subdivides the note value currently selected in the Grid field, to accommodate other rhythmic groupings that aren't binary (multiples of two), including triplets (which can already be selected more easily in the Type selector), quintuplets, septuplets, and so on. For example, selecting a Grid value of 1/4 notes with a Tuplet value of 5 creates a grid of 1/8-note quintuplets—since there will be five grid subdivisions in the space of every 1/4 note.

■ **Randomize.** This is another feature that enables you to humanize the effect of quantization by adding small, random amounts of variation to the resultant position of the quantized notes.

■ **Move MIDI CC.** With this option, controllers related to MIDI notes, such as pitch bend, are automatically moved with any notes that are quantized.

■ **Auto Apply.** Activate this option to immediately apply changes you make to selected events.

■ **iQ.** Applies the looser iterative quantization—and displays the Iterative Strength panel.

■ **Iterative Strength.** This field becomes available when you check the iQ option, and sets the strength level of iterative quantization. With higher percentage values, events are moved closer to the nearest grid increment as specified by your current quantization settings. With lower percentage values, events are not moved as close to the grid setting, allowing for more variations. In other words, 0% strength would not move the notes at all, whereas 100% will move them all the way to the grid increment, as in normal over-quantize mode.

■ **Reset Quantize.** Click this button to undo any previous quantization.

■ **Quantize.** Click this button to apply quantization settings.

Setting Up a Quantize Grid

Previously we've discussed how you can magnetize different elements in the Project window using various Snap modes, as selected by the Snap Type button on the Project window toolbar. Quantization uses this same grid in which to snap selected events.

Know, however, that some Snap modes don't take the grid into consideration, and therefore won't be affected by the currently selected quantization. The mode that *does* work with quantization is the Grid mode; it not only affects movement of events, but also influences where parts are created and where markers will be placed. In other words, selecting an appropriate Grid and Quantize type for the task at hand will help you get the result you want more effectively.

For example, when you're creating a new MIDI part, turn the Snap mode on (from the toolbar), select Grid as the Snap Type, and then select Bar as the Grid Type. As you record the new MIDI event, the newly created event will start at the closest bar from its beginning and will end at the closest bar after you stop recording. In such an example, as you create parts or events, their length could be increased or decreased by only one bar at a time.

Set up an appropriate Snap mode:

1. Enable the Snap On/Off button in the Project window's toolbar.

2. Select the appropriate Snap mode from the Snap Type button.

3. Select the appropriate Grid type from the Grid Type button. For example, if you chose Grid for the Snap type, select from Bar, Beats, or Use Quantize.

4. If you chose the Use Quantize Grid Type, select an appropriate Quantize Type note value (or custom groove template) for your grid.

If in the Snap mode selector you choose Events, Shuffle, or Magnetic Cursor rather than Grid, the quantize value has no effect when you resize or move events.

Setting Quantize Parameters

Because the quantize setting influences how events are quantized, no matter which method you use, it's a good idea to start by setting up how you want Cubase to quantize these events before applying a method.

Set up quantize parameters:

1. Select Edit > Quantize Panel to open the Quantize Panel.

2. If you already have a preset saved, select it from the Presets drop-down menu. Otherwise, complete the following steps.

3. From the Quantize Grid drop-down menu, select a grid value. Which one you select depends on the content you want to quantize.

4. If you want to use tuplets, use the up or down arrow to the right of the Tuplet field to select the appropriate tuplet number. A *tuplet* is a beat subdivision that is greater than four, such as a quintuplet, in which five notes are played within a quarter note. Otherwise, leave this field displaying the Off selection.

5. If you want to create a swing or shuffle feel, select a value from the Swing Factor control. Higher percentages result in more pronounced swing or shuffle feels.

Monitoring Quantize Setup Changes Before Applying Them: Check the Auto Apply check box in the Quantize Panel to monitor changes you make before applying them. When you click Play, you will hear the effect of the quantize settings as you change them in the panel without committing to them.

6. Set the Non-Quantize Range value appropriately by using the up or down arrow. Remember that events within this range are not affected by the quantization.

7. Set the Randomize value appropriately by using the up or down arrow.

8. If you want to use the iterative quantize method, check the iQ box and then set the Iterative Strength value. The higher the value, the more its effect resembles that of the over-quantize method (and at 100% strength is identical).

9. Click the Quantize button to apply quantization.

Once you set quantization properties for an event, you can save those properties to a preset you can use for other events in this project. It's important to know that a song's feel is greatly influenced by its rhythmic definition, which is the result of rhythmic consistency between the instruments and throughout the project itself. Saving your own presets for quantize settings and reusing these presets throughout a project can help achieve this consistency.

Save a quantize setting to a preset:

1. From the Quantize Panel, configure the parameters as desired.

2. Click the Save Preset button.

3. To rename the new preset, Alt-click (PC)/Option-click (Mac) the name in the Select Preset bar, then enter a new name.

Remove a quantize setting from the preset list:

1. From the Quantize Panel's Select Preset drop-down menu, select the preset you want to remove.

2. Click the Select Preset button again and select Remove Preset.

Applying MIDI Quantization

You can apply a quantize setup to a MIDI event in a variety of ways. Here are a few to try out:

■ Apply a standard over-quantize method to already recorded events. Depending on which window is open when you click Apply, this method shifts the start position of selected events to the closest grid line set in the Project window or the current MIDI editor.

- Apply an automatic quantize value during the recording process. This records the note events exactly as you play them, but automatically adjusts their positions in the resultant MIDI part according to the quantize settings of your project. In other words, you can still unquantize events that were recorded with the Auto-Quantize (the AUTO Q button in the Transport panel) feature enabled.

- Apply a quantize value in real time—so that you can make adjustments in real time.

- Use the Quantize Panel, which gives you more control over the effect quantization has on your recorded MIDI note events. For example, using the different parameters available in this panel, you can adjust the strength of the quantization, the swing factor, and the magnetic area of the grid, as well as create a grid for more complex rhythmic values, such as quintuplets and septuplets.

- Apply the Quantizer, a MIDI plug-in, as a track's insert or send effect.

Apply an automatic quantize value during the MIDI recording process:

1. Choose the appropriate Grid Type and quantize preset.

2. Enable the Auto-Quantize (AUTO Q) button on the Transport panel.

3. Start the recording process.

Apply an automatic quantize value during the MIDI editing process:

1. Open the MIDI part you want to edit in the MIDI editor.

2. Open the Quantize Panel and choose the appropriate quantize settings.

3. Check the Auto Apply option in the Quantize Panel. Any changes you make in the Quantize Settings window from this point forward affect the events in the MIDI editor.

Apply a quantize method to selected MIDI events:

1. Choose the appropriate quantize preset from the toolbar.

2. Select the events or parts you want to quantize.

3. Select Edit > Quantize, or press the Q key on your computer keyboard.

Undo quantization on selected events:

1. Select the events or parts you want to unquantize.

2. Select Edit > Reset Quantize.

Creating MIDI Groove Quantize Presets

Cubase also enables you to create a customized quantize setting, which is extracted from the rhythmic content of previously recorded MIDI events. For example, you might record a drum part and get just the groove you are looking for. Because the rhythmic "groove" of the percussions and drum parts is usually something you would want to apply to other musical parts, you can convert the MIDI groove you played into a reusable groove template (called a *groove quantize map*) that can be applied to other MIDI parts.

Rhythmic and Velocity Information: A groove quantize map contains only the rhythmic and velocity information from the MIDI event.

Create a groove quantize map from MIDI events:

1.   In the Project window, select the MIDI part containing the groove you want to save.

2.   Select Edit > Advanced Quantize > Create Groove Quantize Preset.

When you create a groove quantize map, it will appear in the Select Preset drop-down menu of the Quantize Panel, as well as on the Quantize Presets control on the Project window toolbar. Once a groove quantize map is selected, the Quantize Panel will offer a different set of controls from those described previously in this chapter for ordinary quantization, as shown in Figure 26.2. The new controls include the following:

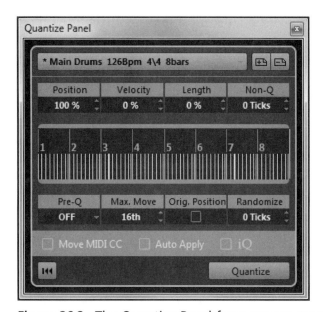

Figure 26.2 The Quantize Panel for a groove quantize map.

■ **Position.** Think of the position parameter as being like the iterative strength, where the position percentage represents the strength of the quantization from the groove's source. The difference between the normal iterative strength value and the position is that the latter influences the groove quantization applied *after* a possible pre-quantize setting.

■ **Velocity.** This indicates what percentage of the groove quantize map's velocity level is applied to the velocity of the selected events. With higher values, the resultant velocities are closer to the groove quantize map than to the original. With lower values, velocities are not changed as much, with no change if the value is set at zero.

■ **Length.** This indicates what percentage of the groove quantize map's length value is applied to the selected events' recorded length. With higher values, the resultant lengths are closer to the groove preset's length than to the original. With lower values, lengths are not changed as much, with no change if the value is set at zero.

■ **Prequantize (Pre-Q).** This quantizes events to a selected note value *before* applying the groove quantize map to increase the rhythmic accuracy of the events.

■ **Maximum Move.** This parameter determines the maximum distance a MIDI event will be allowed to move from its original recorded position, in ticks. (*Ticks* are the smallest time increments inside a Cubase project.)

■ **Original Position.** When this option is selected, the selected MIDI event reverts to its original position on the grid when quantizing.

Inside the MIDI editors, you apply a groove quantize map as you would apply any another quantize type—by selecting the desired events and then selecting that groove quantize map in the toolbar's quantize type field.

Quantizing Audio Events

Before you can quantize an audio event, you must first identify hitpoints within the event, and then "slice" the event into individual beats or sections of the beat. It is these slices that are quantized to the underlying grid.

Understanding Hitpoints

Hitpoints are special markers that can be added to an audio event to, among other things, create audio slices or create groove quantize maps. You can use slices to extract individual sounds from a loop, replace certain slices, or move them around to create new variations.

Hitpoints are created from attack transients that are associated with beats in a rhythmic part, identifying them with special markers. Later, you can use hitpoint markers to slice up the event into separate beats, replacing a single audio event with a series of audio slices in an audio part.

Creating Hitpoints

Hitpoints are used primarily with drum loops. The goal with hitpoints is to separate each beat of the audio event into its own slice; you can then use Cubase's other tools to change the tempo of the event by manipulating the individual slices.

That said, to get the best results, you will often need to fine-tune the marker's location and make sure that your audio content is appropriate for hitpoints. For example, audio with well-defined drum beats works better than material with long, sustained notes. Also, drum beats that have a lot of effects, such as reverb or delay, are harder to slice accurately.

All the following operations assume you have already loaded the event into the Sample Editor.

Create hitpoints and slices:

1. Monitor the sample a few times to count how many bars and beats it has. This will help you later.

2. Enter the sample's time signature in the Sample Editor's Signature field (see Figure 26.3) using the small arrows on each side of the field. Many contemporary drum loop samples in dance-oriented styles use a 4/4 time signature.

3. Adjust the Bars and Beats fields to the corresponding values. For example, if your loop has eight beats, enter two bars (assuming the loop is in 4/4 time). Cubase calculates the audio tempo for the sample automatically.

4. Open the Hitpoints tab in the Sample Editor Inspector, shown in Figure 26.4.

5. Adjust the Threshold slider to the right to add more hitpoints, or to the left to remove unwanted hitpoints. (This control filters "hits" based on how loud they are; the assumption is that the louder the note, the more likely it is to be a major hitpoint.)

6. Click the Beats control and select which hitpoints you want to use—all, 1/4 notes, 1/8 notes, and so on.

7. Click the Create Slices button.

Figure 26.3 Entering the sample's time signature.

Figure 26.4 The Hitpoints tab in the Sample Editor Inspector.

Cubase now creates slices based on the detected hitpoints and closes the Sample Editor window.

Other Hitpoint Functions

Additional hitpoint functions are located within the Hitpoints tab in the Sample Editor Inspector.

- **Edit Hitpoints** enables you to add, move, or delete hitpoints.

- **Remove All** removes all hitpoints from the selected event.

- **Create Slices** creates slices between hitpoints, as just discussed.

- **Create Groove** uses the timing provided by the current hitpoints to create a groove quantize map called Groove. You could create a groove based on the drum loop's timing and apply the same feel to the MIDI bass line, for example.

- **Create Markers** lets you convert existing hitpoints into markers in a project.

- **Create Regions** creates regions within your event, based on hitpoints calculated. This is a good way to isolate recorded sounds for further editing.

- **Create Warp Tabs.** Use this option to create warp tabs that can be time stretched. (We'll discuss this in a moment.)

- **Create MIDI Notes** lets you replace existing recorded notes with MIDI notes, in order to change sounds in a drum track. Learn more in Chapter 31, "Working with Beats and Loops."

Manually edit hitpoints:

1. In the Sample Editor, zoom into the area where you want to add a hitpoint.

2. Open the Hitpoints tab in the Sample Editor Inspector.

3. Click the Edit Hitpoints button in the Inspector.

4. To add a new hitpoint, hold the Alt (PC)/Option (Mac) key and click where you want the new hitpoint to appear. The cursor will become a pencil, and a new hitpoint will appear at the location where you click.

5. To move a hitpoint, drag the hitpoint's marker handle to a new position.

6. To remove a hitpoint, hold the Alt (PC)/Option (Mac) key and click on any existing hitpoint marker handle.

Applying Quantization

There are two primary approaches to quantizing an audio event. First, you can manually create hitpoints and slices, and then apply quantization to those slices. Or you can use AudioWarp technology to time stretch slices to the quantization grid.

Of these two approaches, the AudioWarp approach often produces the best results. When you quantize slices created with hitpoints, you sometimes end up with unwanted space (silence) between the slices. By time-stretching the slices instead, the drum track sounds more complete, not like it was artificially edited.

Quantize with hitpoints:

1. Within the Sample Editor, create hitpoints for the event, as discussed previously.

2. Select Edit > Quantize Panel from the Project window.

3. Select a quantize preset, or configure the quantization parameters as desired.

4. Click the Quantize button.

Quantize with AudioWarp:

1. Within the Project window, select the audio event to quantize.

2. Click the Quantize Presets button on the toolbar and select a preset.

3. For a "looser" quantization, click the iQ (iterative quantization) button on the toolbar.

4. Select Edit > Advanced Quantize > AudioWarp Quantize.

Cubase automatically detects hitpoints for the selected event and creates warp tabs at each hitpoint. The warp tabs are then snapped to the selected quantization grid, stretching the audio slices as necessary.

Applying Quantization to Multiple Audio Tracks

New to Cubase 6 is the ability to quantize multiple audio tracks simultaneously. This is nice if you want to "fix" an entire set of tracks for a live-recorded drum part—if you have separate tracks for bass drum, snare drum, and hi hat, let's say. With multitrack quantization, the individual slices on all selected tracks are grouped and moved at once. (Cubase even creates crossfades and fills in any gaps between slices to ensure seamless transitions without unwanted silence.)

Quantize multiple audio tracks:

1. In the Project window, select the tracks you want to quantize.

2. Select Project > Track Folding > Move Selected Tracks to New Folder. This places the tracks inside a single folder track.

3. Select the folder track.

4. In the Inspector for the folder track, as shown in Figure 26.5, click "on" the Group Editing (=) button. This applies edits made on one track to all tracks in the folder.

Figure 26.5 Enabling group editing for the folder track.

5. Double-click one of audio tracks in the folder to open the Sample Editor.

6. Click the Edit Hitpoints button in the Hitpoints tab of the Inspector, or select Audio > Hitpoints > Calculate Hitpoints to calculate the hitpoints in this event.

7.   Select Edit > Quantize Panel to open the Quantize Panel.

8.   In the Slice Rules section of the Quantize Panel, shown in Figure 26.6, all tracks with hitpoints are listed. For each track, click and drag the "stars" control to assign a priority for that track. The track with the highest priority (highest number of stars) will define where the audio is sliced.

Figure 26.6 The Slice Rules section of the Quantize panel.

9.   Set the Range parameter to determine the minimum distance between two hitpoints on different tracks. Hitpoints within this range are considered as marking the same beat.

10. Set the Offset parameter to determine how far before the hitpoint position an event is sliced.

11. Click the Slice button to slice the events.

12. Set the quantization parameters as desired.

13. Click the Quantize button to apply quantization.

14. In the Crossfades section at the bottom of the Quantize Panel, shown in Figure 26.7, click the Crossfade button to apply crossfades between any overlapping slides.

Figure 26.7 The Crossfades section of the Quantize Panel.

15. If necessary, click the Nudge Left or Nudge Right button to move the crossfade area to the left or right. This may be necessary if the crossfades cut note attacks.

27 Adding MIDI Track Effects

MIDI track effects allow you to transform MIDI events in a track in real time without changing how the events were originally recorded. In other words, a MIDI effect processes the track's events on their way out to the MIDI output port. It's the same way a funhouse mirror transforms your reflection. You do not actually have a big head, small neck, big belly, and small legs—that's just the way your image is processed. MIDI track effects work the same way, leaving the original MIDI image intact while reflecting the processing choices you've applied.

This chapter discusses MIDI effects applied via the MIDI Inserts and MIDI Sends sections of the Inspector area. Because MIDI track effects don't affect the source MIDI events in the track, these modifications do not appear in the MIDI editors—although they do affect all the parts on a track.

Here's a summary of what you will learn in this chapter:

- The role of MIDI effects

- Getting to know Cubase 6's MIDI effects

- How to add or edit MIDI inserts in a MIDI or instrument track

- How to bypass one or several MIDI inserts or MIDI sends

- How to assign a MIDI plug-in effect as the destination for a MIDI send

Cubase 6's MIDI Effects

You may already know about audio effects and how you can use them to make audio tracks sound better or different. In this respect, MIDI effects are similar to audio effects. However, the process is quite different with MIDI than it is for audio.

When you apply a MIDI effect to a MIDI track, you are not processing the sound generated by the MIDI device (a VST instrument or hardware sound module, for instance). Instead, you are using a process that operates in real time as it transforms or adds to the MIDI events recorded on your track (or passing through it from its input) in real time. Because these effects are playing in real time, just like audio effects, you can rest assured that the recorded MIDI events on your track are not modified in any way except at the insert point or send destination where the MIDI effect actually does its processing.

By the way, if you are using an instrument track, as opposed to a straight MIDI track, you can combine both types of effects—audio and MIDI. This gives you even more flexibility in your creative process.

A MIDI effect can be applied to any MIDI track in two ways: through MIDI inserts and MIDI sends. On the other hand, instrument tracks playing through a VSTi plug-in or an external MIDI device can also be processed using MIDI inserts, but not MIDI sends. Both MIDI inserts and MIDI sends transform the MIDI events in real time according to the settings found in the MIDI effect.

Cubase 6 includes a number of plug-in effects for MIDI recording. In addition, plug-ins can be purchased from a variety of third-party manufacturers. For now, however, I'll focus on those plug-ins that come in the Cubase 6 box, detailed in Table 27.1.

MIDI Inserts

The most common way to add a MIDI plug-in effect to a MIDI or instrument track is through the MIDI Inserts section of the Inspector, shown in Figure 27.1. When you are using a MIDI plug-in effect as an insert, you are sending the track's MIDI events through this effect. This effect then generates the necessary MIDI events through the MIDI output port of the track containing the effect. It is the destination VSTi or external sound module's job to actually play the resulting MIDI effect, along with the original recorded MIDI material in this track.

You can have up to four MIDI insert effects on each MIDI track. When a MIDI insert effect is selected from the drop-down menu in each of the track's insert slots, a control panel opens to reveal its settings. You can re-open the insert's control panel at any time by clicking on the Open Insert Effect Editor button above the appropriate insert.

Here are some of the things you can do with MIDI inserts:

■ **Add a MIDI insert effect.** Select a MIDI effect from the drop-down menu in one of the four insert slots.

■ **Edit a MIDI insert effect's parameters.** Click the Open Insert Effect Editor button to display the plug-in's control panel.

■ **Bypass an individual MIDI insert.** Deactivate the plug-in effect you want to bypass by clicking "off" the Activate Insert button. By default, an effect is activated as soon as you select it from the drop-down menu. By deactivating it, you can do a comparison without having to reset your effect each time.

■ **Bypass all MIDI inserts from playback.** Click the Bypass Inserts button at the top of the MIDI Inserts section. The MIDI Inserts section's top-right corner will turn yellow, indicating that the effects are bypassed. Because you can always see the top part of the MIDI Inserts section, you can easily change the status (active or bypassed) of your inserts by using this bar.

Table 27.1 Cubase 6 MIDI Plug-In Effects

Plug-In	Description
Arpache 5	An automatic arpegiattor; when a chord is input, it plays each note of the chord separately.
Arpache SX	An automatic arpegiattor, similar to Arpache 5 but with more advanced functionality.
Auto LFO	Enables you to send continuously changing MIDI controller messages; typically used for automatic MIDI panning.
Beat Designer	MIDI pattern sequencer, used for creating drum parts or patterns.
Chorder	Enables you to assign complete chords to single keys on your MIDI keyboard.
Compressor	A classic dynamic compressor for MIDI data.
Context Gate	Enables selective triggering/filtering of MIDI data, based on selected notes, velocities, and other parameters.
Density	Randomly filters out or adds new notes to the MIDI track.
Micro Tuner	Enables the creation of different microtuning schemes for the selected MIDI instrument.
MIDI Control	Enables you to control up to eight different MIDI controller types on a MIDI instrument.
MIDI Echo	Generates additional echoing notes.
MIDI Modifiers	A duplicate of the MIDI Modifiers section in the Inspector; also includes a scale transposition function.
MIDI Monitor	Used to monitor incoming MIDI events.
Note to CC	Generates a MIDI continuous controller event for each incoming MIDI note.
Quantizer	Changes the timing of MIDI notes by snapping them to a quantize grid.
StepDesigner	Advanced MIDI pattern synthesizer.
Track Control	Provides three ready-made control panels for adjusting parameters on Roland GS– and Yamaha XG–compatible MIDI devices.
Transformer	A real-time version of Cubase's Logical Editor.

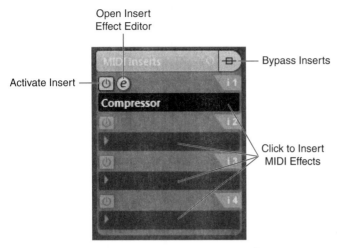

Figure 27.1 The MIDI Inserts section in the Inspector.

MIDI Sends

When you assign a MIDI plug-in effect to an insert slot, it affects the events sent to the MIDI output port of this track, as shown in Figure 27.2. If, instead, you want to use one device to play the original content and another to play the processed information, you can use a MIDI send.

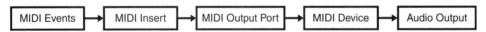

Figure 27.2 The signal path of a MIDI track insert.

One of the big differences between MIDI inserts and MIDI sends is that MIDI sends allow you to route the processed MIDI events generated by the MIDI effect to a second MIDI destination. (For example, you could use a MIDI send to create an echo of a piano track to play back through a guitar sound.) In this fashion, MIDI track sends offer an additional setting for MIDI output ports and MIDI channels.

As you can see in Figure 27.3, the signal from a MIDI send can be routed to two different outputs. If you don't need the effect to play through a different MIDI port and channel, apply the effect as a MIDI insert. However, if you want your effect to play through some other port and channel, or you want to send the MIDI events before or after the volume control setting of the MIDI track, use MIDI sends instead of inserts.

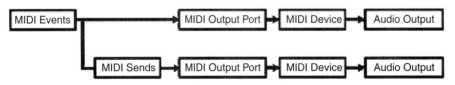

Figure 27.3 The signal path of a MIDI track send.

The MIDI Sends section is not displayed in the Inspector by default. To make this section visible, you need to right-click (PC)/Control-click (Mac) on the track name in the Inspector and check MIDI Sends from the context menu.

Once displayed, you can see that the options for the MIDI sends (shown in Figure 27.4) are similar to the ones in the MIDI Inserts section. In addition to the options explained earlier, below the Select Effect Type field, you will find the MIDI Send Destination selector; this lets you choose the appropriate MIDI port that will be destination for MIDI events generated by the MIDI effect, along with a MIDI channel setting. Finally, the Pre-/Post toggle button lets you choose whether the MIDI events sent to the MIDI send output include the parameters found in the MIDI Modifiers section (the default Post- setting) or exclude them (Pre- setting).

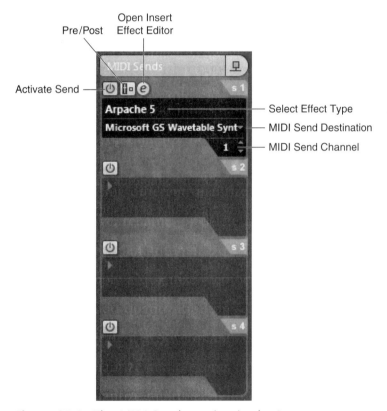

Figure 27.4 The MIDI Sends section in the Inspector.

Assign a MIDI plug-in effect to a MIDI send:

1. Unfold the MIDI Sends section for the selected MIDI track.

2. From the Select Effect Type drop-down menu, choose an appropriate effect.

3. In the MIDI Send Destination field below the MIDI Effect Type field, choose an appropriate destination for the output of the MIDI effect. This affects where the MIDI events generated by the effect will be sent.

4. In the MIDI Send Channel field, select an appropriate MIDI channel for playback.

5. Click the Pre/Post button to send MIDI signals to the send effect before (Pre) or after (Post) MIDI modifiers and insert effects have been applied.

Arranging

28 Arranging in the Project Window

Editing the data inside audio and MIDI events is one thing, but organizing events inside a project's timeline or tracks offers perhaps the most flexible way for a producer to build (and rebuild) entire projects. Creating different mixes, versions, and styles is only possible if the events can be edited in time as easily as building with blocks in a LEGO set. For example, you can split events and parts to move content around, or have an event repeat 16 times to fill an entire track—both options are discussed in this chapter.

You can find editing options inside the Project window in three places—in the Edit menu, through the Project window's context menu in the Edit submenu, and finally, through the editing tools found in the Project window's toolbar. All three locations include the basic Cut, Copy, and Paste commands, in addition to other options specifically designed to give you more control over project editing tasks.

Here's a summary of what you will learn in this chapter:

- How to use the cursor location to split selected events
- How to split events to create moveable blocks of music
- How to move and copy blocks of content defined by a locator range
- How to crop content inside a project
- How to insert additional empty time in a project
- How to use different Cubase-specific Cut, Copy, and Paste functions
- How to resize objects and understand sizing options
- How to shift content inside events or parts
- How to mute objects
- How to lock objects in the timeline
- Revisiting the edit history

Splitting Events

Sometimes you record an audio event that needs editing or even deletion during just part of the event. In this instance, you can split the single large event into several smaller events, and then edit just those parts that need it.

When you want to divide events in this fashion, you have several options at your disposal. The simplest and most common approach is to use the Split (scissors) tool to split an event in two. The exact position of the split is determined by the snap's Grid settings if they are active, or by the location of your click. The result is that you get two events instead of one, as shown in Figure 28.1; the split parts do not have to be of equal duration.

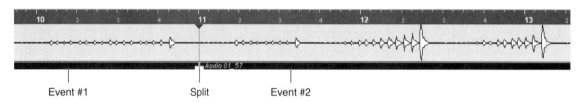

Figure 28.1   An event split into two events.

Split at Cursor

Sometimes it's easier to use the project's cursor position to determine where the split occurs, such as when you need to split all the events across all tracks in a project.

Split selected objects at the cursor's location:

1.   Position the cursor at the desired location.

2.   Select all the objects crossing the cursor at this location that you want to split. All non-selected objects will not be affected.

3.   Select Edit > Functions > Split at Cursor.

Alternatively, you can select the Split tool from the Project window toolbar, as shown in Figure 28.2, then click at the desired split point in the event you want to split.

Figure 28.2   Use the Split tool to split an event.

Split Loop

When you want to create a loop with the objects (parts or events) between two locators, use the locators' positions to determine where the split will occur. After these objects are split, you can select only the objects that occur in this range and copy them elsewhere.

Split objects at the locators' positions using Split Loop:

1.   Position the left and right locators at the desired positions.

2.   Select the objects you want to split.

3.   Select Edit > Functions > Split Loop. Selected objects crossing the left or right locators are now split.

Split Range

You can achieve an effect similar to the Split Loop option by using the Edit > Range > Split command. In this case, however, all the objects within the selected range are split at the start and end positions of the selected range, instead of the range between the locators.

Split a range of selected objects:

1.   Select the Range Selection tool in the Project window toolbar.

2.   Click in the upper-left corner where you want your range to begin and drag over the range and tracks you want to include in this range.

3.   Select Edit > Range > Split.

Range Crop

Another quick way to split objects is to use the Edit > Range > Crop command. Select the objects and range you want to keep, and all the rest will be removed. This technique offers a quick way to build game scene soundtracks, where you build a score around prerecorded elements common to the entire game, but rearrange and crop only the content you want to keep for the current scene.

Set the Range Crop command to a desired range:

1.   Select the Range Selection tool from the Project window's toolbar.

2.   Click in the upper-left corner where you want your range to begin and drag over the range and the tracks you want to include in it.

3.   Select Edit > Range > Crop.

Inserting Silence

The Edit > Range > Insert Silence command performs various tasks, depending on the tool used to make the selection prior to launching this command.

For example, when you select a range using the Range Selection tool, all objects within the selected range are moved to the end point of the range when the silence is inserted, as shown in Figure 28.3. This technique is useful when you want to insert time in the middle of recorded events, but you don't want to apply the change to all tracks.

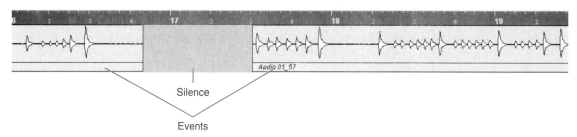

Silence

Events

Figure 28.3 Silence inserted into a selected range.

On the other hand, to insert silence or add time at any point in the project over *all* tracks, use the Object Selection tool, then set the locators' positions appropriately, and then use the Insert Silence command. All events are split at the left locator position and moved after the right locator position, which inserts silence in the range between both locators.

Conversely, if you want to remove the time, including events recorded within this range, use the Edit > Range > Delete Time command. This deletes events within the selected range and moves all events following the range to the start point of the range.

Pasting Functions

Using the Range Selection tool or a combination of the Object Selection tool and the locators, you can copy the content found inside a designated range and paste it back into the project using four different pasting commands: Paste, Paste at Origin, Paste Time, and Paste Time at Origin.

In Figure 28.4, the top track displays a highlighted selection made with the Range Selection tool. This selection was then copied to clipboard using the Edit > Copy command. With the project cursor position always at bar 4, here's what happens depending on the Paste function used:

- Using **Edit > Paste,** the clipboard content gets pasted after the cursor position without moving the content that follows farther along the timeline.

- Using **Edit > Functions > Paste at Origin,** the clipboard content gets pasted at the same place in time. Use Paste at Origin to copy or move content from one track to

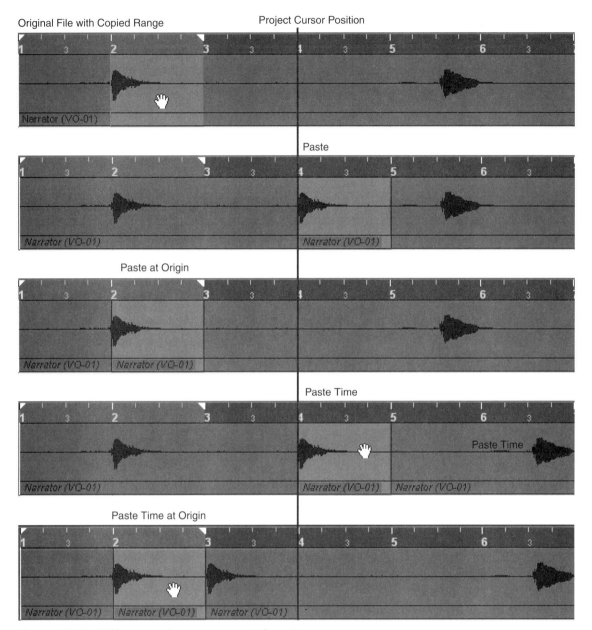

Figure 28.4 Differences between paste functions.

another without changing its position in the timeline. Content following the newly pasted clipboard content does not move either.

- Using **Edit > Range > Paste Time**, the clipboard content gets pasted after the cursor position, moving the content that follows farther along the timeline.

- Using **Edit > Range > Paste Time at Origin**, the clipboard content gets pasted at the same place in time, pushing the content that follows the newly pasted clipboard content farther along the timeline.

Copying Events

Cubase offers the standard copy/paste combination when you need to copy certain selected events from one location to another. Once again, content can be selected with the Range or Object Selection tool. For more specific copying applications, Cubase offers a variety of functions tailored to music production.

Duplicate Command

Select Edit > Functions > Duplicate to make a single copy of selected events or parts. The start time of duplicated events occurs immediately following the end time of the selected object(s) being duplicated.

Figure 28.5 displays different results from a Duplicate action:

- In the top row, a single event is selected with the Object Selection tool and duplicated. As a result, the duplicated event begins immediately after the previous one ends. If you're working with loops, it makes sense to adjust the length of events with the Snap's Grid mode enabled. By doing so, you can avoid creating duplicate copies that aren't aligned with the tempo grid if the event happens to be slightly longer than the grid size.

- In the middle row, two events are selected with the Object Selection tool and duplicated. As a result, the duplicated events begin where the entire selection ends.

- In the bottom row, the Range Selection tool was used to highlight a range that overlaps multiple events, and the range was duplicated. The duplicated range begins where the previously highlighted range ends.

Duplicate objects using the Object Selection or Range Selection tool:

1. Select the appropriate tool (Object Selection or Range Selection).

2. Select the objects or range you want to duplicate.

3. Select Edit > Functions > Duplicate, or press Ctrl+D (PC)/⌘+D (Mac).

Repeat Command

To make more than one duplicate of a range or object selection, consider using the Edit > Functions > Repeat command. This is a great way to repeat looped material several times instead of copying it over and over again. When repeating entire objects, you can share the copies, so when you edit one of the events, all shared repeated copies are automatically updated to reflect those edits. If you want to edit only one copy of the repeated material without affecting the others, either create real copies in the first place,

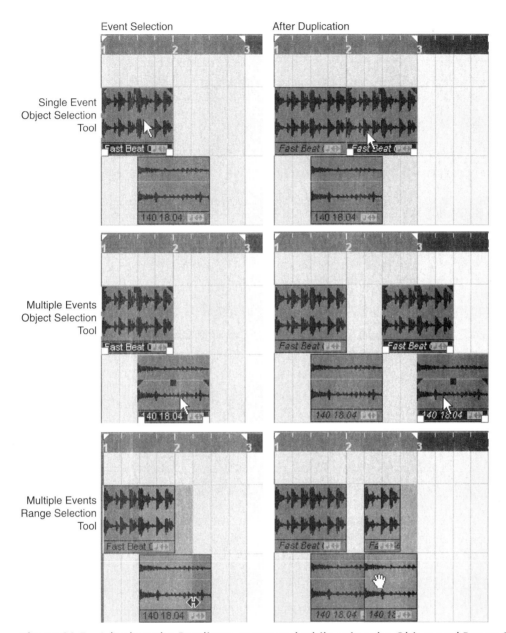

Figure 28.5 A look at the Duplicate command while using the Object and Range Selection tools.

or select the shared copy you want to edit and transform it into a real copy using the Edit > Functions > Convert to Real Copy option.

Cubase asks how many copies you want to make of the selected objects or range. If you are repeating objects, you will also be asked whether you want to create shared or real copies. The Repeat option follows the same behavior as described for the Duplicate option. Also, Cubase always assumes you want to create real copies when you use the Range Selection tool to repeat content.

Shared Copies: With a shared copy, any editing you perform on one instance of the selection will also apply to all other shared copies. In contrast, real copies are distinct entities; editing one real copy does not affect other copies.

When using the Repeat function, you also will notice that the positions of the left and right locators have no effect on the placement of the repeated material. On the other hand, the Grid mode settings for the Snap function play a role in where your repeated objects appear if you have selected objects that do not start or end exactly on grid increments (for example, bars and beats).

Repeat selected objects or ranges over time:

1. Select the appropriate tool (Object Selection or Range Selection).

2. Select the objects or range you want to repeat.

3. Select Edit > Functions > Repeat, or press Ctrl+K (PC)/⌘+K (Mac).

4. When prompted, enter the number of times you want this selection to be repeated.

5. If you have selected objects rather than a range, check the Shared Copies option if you want to do so.

6. Click OK.

Fill Loop Function

Another variation on copying events is offered through the Fill Loop function, which allows you to specify a cycle region between the left and right locators in which events will be repeated. If the last repetition of these events doesn't fit completely inside this area, it will be trimmed to fit within the range defined by the locators.

As with the Duplicate and Repeat commands, you also can use the Range Selection tool to highlight the range that will be used to fill a loop section. This is a great way to create a section structure inside a project in which all selected objects are repeated until they arrive at the right locator position.

Fill an area with selected objects using the Fill Loop option:

1. Select the appropriate tool (Object Selection or Range Selection).

2. Position your left and right locators at the positions where you want the looped repetitions of the current selection to begin and end.

3. Select the objects or range you want to use in the fill.

4. Select Edit > Functions > Fill Loop.

Alternate Fill Option: You also can copy looping content in the Project window by using the Object Selection tool to drag the lower-right handle of a part while holding down the Alt (PC)/Option (Mac) key. Each resulting copy snaps to the end of the previous event or part.

Resizing Objects

Sizing or resizing an object makes it possible to adjust the start and end times of the object without affecting the media file itself. Think of sizing an object as a way to define which portion of the object plays in the project.

Different objects have different sizing restrictions. For example, you can resize an audio event, but not beyond the boundaries of that event's source audio file. The same restriction goes for audio regions: You can expand the event containing the audio region in the Project window beyond the region's boundaries, but not beyond the original clip's boundaries. In terms of MIDI parts or events, you have no such restrictions, because a MIDI part does not actually refer to any content; it only acts as a container for content.

That said, you might want these objects to react differently to the sizing you apply. The Object Selection tool has three resizing modes: Normal Sizing, Sizing Moves Contents, and Sizing Applies Time Stretch. You select a mode by clicking the Object Selection button then clicking the down arrow beneath the button, and then choosing a mode from the resulting context menu.

Normal Sizing

Normally, when you change an event's length by moving its start or end point, the content within the event stays in place and only the start or end point moves, as illustrated in Figure 28.6. Moving the end of the MIDI part in this case (middle segment) moves the end point back in time, whereas moving the start point later in time causes the events occurring before the new start point to be ignored during playback. But the events that were playing during bar 3 in the original version are still playing at bar 3 in the resized version.

Resize objects (events or parts):

1. In the Project window's toolbar, select the Normal Sizing mode of the Object Selection (arrow) tool (a.k.a. the Normal Sizing tool).

2. Select an object to view its resizing handles.

3. Drag the handles in the desired direction.

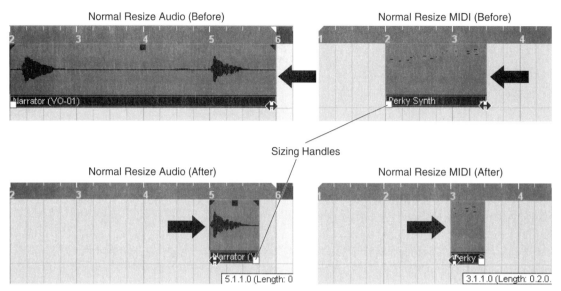

Figure 28.6 Normal sizing audio (left) and MIDI (right).

Sizing Moves Contents Mode

In other instances, you also might want to move the content inside of the object (event or part) when resizing it. This works differently with audio than it does with MIDI events, as you can see in Figure 28.7.

The left example in Figure 28.7 is the audio event; the right example is a MIDI part. In both instances, the top row displays the original content. For the audio event, the start handle is moved forward in time (bottom row), moving the content forward as well, whereas the end point remains unchanged. For the MIDI part, the end handle is also moved forward, unwrapping the MIDI events recorded earlier in time. This is done when the Sizing Moves Contents mode is selected from the Object Selection tool's pop-up menu.

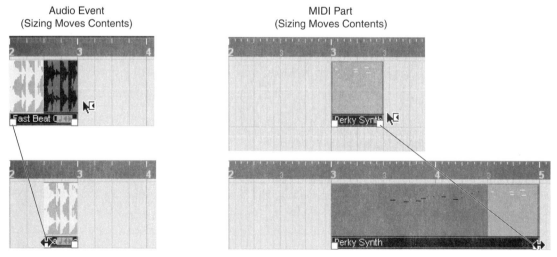

Figure 28.7 Resizing an event using the Sizing Moves Contents mode of the Object Selection tool.

Resize objects while moving their contents:

1. In the Project window's toolbar, select the Sizing Moves Contents mode from the Object Selection tool's pop-up menu.

2. Select an object to view its resizing handles.

3. Drag the handles in the desired direction.

Sizing Applies Time Stretch Mode

The final resizing mode available in the Object Selection tool's pop-up menu enables you to time-stretch objects so that the duration of the events inside is adjusted to fit the new object's size. This stretching can be applied to both audio and MIDI events.

Figure 28.8 displays both types of events being stretched. In the top portion, MIDI events' note length values are adjusted to fit within the new proportion. Note, however, that stretching MIDI events in this fashion can throw off the quantization of your project. That is, if you stretch in a proportion that changes the quantizing of events, you might have to do a bit of editing inside the MIDI editor to get the MIDI events to work with the quantize grid. For best results, try stretching in a proportion that is suitable to the time subdivision currently used in your project.

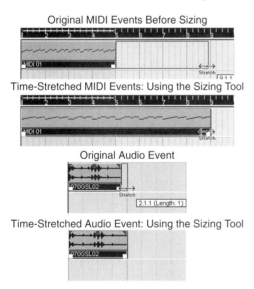

Figure 28.8 Resizing an event using the Sizing Applies Time Stretch mode of the Object Selection tool.

Using this option on audio is a great way to make a drum loop, for example, fit inside a specific number of bars—especially when the tempo difference is minimal. If you look at the audio example in Figure 28.8, you can see that the original content is less than one bar long. Stretching it allows you to loop it an even number of times using the Fill Loop or Repeat options described earlier in this chapter. You can select the algorithm and quality applied to audio through the File menu (PC)/Cubase application menu (Mac) > Preferences > Editing > Audio > Time Stretch Tool Algorithm field. The option you select in this dialog box is applied to all audio events that are stretched using this tool, and the best algorithm for a specific task will depend on the nature of the source material.

Stretch the content of an object while resizing it:

1. In the Project window's toolbar, select the Sizing Applies Time Stretch mode from the Object Selection tool's pop-up menu.

2. Select an object to view its resizing handles.

3. Drag the handles in the desired direction.

You should know that applying a large proportion of time-stretching on an audio file will probably create some major artifacts in the resultant sound. For natural-sounding results, avoid using time-stretching in a proportion greater or less than 25 percent of the original content's length. For MIDI events, there are no such time-stretching limitations. The positions and durations of MIDI events are simply recalculated and re-quantized.

Shifting Events Inside an Object

Adjusting the timing of two takes can sometimes be daunting, and moving the start and end points of an event is not always the best way to go. That's when shifting events inside an object without moving the object's boundaries comes in handy.

Shifting the content inside the event is done by offsetting the position of the audio clip inside the object's start and end points. You also can shift MIDI events inside a MIDI part. In both cases, there is only one condition that applies: The object in which the events are found has to be smaller than the events themselves. For example, if you have MIDI events at bar 1, beat 1 and bar 3, beat 4 within a MIDI part that spans from bar 1 to bar 4, you cannot shift these events inside because the container covers the same area as the events inside the container.

Shift events inside an object:

1. In the Project window's toolbar, select the Object Selection tool.

2. Select the object you want to shift.

3. Hold down the Ctrl+Alt (PC)/⌘+Option (Mac) keys as you click and drag the content within this event or MIDI part to the left or right.

You can use this technique creatively by shifting a drum loop, for example, trying out different beat combinations when playing a shifted event along with other events in the same timeline.

Muting Objects

When trying out ideas inside the Project window, you might want to silence a track by using the Mute button found in the Inspector and Track List area. However, if you only want to mute one or more events within a track, select those events and then select Edit > Mute. The default key command to mute events is Shift+M. After an object is muted, you can unmute it using the Shift+U key command or by selecting Edit > Unmute.

Locking Events

If you've worked hard at positioning events in the timeline, you can lock them in place to prevent time-consuming mistakes. When an object is locked, a tiny lock icon appears in the bottom-right corner of the object next to the end point handle. You lock selected events by selecting Edit > Lock [Ctrl+Shift+L (PC)/⌘+Shift+L (Mac)]. After objects are locked, you cannot move or edit them from the Project window. To unlock objects, select Edit > Unlock or press Ctrl+Shift+U (PC)/⌘+Shift+U (Mac).

Undoing Steps Using the Edit History

When you apply a transformation, such as deleting an object, moving, and so on, each action is saved in a list, which enables you to undo an unlimited number of actions. Although you can undo the last step you made by using the Edit > Undo command, if you want to undo more steps—or steps farther back in the list—you must use the Edit History dialog box. You open this dialog box, shown in Figure 28.9, by selecting Edit > History.

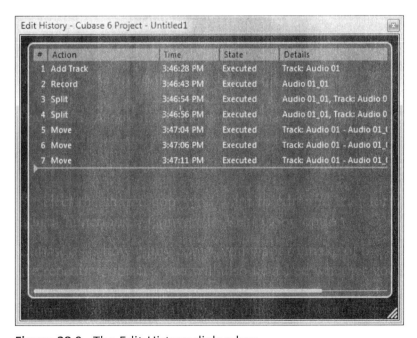

Figure 28.9 The Edit History dialog box.

The Edit History dialog box displays actions on the left and the details about each action on the right. The first actions appear at the top of the list, and the latest ones at the bottom.

The list is separated by a horizontal orange line. Clicking on this line and dragging it creates a selection. All the actions that are included in this selection will be undone. This means that you can undo from the last edit to the first one, unlike in the Offline Process History panel, in which you can edit any single action within the list.

Current Session Only: When you save and close your project, the Edit History dialog box is reset and is not available until you start editing again. That is, it holds only the history of edits you've made during your current editing session.

---

29 Using the Arranger Track

When working on a project, you might find yourself reorganizing the order in which sections of a song play so you can create variations, or simply to find which arrangement works best. To more easily facilitate this type of on-the-fly reorganization, Cubase 6 lets you divide your project into sections and then play these sections in any order you want. You can opt to play section B before section A, or repeat section C five times, or skip section D entirely. It's like working with LEGO blocks; you can construct your recording, start to finish, in whatever order you like.

In Cubase 5 and 6, this is called the Arranger function. (In previous versions of Cubase, it was called the Play Order function; little has changed since, save for the name.) To create this sort of arrangement, you first insert an Arranger track into your project. Within this track you create Arranger events that can then be organized in a type of playlist, called an Arranger *chain*. You can organize the events in a chain however you want—and you can create multiple Arranger chains from your original project.

Here's a summary of what you will learn in this chapter:

- How to enable the Arranger mode

- How to create and manage Arranger events

- How to populate an Arranger chain

- How to manage Arranger events inside an Arranger chain

- How to navigate an Arranger project

- How to convert an Arranger project into a linear project

Creating an Arranger Project

An Arranger project is not different from a normal Cubase project; in fact, it's a normal Cubase project with an Arranger track added. But just as you would save a copy of a normal project and use an alternate version to create musical notation, for example, it makes sense to work on a copy of an existing project to create an alternate version of its arrangement. Furthermore, when you want to create several versions (arrangements) of the same project, it's always easier when you can start fresh with the original project. So save your current project using the File > Save As command, and give the saved version a new name.

Save Project to New Folder: When saving your project, it is not necessary to use the File > Save Project to New Folder option; that's because different arrangements can share the same media files. You can use the Save Project to New Folder option when you are satisfied with the current play order arrangement and you are ready to flatten the play order.

Creating an Arranger Track

Once you've saved the project under a different name, you are ready to start working with the Arranger features. The first step in this process is to create an Arranger track. You will create events on this track that correspond to sections of your recording—one event for the first verse, one for the chorus, another for the second verse, and so forth. You can then rearrange the order of these events to rearrange the parts of your song.

To create an Arranger track, select Project > Add Track > Arranger. You can have only one Arranger track per project.

Loop-Based Recording: The Arranger feature is particularly useful for loop-based recordings. Learn more in Chapter 31, "Working with Beats and Loops."

Working with Arranger Controls

Once you've created this track, you next need to make the Arranger controls visible in the Transport panel.

Make the Play Order controls visible:

■ **In the Transport panel:** Right-click (PC)/Control-click (Mac) in the Transport panel and enable (check) the Arranger option in the context menu.

■ **In the Project window toolbar:** Right-click (PC)/Control-click (Mac) in the Project window's toolbar and enable (check) the Arranger Controls option in the context menu.

Displaying the Arranger controls, as illustrated in Figure 29.1, reveals a number of navigational controls specific to the Arranger track. These controls are also present in the Track List area for the Arranger track. Here's a quick overview of what each of these controls does:

- The **Activate Arranger Mode** button switches Cubase's playback mode from Linear (reads from left to right) to Arranger mode (beginning of playlist to end of playlist).

- The **Current Chain** field displays the current Arranger chain. Click the down arrow to select other chains to play.

- The **Previous Chain Step** button lets you move to the previous Arranger event in the chain.

- The **Next Chain Step** button lets you move to the next Arranger event in the chain.

- The **First Repeat of Current Chain Step** button moves the play cursor to the first occurrence of the Arranger event in the chain.

- The **Last Repeat of Current Chain Step** button moves the play cursor to the last occurrence of the Arranger event in the chain.

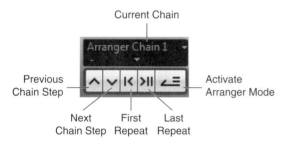

Figure 29.1 The Arranger controls.

For any of these controls to work, the Activate Arranger Mode button needs to be activated (it appears as orange when it is active). And before you can move any Arranger events around, you must first define the events—and add them to a chain.

Creating Arranger Events

A new arrangement created via the Arranger track is called an Arranger chain. Each chain is comprised of multiple steps or events, each step representing a part of the song you've recorded. These events reside in the Arranger track, as shown in Figure 29.2.

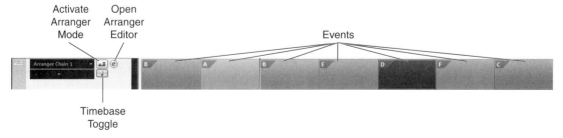

Figure 29.2 Events in the Arranger track.

Create an Arranger event:

1. In the Project window, enable the Snap mode and set the Snap and Grid types as desired. For example, if you don't plan to create Arranger events smaller than bars, set the Snap type to Grid and the Grid type to Bar.

2a. Inside the Arranger track, use the Draw (pencil) tool to click and drag over those measures that represent the section of the song associated with this event. Note that you click and drag *in the Arranger track*, not in any other tracks in the project. This creates a new event in the region you selected.

   OR

2b. Position the left and right locators at the desired start and end positions in the timeline, and then use the Object Selection (arrow) tool to double-click inside the Arranger track. This creates a new Arranger event inside this range.

Exact Measures: By default, Arranger events are created in exact measure lengths. To create an Arranger event less than a measure long, change the Grid Type control in the Info line from Bar to Beat.

A few things to note. First, you can start and end an Arranger event anywhere in the project; you don't have to start with event A in measure 1. Second, the Arranger events do not have to flow in a linear order; that is, event B can come before event A, if you want. Third, Arranger events can overlap, so that two events share selected measures. Finally, not every measure of your project has to be assigned to an Arranger event; any measure that is not part of an Arranger event will not be included in the final recording.

By default, Arranger events are labeled alphabetically in the order they're created—not in left-to-right order in the track. The first event you create, then, is labeled A, the second is labeled B, and so forth. You can, however, rename these events to more logically represent the sections of your song. For example, you could rename one event "Verse 1," another event "Verse 2," and a third event "Chorus."

Rename an Arranger event:

1. Use the Object Selection tool to select the event in the Arranger track.

2. In the Info line, click where the current name appears and type a new name for the part.

If you don't like the Arranger events you've created, you can move them around, without affecting the other tracks in your project. Just click the Object Selection tool and use your mouse to drag any Arranger event to a new position. In addition, you can stretch or shrink an event by dragging the left or right border of an event one direction or another. You can even stack Arranger events on top of each other!

Arranger Track Inspector

You can edit the order of events in an Arranger chain within the Inspector for the Arranger track, as shown in Figure 29.3, or within a special Arranger Editor. The Arranger Track Inspector consists of two panes, the Current Arranger Chain (top) and the Arranger Events (bottom). The top pane is where you organize the events; the bottom pane contains all the events you've created in the Arranger track.

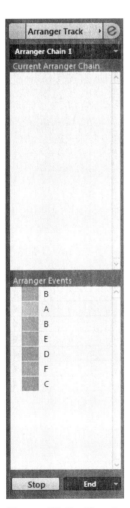

Figure 29.3 The Arranger Track Inspector.

To create an Arranger chain, simply drag events from the Arranger Events pane up to the Current Arranger Chain pane. You can change the order of events in the chain by dragging them up or down the list. To repeat an event consecutively, click the number column and enter the number of times you want the event to play.

Using the Arranger Editor

I find it easier to use the Arranger Editor to create Arranger chains. You can display the Arranger Editor, shown in Figure 29.4, by clicking the Open Arranger Editor control in the Arranger Track Inspector.

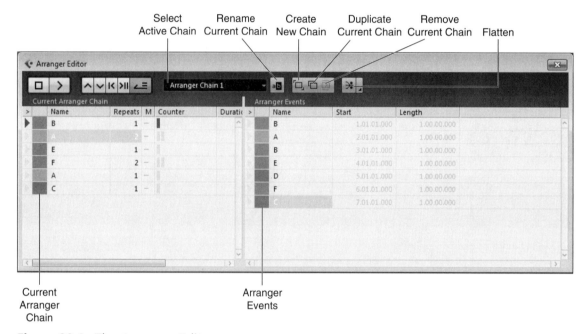

Figure 29.4   The Arranger Editor.

The left side of the Arranger Editor contains the events contained in the current Arranger chain. The right side of the editor lists all events created within the Arranger track. There's a toolbar at the top of the window that contains the Arranger controls, as well as other important commands.

Within the Current Arranger Chain pane are several columns of useful information. The Repeats column indicates how many times an event plays in a row; the Counter column displays this information visually. The Duration column shows the length of the current event (or repeated events), whereas the Song Time column displays the total time of the arrangement.

There are other similarly useful columns within the Arranger Events pane. In addition to the name of the event, the Start and Length columns tell you when, within your original recording, that event starts and ends.

Populating a Chain

There are several ways to add events to an Arranger chain. All involve some variation of clicking and/or dragging with your mouse.

Add an Arranger event to a chain:

■ Click and drag the event's name from the Arranger Events list into the Current Arranger Chain list of the Arranger Editor. A horizontal blue line in the Current Arranger Chain list indicates where the event you're dragging will be inserted. Dragging the same event over an existing instance of that event will increase the number of repetitions for this event in the chain.

■ Double-click on an event in the Arranger Events list to add it above the currently selected event in the chain.

■ Double-click an event in the Track list to add it above the currently selected event in the chain.

Repeating Events: To increase the number of times an event is played in a row, enter a specific value in the Repeats column of the Current Arranger Chain list.

Navigating the Arranger Chain

When playing the project in Arranger mode, Cubase reads the events in the Arranger chain from top to bottom. To enter this non-linear playback mode, enable the Activate Arranger Mode button.

You can also begin playback from any point within the chain. The starting point is always displayed in the Arranger Controls section; select a different event, or click inside any counter display to move the play line to that specific point inside the chain during playback. In addition, you can click the small triangle to the left of any event in the Arranger Editor to immediately skip playback to that location.

Changing the Order of Events

You can change the order of events in a chain the same way you can rearrange tracks in a project: by dragging the event's name to its new position in the Current Arranger Chain list. Once again, a blue line displays where the event will be inserted. To remove an entire row from the Current Arranger Chain list (which includes all the repetitions of an event), right-click (PC)/Control-click (Mac) over the event in the Current Arranger Chain list and choose Remove Touched from the context menu.

Managing Arranger Chains

Each project supports multiple Arranger chains, making it easy to try different versions or structures of the same project. You can manage all your Arranger chains from the Arranger Editor window.

Manage Arranger chains:

■ **Rename a chain:** Click the Rename Current Chain button, and then enter a new name for the chain in the resulting dialog box. Click OK when you are finished.

■ **Create a new chain:** Click the Create New Chain button.

■ **Remove a chain:** Click the Remove Current Chain button. (This option is available only when you've created more than one chain.)

■ **Duplicate a chain:** Click the Duplicate Current Chain button. This option is convenient when you want to keep the current chain's structure but want to experiment with some variations.

Flattening a Chain

When you're done arranging the events in your project, you should convert the events into a linear project. When you engage the Flatten function, Cubase rebuilds your project according to the order of events indicated in the chain. When the process is complete, all names and settings remain the same, but all of your audio and MIDI tracks are split and rearranged in chain order. (The flattened result includes all automation associated with each part that was in the Arranger chain, as well.)

Note that any section of your original project that was not included in the Arranger chain is erased when the project is flattened. That's why it is *strongly recommended* that you save the flattened project under a different name, thus retaining the original project data.

Flatten a play order list:

1. Make sure you've saved a copy of the project containing the Arranger chains.

2. From the Arranger Editor, select the chain you want to flatten.

3. Click the right arrow next to the Flatten button.

4. When the flowchart shown in Figure 29.5 appears, go to the Destination panel and select New Project and Append Chain Name.

5. Go to the Options panel and select the Keep Arranger Track and Open New Projects options.

6. Click the Flatten button.

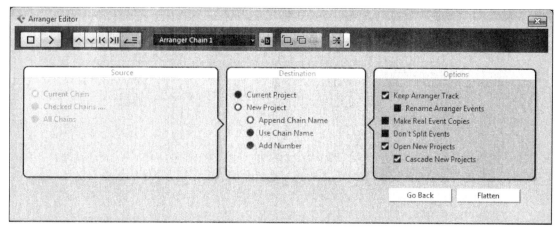

Figure 29.5 Flattening an Arranger project.

Cubase now takes all the different events you've created and rearranges them in the event display, as specified in the Arranger chain. The result is a traditional linear project—assembled from all the individual Arranger events. From here you can continue editing the project or proceed directly to mixing and mastering.

30 Working with Tempo

Here's a summary of what you will learn in this chapter:

- How to add tempo changes using the Tempo Track Editor
- How to edit tempo changes or time signature changes using the Tempo Track Editor
- How to add a tempo change using the Time Warp tool
- How to edit tempo changes using the Time Warp tool
- How to lock the audio tempo to the project's tempo using Warp tabs

Using the Tempo Track Editor

The tempo track in Cubase stores project tempo and time signature changes. Adding tempo changes to a project to slow down or speed up the beat is an essential feature in much non-pop music, but DJs using Cubase to create a track also can use this feature to gradually accelerate the tempo from one section to another. Changing the time signature also offers a convenient way to create a break in the rhythm or when adapting a song with multiple time signature changes inside a project.

The tempo track is not visible by default in Cubase's Project window. Instead, you manage the tempo track from the Tempo Track Editor, shown in Figure 30.1.

There are three ways to open the Tempo Track Editor:

- Select Project > Tempo Track.
- Ctrl-click (PC)/⌘-click (Mac) the Tempo button found in the Transport panel.
- Press the Ctrl+T (PC)/⌘+T (Mac) keyboard shortcut.

The Tempo Track Editor toolbar offers the following tools:

- The **Activate Tempo Track** button is lit when it is enabled, meaning that Cubase will follow any tempo changes found in the tempo track. When the tempo track

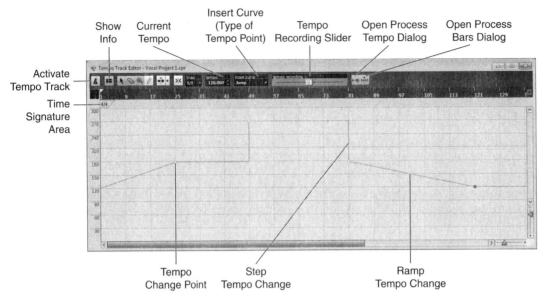

Figure 30.1 The Tempo Track Editor.

is disabled, you can manually set a different tempo in the Transport panel's Tempo field, which is a good way to set a slower tempo for hard-to-play passages when recording in MIDI. When the tempo track is disabled, the word "Fixed" appears next to the Tempo toggle button in the Transport panel, indicating that tempo changes in the tempo track are not in effect. (The default fixed tempo setting is 120 BPM.) Furthermore, whether you are using the tempo track or a fixed tempo setting, the tempo field in the Transport panel will always display the current setting at the playback cursor's location, both during recording or playback and when the Transport is stopped. The time signature changes in the tempo track will still take place as usual, even if the tempo track is disabled, because you will still need these to record events at the proper bars and beat locations.

- The **Show Info button,** when selected, displays the Info line beneath the toolbar.

- The **Object Selection, Erase, Zoom,** and **Draw** tools perform the same functions as they do in other editing environments.

- The **Auto Scroll** and **Snap** buttons offer the same functionality as their Project window counterparts.

- The **Snap** field acts like a quantize grid for tempo changes added with this editor's pencil tool. The selected value determines how the precise positions of individual tempo events are adjusted when you move them or add new ones, or determines the frequency at which the new tempo changes get created as you drag with the pencil.

- The **Current Tempo** field displays the tempo value of a selected tempo event in the tempo display area below. When a tempo event is selected, use the up and down arrows to the right of the field, type in a new tempo value, or drag any tempo event handle to a new position to change its tempo value or time location.

- The **Insert Curve** field selects how the tempo changes when you insert a new tempo point. There are three options: Jump, Ramp, or Automatic. When a jump is created, the tempo stays the same until the next tempo change, at which point it jumps abruptly to the next specified tempo value. When a ramp is created, the tempo moves gradually from one point to another. Selecting Automatic lets Cubase choose between the two options.

- The **Tempo Recording** slider allows you to record tempo changes in real time by moving the slider to the right to go faster or to the left to go slower while the project is playing. Hold down the Shift key while recording tempo changes to get more accurate (finer) control over this slider's values.

- The **Open Process Tempo** button opens the Process Tempo dialog box (see Figure 30.2), which lets you specify a time range to let Cubase determine the right tempo setting to fit this range within a given time. Enter a desired length or end time in the appropriate field, depending on whether you need the project to last a certain amount of time or whether you need the project to reach the end point at a certain time. Click the Process button to let Cubase calculate the rest.

- The **Open Process Bars** button opens the Process Bars dialog box (see Figure 30.3), which lets you add or remove bars (time) by defining a range through the Start and Length fields and then selecting the appropriate action from the Action area.

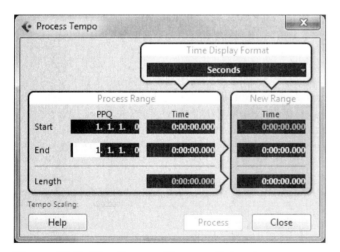

Figure 30.2 The Process Tempo dialog box.

Figure 30.3 The Process Bars dialog box.

The Time Signature area displays the time signature events in your project. When you start a new project, by default you will find a single 4/4 time signature event at the beginning of this bar. You can add several other time signature events along the project's timeline, which will adjust the spacing between bar numbers to reflect how these time signature events affect the number of beats in each bar.

The main part of the Tempo Track Editor is, of course, the tempo display area. This consists of a tempo ruler displayed vertically along the left side of the window and an area where tempo change events appear along the tempo line. Each tempo event is represented by a square handle. When you insert a new tempo event, this line will connect it to existing tempo events on either side of it according to the current Curve and Insert Curve settings.

In the lower-right corner are the horizontal and vertical zoom bars, which enable you to adjust the zoom level for the timeline displayed in the Tempo track, as well as the tempo precision displayed in the tempo ruler, respectively.

Add a tempo change:

1. In the Tempo Track Editor, click "on" the Activate Tempo Track button.

2. Select the Draw tool in the Tempo Track Editor toolbar.

3. Select the desired option in the Insert Curve field.

4. Activate the Snap button if you want the position of newly created tempo events to be adjusted per the Snap mode's current Grid setting. It is recommended that you enable the Snap button if you want tempo changes to occur at the beginning of musical bars.

5. Position your cursor at the time and at the tempo height you want to insert the tempo change, and then click at that point. You can use the Cursor Location field to the left of the ruler to guide you along the vertical tempo value axis.

Add a time signature change:

1. In the Tempo Track Editor, click "on" the Activate Tempo Track button.

2. Select the Draw tool in the Tempo Track Editor toolbar.

3. Click inside the horizontal Time Signature area at the location where you want to insert a time signature change. This adds a time signature using the current value displayed in the Signature field. For obvious reasons, time signature events can be inserted *only* at bar divisions.

4. With the new time signature still selected (a red square appears around the selected time signature), use the toolbar's Signature field to enter the values for the time signature you want to add at this point.

If for some reason you change your mind about any tempo change event, you can move one or several selected tempo events to a new tempo value or time location.

Move a tempo or time signature event:

1. In the Tempo Track Editor, click "on" the Activate Tempo Track button.

2. Click the Object Selection tool in the Tempo Track Editor toolbar.

3. Click on the tempo or time signature event you want to move and drag it to the desired location.

You also can move multiple tempo change events simultaneously by dragging a box to select them. Selected tempo event handles will appear in red, as will the lines between them.

Erase tempo or time signature events:

■ With the Object Selection (arrow) tool selected, click on the tempo or time signature you want to erase and press the Delete or Backspace key. To erase several events, simply drag a box over the desired tempo or time signature events and use the Delete or Backspace key.

■ Select the Eraser tool and click on the events in the tempo track.

Time Warping

The Time Warp feature in the Project window provides a way to match musical (tempo-based) references to linear (time-based) references, such as when you're recording tempo-based music to a time-based video track. This feature adds special markers where you want both references to align. As a result, warp markers are added with tempo values that make it possible for this match to occur.

For example, you can use the Time Warp tool to add tempo changes based on a track that was recorded freestyle (without a metronome), that will follow the MIDI or audio events within that track. Once the start point is determined, create tempo changes that will make bars in the project match up to the recorded events in the track. Because Time Warp markers are locked to the tempo-based ruler (bars and beats), this ruler "warps" to match the linear or time-based ruler.

When using the Time Warp tool, the tempo value of the last tempo event (before the new tab's position) is adjusted accordingly. The Ruler bar turns orange when the Time Warp tool is selected, and inserted tempo changes appear as markers along this bar.

Changing Tempo with Time Warp

There are two Time Warp modes. The default Warp Grid mode transforms the tempo grid into an elastic grid that lets you set the location of bars and beats in relation to absolute time; this is great for matching a tempo grid to an existing audio track with changing tempos. The alternate Warp Grid (Musical Events Follow) mode is better for adjusting tempo-based events to match existing time-based events.

Add a tempo change using the Time Warp tool:

1. Activate the tempo track; the Time Warp tool does not work when the tempo track is not enabled.

2. Enable the Snap function in the Project window and set your Snap mode appropriately. Depending on the grid and quantize types you choose, this forces tempo changes to occur on bars, at the cursor's location, or at an event's start point.

3. Select the Time Warp tool from the Project window toolbar.

4. Click in the Project window at a musical position (bar or beat gridline) and drag it so that it matches a position in the material you're editing—the start of an event, a specific "hit" within an audio event, or a frame in a video clip.

5. When you are satisfied with the location of the tempo change, release the mouse. You will see a tempo change marker appear in the Ruler bar with the BPM value rounded off to the closest integer.

Here are a few additional techniques for working with the Time Warp tool:

■   To only affect the timing of a specific time range, use the Range Selection tool to define this time selection prior to using the Time Warp tool. Clicking to the left of the selected range only affects the tempo before the start point of the range. Clicking inside the selected range affects the tempo inside the range, adding a tempo change at the start, end, and the point where you click. Clicking to the right of the selected range (or after) only affects the tempo after the end point of the selected range. If no tempo events are present, a new tempo change will be added at that point to reflect the time warp entered.

- When using the Time Warp tool inside an editor, a tempo event will also be added at the start of the event or part in the Project window, if there isn't one there already.

- To manually add a tempo event at the current tempo value in order to lock all previous tempo events in place, hold down the Shift key while the Time Warp tool is selected and click where you want the tempo change to occur. The cursor will change into a pencil, and a tempo change will be inserted at the point where you clicked.

After the Time Warp tool is selected, you can see the tempo changes in the Ruler bar and move these tempo changes around by dragging their markers to a new location. You will notice that the cursor changes to a pointing hand as you hover over a tempo change marker.

Locking Tempo with Warp Tabs

To change the timing of a recorded audio event, such as a bass that occasionally drifts away from the drummer's timing or a live recording where the song begins at 109 BPM, and then goes up slightly to 114 BPM and finally ends at 112 BPM, use Cubase's Audio-Warp function. AudioWarp uses the local tempo map to extrapolate the necessary time-stretching so that the sample's tempo always matches the project's tempo.

Time-Stretching Limitations: Although time-stretching can help match the varying tempo of a freely recorded audio event to a somewhat static tempo of a project, applying extreme time-stretching percentages will degrade the audio content's quality. It is advisable to find out what the original tempo of the event is using either Automatic Tempo Detection or Musical mode, as described in this chapter, to set the project's tempo to a BPM value in the same vicinity. For example, setting the project's tempo to 120 BPM while the original sample plays between 90 and 95 BPM does not necessarily represent a successful use of audio warping. The intention of this feature is to fine-tune and tighten rhythmic inaccuracies, not to apply large amounts of time-stretching over the entire event.

Lock an audio event's tempo to the project's tempo using Warp tabs:

1. Open the event in the Sample Editor.

2. If the event does not begin on the first downbeat, before going any further you should edit the event in the Project window or move the Event Start handle in the Sample Editor so that it does. (Enable the Show Audio Event button in the Sample Editor's toolbar if these handles are not already visible.) Matching the start of the event with a recognizable downbeat will make it easier to locate more accurately the first beats of each subsequent measure.

3. Click the Time Warp button in the Sample Editor toolbar.

4. Open the AudioWarp tab in the Sample Editor Inspector.

5. Click the Free Warp button in the AudioWarp tab.

6. Locate a moment in the audio event where the beat doesn't fall where it should according to the tempo grid, click and hold at that point, and then drag the pointer left or right to reposition the beat.

7. Repeat this process at other points inside the event if necessary. The audio content is automatically stretched to match the content between Warp tabs to the current grid.

Changing the Ruler's Display Format: If the ruler does not display bars and beats, now is a good time to change this using the ruler's display settings drop-down menu, found to the right of the ruler in the Sample Editor.

You also can fix rhythmic imperfections or just change the rhythmic content of a drum loop, for example, by adding Warp tabs to a Musical mode–enabled event. Always proceed by defining the audio tempo, enabling the Musical mode, and finally applying the Time Warp tool, as demonstrated here.

Editing Warp Tabs: To move the location of a Warp tab, click the tab and drag it to the desired location. (This operation has no effect on the time-stretching properties or grid location.) To delete a Warp tab, hold down the Shift key and click the tab.

Automatic Tempo Detection

Cubase 6 includes a new Tempo Detection feature that automatically detects the tempo of rhythmic musical content, even if the tempo of that content isn't consistently precise. This is useful for analyzing audio not recorded to a click track, as well as adjusting freely recorded audio to the project tempo. To use the Tempo Detection tool, the audio event has to be at least seven seconds long and have discernable beats; you also have to deactivate Musical mode for the clip.

Automatically analyze the tempo of an event:

1. Select an audio event in the Project window.

2. Select Project > Tempo Detection.

3. This opens the Tempo Detection panel (shown in Figure 30.4). Click the Analyze button.

Figure 30.4   The Tempo Detection panel.

Cubase now creates a rough tempo map for the selected event, and adds tempo and signature tracks to the project. By default, Cubase assigns the project a 1/4 time signature; you can modify this later. In addition, Cubase opens the Time Warp tool for fine-tuning the newly generated tempo map, if necessary.

Analyzing Multiple Events: To analyze the tempo of another event, you must first close the Tempo Detection Panel and then start fresh.

31 Working with Beats and Loops

Cubase's Arranger mode, as discussed in the previous chapter, is an ideal tool for creating drum tracks and loop-based recordings. You don't have to divide your song into major regions; you can instead create shorter Arranger events and use them to construct a recording in building-block fashion.

With loop recording, you start with a few measures of a drum beat and then repeat those measures over and over in a kind of loop. You build up the rest of the song by adding more loops of other instruments; you put the bass on top of the drums, and then layer on keyboards, guitars, synths, strings, vocals; you name it. When you use audio loops in this fashion, you're composing as you record, one loop at time.

The key to successful loop recording, then, is the ability to construct interesting drum beats—and then build on those beats with short loops of other instruments. Creating a composition/recording with loops is really like assembling a structure from a series of building blocks. Anyone can do it, and it's the way that many current recordings are made, especially in the hip hop, techno, electronica, and dance genres.

Here's a summary of what you will learn in this chapter:

- Where to obtain samples and loops for your projects
- How to tempo-match and pitch-match loops to your project
- Four ways to extend loops
- How to enhance a drum loop
- How to replace drum hits
- How to use the Groove Agent ONE drum machine
- How to create drum patterns with the Beat Designer MIDI plug-in
- How to create MIDI tracks from Beat Designer patterns
- How to create interesting loop patterns using LoopMash2

Working with Loops

In recording terms, a *loop* is a short audio sample, typically repeated multiple times to create a longer track in a recording. A *loop-based recording* is constructed primarily from repeated audio loops. A *loop library* is a collection of audio loops or samples, typically distributed on compact disc.

The key thing is that loops are short, they're repeatable, and they're capable of being adapted to a given recording in terms of tempo and pitch. Cubase lets you sample and import all types of audio files; once you have your samples in your project, you can work with them as you would any other audio event to create the perfect loop recording.

Obtaining Samples and Loops

You can obtain audio loops from a number of different sources. You can sample audio from practically any compact disc. You can also import samples from digital audio files downloaded from the Internet. Other loops are sold as part of loop libraries, created expressly for the purpose of creating loop-based recordings. Still more loops can be created on your own, via traditional audio recording, MIDI recording, or by programming a drum machine.

Ripping samples for loops is common practice in many types of music, especially hip hop and R&B. That's because it's relatively easy to sample portions of music available on commercial compact discs. Cubase lets you import entire songs from any CD, or just segments of a song (which are easier to work with if you only want a short sample). The CD tracks are imported as WAV-format audio events, which you can then work with as you would any other event in Cubase.

Don't Sample Without Permission: Many popular musicians use samples in their recordings. Before you sample another artist's music for your own recording, however, you need to obtain that artist's permission and (depending on what kind of deal you work out) pay a flat fee or royalty for use of the prior work. It is illegal to sample a copyrighted recording and then make money from the use of that sample without the owner's permission.

These days it's more common to sample music from digitally downloaded files than from CDs; the music industry is migrating online, after all. Fortunately, Cubase lets you import just about any type of digital audio file, including MP3 and WMA files, so you're good to go with digital downloads.

In addition, many companies (and some professional musicians) offer pre-sampled or specially created loops and samples available for purchase or download. A loop library is likely to contain dozens, if not hundreds, of audio loops that you can use in your recordings; when you purchase a loop library, you're also purchasing the rights to use those loops in your productions. Using a loop library is a great place to start when you're creating loop-based recordings, and it's easy to do; most commercial loops are in WAV format, which is one of the digital audio formats that Cubase imports by default.

I discussed how to import music in all formats in Chapter 7, "Managing Your Media." Refer to that chapter for detailed instructions.

Loop Formats: Cubase imports loops created in the MP3, REX, and REX 2 file formats. (REX and REX 2 are file formats used by the ReCycle loop-production program.) In addition, many commercially available loops are offered in the ACID format; these loops are standard WAV files embedded with tempo and length information. Cubase imports an ACID loop as it would any WAV file, but it uses the embedded information to activate Musical mode and adapt the loop's tempo to the one already set in your recording project.

Matching Tempo

When you import a sample or loop into a Cubase project, it's imported just as it was on the original recording—at the original tempo, and in the original key. That isn't necessarily a good thing, as you need both the tempo and the pitch of the sample to match the tempo and pitch of the rest of your project. It wouldn't do, for example, to have a drum beat playing at 120 beats per minute (bpm) when the rest of your song is playing at 90 bpm.

In Cubase 6, the Musical mode and AudioWarp tools automatically match the tempo of a loop with the project tempo as best as possible—which is sometimes difficult if the loop itself doesn't have a solid tempo. (It also helps, of course, to have your loop be a perfect 4 beats or multiple thereof; it's almost impossible to determine tempo and do the looping thing if you have a loop that runs for 5 beats in 4/4 time.) And, when Musical mode is activated, audio events automatically adapt to any tempo changes you make, just as MIDI events do.

Match the tempo of a sample to the project tempo:

1. In Cubase's Project window, double-click the desired audio event to open the Sample Editor.

2. Activate the Musical mode button on the Sample Editor toolbar.

Matching Pitch

Matching tempo is easy enough to do using Cubase's Musical mode. Matching the pitch of a sample to the rest of your recording, however, is slightly more complex.

Cubase lets you adjust the pitch of an event in real time, but there's no way to magically identify the key and match it to the key of the other events in your project. So you're left with simple transposition—which, of course, occurs without affecting the tempo of the sample. In Cubase 6, you change the pitch of a sample using the Transpose control, found in the Info line for a selected event.

Change the pitch of a sample:

1. In Cubase's Project window, select the event you want to adjust.

2. If you don't currently have the Info line displayed, click the Set Up Window Layout button and check the Info Line option.

3. Go to the Info line and enter a value into the Transpose field. Each whole number you enter transposes the pitch up or down a half-step; enter a hyphen (-) before the number to move down. For example, entering **2** in the Transpose field transposes the event *up* two half-steps. Entering **-2** transposes the event *down* two half-steps.

4. Press Enter (PC)/Return (Mac) on your computer keyboard to lock in the transposition.

Extending Loops

Most loops are relatively short—anywhere from a single measure to four measures long. But four measures do not a song make, which means you need to extend those loops to fill the entire length of the recording.

There are four ways to turn a short loop into a longer one—or, more precisely, a series of shorter loops. The first uses the standard copy-and-paste technique that you're already familiar with.

Extend a loop with copy and paste:

1. Select the event you want to copy.

2. Select Edit > Copy.

3. Move your cursor to the end of the first event (the start of the next measure).

4. Select Edit > Paste.

The drawback to the copy-and-paste approach is twofold. First, it requires four individual steps. Second, it lets you add only one event at a time. But it's an easy way to extend a loop.

The next approach uses Cubase's Duplicate tool, and requires fewer steps than the copy-and-paste approach.

Extend a loop with the Duplicate tool:

1. Select the event you want to copy.

2. Select Edit > Functions > Duplicate.

Cubase now makes a copy of the first event and pastes the copy immediately after the first event.

The duplicate approach is easier than using copy and paste, but you're still working with just one event at a time. If you want to copy more than one instance of an event, a better approach is to use Cubase's Repeat tool. This tool lets you specify how many copies of the event you want to paste back into your project.

Extend a loop with the Repeat tool:

1. Select the event you want to copy.

2. Select Edit > Functions > Repeat.

3. When the Repeat Events dialog box appears, as shown in Figure 31.1, use the Count control to specify how many copies you want to make.

4. Click OK.

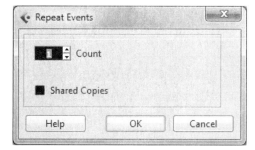

Figure 31.1 Specifying the number of copies in the Repeat Events dialog box.

Using the Repeat tool, if you specify two copies, Cubase places two copies of the event, all in a row following the original event.

If you're not sure how many copies you need to make of your original event, you can let Cubase do the calculation for you via the Fill Loop tool. This tool lets you specify in the ruler the region you want to fill, and then it does the filling for you.

Extend a loop with the Fill Loop tool:

1. In the Project window, Ctrl-click (PC)/⌘-click (Mac) in the ruler at the start of the area you want to fill. This sets the start point.

2. Alt-click (PC)/Option-click (Mac) in the ruler at the end of the area you want to fill. This sets the end point.

3. Select the event you want to copy.

4. Select Edit > Functions > Fill Loop.

The original event is now copied as many times as possible to fill the area specified. This is the easiest way to make your loop fill an entire section of your song.

Creating and Manipulating Drum Tracks

At the heart of most loop-based recordings is the drum track. Whether you use a sampled drum loop, create a drum track with a MIDI drum machine, or record a live drummer, it's important to get that drum beat *just right*.

Cubase offers many ways to create and fine-tune your drum tracks. You can use the AudioWarp and Time Warp functions to tempo-match drum loops and adjust individual hits on or off the beat. You can use audio event editing to copy and rearrange different drum loops within your recording. Even better, you can use VST instruments to create your own MIDI drum tracks. Which approach you use depends on the sound you want to achieve and your own temperament.

Enhancing Drum Loops

Perhaps the easiest way to get a perfect drum track is to use a commercially available drum loop. When you go this route, you typically get anywhere from one to four measures of drums, which you can then loop throughout your entire recording.

The problem with using a commercial drum loop is that you're not the only person in the world using it. Hundreds, if not thousands, of other musicians are using that exact same loop, which means that their recordings will sound similar to yours, at least from the rhythm perspective.

There are ways, however, to add more personality to widely used drum loops. The most obvious method is to edit the loop in the Sample Editor. Add a hit there, take out a hit there, and maybe even alter the feel by moving the snare drum slightly before or after the beat. Any little change you make, no matter how subtle, helps to make that beat your own.

You can create more sophisticated drum patterns by making a long drum groove out of two or more shorter loops. All you have to do is insert one different loop after another, and you end up with a more complex linear groove.

You can also make a simple drum loop sound more sophisticated by stacking a second loop on top of it. Just create two tracks in the project list, and import different audio loops to each track. Make sure the two drum loops sound good together, of course, and that they don't get in each other's way. This will require a little trial and error, but the results can be very interesting.

Replacing Drum Hits in an Audio Track

When you're working with an audio (not MIDI) drum track recorded by a real live drummer, you may not always be satisfied with the sounds of all the drums in the drum kit. Maybe you'd like a punchier bass, or more crack on the snare drum. Short of re-recording the entire drum track, what do you do?

Cubase 6 has the answer to this dilemma, in the form of a new Hitpoint-to-MIDI function. This feature lets you identify specific "hits" in the drum track and replace them with MIDI notes. This way you can slice out a weak live snare drum, for example, and replace it with a perfect-sounding MIDI snare sound.

Replace a drum hit:

1. Open the drum track in the Sample Editor. (This works best if you have each drum in the kit recorded on a separate track; you might then open the snare drum track, for example, or the bass drum track.)

2. Open the Hitpoints tab in the Sample Editor Inspector, as shown in Figure 31.2.

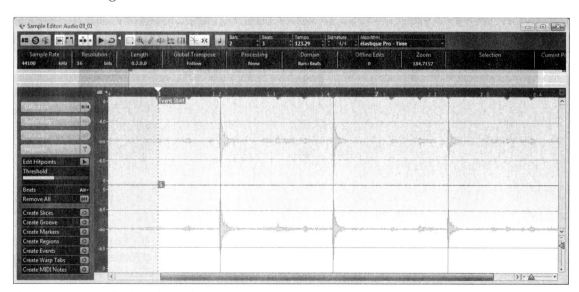

Figure 31.2 Replacing drum hitpoints with MIDI notes.

3. Adjust the Threshold slider to the right to add more hitpoints, or to the left to remove unwanted hitpoints.

4. Click the Beats control and select which hitpoints you want to use—all, 1/4 notes, 1/8 notes, and so on.

5. Click the Create MIDI Notes button in the Inspector. This displays the Convert Hitpoints to MIDI Notes dialog box, shown in Figure 31.3.

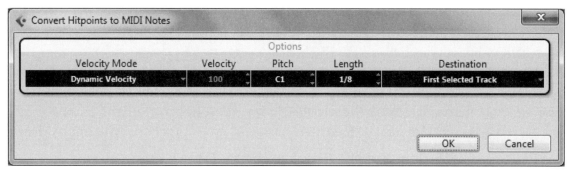

Figure 31.3 Selecting MIDI options for the replaced notes.

6. In the Velocity Mode field, select Dynamic Velocity if you want the volume level of the new notes to track those of the originally recorded notes. Select Fixed Velocity if you want the new drum hits to maintain a constant volume level.

7. If you selected the Fixed Velocity mode, specify the velocity (volume level) in the Velocity field.

8. Specify the pitch for the new notes in the Pitch field.

9. Specify the duration (length) of the new notes in the Length field.

10. Use the Destination field to determine where the new notes should appear:
    - **First Selected Track.** The new MIDI notes are placed on the first selected MIDI or instrument track in your project.
    - **New MIDI Track.** Cubase creates a new MIDI track for the replacement notes.
    - **Project Clipboard.** The new MIDI part is copied to the clipboard so that you can paste it at the desired location on a MIDI or instrument track.

11. Click the OK button.

Using Groove Agent ONE

Although many recordists like working with pre-recorded drum loops, others prefer to create their own grooves using either live drums or a synthesized drum machine. To that end, Cubase 6 includes Groove Agent ONE, a VST instrument that functions as a drum machine and sample player. Groove Agent ONE lets you create your own MIDI drum tracks, just by tapping keys on your MIDI keyboard; it also lets you play back drum tracks using your own or any third-party sample library.

Groove Agent ONE works like any other VST instrument. Before you can use it, you have to load it into your project.

Create a Groove Agent ONE instrument track:

1. From the Project window, select Project > Add Track > Instrument.

2. When the Add Instrument Track dialog box appears, click the Instrument field and select Drum—Groove Agent ONE.

3. Click OK.

A new instrument track is created and set to receive whatever rhythms you create with the Groove Agent ONE.

In addition to being a standard drum machine, Groove Agent ONE also lets you preload a variety of preset drum kits in order to create different drum sounds.

Load a drum set preset into Groove Agent ONE:

1. Click the Open Device Panels button in the drum track's Inspector. This opens the Groove Agent ONE control panel, shown in Figure 31.4.

Figure 31.4 The Groove Agent ONE drum machine control panel.

2.   Click the button to the right of the Presets field and select Load Preset. This displays the Results window.

3.   Double-click the drum kit you want from the list.

The individual drums and cymbals in a drum kit are each assigned to their own pads on the control panel. The pads are arranged into eight groups; click a number button to display the pads in that group. As you can see in Figure 31.4, groups 3 and 4 are where you find the typical drum set sounds in the Pop Kit preset. In this example, the Fat Kick bass drum is activated by pressing the E2 pad in group 4; the Good Snare snare drum is activated by pressing the G2 pad in the same group.

You create a drum part by activating recording for this track and then playing the pads in the Groove Agent ONE controller. You can also create a part by pressing the appropriate keys (in time) on your connected MIDI keyboard or input device.

Using Beat Designer

Cubase 6 offers an even easier way to design drum beats, via the new Beat Designer MIDI plug-in. Assign this plug-in to an inserts channel, and then use it to create sophisticated drum beats; the beats are then played via the Groove Agent ONE drum machine.

Load the Beat Designer plug-in:

1.   Open the MIDI Inserts panel in the drum track's Inspector.

2.   Click the first presets field.

3.   Select Beat Designer from the plug-ins list.

As you can see in Figure 31.5, the available drums and cymbals are displayed in rows on the left side of the Beat Designer window, whereas measures and subdivisions within a measure are displayed in columns along the bottom. Click in any intersection between a row and column to place a note from that particular instrument on that particular beat, or subsection of the beat.

To help you get started, Beat Designer features a variety of preset beats, from Afrique Latino 133bpm to Vinyl Loops 90bpm. To select a preset, simply click the presets field in the Beat Designer window, select Load Preset, and select a preset from the list.

Of course, you can also use Beat Designer to create your own custom beats. Doing so is as simple as clicking where in the measure you want a particular drum or cymbal to sound.

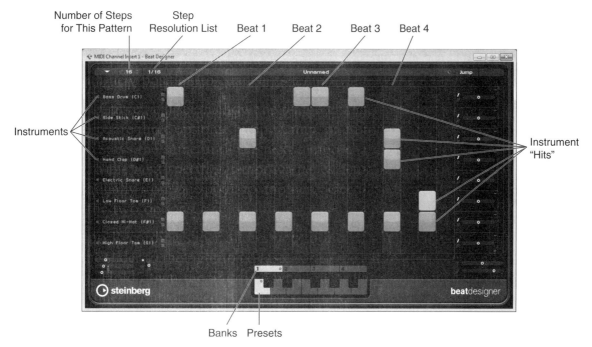

Figure 31.5 Cubase 6's MIDI Beat Designer.

Create a drum beat:

1. Pull down the Step Resolution list and select the subdivisions you want for this beat. For example, if you want to create a beat with only quarter-note downbeats in 4/4 time (four quarter notes to a measure), select 1/4. To include eighth notes in your pattern, select 1/8. To create a more sophisticated pattern using sixteenth notes, select 1/16.

2. Adjust the Number of Steps for This Pattern control to determine how many steps are included in this pattern. For example, if you selected 1/8 for the Step Resolution and want to create a four-measure pattern, enter 32. (That's 8 eighth notes per measure times 4 measures.)

3. The grid now adjusts itself per your instructions. Click in the appropriate space in the grid to add a note for the selected instrument at the selected point in the beat.

4. To remove a previously entered note, click the note again.

You can create 12 separate patterns for each of the four individual banks. The banks are selected by clicking the numbered buttons above the keyboard at the bottom of the window; the patterns within a bank are selected by clicking a key on the keyboard.

Swing Rhythm: By default, Beat Designer creates "straight" rhythms to an eighth or sixteenth note grid. To create a triplet-based swing or shuffle rhythm, adjust the Swing 1 control accordingly.

Once you've created a pattern, of course, you should save it as a new pattern in Beat Designer's Pattern Bank. You can then call up the pattern (load the new preset) for use later in this project or in future projects

---

Save a drum pattern:

1. Click Beat Designer's Presets field and select Save Preset.

2. When the Save Pattern Bank dialog box appears, enter a name for the pattern.

3. Click OK.

Finally, you can convert the drum patterns you create into MIDI or Groove Agent ONE instrument tracks. Doing so creates a new MIDI event, which you can then work with as you would any drum loop.

Convert a drum pattern into a MIDI part:

1. Within the Beat Designer window, select the bank and preset for the pattern you want from the keyboard display.

2. Click and drag the pattern from the keyboard display onto the desired position on the MIDI or instrument track in the Project window.

This creates a new MIDI event on the selected track. Each note in the event represents a piece of the drum pattern you created with Beat Designer.

Using LoopMash2

When you need creative new ways to work with loops in your recordings, turn to Cubase 6's LoopMash2 VST instrument. It's a powerful tool for slicing and reassembling rhythmic patterns, in real-time.

LoopMash2 loads the same way as any VST instrument, in its own instrument track.

Create a LoopMash instrument track:

1. From the Project window, select Project > Add Track > Instrument.

2. When the Add Instrument Track dialog box appears, click the Instrument field and select Synth > LoopMash.

3. Click OK.

LoopMash2 comes with a variety of preset patterns. It's probably good to start experimenting with these presets before you begin importing your own loops into the instrument. To load a present, click the presets field, select Load Preset, and then select a preset from the list.

The LoopMash control panel, shown in Figure 31.6, includes eight tracks of sounds; each track is comprised of multiple sliced loops. Move the slider beside each track to the right to play more slices in the track. Move the slider to the left to play fewer slices.

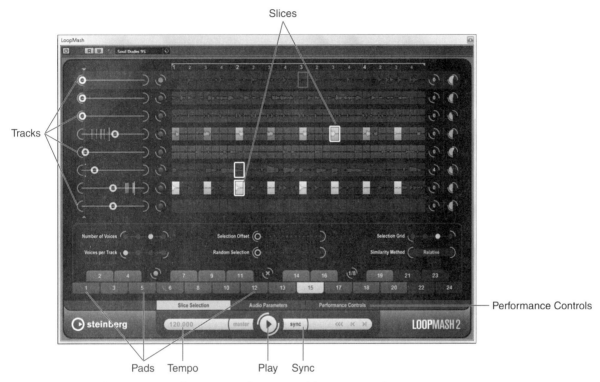

Figure 31.6 Using LoopMash2 to "mash" several loops together.

Along the bottom of the LoopMash window are 24 pads. Each pad activates a predefined selection of tracks. Click a pad to hear the selected rhythmic mix.

Play a LoopMash mix:

1. Turn "off" the Sync control.

2. Click the Performance Controls button.

3. Click the Play button.

4. Click a pad to change the mix. You'll see different tracks light up, depending on the pad you select, and hear those tracks in the playback.

You can change LoopMash mixes in real time. You don't have to stop the playback to select a different pad/mix.

Naturally, you can import your own loops into LoopMash. When you import a loop, LoopMash analyzes the audio material and slices the loop into eighth-note segments. Import additional loops to create more complex patterns; LoopMash automatically makes all your loops fit together.

Import loops into LoopMash:

1. From the main Cubase window, select Media > MediaBay.

2. From the MediaBay, navigate to the loop you want to import.

3. Drag the loop from MediaBay onto an empty track in the LoopMash window.

Once you've populated several tracks in the LoopMash window, you can experiment with all of the instrument's various controls and parameters.

Mixing and Mastering

32 Using the Mixer

After you've recorded and edited all the tracks of your project, it's time to turn all those tracks into a finished recording. This is typically a two-step process. The first step is to mix all those tracks so that you get the overall sound you want, complete with any necessary processing and equalization. The second step is to add master effects and export the mix to a stereo audio file, suitable for final distribution on compact disc or other appropriate media.

Mixing your project involves finding the perfect balance between all the tracks you've recorded. Some tracks need to fade into the background, while others need to take a more prominent position; some tracks may require additional processing or equalization, but some may prove superfluous and need to be muted or deleted. That's what you do during the mixing process—adjust this track and that to create the overall sound you want.

Most recordists conduct their mixing operations in Cubase's Mixer; it's where you adjust the relative volume levels of individual tracks, as well as mute any tracks you don't want to include in the final mix. At first glance, the Mixer duplicates most of the channel settings described in previous chapters of this book. But it does so in a way that makes the mixing process more efficient and effective, by presenting all these settings in an interface that resembles a traditional physical mixing console.

Here's a summary of what you will learn in this chapter:

- How to recognize the different areas of the Mixer panel
- How to save channel settings and apply them to other channels inside the Mixer panel
- How to customize the Mixer to fit the tasks at hand
- How to find and use the input and output busses in the Mixer
- How to use the Can Hide functionalities of the Mixer
- How to create a great-sounding mix

Understanding the Mixer Areas

You open the Mixer panel by clicking the Mixer button on the toolbar, by selecting Devices > Mixer, or by pressing the F3 button on your computer keyboard. The main purpose for the Mixer is to offer a single interface to control all channels in a project. As you can see in Figure 32.1, however, the Mixer offers more than just individual channel controls (which are mirrored in the Inspector and VST Channel Settings panel). To that end, the Mixer is comprised of the following areas:

■ The **Common panel,** located on the far left of the Mixer, displays a series of controls that affect all channels in the Mixer.

■ The **Channel strips** let you adjust levels and other settings for each input, audio, MIDI, and output channel in your project.

■ The **Extended Mixer,** located above the main Mixer controls, displays insert and send effect settings, EQ settings for audio and group channels, output levels, and an overview of settings applied to a channel.

■ The **Routing panel,** located at the very top of the Mixer, displays input and output bus assignments and controls for each channel in the project.

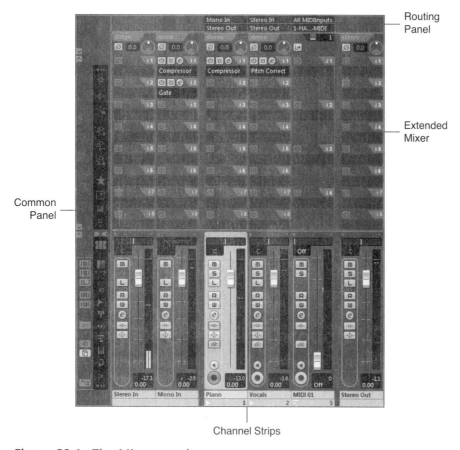

Figure 32.1 The Mixer panel.

Common Panel

The Common panel found on the left of the Mixer (see Figure 32.2) controls global settings for this Mixer panel, as well as for its appearance and behavior. Here's a look at each item in the panel, from top to bottom.

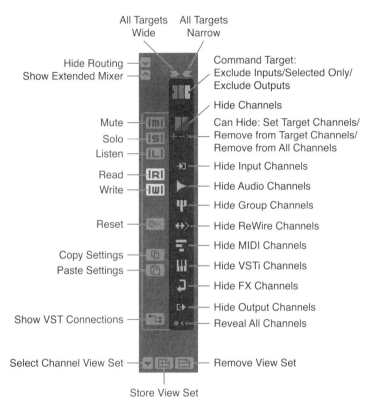

Figure 32.2 The Common panel found on the left of the Mixer panel.

When you need to have an overview of all EQ, send or insert FX settings, or you want to see which effect is loaded where, the Show Extended Mixer button offers a way to reveal the extended portion of the Mixer. When the extended portion of the Mixer is visible, the Show Extended Mixer button turns into the Hide Extended Mixer button; click this button to hide the Mixer.

All Targets Wide/All Targets Narrow buttons make all channels in the current Mixer wide or narrow, respectively. The same settings appear individually on each channel, enabling you to make them narrow or wide independently. But when you click here, all channels change to wide or narrow at the touch of a button. When a channel is displayed in Narrow mode, all of its functions remain active; however, some of the controls are hidden, allowing more channels to fit on your desktop. This becomes convenient when you are working with a project that has more channels than can fit in your current desktop resolution.

The global Mute, Solo, Listen, Read, and Write buttons in the Common panel resemble those on individual channels. Although changing one of these buttons on an individual channel won't affect the others, changing the state of one of these buttons in the Common panel toggles that function off for *all* channels available in the Mixer panel. Whenever one or more tracks in the Mixer panel is muted, the global Mute indicator button in the Common panel is lit. Clicking this global button in the Common panel cancels all current mute settings, unmuting all channels in the project. The Listen and Solo buttons play a similar role in the sense that they are lit when one or more tracks is in Solo or Listen mode. Clicking the corresponding global button in the Common panel then deactivates the solo or listen monitoring for all channels in the project. The global Read and Write buttons in the Common panel can be used to activate or deactivate the read or write automation status on all channels. If one or more channels is already in Read or Write mode, the Mixer panel is lit as well to indicate that a channel is currently actively reading or ready to write automation.

The Reset button resets all the channels or only the selected channels in the Mixer. When you reset a channel, you deactivate all solo, mute, EQ, insert, and send effect settings. The Volume fader also is set to 0 dB (that is, no gain change applied to the source signal) and pans to center position.

If you want to copy the settings of a selected track to another, use the Copy First Selected Channel's Settings and Paste Settings to Selected Channels buttons. For example, if you want to have the same EQ, insert, and send settings on several vocal tracks, you can make the settings on a first channel, and when you are satisfied with these settings, you can copy and paste them to one or more channels. Subsequently, all the channels to which you copied these settings will be the same.

Copy a channel's settings to another channel:

1. Adjust the settings of the channel you want to copy.
2. Be sure this channel is selected in the Mixer.
3. Click the Copy First Select Channel's Settings button. The Paste button will become active.
4. Select the channel to which you want to paste the copied settings.
5. Click the Paste Settings to Selected Channels button in the Common panel.
6. You can repeat this paste operation to any number of channels by selecting the channel and clicking the Paste button again.

The Show VST Connections button does the same thing as the VST Connections option found under the Devices menu; it brings up the VST Connections window, allowing you to make modifications to the current input and output bus configurations.

On the right side of the Command panel is a black strip with a series of icons, which are actually buttons. The top button includes three Command Target buttons that toggle on and off the ability to exclude all input busses, the currently selected channels, or all output busses from key commands. To exclude inputs from key commands, enable the left button. To only apply key commands to selected channels, enable the center button. Finally, to exclude output busses, enable the right button.

Below this group of three buttons is the Hide Channels button; toggle this button to switch on and off the ability to hide individual channels. Beneath this button is another set of toggles that sets target channels to Can Hide, removes Can Hide from target channels, and removes Can Hide from all channels.

The remaining buttons in the black strip hide from view all channels of this particular class in the Mixer panel. These are, from top to bottom, input channels (busses), audio channels, group channels, ReWire channels, MIDI channels, VST instrument channels, plug-in FX channels (send effects), and output channels (busses). Hiding a class of channels does not influence the output, but it does make it easier to navigate the Mixer when the project has a large number of channels and you need to work on a specific class of channels. You can unhide all hidden channels by clicking the Reveal All Channels button at the bottom of this strip.

At the bottom of the Common panel are the Store View Set and Remove View Set buttons, which let you save a set of Mixer display options as a preset and retrieve it later from the Select Channel View Set menu. Creating your own presets enables you to customize the Mixer to display the information you need to see for specific tasks, such as audio recording, mixing, or any other task you frequently need to perform in this window.

Store a channel view set:

1.   Set up the Mixer view options appropriately so that they display the information to which you want to have quick access.

2.   Click on the Store View Set button.

3.   Enter a name for your preset—for example, Audio EQ if you chose to display only audio channels with their EQ settings displayed in the extended panel.

4.   Click the OK button.

Remove a channel view set:

1.   Select the view from the Select Channel View Set menu.

2.   Click on the Remove View Set button.

You can use up to three Mixer panel configurations with Cubase. Take advantage of this feature to organize your mixing environment in a way that suits you best. For example, you can choose to display all MIDI channels in one Mixer and audio channels in another. Access the additional mixers you create (labeled as Mixer 2 and Mixer 3) through the Devices menu.

Channel Strips

The main part of the Mixer consists of control strips for different types of channels, as shown in Figure 32.3.

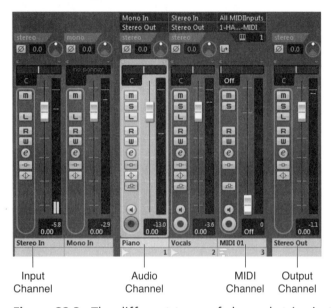

Figure 32.3 The different types of channel strips in the Mixer panel.

- **Input channel strips** let you control the levels and assign effects for each of the audio input channels in your project. You will have as many input channel strips as you have audio input channels.

- **Audio channel strips** let you control the levels and assign effects for each of the audio tracks in your project. You will have as many audio channel strips as you have audio tracks.

- **MIDI channel strips** let you control the levels and assign effects for each of the MIDI tracks in your project. You will have as many MIDI channel strips as you have MIDI tracks.

- **Output channel strip** lets you adjust the output level and other settings for your entire project. There is one output channel strip per output bus in your project.

Each type of channel strip is discussed in more detail in that appropriate section of this book. In general, each strip contains a level slider; pan control; mute, read automation, and write automation buttons; an edit channels setting button; and inserts and EQ bypass buttons. Some types of channel strips include additional controls; for example, audio and MIDI channel strips include Monitor and Record Enable buttons, for use when recording.

Extended Mixer Panel

The Extended Mixer panel is visible to Cubase users when you click on the Show Extended Mixer button at the left edge of the Common panel. When the Mixer is in extended mode, the corresponding portion of the Common panel reveals an additional set of options (see Figure 32.4).

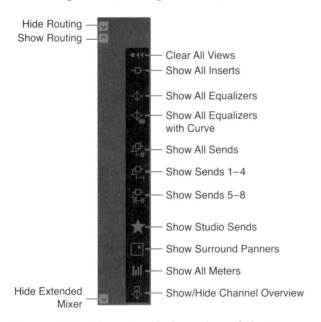

Figure 32.4 The extended portion of the Common panel in the Mixer panel.

When you click one of the view options in the Common panel, all channels in the current Mixer will display the same type of information. For example, clicking the Show All Inserts button in the Common panel switches the display format of all channels to show insert settings in the extended portion of the Mixer. You can, however, change the displayed extended panel for a specific channel by selecting a different display option for this channel. As with the options found in the lower part of the Common panel, the global options here can also be set independently for each channel in the Mixer.

Note that changing the display format for mixer channels does not in any way change their settings—it only affects the type of information that is displayed.

Depending on which option you choose to view in the extended Mixer area, different panels will appear. For example, there are no MIDI EQ settings in the Extended Mixer panel; when you choose to display the EQ for other channels, the MIDI channel's Extended area is grayed out.

As an example, the MIDI insert's Extended panel displays the four insert settings shown in Figure 32.5. Each insert has the following functions:

■ Activate insert

■ Open insert editor

■ Select plug-in (insert effect)

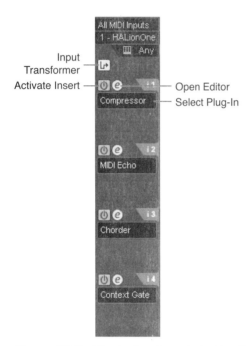

Figure 32.5 Displaying inserts in the Extended MIDI channel panel.

Audio inserts have the same controls as the MIDI inserts; however, the list displayed in the Insert Selection menu is different.

As another example, both extended EQ display options offer the same controls in different display options, as shown in Figure 32.6:

■ An On/Off button to enable or disable the EQ band

■ Gain control (top slider)

■ Frequency control (second slider)

■ Q setting (third slider)

The settings displayed in the Extended panels are the same settings that are available in the Inspector area of each track, and you can click on the e button (Edit Channel Settings) next to the channel's Level fader to open that channel's additional settings panel.

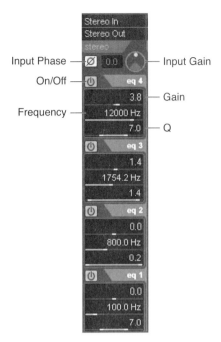

Figure 32.6 Displaying EQ settings in the Extended audio channel panel.

Routing Panel

The Routing panel, found at the very top of Cubase's Mixer, lets you choose the input and output busses for audio channels and input and output MIDI ports for MIDI channels.

If you don't see the Routing panel, shown in Figure 32.7, click on the Show Routing button in the upper-left corner of the Mixer. To hide the panel once again, click on the Hide Routing button that appears in place of the previous Show Routing button. Use the Routing panel to set up multiple track inputs, instead of going through the Inspector area.

Figure 32.7 The Routing panel found in the Mixer panel.

Working with Mixer Settings

Besides saving Mixer channel views, described earlier in the "Common Panel" section, there are a few other Mixer settings you can save. After a setting is saved, you can load it later, applying these saved settings elsewhere in the Mixer. These options are available by right (PC)-/Control (Mac)-clicking over any channel in the Mixer. The settings you save are those of the currently selected channel. Similarly, the Load Selected Channels option loads the saved Mixer settings in all selected channels. Saving selected channels also allows you to store bus routing.

The Save/Load All Mixer Settings function saves all the current audio channel settings so that you can retrieve them later by using the Load All Mixer Settings function. To load saved Mixer settings, you simply need to select the appropriate channel, select the load setting option desired, look for the file on your media drive, and load it in the Mixer panel.

In the same context menu, you also have the option to link or unlink channels. When channels are linked, the volume, EQ and send effect settings, bypass insert, and bypass send effect settings you apply to one channel also affect all the other channels linked to this one.

Link or unlink channels in the Mixer panel:

1. Select the first channel you want to link.

2. Shift-click on the other channels you want to link with this first channel.

3. Right-click (PC)/Control-click (Mac) on one of the selected channels.

4. Select the Link Channels function from the context menu.

5. To unlink the channels, select one of the linked channels, and then select Unlink Channels from the same context menu.

Using Hold Peak: You can enable/disable the Hold Peak option by clicking inside the VU meter of any channel inside the Mixer.

Adding Tracks Inside the Mixer: Add tracks to a project from within the Mixer by selecting the Add Track option in the Mixer's context menu. The track is added to the right of the currently selected track; it also appears as a new track in the Project window.

To edit all channel settings in a single window, open the Channel Settings window, shown in Figure 32.8. To open this window, click the Edit Channel Settings button in either the Inspector's Channel section, the Track List area, or the Mixer panel.

Editing the Input Bus Channels

The input channel strips monitor the levels and effects of the audio busses that provide inputs to your project. As such, they offer similar controls found in other channel strips, with one significant difference—you can't solo an input bus.

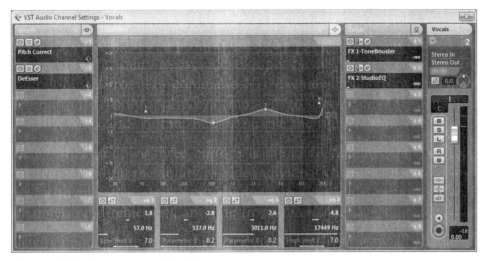

Figure 32.8 The Channel Settings window.

You use the input channel strip in Cubase to monitor the signal as it enters the input of your audio hardware, and then adjust its level accordingly. After an input bus is active, it becomes available at the top of the audio channels.

Change the physical input or output assigned to a bus:

1. Select Devices > VST Connections to open the VST Connections panel.

2. Select the Inputs tab.

3. Select the appropriate bus.

4. Select the desired input path on your audio hardware from the available selections in the Device Ports column.

Renaming Busses: You can rename busses inside the Mixer by double-clicking the current bus name at the bottom of its channel strip and entering a new name for this bus.

Editing the Output Bus Channels

The number and type of output bus channels available in the Mixer correspond to the output bus channels previously created in the VST Connections panel. How you use these outputs is contingent upon the project at hand and the number of available outputs on your audio hardware.

Depending on how you set up your system or how many separate audio outputs your audio hardware offers, you will generally use the two main outputs of your audio hardware to monitor your project in stereo. If there are more than two outputs on your audio hardware, you can use these as additional output busses. These could be used to feed an external effect processor, a headphone amplifier, another recording device, or a multispeaker monitoring system typical in surround systems. For more on this, take a look at Chapter 6, "Using the Control Room Mixer."

Each output bus created in the VST Connections panel appears when output bus channels are visible in the Mixer. You also can change or create bus output configurations through the VST Connections panel. If your audio hardware only offers a stereo output pair, creating a single stereo output bus and perhaps two mono output busses should be enough because you can't separate the signal on its way out, anyway (besides the two mono signals). If you want to group a series of channels and control or process their audio signal as one subgroup in the Mixer, you should use a group channel rather than a bus.

You can send any audio channel (audio, VSTi, ReWire, and group channels) to any active bus or group channels.

Output busses, like other audio channels, can also have up to eight assignable inserts, but have no sends. Assigning effects to output busses can be useful when you want to optimize the overall level of a project with compression/limiting or some other dynamics processing, apply dithering to reduce the bit depth of your project's audio output from 32 (or 24) to 16 bits per sample, or simply add a subtle reverb to the entire mix.

Then again, output busses don't have to be used only for mixing purposes. The last two insert effects—inserts 7 and 8—are post-fader, contrary to the typical pre-fader insert configuration. As mentioned in the tip called "Preparing a 16-Bit Mix-Down," dithering plug-ins (or corresponding hardware inserts) should always be the last insert effect in the chain, placed in post-fader insert slot 8 on the final output bus for your mix.

Preparing a 16-Bit Mix-Down: If you are preparing your project for a final CD mix-down and you want to convert the files from 32- or 24-bit to 16-bit resolution (required for most CD burning programs that don't offer their own dithering options for source files at higher bit depths), you should apply the UV22 dithering plug-in effect as your last insert effect for the output bus containing the audio content, in one of the post-fader insert slots 7 or 8.

Using the Can Hide Function

With a hardware mixer, hiding what you don't need is not an option. But in Cubase's Mixer, you can easily hide those tracks you're not currently using—which makes effective use of limited screen real estate and makes the Mixer easier to use.

When working with large projects, the number of channels displayed in a Mixer can become overwhelming. The ability to hide things can also be useful when working with ghost tracks, or tracks that you use to place events temporarily but are not part of your mixing process. Hiding them from view makes it easier to focus on the tasks at hand.

> **Ghost Tracks:** *Ghost tracks* are audio or MIDI tracks that contain shared copies of events used in another track for doubling parts or alternate processing. A ghost track can also be the disabled original track you're keeping as a reference.

I discussed the Common panel's Hide buttons, but hiding all audio channels or instrument channels might not be what you had in mind. One way to deal with this is to use the Can Hide functionality, which allows users to flag certain channels as "hideable." Once a channel is flagged as a Can Hide channel, clicking the Mixer's Hide Channels Set to Can Hide button hides this and all channels from view. Hidden channels still play unless they were muted before they were hidden. Because this process is twofold, let's start by looking at how to set this Can Hide flag.

Set individual channels to Can Hide:

1. Click the down arrow at the top of any channel strip.

2. Select the Can Hide option.

The Hide Channels Set to Can Hide button found in the Common panel of the Mixer, along with the three symbols below it, are a part of the Can Hide set of features available in the Mixer's Channel menu. The main Hide Channels button hides all channels that are flagged as Can Hide. You can unhide all channels by disabling this button.

Set a selection of channels as Can Hide:

1. Set the Command Target button in the Common panel to Selected Only.

2. Select the channels you want to set as Can Hide. Hold Ctrl (PC)/⌘ (Mac) down when clicking on channels to select as many channels as you want.

3. Click on the Set Target Channels to Can Hide button.

Use the other Can Hide functions to remove the Can Hide flag from selected channels or from all channels at once.

What Makes a Great Mix?

So far in this chapter we've discussed the mechanics of using the Mixer. Beyond all this button pushing and knob twiddling, however, lurks a larger and more important question: How do you create a great-sounding mix?

Unfortunately, there are no hard-and-fast rules for what sounds good and what doesn't; at the end of the day, you have to treat each project individually and trust your ears. I can, however, offer some general advice that might provide guidance when it comes to mixing your own projects.

- The most important track is almost always the lead vocal track. If the lead vocal gets buried in the mix, you haven't done your job. Listeners want to hear the lead vocals, which means mixing them up—or sending the other tracks to the background.

- It's easy to create a mix that's too busy. When you have too much happening in the background, either instrumentally or vocally, it detracts from the lead vocal—which is, I repeat—almost always the most important part of the mix. Don't get carried away by the unlimited number of tracks that Cubase lets you work with; sometimes a simpler mix is better.

- Along the same lines, don't fall in love with subsidiary parts. That bass line may be super hip and in the groove, but if it's too busy you may have to simplify it. No matter how cool it is, it's there to support the lead vocal, not to function as a solo track.

- Proper stereo placement is important. Seldom do you want to place important vocals or instruments hard left or hard right in the mix. Off-center placement is fine for auxiliary tracks (rhythm guitar, piano accompaniment, and so on), but for the main tracks (lead vocal, drums, bass), placement in the center of the sound field is the least distracting way to go.

- Don't make it too perfect. The best recordings are seldom the most flawless ones. When mixing tracks, feel matters more than technical precision. The best-sounding take is often the one with a lot of energy and a few minor mistakes, not the one with zero mistakes and a machine-like soul. Bottom line, most listeners will never hear the details (and flaws) that you do in the studio.

- Remember that most people will listen to your recording in the car, or on an iPod, on their computers, or on an otherwise less-than-perfect audio system. The sound you hear on your studio monitors will almost always be better than what most listeners will hear on their home or portable audio equipment. Consider making a "pre-mix" that you can play on various audio setups to hear for yourself what the average listener will hear. (In the old days, some top producers would feed their recordings through a cheap car speaker connected to the mixing console, to hear how things would sound to a teenager cruising around town.)

Overall, it's important to think like a producer during the mixing process—not like a musician. It's the final sound that's important, not any individual part, even if you played it yourself. Be as ruthless as you need to be to cut and fade and otherwise mold the individual tracks to achieve the most effective mix.

33 Working with FX Channel Tracks

FX channel tracks are similar to auxiliary returns on a hardware mixer or console. On hardware mixers, aux returns are often used to incorporate the output from external effect modules into the mix. Although they also can be used this way in Cubase, more often the effects are actually software plug-ins on the FX channel itself.

You can add up to 64 FX channels per project in Cubase, and each of them can hold a chain of up to eight plug-in effects. Audio signals can be routed to FX channels using the send controls available in every audio, instrument, group, or ReWire channel. If there is no source signal routed through it via sends from other channels, an FX channel is silent.

Here's a summary of what you will learn in this chapter:

- How to create an FX channel
- How to work with sends
- How to use FX channels as a send destination
- How to bypass FX channels and send destinations

Understanding the FX Channel Options

The main purpose of FX channel tracks is to process audio sent from several channels simultaneously by passing the combined signal through the same audio plug-in. In comparison, audio insert effects on each source channel can only process the audio signal of the channel where they reside, and the options for adjusting the mix level between the source and processed signals are a bit more limited.

The perfect example for an FX channel is when you need to add some reverb to drum tracks, where each instrument in the drum kit has been recorded on a separate track. To make all the drums and cymbals sound like they were recorded in the same room or environment, it makes sense to apply a common reverb to all of these tracks. This is in contrast to loading multiple instances of the same reverb as inserts on each drum channel, which would not only take more time to set up, but it would also reduce the number of insert slots available, increase the resources required to process each signal individually, and force you to update effect levels in every channel whenever a change is required.

At its core, the FX channel track in Cubase is very similar to a group channel or an audio channel. It offers the same volume, pan, mute, and solo controls, but it also offers a few distinct features of its own. You can't choose the input bus for an FX channel track because it receives its signal exclusively via sends from other audio channels (which include group and instrument channels, but not their MIDI counterpart). This also means that you can't record any audio into an FX channel track, but you can certainly record the output of an FX channel track. Because the main purpose of an FX channel track is to provide effects to audio from other channels in your project, the sends from an FX channel cannot be routed to another FX (or group) channel.

Add an FX channel track to a project:

1. Select Project > Add Track > FX Channel.

2. In the Add FX Channel Track dialog box (see Figure 33.1), select a track configuration from the drop-down menu. This determines how the effect will process the signal going through it. Keep in mind that most current plug-ins are configured for stereo audio processing.

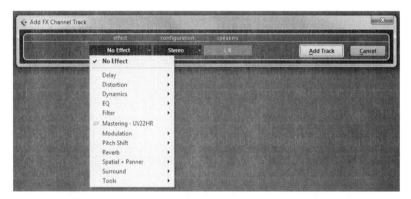

Figure 33.1 The Add FX Channel Track dialog box.

3. Select the desired plug-in from the Effect drop-down menu. If you are not sure which plug-in you want to use at this point, you can leave the plug-in field set to No Effect and change it later. This will simply create an empty FX channel, which can also serve to send an audio signal to an external source.

4. Click OK.

Using Audio Track Sends

FX channels receive their input from other channels through the Track Sends feature. The term *sends* comes from the fact that, in addition to the channel's main output assignment, you are also "sending" the signal to another destination. Send controls are completely independent from each other and from the main channel controls. That's why they are so convenient.

Understanding Send Effects

With a send effect, the audio stays in the signal path until it reaches the output bus, where it is sent to the selected plug-in. The processed signal is then available to be sent to the monitor mix, or to the final mix-down. Because send effects are added at the very end of the signal path, they are best suited for effects such as reverb and delay.

Managing Audio Track Sends

Before you can send a track's input to an FX track effect, however, you must first create the FX track, as just discussed. You can then control the sends for an audio or MIDI track from the Sends section of that track's Inspector, as shown in Figure 33.2.

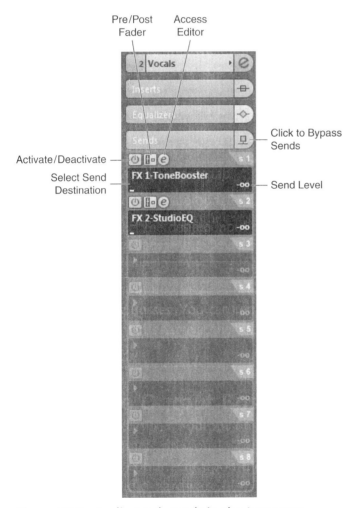

Figure 33.2 Audio track sends in the Inspector.

The Click to Bypass Sends button lights up whenever one of the eight sends in the track is active. When all the sends are bypassed, the button lights up yellow; it lights up blue when the sends are active. Click this button to bypass all sends at once without changing any settings in this section. To bypass a single send, simply deactivate it. Deactivating the track itself will also disable its sends.

For each audio track send, there are three buttons above the Select Send Destination field —the Activate/Deactivate toggle button, the Pre-/Post-Fader toggle button, and the Access Editor button, which (unless the send destination is an output bus for physical outputs on your audio hardware) opens the panel for the plug-in insert in slot 1 of the destination track, where you can change parameter settings. Below these three buttons is the Select Send Destination field, which displays the name of the send destination when one has been assigned. Send destinations can be FX channels, output busses, or group channels.

If a send destination is an output bus to physical audio ports, the Access Editor button is inactive, as it is while the destination FX/Group channel has no plug-ins. The Access Editor button is active only if the destination channel has an insert plug-in effect in slot 1 (that is, if slot 1 is empty, the button is inactive *even if the destination channel has active plug-ins in its other slots*).

As noted, to assign a send to any destination, this destination has to exist beforehand. Changing the name of the destination track alters the name that appears here. Once a destination has been assigned, sending a signal to this destination is done by dragging the Send Level bar or by entering a numeric value in the Send Level value field. This controls how much signal from this track you want to send to the selected FX channel track. Audio sent to an FX channel track (which then routes the signal through audio plug-in effects inserted into its signal chain) is processed at the level at which it is received. The more signal you send to the effect, the more processed sound you will hear for this audio signal. The idea is to give you control over how much processed signal you want to hear for each individual track without having to load multiple instances of plug-in effects on the source tracks.

You can have only a total of eight send destinations per audio track, but you can create up to 64 FX channels. This means that the send destinations from each channel can be completely different from the others. For example, you might have 10 FX channel tracks in which audio track 1 uses sends 1 through 4, and audio track 2 uses sends 1 through 4 as well, but in both cases, the signal might be sent to different FX channel tracks altogether, with track 1 going to FX channel tracks 1, 2, 3, and 4, and track 2 perhaps sending its signal to FX channel tracks 3, 5, 7, and 9.

Send an audio track to an FX channel track:

1. Unfold the Sends tab in the Inspector area of the audio track.

2. Select the desired send destination from the drop-down menu in the Select Send Destination field. You can also send an audio signal to a group channel (if one exists) or an output bus.

3. Activate the sends.

4. Select Pre- or Post-Fader, as desired.

5. Raise the level sent to the effect until the desired effect is reached.

Adjusting the Overall Level of an FX: To adjust the overall level of the effect in the mix, you can simply adjust the FX channel's volume level. Changing this level affects the signal from all audio tracks that are being routed through that FX channel.

After completing these steps, you need to fine-tune both the level being sent to the FX channel from each source channel and the level returning to the mix from the FX channel until the appropriate blend is found.

To send the signal from one track to more than one send destination, repeat the same steps mentioned earlier in this section for another send destination. Unlike insert effects, each send effect is processed in parallel, not in series. The slot numbers used for each of the eight potential sends from a channel do not affect the resulting sound.

Figure 33.3 shows how a sends signal is routed. (In Post-Fader mode, the signal sent to the effect is taken after the audio track's channel volume level and volume settings.) As you can see, there are many places where you can bypass an effect. The following list describes the differences between each type of signal bypass and how you can use each one.

■ **Bypass/activate the signal sent to all send destinations in a track.** Use the Click to Bypass Sends button found in the Sends tab's title bar (in the Inspector area of the audio track).

■ **Bypass/activate the signal sent to one send destination in a track.** Use the Activate/ Deactivate button found above the name of that send destination (which in the case of FX channel destinations will display the name of the effect in its first insert slot) in the Track Sends section in the audio track's Inspector area.

■ **Bypass all the tracks sent to the same effect.** Use the Bypass button found on the FX channel Track List or in the FX channel's settings.

Sending a Signal Outside Cubase: You can also use sends to route your signal to additional output busses on your audio hardware. This might come in handy when you want to process the signal with a hardware device rather than a soft-ware-based plug-in, as well as for creating additional cue mixes and broadcast feeds. To route your signal through a piece of hardware outside Cubase, create a

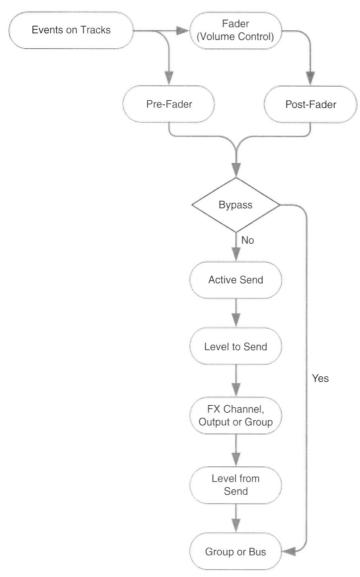

Figure 33.3 The audio send signal path diagram.

new external FX connection in the VST Connections panel. After the connection is created, select the corresponding external FX from the FX selection menu.

Managing FX Channels Through VST Connections

For projects involving many FX channels, adding and managing this type of channel can be performed inside the VST Connections panel, shown in Figure 33.4, which is accessible by selecting Devices > VST Connections. The Group/FX tab of the VST Connections panel provides a few easy ways to create FX channels, rename them, and change their output settings with a few clicks.

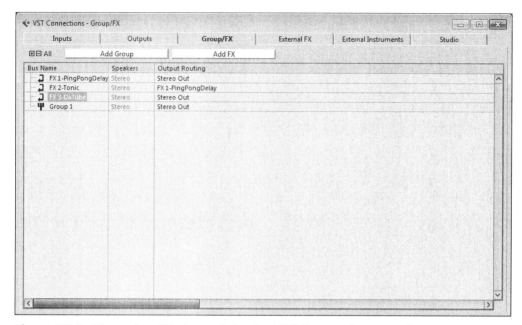

Figure 33.4 Managing FX channels in the VST Connections panel.

- **Add an FX channel.** Click on the Add FX button or right-click (PC)/Control-click (Mac) in the Bus Name column and choose Add FX Channel from the context menu.

- **Remove an FX channel.** Right-click (PC)/Control-click (Mac) over the bus name and then select Remove Channel from the context menu.

- **Change the output of an FX channel.** Click in the Output Routing column next to the desired FX channel and choose another output bus from the context menu.

34 Adding Equalization

The sound of an instrument or voice stretches across a large band of frequencies. By adjusting specific frequencies—increasing some and decreasing others—you can dramatically affect the sound of your recordings.

For that reason, equalization (EQ) is an essential part of the recording and mixing process today. It's the secret weapon of the savvy recording engineer and can make or break the sound of a recording. It's also typically one of the last parts of the mixing process; you apply EQ to your mix just before you move into the mastering process.

That said, equalization can be used at any point in your project, either correctively or creatively. Too much equalization, and you might lose the purity of a well-recorded original sound. On the other hand, a subtle boost or cut of a given frequency can make a vocal sound warmer, give a snare drum more "crack," clean up a muddy bass guitar, or make a lead guitar cut through the backing instruments.

Here's a summary of what you will learn in this chapter:

- Understand the three components of equalization—frequency, gain, and Q

- How to adjust the EQ controls in the Channel Settings window, Track Inspector, and Extended Mixer

- How to use the EQ graph to adjust EQ graphically

- How to save and recall EQ presets

- How to apply different filter types

- How to carve an EQ hole

Understanding Equalization

Equalization shapes the tone of a signal by boosting or cutting selected frequency ranges. Each track you create in Cubase can be equalized separately, or you can equalize your entire recording by using EQ during the output stage.

When you add EQ to a track or recording, there are three settings you have to specify—the frequency you want to boost or cut, the amount you want to boost or cut that frequency, and the "Q" level. This section examines each of these concepts separately.

EQ After Recording: You can add EQ at any point in the recording or mixing process—even when you're laying down the initial tracks. That said, many engineers prefer to add EQ after the recording has been made and other effects have been added; this way you're equalizing the final sound you'll hear, after all the other recording tricks have been applied.

Frequency

The Frequency control determines which frequency is affected by the chosen equalization. You can choose any frequency within the standard 20–20,000 Hz range to boost or cut. That means you could choose to increase the volume of the 500 Hz frequency, or decrease the one at 8,000 Hz.

Gain

The Gain control lets you specify how much you want to increase (boost) or decrease (cut) the selected frequency. Volume level is measured in decibels (dB), and that's how you specify the boost/cut level. Cubase lets you boost or cut the frequency up to 24dB—that's a +/−24dB range for each frequency you equalize.

Q

The Q (Quality Factor) level specifies the bandwidth (that is, the width of the frequency range) that is affected by the boost or cut. The lower the Q value, the greater the width affected; the higher the Q value, the narrower the width.

More precisely, the Q level corresponds to a set number of octaves that are affected by the EQ boost/cut. For example, a Q of 0.7 affects a bandwidth of two octaves; a Q of 1.4 affects one and a half octaves; and a Q of 2.8 affects one octave. That's why a lower Q number affects a wider frequency range.

A narrow Q is useful for isolating a problematic frequency, such as a 60-Hz cycle, that is often associated with electrical equipment. A wide Q is useful to enhance or reduce a large area of the harmonic structure of a sound, such as boosting the high end of the sound.

Magic Q: Many professional recording engineers believe that the "magic Q" setting is 1.0, which corresponds to a 1 1/3-octave range. This happens to be the bandwidth that best matches how different instruments cover the different frequency ranges. For more melodic instruments, you can broaden the frequency range covered by using a lower Q number; for less melodic instruments, such as drums, you can use a higher Q number.

Adding EQ

There are three ways to add EQ in Cubase—in the Channel Settings window, in the Extended Mixer, and in the Equalizer panel of the track Inspector. All three methods add the exact same EQ; which method you use depends on how you like to work.

Each of these equalizers is a four-band equalizer. The four bands are displayed from high to low; within each band the controls are, from top to bottom, gain, frequency, and Q level.

Adjust EQ controls:

1. Start with the lowest frequency you want to equalize.

2. Click "on" the power button for the first EQ setting control.

3. Drag the slider bar in the Frequency control to the frequency you want to adjust. Alternately, double-click the frequency value and enter a new value between 20 and 20,000 Hz.

4. Drag the slider bar in the Gain control to determine how much you want to boost or cut the selected frequency. Alternately, double-click the gain value and enter a new value between −24 and +24.

5. Click the Band Type control and select the desired filter type from the context menu. (See "Applying Filter Types" later in this chapter.)

6. Drag the slider bar in the Q control to adjust the slope of the filter for this band. For bandpass filters (the only mode available for EQ bands 2 and 3), at a given amount of gain increase or decrease, smaller Q values result in wider bands, whereas higher values result in narrower bands.

7. Repeat these steps for each additional frequency range you want to adjust.

You can bring back each value to its default position in the EQ by Ctrl-clicking (PC)/⌘-clicking (Mac) on the appropriate field. You also can do before/after comparison listening by deactivating an EQ band. This acts as a band bypass. When you deactivate an EQ band, its settings remain unchanged.

EQ in the Channel Settings Window

Perhaps the most versatile way to adjust EQ is in Cubase's Channel Settings window. You open the Channel Settings window for a given channel by selecting that track in the track listing, and then clicking the Edit button at the top of the Inspector.

The Equalizers panel (see Figure 34.1) rests in the middle of the Channel Settings window. There's a big EQ graph at the top of this section; below are the four EQ controls.

Beyond setting the EQ controls individually, as previously discussed, you can also change EQ directly from the EQ graph, using your mouse. The display represents

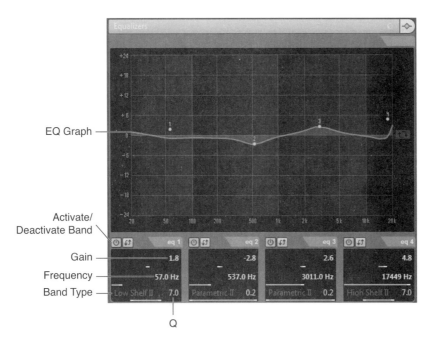

Figure 34.1 The Equalizers panel in the Channel Settings window.

the current EQ settings for the selected audio track; each band is represented by a point along a centered horizontal line. This center line represents an EQ in its default state, which implies that no boost or cut has been made to the audio at the frequency. Frequencies are displayed from low on the left to high on the right of the display. The space above the centered line represents a gain boost, whereas the space under the centered line represents a cut.

Any changes you make in the Equalizers panel are visible here, so you can use this area to quickly glance at the curve produced by your current EQ settings for this track. However, the EQ curve can also be used to change your EQ settings for the track graphically.

Adjust EQ settings using the EQ graph:

- **To add an EQ band:** Cubase includes a four-band equalizer. Click where you want to add a new EQ band on the EQ's curve. The band numbers correspond to their respective frequency ranges. This means that where you click in the display influences which band number appears. If you want to use a low-shelf, low-pass, high-shelf, or high-pass filter, you will need to click near the left or right extremities of the display, depending on the band you want to activate.

- **To change the gain:** Hold the Ctrl (PC)/⌘ (Mac) key down while you drag the band's handle up or down in the display.

- **To change the frequency without affecting the gain:** Hold the Alt (PC)/ Option (Mac) key down while you drag the band's handle right or left in the graphical display.

■   **To change the band's Q:** Hold the Shift key down and move your mouse up to increase the width of the Q (the Q value will actually go down), and move your mouse down to decrease the width of the Q (the Q value will actually go up).

EQ in the Track Inspector

In addition, the Inspector for each audio track includes an Equalizers tab, shown in Figure 34.2. Display this area by clicking the Show Active Equalizers button. In addition to the individual EQ bands, this tab also includes an Equalizer Curve section. This is an editable curve, just like in the Channel Settings window; click any point on the curve to adjust the EQ.

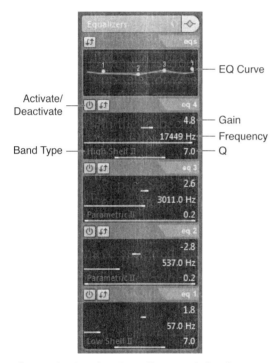

Figure 34.2 The Equalizers tab in the Inspector.

EQ in the Extended Mixer

If you're using the Mixer in Extended view, you can make these same EQ adjustments there. To display the EQ view, shown in Figure 34.3, click the down arrow at the bottom right of the Extended panel and select EQs. (To display the EQ view with an Equalizer Curve section, select EQs Curve, instead.)

Applying Filter Types

Cubase offers several types of filters for its equalizer. Not all of these filters are available for all EQ bands; EQ1 and EQ4 bands share an identical set of features, whereas the EQ2 and EQ3 bands share a different set of identical features.

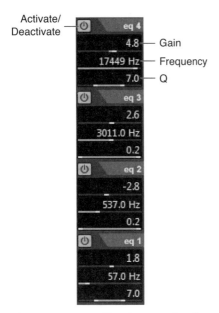

Figure 34.3 Adjusting EQ in the Extended Mixer.

You select a filter type by clicking the Band Type control in the EQ view and choosing from the options in the menu. The available filters include the following:

■ **Low Pass I and II.** The low pass filter usually associated with EQ band 4 filters out the high frequencies. The Low Pass I filter is unaffected by the Q value. With Low Pass II, a resonance filter creates a bump at the center of the band; the narrower the Q, the more pronounced this bump will be.

■ **High Pass I and II.** The high pass filter usually associated with EQ band 1 filters out the high frequencies.

■ **Band Pass I and II.** These filters are available for all four EQ bands. Band Pass I mode works well in most corrective EQ situations. The Band Pass II filter offers a slightly narrower resonance (or Q) at the center of the band's frequency; this is ideal in situations where a precise band filtering effect is required.

■ **Low Shelf I, II, III, and IV.** These filters are available for EQ band 4; each one of these shelves offers a different resonance "bump" or "dip" at the cutoff frequency point. A bump occurs when the resonance is applied in the same direction as the gain and a dip occurs when the resonance is applied in the opposite direction of the gain. Some of these differences will be more perceptible when using a very narrow Q; the narrower the Q, the greater the amount of "bump" or "dip." For example, the Low Shelf II has a "dip" and Low Shelf III has a "bump," whereas the Low Shelf IV offers a combination of both.

■ **High Shelf I, II, III, and IV.** These filters are available for EQ band 1; as with the low shelf filters, each one of these shelves offers a different resonance "bump" or "dip" at the cutoff frequency point.

It may be easier to visually show how some of these filters work. Figure 34.4 displays the equalization curves distinctive to High Shelf, Low Shelf, Low Pass, and High Pass filters.

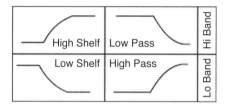

Figure 34.4 The different types of filters available in each audio channel EQ.

Using EQ Presets

Although it's more effective to adjust EQ manually (you can make more precise and relevant adjustments), Cubase does provide some handy preset EQ levels that can speed up the equalization process. These EQ presets are a good starting point for basic equalization; you can always tweak them for your personal use. To access these EQ presets, click the Preset Management button and select an instrument or sound closest to what you'd like to achieve.

You can also save your own custom EQ settings as a new preset, which makes it much easier to recall your settings in future projects.

Store/recall/rename an EQ as a preset:

■ **Store a preset:** Click the Preset Management button in the EQ panel. At the bottom of the pop-up menu, which includes many presets included with the Cubase program, select Save Preset.

■ **Select a preset:** Click the Preset Management button and select a preset from the same menu, or select From Track Preset at the bottom of the menu to browse and extract an EQ preset from one of your stored track presets.

■ **Rename a preset:** Click the Preset Management button and select Rename Preset, type in a new name, and click OK when you are finished.

Carving EQ Holes

There are two primary reasons to apply EQ—to adjust the timbre of the sound, as I've been discussing, and to make room for certain instruments (or vocals) in the mix. This second approach is called *carving EQ holes,* because you use equalization to "carve out" a hole where a specific instrument can sit.

The most common use of EQ carving is to make vocal tracks stand out in the mix. Because vocal intelligibility relies on frequencies in the 1,000–4,000 Hz range, if you cut this range in other instruments, such as guitars and keyboards, you reduce the overlap with the vocals. This technique leaves most of this range to the vocals alone, which makes them easier to hear and understand in the mix.

Another use of EQ carving is to reduce competition among similar instruments. A good example of this is the pairing of bass guitar and bass drum, which both compete in the lower frequency ranges. To make the bass guitar more prominent and the bass drum punchier, cut the bass guitar at 60 Hz and boosting it at 100 Hz; correspondingly, boost the bass drum at 60 Hz and cut it at 100 Hz. This reduces the competition between the two instruments, and makes the bottom of the mix slightly less muddy.

35 Working with Group Channel Tracks

A group channel track offers a way to assign the output of different audio channels to a common set of controls. By adding automation or effects to this group, you affect the summed output of all audio channels assigned to this group. For example, if you don't have a multiple-output sound card, you could assign the audio outputs from various tracks to several group tracks and use these groups as submixes. Typically, you might send all the drum and percussion tracks to one group, all the backing vocals to another group, and the strings (if you have violins, violas, cellos, and contrabasses, for example) to another group. Then, if you want to increase the level of the string section, all you have to do is raise that group channel fader, rather than raise the individual audio channel faders for each string instrument.

Here's a summary of what you will learn in this chapter:

- How group tracks work
- How to create a group channel track
- How to use a group as a submix group fader

Anatomy of a Group Track

Group tracks do not contain any audio or MIDI events; as a result, in the Project window group tracks display only relevant automation information, as shown in Figure 35.1. The Inspector for a group track offers similar controls to an audio track, with a few exceptions:

- You can't record on a group track, so it has no Record or Monitor button.
- Group tracks are summing busses, taking their input from other channels assigned to them. As a result, you won't find any input selection fields. You can, however, assign the output of the group to a desired bus (or even another group channel).
- There are no track presets available for group tracks.

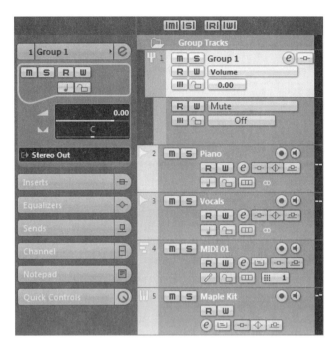

Figure 35.1 A group track in the Project window.

Using Group Channels

A group channel appears in the Mixer whenever a group track is created in the Project window. After a group track is created, you can assign the output of other tracks to it in the Inspector or the Mixer window.

Groups are used as summing outputs only; you can assign other channels to play through them and then process all the channels sent to a particular group with one single set of controls. For example, if you have multiple tracks for the microphones on your drum kit, you can assign all these individual tracks to play through a stereo "drums" group channel and instantiate a limiter as an insert effect on this group channel. This limiter is thereby applied to the entire stereo drum submix, ensuring better control over the sum of all your individual drum instruments.

In this example, applying limiting to the group channel does not prevent you from applying individual dynamic controls or EQ settings to each channel that has been routed to the group channel. Moreover, when you want to change the overall level of the drums in your mix, you will only need to adjust the group channel's level instead of all individual volume levels for each drum microphone channel.

Group channels are useful for creating submixes, in which the output from a series of related tracks are summed. You can then use the group's fader as a general level control for all tracks routed to it. (Note that panning is still applied to individual tracks, not to the group channel as a whole.)

You can create a group channel track in a number of ways:

■   From the Project window, select Project > Add Track > Group Channel.

■   In the VST Connections window (F4), select the Group/FX tab and click on the Add Group button.

■   In the Project window, right-click (PC)/Control-click (Mac) in the Track List and select Add Group Channel Track from the context menu.

■   In the Mixer window, right-click (PC)/Control-click (Mac) anywhere and select the Add Track > Group Channel command from the context menu.

Use a group as a submix group fader:

1.   Create a group channel track in the Project or Mixer window.

2.   Name this group appropriately. The group's name will appear in the pop-up selector when you select an output destination for any audio track or channel.

3.   In the Inspector's Channel Settings panel for the first channel in the group, click the Output Routing field and select the group's name from the menu.

4.   Repeat Step 3 for all the channels you want to send to this group or any other group channel.

After you have assigned the outputs from various audio or VSTi channels to the same group channel, you can either adjust their relative levels individually, or use the group channel's fader to adjust the overall level being sent to the master output bus.

я

36 Writing and Reading Automation

Not every mix is static. Oftentimes you need to increase or decrease the volume of an instrument over the course of a track; for example, you may want to turn up a guitar during a solo section, but then turn it back down when the vocals come back in.

In Cubase, changes you make to volume levels, panning, and other settings over the course of a mix are captured via the Automation feature. That is, the changes you make are automated—and captured in a separate automation subtrack.

Cubase supports two basic automation recording techniques. First, you can create mix automation in real-time by writing the volume, pan, and other parameter changes you make in the Mixer window—or anywhere that real-time controls are available in Cubase. Secondly, you can also create automation by drawing automation curves in the automation subtracks.

Owning a remote control surface definitely makes it more convenient to automate a mix when compared to using a mouse alone, but either way, the automation subtracks are always easy to access and can be edited at any time. Also, if you're used to the Mixer environment, recording automation may feel more comfortable to you when the Mixer window is visible. On the other hand, editing previously recorded automation might be easier if done through the Project window.

Here's a summary of what you will learn in this chapter:

- How to use the Read and Write buttons to record and play back automation
- How to record channel and plug-in parameter automation
- How to change the automation mode
- How to use the Automation Panel to control automation settings
- How to draw channel settings automation values in an automation track
- How to add automation using the Line tools
- How to hide and remove automation subtracks

Using the Read and Write Buttons

You can set the levels and pans of audio channels in the Mixer or Inspector without using automation, just as you would on a normal mixing desk. This enables you to adjust the level and position of your tracks in the mix without adding automation to them. As long as the Write or Read Automation buttons (found in the Common panel on the left of the Channel Mixer window) are not activated (not lit), the faders, pan, and any other effect settings stay at the same position. When the Read Automation button is disabled in the Common panel, Cubase will not read any existing automation in your tracks. However, disabling automation doesn't mean that you lose the automation you have previously recorded.

Read and Write Automation buttons are available to record and play back mix automation for each channel in the Mixer window, the Track List, the Channel Settings panel, or the Channel section of the Inspector. Use the Write button to record the automation and the Read button to enable playback of any automation data contained in this track's automation subtracks (whether created in real time with the Write button, or drawn using the mouse).

To activate the automation writing process, click the Write Automation button of the desired channel, as shown in Figure 36.1. Clicking this button in any of the mentioned areas activates the same function in all subsequent windows where the channel is represented (the Inspector, the Track List, the Channel Settings panel, and the Mixer window).

Read
Automation

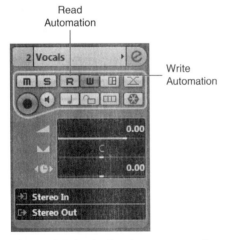

Write
Automation

Figure 36.1 Activating automation for a selected channel in the Inspector.

By clicking the Write Automation button directly in the channel, you activate the writing automation functions for this channel only. If you want to activate the automation writing mode for all channels at once, you can enable the global Write Automation button found both at the top of the Track List and in the Common panel of the Mixer window, shown in Figure 36.2. Whether you enable writing of automation on one or all channels depends on what you want to achieve.

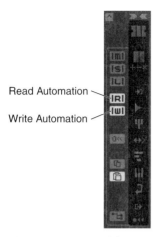

Figure 36.2 Enabling automation for all channels at once in the Mixer's Common panel.

When you activate the Write button on a channel or in the Common panel of the Mixer, Cubase is ready to record any change you make in parameter settings during playback. This includes all channel controls, insert and send effects, VSTi control panels, and Inspector parameters, for example. Bear in mind that writing of automation is completely independent of the recording function on audio or MIDI tracks. If you don't move a given parameter, Cubase will not record any data for this parameter.

After you have recorded automation, you need to activate or enable the Read Automation button in order for Cubase to read whatever automation you have recorded. Otherwise, the information is present, but your automation is not read during playback. As with the Write Automation button, the Read Automation button is available in several windows inside your project, and enabling it on a channel in one window enables it in all the other windows as well. The global Read Automation button found at the top of the Track List and in the Common panel of the Mixer window also activates the Read option for all channels at once.

Writing Channel Track Automation

This section describes how to record the most common type of automation: track automation. This type of automation is associated with a Mixer channel (also seen as a track in the Project window), as well as MIDI and audio channel settings. Automation is frequently used to change the volume or pan of a track in the course of a project, to alter the parameters of its sends or insert effects, to mute a track or its effects by enabling the Mute button, or bypassing one or several inserts or sends at a time. The actual settings you can write in real time are determined by the track class itself.

Write channel automation in real time:

1. Open the Mixer window.

2. Activate the channel's Write Automation button. This button is lit when active.

3. Position your playback cursor and click the Play button on the Transport panel (or press the spacebar) to start playback.

4. Move the appropriate faders, knobs, switches, and so on as the track plays.

5. Stop playback when you're done.

After automation has been written, you can listen to it by activating the Read Automation button and bringing the play cursor to the same location you started writing this automation. Click the Play button to see (and hear) the automation on this channel.

After your automation is written into the track, you can use the channels' automation subtracks to view the automation curves for each setting that was automated. I'll get into this a little later in the chapter.

Writing Parameter Automation

Writing real-time parameter changes in a plug-in effect, such as a VSTi or send effect, is quite similar to automating channel settings in a track. However, automation events for VST effects and software instruments are recorded in separate tracks and subtracks, created automatically by Cubase as soon as you move any of the controls of an effect or VSTi when the Write Automation button is activated inside the plug-in's control panel. (This can be a VSTi or VST effect plug-in.)

This type of automation is normally used to change the parameters of effects or a VSTi, creating dynamic changes in the plug-in over time during playback. For example, you can automate the Cutoff frequency by moving this parameter in the VSTi's control panel (provided there is such a parameter on the instrument itself).

Write automation for plug-in parameters in real time:

1. Open the desired effect's control panel.

2. Activate the Write Automation button found inside the panel. This button is lit when active.

3. Position your playback cursor and click the Play button on the Transport bar (or press the spacebar) to start playback.

4. Move the appropriate faders, knobs, switches, and so on. You might need to consult the documentation provided with the effect to find out which parameters are automatable because this varies from one effect to the next.

5. Stop the playback when finished.

Once automation has been created in a track, you can listen to it by activating the Read Automation button, as mentioned earlier in this chapter.

About Automation Modes

An automation mode determines how Cubase behaves when you change parameters with the mouse or a remote control surface; different modes can be used depending on the type of automation you want to perform.

Cubase 6 offers three automation modes: Touch (default), Auto-Latch, and Cross-Over. They differ in their "punch out" behavior.

- With **Touch** automation, the program starts writing automation as soon as you press or move any control for a parameter, such as the Volume fader, and stops writing when you release the mouse button.

- With **Auto-Latch,** the program starts writing the automation as soon as you press or move any control, and stops writing when you stop playback or deactivate the Write Automation button. In other words, the last automation value is continuously written until you turn off the Write Automation button within the channel mixer found in the Inspector area or in the Mixer window. This mode is useful if you want to write over a long section containing previously recorded automation that you want to replace. It is also useful when you are using an external control surface to control your mix. Because Cubase has no way of knowing which control you want to rewrite, it starts writing as soon as you move a control and keeps writing the value sent by this control (overwriting any existing automation for the particular parameter) until you stop playback or disable the Write Automation button. Make sure, however, that you don't touch any other controls when doing this; otherwise, you might end up replacing automation by mistake. Note that this also applies for some VSTi and VST plug-in effects parameters.

> **Locking Automation Once Completed:** Once you are happy with a track and its automation, that's a good time to lock it in place with the Lock button found in the Track List area. By locking a track, you can avoid unintentionally overwriting existing automation data.

- **Cross-Over** automation works much like the Auto-Latch mode, with one exception: As soon as your playback cursor crosses a previously recorded automation curve point, the write process is automatically turned off.

> **Change the automation mode:**
>
> 1. In the Project window, click the Global Automation Mode button in the toolbar (see Figure 36.3).
>
>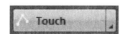
>
> **Figure 36.3** The Global Automation Mode button in the Project window's toolbar.
>
> 2. Select the desired automation mode from the drop-down menu.

Managing Automation with the Automation Panel

You can manage most of Cubase's automation functions with the Automation Panel, new to Cubase 6. You display this panel by clicking the Open Automation Panel button (the down arrow next to the Global Automation Mode button) on the Project window toolbar.

As you can see in Figure 36.4, the Automation Panel consists of a toolbar and four columns. The toolbar contains the following functions:

- **Activate Read for all tracks** enables all Read buttons on all tracks of your project.

- **Deactivate Read for all tracks** disables all Read buttons on all tracks of your project.

- **Activate Write for all tracks** enables all Write buttons on all tracks of your project.

- **Deactivate Write for all tracks** disables all Write buttons on all tracks of your project.

- **Global Automation Mode** lets you select which of the three automation modes (Touch, Auto-Latch, or Cross-Over) to use for your project.

- **Trim** lets you add or remove automation data from a previous pass.

- **Functions** provides access to the following automation-related functions: Delete All Automation in Project, Delete Automation of Selected Tracks, Delete Automation in Range, Freeze All Trim Automation in Project, and Freeze Trim Automation of Selected Tracks.

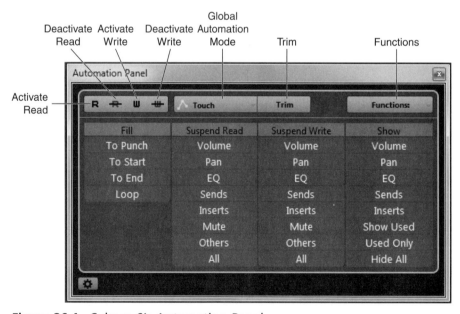

Figure 36.4 Cubase 6's Automation Panel.

Actions accessible from the Automation Panel can be applied to selected tracks or ranges in the Project window.

The four columns in the Automation Panel offer quick access to various automation-related options. These columns include the following:

■ **Fill** options define what happens in a specific section of your project when you punch out of a running automation pass. Options include To Punch, To Start, To End, and Loop. You can select fill options individually, or combine fill options by selecting multiple options at a single time.

■ **Suspend Read** excludes selected parameters from the reading of automation data. Parameters include Volume, Pan, EQ, Sends, Inserts, Mute, Others, and All.

■ **Suspend Write** excludes selected parameters from the writing of automation data. The same parameters are available as with the Suspend Read column.

■ **Show** opens the automation tracks for the selected parameters.

Drawing Automation

If working with a remote control surface is not for you, if you need to perform some fine-tuning on your automation, or if you simply want to set a curve to a specific value using a specific curve shape, perhaps drawing the automation is the better approach. By drawing your own automation, you can make much more precise changes than you can by physically riding the sliders in real time.

This section describes how to add automation curves into an automation subtrack for any channel.

Draw channel settings automation curves in an automation subtrack:

1. In the Project window's Track List area, select the track for which you want to create automation events.

2. Hover your cursor over the bottom-left corner of the selected track to display the Show/Hide Automation button (small arrow); click this button to reveal the first automation subtrack, shown in Figure 36.5.

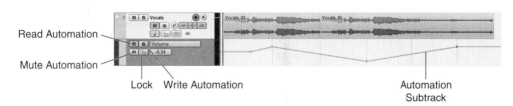

Read Automation

Mute Automation

Lock   Write Automation

Automation Subtrack

Figure 36.5 Working with an automation subtrack.

3. Enable the Read Automation button for this track/channel (and/or the particular automation subtrack).

4. Select the parameter you want to automate from the Parameter field. If the parameter you want to automate doesn't appear in this list, click the More option to display a dialog box revealing additional automatable parameters available for this track. Select the one you want and click OK to return to the subtrack. At this point, the Parameter field should display the parameter you just selected.

5. If there is currently no automation for this parameter, a colored flat horizontal line appears within this subtrack in the Event Display area. Select the Draw tool in the Project window toolbar.

6. To add a curve point, click near the location inside this lane where you want to add an automation value. If you want to create a ramp between two points, release the mouse button. However, if you want to create a curve, drag your mouse to the next desired location and value.

7. Repeat Steps 5 and 6 to add more automation curve points along this parameter's subtrack.

Note that an automation curve point is added at each location where you click, as long as you are using the Pencil or Draw tool and stay inside the subtrack's boundaries.

Adding Additional Automation Events

If you want to add automation events to another parameter for the same channel, you can either select another parameter from the Parameter field to display a new parameter in the same subtrack or hover over the bottom-left corner of the automation subtrack and click the newly visible Append Automation Track button. When the new subtrack is visible, repeat Steps 3–6 from the previous list.

Note that choosing a different parameter in a subtrack that already contains automation does not remove or cancel the automation it holds. When a track contains recorded automation events for a given parameter, an asterisk appears after this parameter's name in the Parameter selector field for the automation subtrack. These asterisks help you quickly spot which parameters already contain automation, which makes editing and troubleshooting much more efficient.

After you've recorded automation on a track, you can select the Show All Used Automation option available in the Track List's context menu (right-click on PC or Control-click on Mac). You can add automation to several parameters by using a single subtrack, changing the parameter's name to view, or adding new automation, and after you are done, reveal all automation subtracks containing events. Remember that each parameter has its own subtrack.

Drawing Shapes

Under the Line tool are several drawing shapes: Line, Parabola, Sine, Triangle, and Square. These tools can be used to create specific automation values, such as pan effects. You can also use the Parabola and Line tools to create consistent automation curves instead of drawing curve points freehand-style.

Add automation using the Line tools:

1. Select the drawing shape you want to use for the Line tool.

2. Select the desired track and expand its automation subtracks.

3. From the Parameter selection field, select the parameter for which you want to create some automation curve points. You also may append additional automation subtracks if you want.

4. If the parameter you want to automate doesn't appear in this list, click the More option to display the Add Parameter dialog box. This dialog box reveals additional automatable parameters available for this track; select the one you want, and click OK to return to the subtrack. At this point, the Parameter field should display the parameter you just selected.

5. Click and drag the cursor in the automation track to add curve points.

Hiding and Removing Automation Subtracks

When working with automation, you can hide automation subtracks that you don't need to see in order to clean up your working area. Hiding automation subtracks does not prevent their automation from being read. If you don't want to hear the changes made by automation, simply turn off the Read Automation button for this track—or at the top of the Track List if you want to globally disable reading of *all* automation in this project. At any time, you also can mute only a specific type of automation by clicking the Mute Automation button for the subtrack that is displaying that parameter in the Track List.

Hide automation subtracks:

■   **To hide all automation subtracks,** select the Hide All Automation option from the context menu. This appears after right-clicking (PC)/Control-clicking (Mac) anywhere in the Track List.

■   **To hide automation for one track,** click the Show/Hide Automation button for this track (the arrow pointing up in the lower-left corner of the track containing the automation subtracks). Note that this button becomes visible only when your mouse cursor rolls over this corner of the track's entry in the Track List.

■ **To hide only one automation subtrack,** click the Show/Hide Automation button of the subtrack above it (the minus sign in the upper-left corner of the subtrack containing the automation you want to hide).

Remove automation subtracks:

■ **To erase all automation events for a subtrack's parameter,** select the Remove Parameter option from the Parameter field of this subtrack. This removes the automation subtrack, as well as all the automation curve points on the selected subtrack.

■ **To erase some of the automation events on a subtrack,** select them by using the Selection tool or Range Selection tool and delete them by pressing the Delete or Backspace key. You also can click on the selected automation events (curve points) using the Eraser tool.

■ **To remove unused subtracks that might have been left behind after editing,** select the Remove Unused Parameters option from the Parameter field in one of the subtracks.

Editing Automation

After you've recorded automation, editing it is not very different. You can use the Mixer window to edit automation in real time through the Write/Read Automation buttons or by editing automation parameters in their respective automation subtracks in the Project window.

View the automation previously recorded:

1. In the Project window, right-click (PC)/Control-click (Mac) in the Track List.

2. Select the Show Used Automation option from the context menu. If you want to see all automation recorded on all tracks, select the Show All Used Automation, instead.

You will probably notice that some parameters do not allow intermediate values. This is the case for switch type parameters, such as a Mute, Bypass, or Sustain Pedal MIDI message. Because these parameters are either on or off, there are only two acceptable values: 0 or 127. When editing their automation, you can only enter these values, and the curve points will automatically jump between these minimum and maximum values.

Using Write Automation

To edit existing automation data using the Write Automation button on a channel, you just need to write over the automation again. If Touch is selected as the automation mode, as soon as you touch a control (by clicking on it and holding it or moving it to a new location), the old automation is replaced by new values, until you release the mouse. At that point, if the Read Automation button is also active, from that point forward Cubase continues reading existing automation on the parameter's automation subtrack. (To ensure that the transition back to the existing automation values is smooth, the Automation Return Time field allows you to specify how long this transition should be after you release the control.)

Using Automation Subtracks

When you open a parameter subtrack containing recorded automation, you will notice that curve points (handles) appear along the automation line. Here's a look at how you can edit the points on this line.

Edit recorded automation in a subtrack:

- **To move an existing curve point.** In the Project window, select the Object Selection tool and move the curve point to a new location by clicking it and dragging. Note that the quantize grid settings, if the Snap is active, influence exactly where in time you can move this automation.

- **To move several automation curve points simultaneously.** With the Object Selection tool, drag a selection box over the points you want to move. The selected curve points become red. Click and drag one of the selected points to the new location. You also can Shift-click on several points if you want to edit non-continuous points instead.

- **To draw over existing automation.** In the Project window, select the Draw, Line, Parabola, Sine, Triangle, or Square tool from the toolbar and click where you want to start drawing over the existing automation and drag your tool until the point where you want to stop replacing the existing automation. The first and last points where you draw this automation automatically create a connection to the existing automation line. You can use the different options associated with each tool to create different shapes; for example, use the Ctrl (PC)/⌘ (Mac) key to invert the parabola curve.

- **To erase existing curve points.** Click on the point or drag a range over several automation curve points using the Object Selection tool. After the desired points are red, press Delete, Backspace on your keyboard, or use the Eraser tool to erase them.

- **To move or erase all automation curve points on a subtrack.** Right-click (PC)/Control-click (Mac) over the desired subtrack's Track List area and select the Select All Events option from the context menu. After they are selected, you can move or erase these automation curve points. Note that if you want to remove all automation for a parameter, you can also use the Remove Parameter option from the subtrack's Parameter field.

Moving Along Events with Their Automation: Quite often, you start working on a project, record events, and add automation to subtracks below these events. But if you need to move these events, it would be nice if the automation could move along with it. The Automation Follows Events option does exactly that: It keeps the automation attached to the event. When you move the event, the automation moves with it. You can enable this option by selecting Edit > Automation Follows Events.

37 Mixing for Surround Sound

Cubase 6 offers the possibility of mixing in several surround modes, as well as in traditional stereo mode. When it comes to an audio recording mix, the word "surround" refers to a multichannel positioning system, rather than a standard stereo (left/right) positioning. The advantage of mixing in surround is that beyond the left/right field available in stereo mixes, you can literally place your sound anywhere in space around the listener by using various surround configurations. Surround mixing is particularly effective—and necessary—with video projects, where you want the soundtrack and sound effects to surround the listener.

Here's a summary of what you will learn in this chapter:

- How to create a child input or output bus

- How to use the SurroundPanner

- How to mute speakers in the SurroundPanner

- How to edit the routing of an insert effect in a surround output bus configuration

- How to export a surround mix

Multichannel Configurations

Cubase offers a number of different multichannel surround configurations; which configuration you choose depends on the surround standard you want to use and the room for which you are mixing. For example, a surround movie soundtrack typically uses a 5.1-channel configuration, with three front speakers (left, center, and right, located in front of the listener), two surround speakers (left and right, located to the sides of the listener), and a single subwoofer. The subwoofer reproduces the lowest bass notes in the Low Frequency Effects (LFE) channel.

Table 37.1 details the various surround modes supported in Cubase 6.

To use surround mixing in Cubase, you must create a surround output bus that is connected to multi-output audio hardware. You also could create a surround input bus, but your input sources and audio tracks don't have to be multichannel in order to be routed to a surround output bus. When any audio channel is sent to a surround

413

Table 37.1 Surround Sound Modes

Mode	Description
5.1	This is the most popular surround sound format, with three front channels (left, center, and front), two side-mounted surround channels (left and right), and a single LFE (subwoofer) channel. This format is used in both Dolby Digital and DTS systems.
5.0	The same as the 5.1 format, but without the LFE channel.
LRCS	Left Right Center Surround, a four-channel system with three front channels (left, center, and right) and a single surround channel positioned behind the listener. This is the original surround format, first appearing in movie houses as Dolby Stereo and in the home as Dolby ProLogic.
LRCS+Lfe	The same as LRCS but with an added LFE (subwoofer) channel.
LRC	Left Right Center, essentially the same as the LRCS format but with only front channels (no surround channel).
LRC+Lfe	The same as LRC but with an added LFE (subwoofer) channel.
LRS	Left Right Surround, essentially the same as the LRCS format but with no front center channel.
LRS+Lfe	The same as LRS but with an added LFE (subwoofer) channel.
Quadro	A four-channel system for music, replicating the original quadraphonic recordings of the 1970s. This places two speakers (left and right) in the front, and a matching two speakers (left and right) behind the listener.
Quadro+Lfe	The same as the Quadro format, but with an added LFE (subwoofer) channel.
6.0 Cine	A six-channel setup for movie soundtracks, utilizing three front channels (left, center, right) and three surround channels (left, center, right).
6.0	A six-channel setup for music, utilizing two front channels (left and right), two side channels (left and right), and two rear surround channels (left and right).

output bus, the SurroundPanner appears in the channel's panning area, replacing the pan position value display, offering you control over more than the typical left and right channels in a stereo mix.

You can also choose to route an audio channel (disk-based, VSTi, ReWire, or FX channel) to a specific set of outputs within the surround bus channels. In that case, the pan control would remain the same, as if you were routing the signal through a mono or stereo output bus. Figure 37.1 shows how an audio channel displays the pan control when it is assigned to a surround output bus on the left and to a stereo output bus on the right.

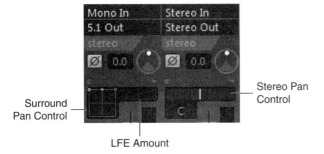

Figure 37.1 An audio channel with a surround pan control (left) and stereo pan control (right).

Mixing in surround requires multiple-output audio hardware to monitor the signal sent to these additional outputs. It also requires an external multichannel monitoring system to support surround mixes.

Creating a Surround Bus

To work with surround configurations, you need to create surround output busses. These are created in the VST Connections panel by selecting one of the multichannel configurations in the Add Output Bus dialog box.

After you have created a surround bus (input or output), you can associate each channel in the bus with an ASIO device port (that is, an individual input or output on your audio interface). How many ASIO device ports you need depends on the surround configuration you choose. For example, a 5.1 configuration will create a six-channel configuration, whereas an LCRS configuration uses only four channels.

When you want to assign an audio channel to a surround bus, you can decide to route the output directly through one of the individual channels in the surround bus, or to all the channels at once, where its exact location will be determined by the position of the SurroundPanner. When a channel is routed directly to a single channel within the surround bus, the pan area of the channel does not offer a surround panning option.

After a surround bus is created, you can also create child busses. A child bus offers a convenient way of routing an audio channel through a specific set of outputs that forms part of a surround bus. For example, you can create a stereo child bus within a 5.1 surround configuration, where the left and right channels are grouped within the surround bus.

Routing an audio channel through a stereo child bus (consisting of two audio outputs on your audio interface) allows you to control where the sound will occur in that child bus, so you will have a stereo Pan control rather than a surround Pan control. In other words, creating a child bus can make it easier to route audio through a surround bus, yet keep a stereo control (affecting both channels) when adjusting the pan and volume for this channel. For example, if you are creating a surround input bus to capture a multichannel performance or surround atmosphere, you can create child busses to represent the left/right pair and then a left surround/right surround pair. When adjusting the level of the inputs, changing the volume for the left side will also affect the right side as they are being grouped inside the surround bus configuration.

Create a child input/output bus:

1. Open the VST Connections window and select the surround bus within which you want to create a child bus.

2. Right-click (PC)/Control-click (Mac) on the selected surround bus and choose Add Child Bus to [your surround configuration's bus].

3. Select the appropriate Child Bus submenu option that you want to create.

Notice that the ASIO device ports assigned to the newly created child bus are also being used by the surround bus. Reassigning these ports in the child bus also changes them in the surround parent bus.

Surround Routing Options

When working with surround busses, both as input and output, many routing options are available.

Depending on which routing option you choose, several pan control options are available. Table 37.2 offers a quick look at the surround signal routing options and the types of pan control offered by each.

Table 37.2 Surround Signal Routing Options

Source	Destination	Pan Control
Mono	To single channel inside the surround bus	None. The output channel is mono and is heard through the associated ASIO device port.
Mono	To child bus inside the surround bus	It is handled as a standard stereo or multichannel, depending on the child bus configuration. The pan might affect the surround position or any other location, depending on the current parent bus configuration. For example, if the bus is in 5.1 (six channels) and the child bus set as an LCR subset (three channels), the channel will display the SurroundPanner to control the location. On the other hand, if your child bus is stereo (left/right), the mono channel will be panned between left and right (not surround panned, even though it is part of the surround configuration).

Table 37.2 *(Continued)*

Source	Destination	Pan Control
Mono	To a surround bus	The SurroundPanner positions the signal anywhere within the current surround bus configuration.
Stereo	To stereo child bus inside the surround bus	See above—this is the same as with a mono signal sent to a stereo child bus.
Stereo	To a surround bus	The SurroundPanner positions the signal anywhere within the current surround bus configuration.
Surround	Surround	No pan control; all channels play in the same channel as they came in from. You should avoid sending a multichannel input signal configuration into another multi-input signal configuration or into a mono or stereo output bus. For example, avoid sending a 5.1 multichannel input signal to an LCRS output bus. Doing so results in loss of sound positioning precision.

SurroundPanner V5

SurroundPanner V5, updated for Cubase 6, is automatically available in a channel's pan control area in the Mixer window (and optionally in the Inspector) when mono or stereo audio channels are routed through a surround output bus or a multichannel child bus (but not a stereo child bus). You can position and automate the position of the sound within the surround configuration by dragging the small dot inside the surround pan display.

To open the full SurroundPanner V5 window for a track, as shown in Figure 37.2, double-click the pan control area for that track in the Mixer or Inspector. This full display offers more precision and greater control over the setup and behavior of the panner.

The upper part of the SurroundPanner V5 window offers a representation of the speaker placements and the position of this channel's sound in relation to the speakers. The lower part offers a variety of controls over the behavior of the SurroundPanner itself. Note that the actual number of speakers and how they appear in the upper part depends on the current surround output bus configuration.

To roughly position this instrument in the surround field, use your mouse to drag the sound source to a new position within the SurroundPanner display. To fine-tune the position, use the positioning controls (knobs) underneath the visual display. And, in configurations with a low frequency effects (subwoofer) channel, use the LFE Level control to set the volume level of the subwoofer channel.

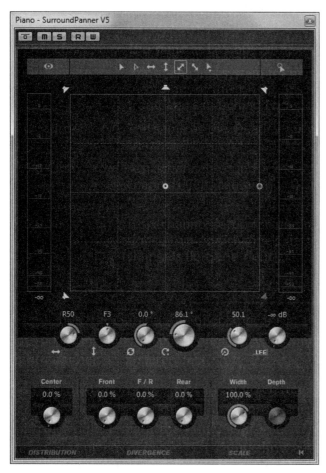

Figure 37.2   SurroundPanner V5.

Mute speakers in the SurroundPanner:

■   Alt-click (PC)/Option-click (Mac) on the speaker you want to mute.

■   Repeat the operation on the same speaker to unmute it.

You can automate the SurroundPanner as you would any other channel automation described in Chapter 36, "Writing and Reading Automation."

Routing Effects in Surround Outputs

As you might have anticipated, using effects in Surround mode is a slightly more complex issue because most effects are designed to work on two channels rather than four, five, or six channels. To that end, Cubase offers some surround plug-ins and support for surround-compatible plug-ins from third parties through a special signal path diagram, which is accessible in the Channel Settings panel for the surround output bus.

This routing also is available for any stereo or mono channels; however, the surround configuration only shows up when you are editing a multichannel track (recorded from a multichannel input) through a multichannel output bus.

By default, the Insert Routing panel is not visible; to display it, right-click (PC)/Control-click (Mac) anywhere in the window and select Customize View > Insert Routing.

Each vertical line in this display corresponds to a channel (ASIO device port) in the multichannel track, routed to its corresponding output bus channel. By assigning multiple instances of the same effect to different channels in the bus, you can use effects on all channels in the bus. Lines that are interrupted by handles before and after the insert effect indicate that the signal will be processed by this effect on this channel inside the bus.

To change the routing of an effect in a multichannel setup, double-click on the routing lines next to the effect you want to route. The Routing Editor dialog box, displayed in Figure 37.3, opens and displays three types of paths: broken lines with boxes (L, R), broken lines without boxes (C, LFE), and passing lines (Ls, Rs). The connector at the top represents the input of the insert, and the connector at the bottom represents its output. If a line is broken with a box on each side of the connector, it means that the signal is routed through the effect. If a line is broken without boxes, the signal is muted from this point on in the signal path. In the same figure, this is the case for the two center lines (channels).

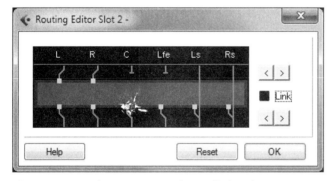

Figure 37.3 The Routing Editor dialog box.

If the line passes through without breaking, it means that the signal bypasses the effect altogether. You might decide to process a channel with a plug-in, yet send the output of this plug-in to another channel. For example, you could process the left and right surround channels with a reverb and send the output of this reverb effect into the left and right channels instead; in this example, the left and right channels will contain both the source signal bypassing the reverb and the reverb's processed output, which contains the signal originally found on the left and right surround channels.

The set of arrows separated by the Link check box moves the input channels or the output channels left or right to modify the routing. When the Link check box is active, both the input and output channels will move together.

Edit the routing of an insert effect in a surround output bus configuration:

1. Open the VST Output Channel settings for the Surround bus.

2. Assign the desired effect to the insert effect's slot.

3. Double-click the routing diagram. The Routing Editor dialog box will appear.

4. Check or uncheck the Link option, according to your needs (see the description from a moment ago).

5. Click on the input arrows (top pair) to move the connections to the desired channels.

6. Click on the output arrows (lower pair) to move the connections to the desired channels.

7. Click OK when you are finished.

Exporting a Surround Mix

After you have completed your surround mix, you can export it as you would export a normal final stereo mix. The only difference with a surround mix is that you can choose an additional number of output file formats in the File > Export > Audio Mixdown dialog box. Make sure you select the appropriate multichannel bus output in the Channel Selection pane; this is necessary for Cubase to create the proper surround mix.

38 Mastering and Exporting the Final Mix

You have now come to the final part of your Cubase recording project, where you take everything you've done up to this point and prepare it for distribution. This process is called *mastering*, and it creates the master files that end up on a shiny new compact disc or are uploaded to the Internet.

Although most of this chapter discusses how to master a final mix and then export that mix to a file, understand that exporting any track, part of a track, the audio rendering of an effect to create a sample, or a specific loop inside a project is performed in quite the same way. The same precautions need to be taken to ensure the quality of the exported mix is good and the same output file format options are available, regardless of the purpose for the export.

Here's a summary of what you will learn in this chapter:

- How to export your final mix as an audio file
- Understanding different audio formats
- How to enter information that will be embedded in broadcast wave files
- Tips on mastering
- How to set up dithering on your final mix-down
- The importance of backing up your work
- How to export a project to an OMF format

Audio Exporting Options

After you are satisfied with your mix and you want to render a final mix-down, you use Cubase's Export Audio Mixdown function [File (PC)/Cubase (Mac) > Export > Audio Mixdown. This function also lets you export a specific selection, a track containing effects, or a VSTi or ReWire track.

The Audio Mixdown function does not, however, export MIDI tracks for non-VSTi devices, such as ReWire devices, unless two conditions are met: the Real-Time Export option must be selected, and the external MIDI devices have to be configured using the

VST Connections, as described in Chapter 10, "Using VST and MIDI Instruments." The following steps assume that you have already configured your VST Connections accordingly and have previously converted your MIDI/instrument tracks into audio tracks, as described in Chapter 17, "Navigating MIDI Tracks."

Export your final mix as an audio file:

1. Mute the tracks you don't want to include in your audio mix, and unmute those you do want to include.

2. Position your left locator where you want to begin the audio mix and the right locator where you want to end the audio mix-down. (If your mix includes reverb and delay effects, be sure to position your right locator *beyond* the last audio and MIDI events in your tracks, leaving enough time for the reverb decay or delay repeats to fade out completely at the end of your mix-down file.)

3. If you want to export the automation when rendering a mix-down, be sure all the appropriate Read Automation buttons are enabled.

Subzero!: The output bus used for rendering an audio mix-down should not clip at any time during playback. Clipping causes distortion in your final mix-down. So, be sure your levels stay below zero dBFS (decibels, full scale) at all times and that the clip indicator in this bus does not light up.

---

4. Select File (PC)/Cubase (Mac) > Export > Audio Mixdown. The Export Audio Mixdown dialog box appears, as shown in Figure 38.1.

5. In the Name field, enter a name for your exported file.

6. Click in the Path field to select an appropriate folder in which to save this file.

7. Use the File Format section to select the appropriate file format for the audio mix-down. Depending on the file format, various additional options will appear in this section. If you are preparing an audio mix-down to burn on a CD, for example, chances are you will select a WAV or AIFF format. For Web distribution, MP3 (MPEG 1 Layer 3 File) or WMA (Windows Media Audio File) may be more appropriate. The Wave64 format should be selected when you expect the resulting file size will be greater than 2 gigabytes.

8. In the Channel Selection panel, select the appropriate bus you want to mix down. You can optionally choose only a specific channel as the source for your mix-down, such as a VSTi, Group, FX or audio channel.

9. In the Audio Engine Output section, set the sample rate and bit depth you want to use for your exported file.

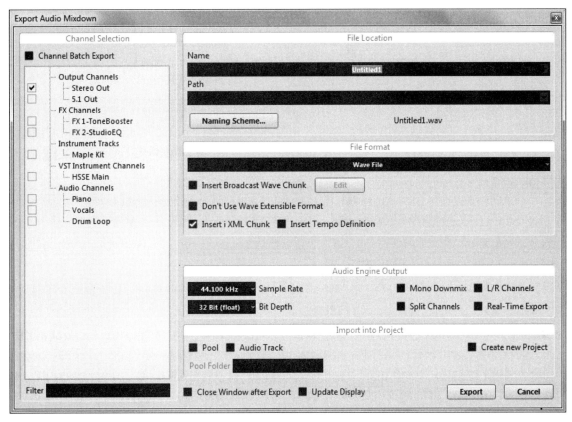

Figure 38.1 The Export Audio Mixdown dialog box.

10. In addition to creating a stereo mix-down file, you can also check the Mono Downmix option to render a mono file or select the Split Channels option to split a stereo mix into two files (which will have "Left" or "Right" appended to their file names).

Splitting Stereo Files: Note that when you go to the Audio Channels area of the Export Audio Mixdown dialog box and select the Stereo Split option, Cubase creates a left and a right mono file, rather than a single stereo interleaved file. This might save some steps if you need to use this file in another audio application that doesn't directly support stereo interleaved files, such as Pro Tools.

---

11. Check the Real-Time Export option only if needed. Real-time export is particularly useful when you are rendering external MIDI devices, as described in Chapter 17.

12. If you want to automatically import this file into the Pool or add it as a new track in your project, check the appropriate options in the Import into Project section.

13. Check the Update Display option if you want to monitor the levels during mix-down. If a clip occurs, you can see it and adjust the levels appropriately to avoid the problem.

14. Click Save when you are finished.

If you have enabled the Audio Track option in the Import into Project section, Cubase will create a new audio track. After the newly created track is in place, be sure to mute the source tracks for this new track (containing the audio mix-down).

If you have chosen not to import the audio rendering of your mix back into your project, you can proceed with your work as usual, continuing whatever work needs to be done, or save and close your project and start working on the mastering of your album, as discussed later in this chapter.

Choosing an Audio Format

For the highest quality audio, which is what you want if you're mixing for CD duplication, you can export your final mix in two lossless formats: WAV and AIFF. Both are standard formats and compatible with Mac and PC platforms. You can also use the Wave64 file format, which supports file sizes larger than 2 gigabytes.

If you're mastering directly for digital distribution, you probably don't want to go the lossless route, as this creates unwieldy file sizes. Instead, digital distribution favors smaller-sized, lower-quality compressed file formats. Cubase supports a variety of these download-friendly formats, including Microsoft Windows Media (PC only), MP3 (from MPEG 1 Layer 3), and Ogg Vorbis. Because these formats were developed with the Web in mind, they make it easy to stream or distribute content over a low-bandwidth system. As a result, a certain amount of audio data compression is applied to these file formats. The more you compress the files, the smaller they are, but this also directly affects sound quality—the higher the compression, the worse the sound quality. All these compression algorithms are *lossy*, meaning that they irretrievably remove sonic information from the original file when saving it into this new format, and by doing so they reduce sound quality as well.

Recommended Formats: If CD is your end medium, use either the WAV (Windows) or AIFF (Mac) formats. If you're preparing a song for Internet download, use the MP3 format. (MP3 is more universal than WMA.)

By the way, don't confuse data compression, which is used to compress the size of a file, with dynamic compression, which is used to control the dynamics of the audio signal. Compression of the dynamic range in audio material does not influence the size of the file, although it does decrease the audio quality. You will have a chance to experiment with compression settings for these digital audio file formats and will have to find a compromise that you are comfortable with in the end.

What Is Ogg Vorbis?: Ogg Vorbis is an audio compression format that is roughly comparable to other formats used to store and play digital music, such as MP3 and other compressed digital audio formats. It is different from these other compressed formats because it is completely free, open, and unpatented. Learn more at www.vorbis.com.

Adding Metadata

Now that your project is ready to be exported, it might be a good time to add information about who created the files. This information is called *metadata*, and you create it through Cubase's Broadcast Wave properties function. The information you enter here is embedded in all the digital audio recordings/renderings you create in WAV format. Think of embedding this metadata as a way to label and keep track of your intellectual property; it lets everyone who uses your file know you are the owner.

Broadcast wave information contains three basic fields: a description, an author, and a time-stamped reference based on the timeline in your source Cubase project. This last bit of information can be useful when exchanging files with video editors, for example.

Enter metadata that will be embedded in broadcast wave files:

1. Select File (PC)/Cubase (Mac) > Preferences.

2. Under Record, select Audio > Broadcast Wave. The Record-Audio-Broadcast Wave panel will appear in the right portion of the dialog box (see Figure 38.2).

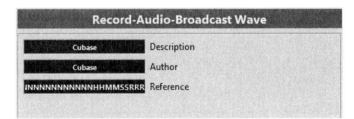

Figure 38.2 The Record-Audio-Broadcast Wave information panel.

3. Enter any information you want in these fields. Remember that this information will be embedded in the audio files.

4. Click Apply then OK.

When you export a project using the File > Export > Audio Mixdown option, the Export Audio Mixdown dialog box offers an option to insert the broadcast wave chunk into the exported audio files. Checking this option will add the information you just added to the files. At that point, you can choose to edit this information further by clicking on the Edit button. This opens the Broadcast Wave Chunk dialog box, where you can change the information embedded into the audio file, as displayed in Figure 38.3.

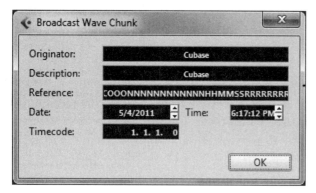

Figure 38.3 The Broadcast Wave Chunk dialog box.

About Mastering

Mastering is the art of subtlety and involves adjusting a collection of final mixes so that they all sound coherent and cohesive when played sequentially. From the first mix you did two months ago to the one you just created this morning at 4:00 a.m., they should all have the same quality, sound level, and dynamic intensity. Think of mastering as the art of giving an album its soul.

When preparing an album, mastering is a must before pressing your master copy. The mastering process is used to reduce the aforementioned differences between various mixes by patching together every song in a one- to two-day span—listening to them in the order they will appear on your album and correcting the overall harmonic colors and dynamic range of your songs as necessary. You can also master a given recording for playback on different devices and media, such as compact disc versus online downloading.

It is also a good idea not to master your album with the same listening reference as you used for the recording and mixing process because your ears have probably grown accustomed to this sound and may no longer be as critical to some aspects or coloring of the music. Furthermore, if your monitoring system is adequate at best, you will probably benefit from a professional mastering facility rather than a home studio mixing environment because the better facilities provide the best all-around listening and processing equipment to truly isolate problems in the consistency between your songs, not to mention provide a fresh pair of ears listening to your project. This can add a whole new untapped dimension to your project, which is especially true if this is to be a commercially distributed album. No matter what the proponents of home-based recording might say, there will always be a difference in quality between a home studio filled with inexpensive equipment and low-quality components, and a quarter-million-dollar mastering facility in which every piece of equipment in the room is meant to optimize your sound.

Mastering Engineers: Probably the *most* valuable asset in the pricey mastering studios is the technical expertise and years of experience that a professional mastering engineer can bring to bear. Mastering engineers have the ability to produce results that are consistent in varied playback environments, which will definitely save you a lot of time on trial and error every time your mix is played on a different system.

When you use a professional mastering studio, you may need to provide your entire Cubase project or just your exported stereo WAV/AIFF files. Consult with the mastering engineer beforehand so you'll know what they need—and maybe save yourself a little work, in the process.

If you don't have the financial resources or you don't feel the need for professional mastering because your project is for small and local distribution only, you can use Cubase's mastering features to do the job yourself. Know, however, that there are no fixed recipes and no settings that can apply to every situation; rather, there are pointers that should help you get the most out of a mastering session.

That said, here is some advice worth considering:

- Mastering is *not* where you mix your songs. If you are not satisfied with a mix, you should remix it rather than try to fix it at the mastering stage.

- This might be very obvious to most people, but just in case: *Never* master an album using your headphones as a reference. The proximity of headphones gives you false information about the depth of field and presence of certain musical events. Also, most people do not listen to music through headphones; they listen to it through loudspeakers.

- If you are unsure about how your mix sounds, try listening to music in a similar style that sounds like how you want your music to sound. Then try to emulate these qualities.

- Another way of evaluating your mix-in progress is by listening to it in varied environments, such as on a car stereo, from the room next door, or at a friend's place.

- When exporting your audio mixes in Cubase for the mastering process, use the highest quality available. If you have worked in 96 kHz, 32-bit stereo format and you have a reliable system that can reproduce these specifications, go for it. You can always convert your final result after the mastering process to 44.1-kHz, 16-bit stereo format.

- Remember that the fresher your mind and ears are, the better mastering process you'll have. So avoid starting a mastering session after a long day of work or immediately after mixing the last song on your album.

- Before you start your mastering session, sit down and listen to all the songs in order with your notepad and a pencil in hand. Take notes on inconsistencies between songs, keeping the entire album in mind. That is, you want the individual songs to fit comfortably with one another, in terms of volume level, equalization, and general tonal quality. This is where you pull out your master insert effects and master EQ, to create the best sonic match between the different songs.

- Generally, there are two important things that you want to adjust in a mastering session, and these should be kept in mind throughout the entire mastering process of a single album: EQ and dynamics. Both should be consistent from song to song.

- When tweaking the EQ, you are not trying to reinvent the mix, you are just tweaking it. Give the bass more definition, add presence to the vocals and crispness to the high end, and most of all, be sure that all songs have the same equalization qualities.

- Dynamics give punch and life to a mix. Be sure all your tracks come into play at the same level. This doesn't mean they should all be loud or soft, but they should be consistent with the intensity of the song. If a song is mellow, it can come in softer, but the soft intensity in one song has to be consistent in relation to the soft intensity of another song. As with EQ, consistency is the key.

- Any changes you make during the mastering process should be subtle ones—tweaks rather than dramatic changes. You don't want to alter your mix, you want to improve upon it. That means giving the bass just a hair more definition, or making the high end just a tad more crisp. This is not the point to decide to change the entire sound of a song; if you don't like what you're hearing, stop mastering and do a remix, instead.

- There are more and more software packages out there that do a pretty good job at EQing and compressing audio. Steinberg's WaveLab, Izotope's Ozone, various Waves plug-ins (including the famous L1/L2/L3 Ultramaximizer and L3 Multi-maximizer, the S1 Stereo Imager, the Renaissance Equalizer, and the Renaissance Compressor), and IK Multimedia's T-RackS are just a few of the tools you can use to help you get the most out of your home mastering session.

About Dithering

If you're mastering for compact disc or digital distribution, you need to add *dithering* to your master mix as a master insert effect. Put simply, dithering helps to reduce the potential for digital distortion in your recording, especially when you record in a 24- or 32-bit environment and then create a 16-bit master for CD or digital download.

Dithering works by adding a low level of random noise to your project, but in a way that masks actual noise. It's virtually inaudible to the listener.

Burning Your Own CDs: Many independent musicians create their recordings with Cubase and then burn their own CDs for sale at gigs or over the Internet. Although just about any digital audio player can be used to create CDs, you probably want to use a program geared for professional CD burning. These programs burn CDs to official Red Book specifications, and offer a variety of useful features not found in enduser-oriented programs.

Why not just record in a 16-bit environment? It's simple. Using 24-bit or higher resolution during the production process increases the potential dynamic range of your project, while reducing the possibility of any audible noise being introduced as a result of the digitization process itself. It also increases the signal-to-error ratio, which is the degree of rounding determined by the "resolution" or bit-depth. This error is more noticeable when signals are recorded at low levels or as they fade out to a lower level in reverb, for instance—especially if their levels get significantly boosted later in the mixing process.

As you saw earlier in this book, this signal-to-error ratio (in theory) is around 146 dB in a 24-bit recording and 194 dB in a 32-bit recording. Such a ratio suggests that when you record a sound using 32-bit resolution, your theoretical dynamic range is 194 dB, a signal-to-error ratio that is inaudible and negligible by any standards. Of course, in practice, you rarely get such impressive signal-to-noise ratios due to many noise-generating elements before and after the audio hardware's converters, but the ratios are consistently more impressive when you are using higher bit rates.

All that said, when you transfer a stereo mix-down to a 16-bit medium, such as compact disc, you need to bring this precision down to 16-bit. There are two primary approaches you can employ to accomplish this reduction in bit depth: truncating and dithering.

Truncating simply cuts the least significant portion of the digital word that exceeds the 16-bit word length. This is not the recommended approach, as the eight digits you get rid of are often noticeable, especially in reverb trails or harmonics of instruments at low-level intensities. Cutting them off usually adds what is known as *quantization error*. The digital distortion of the original audio waveform produced by quantization error (in essence, a rounding error due to the word length not offering enough amplitude levels to accurately depict the waveform) sounds unnatural to human ears. You are probably familiar with some extreme examples of this, in the 8-bit audio used by certain children's toys and vintage computers or game systems.

A good solution to this problem is to add a special kind of random noise to the sound when you need to bring down the resolution. This random noise is *dither noise*, and it randomly changes the last bit in a 16-bit word, creating a noise at −98 dB, which is pretty low.

Because dithering is—and should be—the last step in your mix-down process, it should only be added when you are exporting the final mix-down directly to a 16-bit sound file. Because of this, load the UV22HR dithering plug-in into the last insert slot of your output bus—number 8, which is a post-fader insert.

Set up dithering on your final mix-down:

1. Open the Mixer window.

2. Click the Edit button for the master output bus.

3. When the VST Output Channel Settings dialog box appears, click the final Inserts slot and select Mastering – UV22HR.

4. In the UV22HR panel, shown in Figure 38.4, select 16 for output bits, Hi for dither level, and Auto Black.

Figure 38.4 The UV22HR control panel.

5. Close the control panel and make sure the blue Inserts State button is clicked "on" for the output bus in the mixer.

With this final option set, you are now ready to export your mix to an audio file.

24-Bit Mix-Downs: In certain cases, you may want to export your stereo mixdowns at 24-bit resolution. For example, more sophisticated CD-creation programs such as WaveLab, CD Architect, Nero, Jam and others may offer their own tools for fine-tuning mixes, including various dithering algorithms. In these instances, it may be preferable to export your mixes at 24-bit or higher resolution for use with these programs. Also, if a mix-down is going to be turned over to a mastering engineer for professional mastering, 24-bit files with no dithering (and generally, no EQ or dynamics processing on the main output bus) are the norm.

Backing Up Your Work

It's essential to make backup copies of your work during the course of a project. Not only does creating a backup prevent you from having to rerecord your material if you make mistakes and erase files, but it is also a good way to keep source material from being lost because of hard drive crashes. Another good reason to back up files as you are working with them is that you can always go back and change things later in an arrangement or create a new arrangement altogether by using the source material rather than the master two-track recording.

If these are not good enough reasons for you, consider this last piece of advice: When you are working on a project for someone else and charging studio time, it's doubtful that your client will be impressed by your work if you lose some of their recordings!

There are many ways to do backups inside and out of Cubase:

- Select File (PC)/Cubase (Mac) > Back Up Project. This is probably the quickest way to create a backup, but only once your project is nearly completed, especially if you enable the Freeze Edits and Remove Unused Audio options in this command's dialog box.

- Create an Archive folder containing all the audio present in the Audio Pool of your project by selecting Media > Prepare Archive. This prompts you to select a destination folder where a copy of all the audio files used in the Pool are copied, making it easy to save this folder on a backup medium, such as a DVD-R or CD-R, DVD-RW or CD-RW, tape backup, or removable media drive. Once you have consolidated all the audio files this project uses into its Audio subfolder, you can be sure that copying this project folder to an archive medium will include all the files it requires (including the .CPR project file itself). Be sure to also include any video files used by the project in your backup, if applicable.

- Use your DVD/CD creation software to create a data disc that contains all the source material (audio, arrangements, song, preset, and setting files) used for this project, labeling your DVD/CD accordingly.

- Use backup software or disk imaging software to create a backup image of your files, either to disk or tape.

Keeping in mind that computer crashes occur quite unexpectedly, and that disc failures are not as infrequent as you would want, making backup copies of your work makes sense—even after each working session. This way, you reduce the amount of time lost if something bad ever happens.

Reading the documentation provided with your DVD/CD burning and backup software to understand how it works and how you can retrieve information from backup discs and tapes might prove useful (especially in a crisis!), so take a little bit of time to familiarize yourself with these options.

OMF Export Options

When you want to use your Cubase files in other applications—to use a third-party mixing or mastering program, for example—you use Cubase's OMF Export option. This option enables you to save your project in a platform- and application-friendly format.

OMF is friendly in the sense that this is a standard supported by more applications than the current .CPR or Cubase Project file might be. In other words, if you stay within Cubase, you won't need to use the OMF export format, but if your project needs to be added to another application, such as Final Cut Pro or Avid, exporting to OMF format will save everyone lots of time because the volume and fade settings will be retained in the OMF version of your project, as well as the positions of the all the audio events within it. This implies that you won't have to re-import and position all your audio content in another application.

Exported OMF files retain references to all audio files that are played in the project (including fade and edit files) and do not include unused audio files referenced in the Pool. They won't contain any MIDI data either, so it's important that you convert all your MIDI parts into audio events and render any tracks with inserts or send effects and include these "flattened" tracks when exporting the project to OMF. If your project contains a video file, the only thing that will be included in the OMF file are the start positions of video events. You will need to manually import video files later in the other OMF application.

Export a project to an OMF format:

1. Select File (PC)/Cubase (Mac) > Export > OMF. The Export Options dialog box will appear (see Figure 38.5).

2. Check which tracks should be included during the export, or click the Select All button to include all the audio tracks in the project. Because the OMF file interchange format only includes audio and video content, you will need to have exported VSTi, ReWire, and MIDI tracks to audio tracks previously if these need to be included in the OMF export.

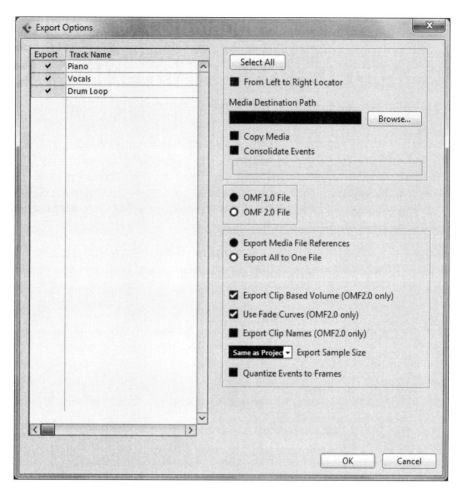

Figure 38.5 The Export Options dialog box.

3. Select the From Left to Right Locator option if you only want to export a specific section of your project timeline.

4. By default, files being exported will be placed in a subfolder under the location where the OMF file will be saved. If you would like to save the audio assets somewhere else, click the Browse button to specify a location for the exported content.

5. The Copy Media and Consolidate Events options allow you to either copy all the source media into the OMF export document's audio subfolder or to consolidate only the portions currently used by the project. Consolidating events requires less space because it does not copy any portion of the source audio file outside an event's boundaries. That being said, if space is not an issue and you would like to have access to the extra audio content later, the choice is there for you. When the Consolidate Events option is checked, you can set the "handle" length in milliseconds. This corresponds to the audio content outside the current event boundaries within the source audio file. Leaving a bit of time before and after will ensure that you can fine-tune or modify the event's boundaries later if necessary, for example to adjust fade lengths.

6. Select the desired OMF file version (1.0 or 2.0), depending on which OMF version is supported by the application in which you plan to import the file later. You might want to check with the studio where you need to bring this file before you make a selection here.

7. Select whether you want to include all audio data used in the project inside one large OMF file (Export All to One File) or use references to external files only (Export Media File References). If you choose the latter option, be sure to include all those source media files, as well as the OMF file itself, on the backup copy that you bring to the other studio. If you know that everything will fit on a CD or DVD-R (or DVD-RAM), you might be better off creating a self-contained, all-in-one OMF file to ensure that there are no missing files.

8. If you are exporting to a 2.0-compatible OMF file, you will often choose to include the fades and volume settings for each event. To do so, check the Export Clip Based Volume and Use Fade Curves options.

9. By default, the current project's sample size and sample rate are selected for the OMF export, but you can specify another resolution and sample rate for the exported files.

10. Click OK.

11. When prompted, enter a name for the exported OMF file.

12. Click the Save button when you are finished.

At this point a single OMF file is created, which includes all the checked tracks. All the files are saved inside the destination folder.

Tempo Data: Tempo data is not transferred when exporting to an OMF file.

Managing

39 Customizing Your Project

Once you start getting comfortable with Cubase, working habits will also start settling into place. That's when you'll start wondering whether you can customize where tools are laid out and how you can more efficiently do the actions you perform the most often. This chapter discusses ways that you can customize settings and create reusable documents to suit your working preferences and habits.

Here's a summary of what you will learn in this chapter:

- How to create and organize your Workspaces

- How to create a project template

- How to customize key commands

- How to create a macro and add commands to it

- How to use a macro in a project

- How to change the appearance of a toolbar and save this customization

- How to show/hide Transport panel sections

- How to create customized track controls for the Track List area and select customized settings

Creating and Organizing Workspaces

Given all the possible windows and controls necessary in even a moderately sized recording project, screen real estate and the layout of those windows are of primary importance. As such, Cubase's Workspace feature helps you organize your on-screen Workspace.

Workspaces provide an easy way to recall a particular window layout for your Cubase project, such as a useful view for editing events, or a wide Mixer panel for the mixdown phase of a project. Workspaces are saved along with the project file or can be saved as presets that are available for all projects in Cubase. Workspaces and Workspace presets retain the current position and state of windows inside a project, but not the project-specific content within windows, such as a part loaded in a particular editor or the size of the main Cubase window on the desktop.

Create a Workspace:

1. Open and organize the windows you want to display on your desktop.

2. After you are satisfied with the layout, select Window > Workspaces > New Workspace.

3. When the New Workspace dialog box appears, enter an appropriate name for this Workspace.

4. Repeat these steps to create additional Workspaces.

5. Select Window > Workspaces > Organize.

6. When the Organize Workspaces window appears, as shown in Figure 39.1, click the Locked option next to the newly created Workspaces. (This prevents the layout from being overwritten by mistake; you can still move windows around afterward, but recalling the Workspace returns all windows and panels to their saved states and locations.)

7. Check the Use IDs option.

8. Click the ID column next to the first Workspace and select an appropriate ID number. (The ID number determines the position of the Workspace in the Workspaces submenu.)

9. Select ID numbers for the other Workspaces.

10. Click OK when you are finished.

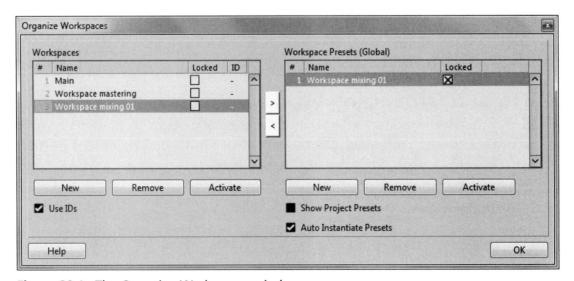

Figure 39.1 The Organize Workspaces window.

Organize your Workspaces:

1. Select Window > Workspaces > Organize.

2. Select the Workspace you want to act on.

3. Click the Remove button if you want to remove a layout from the list. Click the New button to save the current Workspace, or click Activate to apply the display attributes of the selected Workspace to your current project.

You can create several Workspaces and recall them through a set of customized key commands. You'll find more on how to customize key commands later in this chapter.

Creating Templates

When we work, we often start with basic settings. For example, if you have a favorite VSTi that you load for drums, a favorite window layout, a typical bus routing, or a number of tracks that you always name the same way, you might consider creating a *template*.

Templates are Cubase project documents that are saved in a Template folder. Saving a project as a template before you start recording events into it allows you to save all these settings, including preferences, output and input settings, and all the previously mentioned settings.

To use a template, select File (PC)/Cubase (Mac) > Create New Project. This opens the Project Assistant, shown in Figure 39.2. Click the More tab to view all the template files you've created.

Create a project template:

1. Organize your project as you normally do. For example, if you often start from a guitar, vocal, synth bass, and drum machine setup, create a project with at least two audio tracks and two MIDI/instrument tracks, make the VST Instruments panel visible, set up the appropriate connections, and so on.

2. When you are satisfied that this is a worthy template—in other words, that all the setup steps you just took to get here are worth saving for the next time around—select File (PC)/Cubase (Mac) > Save As Template.

3. When the Save as Template dialog box appears, enter a name for your template into the New Preset field at the bottom of the dialog box. The exact name you enter for this saved template file will appear as an option in the New Project dialog box from now on.

4. Click the OK button.

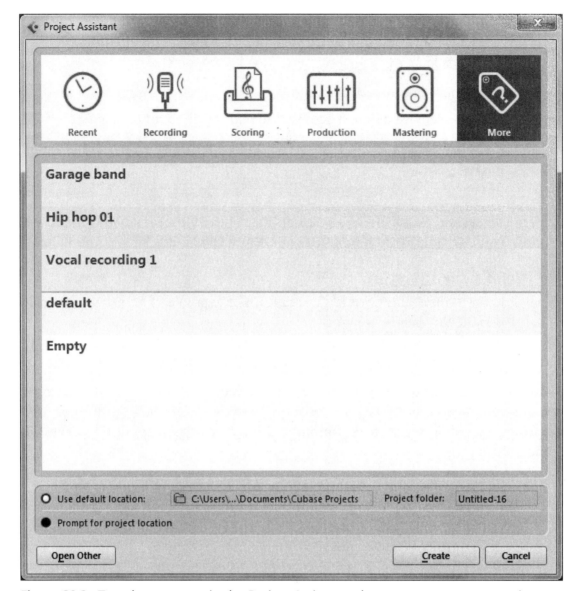

Figure 39.2 Templates appear in the Project Assistant when you create a new project.

Because templates are just like regular project files, you can use Windows Explorer or the Mac Finder to rename or delete them from your hard drive and subsequently change the template list. This also means that you can save audio and MIDI events within a template file if necessary.

Editing the Default Project: Another way you can customize your environment at startup is to edit the Default template. To edit this default file, open it, make the desired changes, and save it.

Customizing Key Commands

Throughout this book, references are made to key commands, also known as keyboard shortcuts. Although Cubase provides a default set of key commands for a number of functions and operations, you can change these default settings to reflect your working habits better and add some of your personal favorites to the existing key commands.

The commands that can be associated with keyboard shortcuts are found in the Key Commands dialog box, which you open by selecting File (PC)/Cubase (Mac) > Key Commands. As you can see in Figure 39.3, all the key commands are grouped by category in the Commands list area; you can also use the Search box to search for specific commands. The keyboard shortcut associated with a given command is displayed in the Keys list on the right.

Figure 39.3 The Key Commands dialog box.

Customize a key command:

1. Select File (PC)/Cubase (Mac) > Key Commands.

2. In the Key Commands dialog box, select the Cubase function to which you want to assign a keyboard shortcut. Categories are represented by little folders. You either double-click to open or close them or click on the

plus signs to their left (or their "disclosure triangle" buttons on a Mac) to reveal the actual commands found within the desired category folder.

3. Click inside the Type in Key field to make it active. If the selected item already has a key command associated with it, the Keys field (above) will display the associated key or key combination.

4. Press the key or key combination (for example, Alt+G on the PC or Option+G on the Mac) you want to associate with the currently selected item. If the key or key combination is already assigned to another function in Cubase, the name of this function will appear in the Assigned To area below.

5. Click the Assign button to associate the keys you entered with the selected function. The keys should appear in the Keys area above. If another key command was previously assigned to the selected item, it will be replaced by the new one you just created.

6. Click OK to close the dialog box.

Within the Key Commands dialog box, the Recycle Bin (Delete) icon below the Keys area removes the keyboard shortcut associated with a selected command. The Presets field below manages the previously saved presets or enables you to save a preset to memory.

Note that there are already presets available for Cubase VST and selected other applications. Using the same shortcuts to do the same tasks from one software program to the next can make sense, so if you're used to working with a specific set of keyboard shortcuts, this dialog box customizes the key command associations to better meet your needs.

Using Cubase Macros

Using Cubase macros is a way to save a sequence of tasks that you perform regularly, one after the other. For example, you might often need to quickly create four audio tracks and a marker track, select a window layout, and select a zoom level. Performing these tasks can take many steps—or only a single step when programmed as a macro command.

Create a macro:

1. Select File (PC)/Cubase (Mac) > Key Commands.

2. In the Key Commands dialog box, click the Show Macros button. This reveals the Macros section at the bottom of the dialog box, as shown in Figure 39.4.

3. Click the New Macro button to add a new macro in the Macros area.

4. Double-click the new macro's name and type a new name for it.

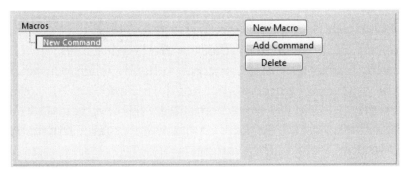

Figure 39.4 Creating macro commands in the Macros section of the Key Commands dialog box.

Now your new macro is created, but it won't do anything. Let's add commands to it.

Add commands to a macro:

1. In the upper portion of the Key Commands dialog box, click on the category of command you want in the Commands area.

2. Select the command you want to add to your macro.

3. Click the Add Command button in the Macros section. The selected command now appears in the Commands list area of the Macros section.

4. Repeat the previous steps for each command you want to add to your macro.

5. When you've finished adding commands to your macro, click OK to close this dialog box.

When you launch your new macro, the commands you have just entered will be executed in the order in which you entered them in the macro. Note that as you get more experienced with key commands and macros, not only can you assign a key command to any macro, but you can also launch one macro from within another.

Use a macro in a project:

1. Once any macros have been created in Cubase, they appear in the Edit > Macros submenu.

2. To execute the series of commands in a given macro, select that macro from the submenu.

Customizing Toolbars

Cubase enables you to easily change the tools that are displayed in a window's toolbar and save these layouts for further use. This can come in handy when you need certain tools during one part of your creative process, but not during another. Also, depending on the resolution currently selected for your computer's display, you may not have enough space on-screen to display all the tools at once—this may particularly be the case with the Project window toolbar, for example.

Change the contents of a toolbar:

1. Right-click anywhere in the toolbar. A context menu displays all the options available for this toolbar. The toolbar elements with check marks next to them are currently visible, whereas the others are not.

2. Select an option with a check mark to hide it from the toolbar, or select an option without a check mark to enable its display in the toolbar.

You can also save these customizations and select them later from the same context menu. This is a very useful technique that you should try to incorporate as soon as possible in your learning process with Cubase.

Save a toolbar customization:

1. Right-click anywhere in the toolbar and select Setup from the context menu.

2. The Setup dialog box now appears, as shown in Figure 39.5. Items that appear under the Visible Items column are currently visible, whereas the items in the Hidden Items column are not.

3. Use the arrow buttons in the center to move items between the left and right columns. You can also use the Move Up and Move Down buttons to change the order in which the visible items will appear from left to right in the toolbar.

4. Once you are satisfied with your changes, click on the disk icon at the bottom of this dialog box to save the changes into a preset. Note that clicking on the Recycle Bin (Delete) icon deletes the preset currently displayed in the Presets field.

5. Another dialog box will appear, prompting you to enter a name for your preset. Enter a descriptive name for your preset. The name you enter here will appear in this dialog box's Presets selection field.

6. Click OK twice to return to the previous window.

7. The newly created preset can now be selected from this toolbar's customization context menu.

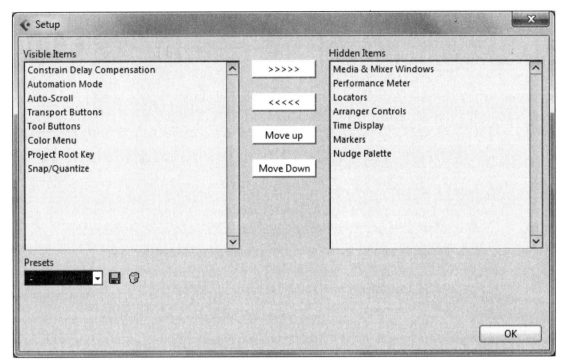

Figure 39.5 The toolbar Setup dialog box.

If you want to return the toolbar to its default state, you can do so by selecting the Default option in the same context menu, or you can choose to display *all* the available toolbar items by selecting the Show All option instead.

Customizing Your Transport Panel

You can choose to hide certain portions of the Transport panel if you don't need them or if you want to free up some valuable desktop space. Later, you can choose to re-display any hidden areas of the Transport panel.

Show/hide Transport panel sections:

1. Right-click (PC)/Control-click (Mac) anywhere on your Transport panel (except inside value fields that can be changed with your cursor).

2. From the pop-up context menu, check the sections you want to see and uncheck the sections you don't want to see.

Customizing Track Controls

Although working with controls in the Track List is convenient, sometimes dealing with all the controls available might become cumbersome and confusing. Certain controls are used only during the recording process, whereas others are used only during the editing process. Furthermore, some users might never use a particular control from the Track List, using the Inspector or Mixer panel instead, whereas others might never use the Mixer panel and only use the Track List.

You can customize the controls that are displayed in the Track List, save these settings for each track class, and recall them later when you need them.

Create customized track controls for the Track List area:

1. Right-click (PC)/Control-click (Mac) anywhere within the Track List and select the Track Controls Settings option, or select the same option from the Track Controls Settings drop-down menu that can be opened via the button at the top left of the Track List area.

2. When the Track Controls Settings dialog box appears, as shown in Figure 39.6, select the desired track type from the Track Type drop-down list in the upper-left corner of the dialog box. The control elements on the left side are currently visible in the Track List. The control elements on the right are available, but not currently visible. Before creating a preset, let's look at an existing one to see whether there's already a preset that would suit your needs.

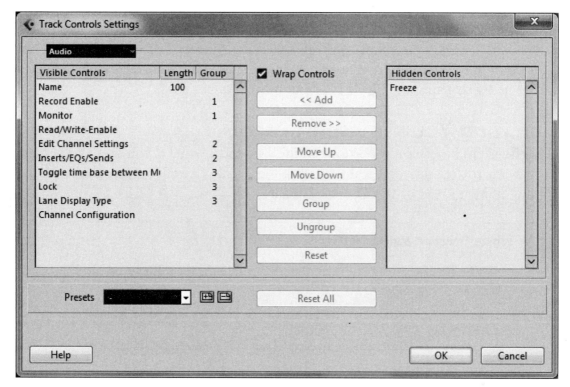

Figure 39.6 The Track Controls Settings dialog box.

3. From the Presets menu in this dialog box, select the appropriate preset to see its current track control settings.

4. To add a control to the current preset, select the control under the Hidden Controls column on the right and then click the Add button.

5. To remove a control from the current preset, select the control under the Visible Controls column on the left and then click the Remove button. As you probably noticed, the selected control will move from one side to the other. You can also change the order in which the controls appear in the Track List area.

6. Select the control that you want to modify in the Visible Controls area and click the Move Up or Move Down button to move this control to a new position in the list. To make sure two or more controls always stay together on the same line when you resize the Track List area, you can group them.

7. Select the first control you want to group; then Ctrl-click (PC)/⌘-click (Mac) on the other controls you want to group together. Note that if a control is already in a group, you'll need to ungroup it first, before you can group it with another control.

8. Click on the Group button to group the controls.

9. Repeat Steps 4 through 8 until you are satisfied with the results.

10. Click the Add Preset button (the "+" button next to the Presets list) to create a new preset.

11. Enter the desired name in the field and click OK.

12. Click OK once again to return to the Project window.

Remember that you can always remove unwanted presets by selecting them in this dialog box and clicking on the Remove Preset button (the "-" button next to the Presets list).

To select a customized track control setting, select the appropriate preset from the Track Controls drop-down menu found at the top-left corner of the Track List area.

40 Optimizing Your Project

As projects grow in size, so does the real-time processing demand on a computer's CPU, which eventually can cause the project to outgrow the computer's limited resources and require more processing power than what is available. Although this might sound a bit limiting creatively, it doesn't always have to be this way.

Naturally, you can invest in a newer, faster computer for your recording and mixing chores, and with the rapidly decreasing prices of computers today, that may not be a bad option. But you don't have to spend good money on a new computer; you can get your project done with the resources that are available to you today. All you have to do is learn how to manage the resources you have available and optimize your project when these resources are running low.

Here's a summary of what you will learn in this chapter:

■ How to disable unnecessary audio tracks to reduce disk access

■ How to use offline processing instead of online (real-time) processing to reduce CPU load

■ How to free up resources by freezing audio channels, object edits, real-time processes, and VST instruments

■ How to use folder tracks to group and control several tracks together

Disabling Audio Tracks

After you start recording audio inside a project, you will gather more audio takes than needed in the final version, because you will most likely have different takes from which to choose and different versions of the same audio content. You might also create several working tracks along the way that are not used anymore. These tracks take up valuable system resources, as they are all loaded into your system when you open the project. After a while, these tracks will drag down the performance of your project.

> **Muting Tracks:** Simply muting audio tracks only mutes their output level, and doesn't prevent them from being loaded into your system.

To avoid this, you can disable audio tracks that are not currently being used in your project. This offers the advantage of shutting down all disk activity related to the audio content found on these tracks, while the tracks still remain in your project in case you need them later.

> **Disable audio tracks:**
>
> 1. Right-click (PC)/Control-click (Mac) in the Track List area for the track you want to disable.
> 2. From the context menu, select Disable Track.

You can re-enable a track after it has been disabled by repeating this operation. The option in the context menu is replaced by Enable Track instead.

Processing VST Plug-Ins Offline

VST plug-in effects, as you saw earlier in this book, can be added as inserts or used as send effects on an FX channel track. When doing so, you are processing the audio in real-time, as described in Chapter 13, "Using Insert Effects." You also can apply VST plug-in effects available on your computer to a file directly, if you want to affect only a portion of a track or don't want to add real-time processing load on your computer's CPU.

Remember that when you apply one of these *offline process* effects to all or part of a selected object, the processed result is saved in a special file, leaving your original file intact. This new file is seamlessly integrated into your project. In other words, you won't even feel or see it's a different file, other than the fact that this portion is processed.

Because VST plug-in effects vary from one to another, I will not discuss the specific settings of these plug-ins, but understand that you can use these effects in an offline process (non-real-time) the same way as you would use them in an online process (real-time). The only difference is that with offline effects you don't have the flexibility to vary their parameters over the range of time that will be affected by this processing.

> **Add a plug-in effect to a selected object:**
>
> 1. Select all or part of the desired object in the project's timeline.
> 2. Select the desired plug-in from the Audio > Plug-Ins submenu.

3. Make the appropriate adjustments in the plug-in's control panel. To preview the result, click the Preview button.

4. When you are satisfied with the settings, click the Process button.

Using the Freeze Function

Many effects, edits, VST instruments, and automation tasks are occurring whenever you press the Play button with a full project going. When you need more processing juice than your computer can muster, but you don't want to render tracks permanently in case you'd like to change something, think of freezing them.

Freezing renders a new audio event incorporating all that track's processing and loads it up in an invisible audio channel. Then it locks the event, track, VSTi, or plug-in effects, saves their settings, and unloads them from memory until you decide to change something, such as a cutoff frequency parameter on filter, for example.

If you like trying different things while you are composing, chances are you might load up your memory with instances of VST instruments, giving you access to many layers of sound. This layering is what makes using Cubase such a great experience. What's not so great is when you run out of resources and your computer starts its "I've had enough" routine, crackling the sound, jerking playback, and exhibiting other related computer behaviors.

In the following sections, I'll discuss several techniques that let you free up some valuable processing power, while keeping the option of change conveniently close enough that you won't feel like you are spending most of your time dealing with problems during playback.

Freezing an Audio Channel

The Freeze Audio Channel button found in the Audio Settings section of the Inspector (shown in Figure 40.1) renders a temporary audio file of the audio track, including all its pre-fader insert effects in slots 1–6. You can still adjust the track's volume, pan, EQ, and Sends parameters. To unfreeze an audio channel, click on the Freeze Audio Channel once again; this time, the button is orange. A dialog box prompts a selection:

■ Unfreeze erases the temporary audio rendering and unlocks the audio channel.

■ Keep Freeze Files keeps the temporary audio rendering in case you need to re-freeze. If an error occurs that prevents you from getting the same result you had before you froze, and the freeze file is no longer available, you won't be able to get the same process, even though the original unprocessed file will still be there.

Figure 40.1 The Freeze Audio Channel button.

Freezing Edits

The Freeze Edits option makes it possible to write all the offline processing added to an event in this project to a new file on a media drive, or to replace the original file with the new, processed version. When you freeze edits, the original always remains on the drive unless it is used only once in the project. Freezing the edits of an event that's used in more than one place in a project automatically prompts you to save to a new file.

Freeze events that have insert effects applied:

1.   Select the appropriate audio event.

2.   Select Audio > Freeze Edits.

If there is only one edited version of the selected event, you are prompted to either replace the original file or create a new file. If the selected event has multiple edit versions, you are prompted to either apply the processing to the current version of the event or to create a new event.

Freezing VSTi

In this situation, you use Cubase's Freeze function to create a temporary audio render of the VSTi for all MIDI events routed through the selected VSTi you chose to freeze. As a result, the MIDI track becomes locked from editing and muted, the VSTi unloads from memory, and Cubase creates a special audio rendering corresponding to the result of the MIDI events going through the VSTi. This offers the advantage of hearing what you heard before—MIDI events playing through a VSTi—without the resource real estate required by VSTi.

The frozen audio will not appear in the project as a separate audio channel, but will continue to be controlled in the Mixer panel through its VSTi channel. So, any volume, EQ, or routing will continue to have an effect on the sound.

If you later want to change something in the MIDI track, you can unfreeze the VSTi, change the MIDI, and refreeze again. Once a VSTi is unfrozen, the freeze file is removed from its special Freeze folder, which can be found inside the project's main folder. Note that parts that are muted will not be frozen. In other words, the result of a freeze, in terms of what you hear, is identical to the VSTi generating the sounds in real-time.

Freeze a VSTi:

1.   Open the VST Instruments window.

2.   Click on the Freeze button next to the desired VSTi.

3.   When the Freeze Instrument Options dialog box appears, as shown in Figure 40.2, choose to either freeze the instrument only or the instrument and all channels to which it is applied. This lets you freeze all channels using the same VST instrument simultaneously, if you wish.

4.   Check the Unload Instrument When Frozen option to free up more system resources.

5.   Click OK.

Figure 40.2 The Freeze Instrument Options dialog box.

Cubase will now create the audio render. This might take anywhere from a few seconds to a few minutes, depending on the complexity of the process and the computer resources available.

When a VSTi is frozen, the Freeze button will appear orange, and you won't be able to make any changes to the MIDI tracks being sent to this VSTi. To unfreeze a VSTi, click the Freeze button again.

Using Folder Tracks

Folder tracks, as you might have guessed, are used as folders into which you can put any combination of track classes, including other folder tracks. You can use folder tracks as you would use folders in your computer, grouping related tracks into a single folder which you name appropriately. You can also hide the folder track to give you more working space on your screen, or mute or soloing its entire contents with a single click.

For example, if you have several percussion tracks, you could create a folder, name it "Percussion," and drag all these tracks inside it. When you're not working on your percussion tracks, you can fold up the folder track to minimize the space that these tracks would otherwise use in the Track List. When the time comes to edit these tracks, all you need to do is unfold the folder track to reveal all the tracks and controls inside.

When tracks are moved inside a folder track, a folder part is created in the Event Display area, which graphically represents the contents of the folder track even when it is minimized.

The Inspector for a selected folder track only contains one section. This section contains the name of the tracks you moved inside the folder track. Whenever you click on the name of a track in this section, that track's Inspector area is displayed below the Folder section (also in the Inspector area, as shown in Figure 40.3).

Figure 40.3 The Inspector settings for a folder track.

At the top of the folder track's Inspector are some buttons that are also found in other track classes (and explained previously). These buttons affect all the tracks inside the folder track simultaneously. For example, clicking the Mute button for a folder track in the Inspector or the Track List mutes all the tracks inside the folder track. Similarly, clicking the Lock button locks all these tracks from editing. As you would guess, this makes recording, monitoring, muting, soloing, or locking multiple tracks simultaneously very easy.

Move tracks into a folder track:

1. In the Project window's Track List, click and drag the track you want to move to a folder track.

2. When a green line appears within your folder track, drop your track into it by releasing the mouse button.

3. Repeat this process to add additional tracks to the folder. You can drag multiple consecutive tracks simultaneously into a folder track by clicking the first track in the Track List area, and then Shift-clicking the last track you want to move into the folder track. To move nonconsecutive tracks, use the Ctrl (PC)/⌘ (Mac) key to select your tracks before dragging them.

To remove tracks from a folder track, simply drag them outside of the folder track in the Track List, just as you moved them inside of it.

When tracks are added to a folder track, a folder part is created. As you can see in Figure 40.4, the folder part displays the position and colors used by the parts on the tracks it contains. In this example, the folder track has been unfolded, showing the details of these tracks. You can click the track's Folder icon (to the left of the Mute button) to toggle the folded/unfolded states of selected folder tracks. You also can rename folder tracks as you would any other tracks through the Inspector area.

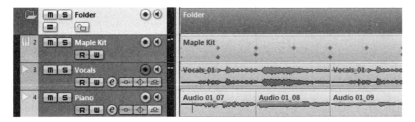

Figure 40.4   Folder parts appear in the folder track.

Rename a track by using the Inspector:

1. Click in the name box at the top part of the Inspector for the selected track.

2. Type a new name for your track.

Index

A

Access Editor button, 384
accessing
    MIDI port settings, 23
    Patch Banks, 122
    Pool, 157
ACID loops, importing, 240
Acoustic Feedback button, 266–267
actions, Offline Process History process, 238
Activate Arranger Mode button, 333
Activate/Deactivate Insert button, 150
Activate Metronome Click (CLIK) button, 78
Activate Project button, 173–174
Activate Tempo Track button, 341
activating. *See also* starting
    Note Expression, 275–276
    VST instruments, 116
activity indicators, 130–131
Add Audio Track dialog box, 96
Add External FX dialog box, 55
Add FX Channel Track dialog box, 382
adding
    audio tracks, 66–67
    automation events, 408
    commands to macros, 443
    Controller Lanes, 272
    dithering, 429–431
    EQ (equalization), 245, 389–396
    FX channels, 22, 387
    input insert effects, 153
    insert effects, 82, 261
    instrument tracks, 70–71, 87
    metadata, 425–426
    MIDI (Musical Instrument Digitial Interface)
        controllers, 41
        devices with Device Manager, 119–125
        effects to tracks, 309–314
    notes, 261
    Patch Bank lists, 122
    presets, 123
    reverb, 249
    silence, 221, 320
    tempo changes, 344
    tracks, 185–186, 455
        insider Mixers, 376
        overdubbing, 103–104
Add Input Bus dialog box, 53
Add Instrument Track dialog box, 113, 362
Add MIDI Device dialog box, 120
Add Output Bus dialog box, 415
advanced quantizing, 296
advantages of VSTi (VST instruments), 114, 115
aftertouch information, 15
AIFF files, 90
Alesis MasterControl products, 34
algorithms, compression, 424
alignment
    audio, troubleshooting, 56
    locators, 129–130

amplifier racks, 6
amplitude, 10
analog sound, 10–11
analyzing
    Pool, 160–162
    tempo, 349
applications
    audio, 44–45
    closing, 31
    DAW (digital audio workstation), 3
    ReCycle, 90
    ReWire, 137–142
    running, simultaneously, 44–45
applying
    Arranger Editor, 336–337
    Arranger tracks, 331–339
    Beat Designer, 360–362
    beats, 351–364
    Compressor effects, 246
    Control Room Mixers, 75–84
    DeEsser effects, 247
    devices, Inspector, 124–125
    Draw tool, 260
    drum maps, 282–285
    effects, 144
    EQ (equalization), 393–395
    filters, 88
    folder tracks, 454–455
    Freeze function, 451–453
    FX channels, 381–387
    Groove Agent ONE, 358–360
    group tracks, 397–399
    In-Place Editor, 255–256
    insert effects, 143–156
    instrument presets, 87
    Key Editor, 265–271
    lanes, 109
    Line tool, 260–263
    LoopMash2, 362–364
    loops, 351–356
    macros, 443
    MediaBay, 85–87
    MIDI (Musical Instrument Digital Interface)
        effects, 309–314
        functions, 292–293
        lanes, 134
        quantizing, 300–301
    Mixer, 367–380
    Notepad, 198
    offline resources in the Pool, 167
    online audio effects, 229
    Overview line area, 188–189
    pitch shifts, 234–236
    Pool, 157–167
    processing, 228, 229
    quantizing, 295–298
    Read Automation button, 402–403
    regions, 223–224
    reverb, 249

applying (*Continued*)
ReWire, 137–142
Sample Editor, 215–225
Step Input mode, 273–274
tempo, 341–349
Virtual MIDI Keyboards, 135–136
VSTi (Virtual Studio Technology instruments), 111–119
Write Automation button, 402–403
zoom tools, 189–190
archiving, Pool, 165–166
areas
Mixer, 368–375
Project window, 171–184
Sample Editor, 215–217
Arranger Editor, applying, 336–337
Arranger tracks, 184, 331–339
chains, managing, 338–339
events, 333–335
Inspector, 335–336
projects, creating, 331–333
arranging in Project windows, 317–330. *See also* managing
ASIO (Audio Stream Input/Output), 18, 416
DirectX Full Duplex drivers, 35–36
drivers, 34, 35–36
port settings, 42
assembling
master MIDI takes, 134–135
master takes, 109–110
assigning
drum tracks, 283
MIDI plug-in effects to sends, 313
programs to MIDI tracks, 124–125
associating attributes, 89
Attack control, 247
Attribute Inspector panel, 89
attributes, associating, 89
audio
activity indicators, 130–131
alignment, troubleshooting, 56
applications, 44–45
channels, 19, 21–22
freezing, 451–452
routing, 415
strips, 372
clips, 25–26
connections, 18–22, 47–60
DAW (digital audio workstation), 3
drivers, 19, 34–36
editing, 216
new features, 6
processing options, 227–241
effects, adding, 245
events, 25–26
overlapping, 211–212
quantizing, 303–308
Sample Editor, 216
snap points, 224–225
exporting, 421–424
files, ReWire, 137
formatting, 424–425
hardware configuration, 35
importing, 90–94
interfaces
connections, 32–34
devices, 32
MIDI tracks, converting, 203–204
monitoring, 47–60
overview of, 9–13
parts, 26–28
plug-in effects, 146–149

Pool, 157–167
port setup, 41–44
processing effects, 144, 228–229
real-time stretching, 4
recording, 5, 95–101. *See also* recording
regions, 25, 26
slices, 25, 26
tracks, 20. *See also* tracks
creating, 66–67
disabling, 449–450
Inspector, 180
navigating, 205–212
presets, 67–70
replacing drum hits, 357–358
setup, 205–209
video, importing, 93–94
Audio Channel Settings panel, 211
Audio Mixdown function, 421
Audio Part Editor, 28
Audio Stream Input/Output. *See* ASIO
Audio tracks, 184
AudioWarp, 239–241, 306, 353
Audition button, 219
Audition Loop button, 219
Audition tool, 266
Auto Apply checkbox, 299
Auto Apply control, 298
Auto Fades dialog box, 208
Auto Fade Settings button, 207
Auto-Latch automation, 405
automation
channel tracks, 403–404
drawing, 407–409
editing, 410–412
events, adding, 408
lanes, 183
managing, 406–407
modes, 405
offline processing, 228
parameters, 404
viewing, 410
Automation feature, 401–412
Automation Panel, 406–407
auto monitoring preference setup, 48–50
Auto-Quantize button, 129
Auto-Scroll button, 175, 219, 267
Auto Select Controllers button, 268

B

background processes, 44
backups. *See also* saving
files, 431–432
projects, 165
banks, sound, 15
Bank Selector field, 197
bass, overdubbing, 103
baud rates, 14
Beat Designer, applying, 360–362
Beatles, 103
beats, 98
applying, 351–364
drums, 356–363. *See also* drums
beats per minute. *See* BPM
bend, pitch, 14
bits, 11
bits per second (bps), 14
depth, 13
booths, recording, 57
BPM (beats per minute), 100

bps (bits per second), 14
Broadcast Wave Chunk dialog box, 426
browsers, media, 85. *See also* interfaces
buffer sizes, 36
    modifying, 43
building MIDI tracks, 133
burning CDs (compact discs), 429
busses, 19, 371
    Control Room Mixers, 76
    input, 20, 51–53
    output, 20, 53–54
    stereo child, 415, 416
    surround sound, 415–416
    USB (universal serial bus), 33. *See also* connections; USB
        (universal serial bus)
Bypass button, 150
bypassing
    sends, 383, 384
    signals, 385
Bypass Inserts button, 151
Bypass Send Effect button, 140

C

Card Options, 36
carving EQ (equalization) holes, 395–396
CDs (compact discs), 13
    burning, 429
    tracks, importing, 91–92
chains
    Arranger tracks, 333–335. *See also* Arranger tracks
    flattening, 338–339
    managing, 338–339
Channel column, 281
channels
    audio, 19, 21–22
    automation, enabling, 403
    configuring, 201
    copying, 370
    destination, 384
    faders, 201
    freezing, 451–452
    FX
        adding, 22, 387
        applying, 381–387
        deleting, 387
        managing, 386–387
        navigating options, 381–382
    group tracks, applying, 397–399
    instruments, creating, 113
    LFE (Low Frequency Effects), 413, 419
    linking, 376
    MIDI (Musical Instrument Digital Interface), 23–24
    multichannel setups, surround sound, 413–415
    multiple MIDI, recording simultaneously, 132
    ReWire, 137–140
    routing, 415
    Strings, 21
    strips, 372–373
        input, 376–377
        output, 377–378
    tracks, automation, 403–404
    unlinking, 376
    view sets
        deleting, 371
        saving, 371
Channel section, Inspector, 209–211
Channel Settings
    panels, 210–211
    windows, 391–393

child busses, stereo, 415, 416
classes, tracks, 184–185
Click button, 54, 98
Click to Bypass Sends button, 383
click tracks, 98–101
CLIK (Activate Metronome Click) button, 78
clips, 29
    audio, 25–26
    Pool, 157–167
clocks
    setup, 43
    sources, setup, 95
closing applications, 31
Color menu, 177
Color tool, 177
columns, customizing Pool, 158
comb filtering, 234
commands
    customizing, 441–442
    Duplicate, 322
    Freeze, 154
    O-Note, 291–292
    Range Crop, 319
    Repeat, 322–324
    Split at Cursor, 318
    Transpose, 287–288
    Undo, 329–330
Common panel, Mixer, 369–372
    automation, enabling, 403
compact discs. *See* CDs
comparing insert effects and send effects, 144–146
compatibility
    ASIO (Audio35 Stream Input/Output)
    MIDI (Musical Instrument Digital Interface), 56
    ReWire applications, 138
comping, 109
complex waveforms, 10
compression
    algorithms, 424
    Ogg Vorbis, 425
Compressor, 245–247
Computer Management window, 37
configuration
    audio hardware, 35
    busses, 19
    channels, copying settings, 370
    DirectSound drivers, 36
    metronomes, 99
    MIDI (Musical Instrument Digital Interface), recording,
        270–271
    Mixer, 375–376
    multichannel setups, 413–415
    peripherals, 31–46
    project setup, 63–66
    Quick Controls, 199
    ReWire, 137–139
    surround sound, 415–416
    tracks, 72
    VST instruments, 112–114
connections
    audio, 18–22, 47–60
    Control Room Mixers, 77
    External FX tab, 54–56
    external instruments, 56–57
    FireWire, 33. *See also* FireWire
    Group/FX tab, 54
    input, 51–53
    interfaces, 32–34
    MIDI (Musical Instrument Digital Interface), 22–25
    output, 53–54

connections (*Continued*)
  saving, 58–60
  Studio connection tab, 57–58
  Talkback, 81
  VST (Virtual Studio Technology) setup, 51–58
connectors, MIDI (Musical Instrument Digital Interface), 15–18
Constrain Delay Compensation button, 174
Content Vertical Zoom bar, 189
context menus, 25
Control Change information, editing, 260
Controller Display area, 272
Controller Lanes, 272
controllers
  events, adding, 261
  Note Expression, mapping, 276–277
Control Room Mixers, 75–84
  disabling, 57
  inserts on, 154–156
  monitoring, 77–84
  navigating, 76–77
Control Room Overview. *See* CRO
controls, 14, 206–208
  Arranger, 332, 333
  Attack, 247
  Auto Apply, 298
  Channel section, 210
  EQ (equalization), modifying, 391
  Frequency, 390
  Gain, 390
  Grid Display, 297
  insert effects, 150–151
  iQ, 298
  Iterative Strength, 298
  Make-Up, 246
  Move MIDI CC, 298
  Non-Quantize Range, 297
  pan, 414
  Play Order, viewing, 332
  Quantize, 298
  Quantize Catch Range, 297
  Quantize Grid, 296
  Quantize panel, 296–298
  Randomize, 298
  Ratio, 246
  Reduction, 247
  Release, 248
  Reset Quantize, 298
  Select Preset, 296
  Swing Factor, 297
  Threshold, 246
  Track Pan, 196
  tracks, customizing, 445–447
  Track Volume, 196
  Transport, 175–176
  Tuplet, 297
  zoom, 173
control surfaces, 33
converting
  drum patterns into MIDI parts, 362
  MIDI tracks to audio, 203–204
  O-Note Conversion tool, 291–292
Convert VST3 option, 290
copying
  chains, 338
  channels, 370
  events, 322–325
  loops, 354
  tracks, 203
copyrights, 352
cost of microphones, 244

CPR (Cubase PRoject) files, 61
creating. *See* formatting
CRO (Control Room Overview), 77
crossfades, 110
Crossfades section, 308
cross-over automation, 405
Cubase PRoject files. *See* CPR files
Cube-shaped preset management button, 150
Cubit, 4
Current Chain field, 333
Currently Edited Part button, 269
Current Tempo field, 343
cursors, Split at Cursor command, 318
curves, drawing, 407
customizing
  Auto Fade settings, 208
  Channel Settings panels
  commands, 441–442
  drum maps, 284–285
  Pool columns, 158
  presets, 89
  projects, 437–447
  regions, 223
  toolbars, 444–445
  track controls, 445–447
  Transport panel, 445
  VST instruments, 112–114
cutting, 221
Cycle mode, 133
  recording, 108–109
cycle playback, ReWire, 139
Cycle Record mode, 128–129

D

data, 14
DAW (digital audio workstation), 3
DC Offset process, 237
decimal points, 13
decreasing values, 64
DeEsser, 247–248
Default Location option, 63
default projects, editing, 440
Define Locations, 85–86
delay, 48. *See also* latency
  Constrain Delay Compensation button, 174
  tracks, 196
  values, 55
Delay slider, 207
Delete Doubles function, 292
deleting. *See also* removing
  automation subtracks, 409–410
  chains, 338
  channel view sets, 371
  Controller Lanes, 272
  drum maps, 285
  files, 164
  FX channels, 387
  notes, 221–222
  Offline Process History process, 238
  quantization settings from presets, 300
  tempo, 345
  tracks, 455
depth, bits, 13
destination channels, 384
detecting, Tempo Detection feature, 348–349
Device Manager, adding MIDI devices, 119–125
devices
  audio drivers, 19
  FireWire, 39

Inspector, applying, 124–125
interfaces, 32
maps, 119
MIDI (Musical Instrument Digital Interface), 14
    adding with Device Manager, 119–125
    interfaces, 33
    managing, 121–124
    removing, 124
    synchronization, 15
ports, 19
presets, adding, 123
remote, 40–41
setup, 38–44
USB (universal serial bus), 39
Device Setup dialog box, 38, 39
Device Setup VST Audio System setup page, 42
dialog boxes, 25
    Add Audio Track, 67, 96
    Add External FX, 55
    Add FX Channel Track, 382
    Add Input Bus, 53
    Add Instrument Track, 113, 362
    Add MIDI Device, 120
    Add Output Bus, 415
    Auto Fades, 208
    Broadcast Wave Chunk, 426
    Device Setup, 38, 39
    Dissolve Part, 291
    Drum Map Setup, 283
    Edit History, Undo command, 329–330
    Envelope, 231
    Export Audio Mixdown, 423
    Export Options, 433
    Fade In, 232
    Freeze Instruments Options, 453
    Gain, 232
    Key Commands, 441, 442
    Metronome Setup, 99
    MIDI Controller Setup, 273
    MIDI Merge Options, 290
    MIDI Transpose Setup, 288
    Noise Gate, 233
    Normalization, 234
    Offline Process History, 238
    Preset Name, 60
    Process bars, 343
    Process Tempo, 343
    Project Setup, 64, 95, 188
    Repeat Events, 355
    Routing Editor, 419
    Save as Template, 439
    Save Preset, 89
    Toolbar Setup, 445
    Track Controls Settings, 446
    VST Input Channel Settings, 152
digital audio, 9–13. *See also* **audio**
digital audio workstation. *See* **DAW**
Dim button, 81
direct monitoring, 50–51
DirectSound drivers, configuration, 36
DirectX, Full Duplex drivers, 35–36
disabling
    audio tracks, 449–450
    Control Room Mixers, 57
    metronomes, 98
disadvantages of VSTi (VST instruments), 114, 115
discrete mixes, setup, 83–84
displacement, molecules, 10
display areas, Key Editor, 271–273
Dissolve Parts function, 290–291

distortion, 150
dithering, adding, 429–431
downloads
    loops, ripping samples for, 352–353
    online, 13
dragging. *See also* **moving**
    events, 61, 167
    files, 90
drawing
    automation, 407–409
    shapes, 409
Draw tool, 177, 260, 267
drivers
    ASIO (Audio Stream Input/Output), 34, 35–36, 42
    audio, 34–36
    devices, 19
    DirectSound configuration, 36
    Full Duplex (DirectX), 35–36
    MIDI (Musical Instrument Digital Interface), 36–38
    peripherals, 32
dropping files, 90. *See also* **moving**
Drum Editor, navigating, 279–282
Drum Map
    menu, 197
    Setup dialog box, 283
drums, 10
    Beat Designer, 360–362
    Groove Agent ONE, applying, 358–360
    loops, 356–362
    maps, 282–285
    MIDI (Musical Instrument Digital Interface)
        editing tracks, 279–285
        quantizing drum parts, 285
    O-Note Conversion tool, 291–292
    overdubbing, 103
    parts, 282
    patterns
        converting into MIDI parts, 362
        saving, 362
Drumstick button, 282
Duplicate command, 322
Duplicate tool, 355
duplicating chains, 338
duration, notes, 13
dynamic range, 12

E

echoes, 143
Edit History dialog box, Undo command, 329–330
editing, 3, 5
    Arranger Editor, applying, 336–337
    audio, 216
        new features, 6
        processing options, 227–241
    Audio Part Editor, 28
    AudioWarp, 239–241
    automation, 410–412
    buttons, 219
    Control Change information, 260
    freezing, 452
    functions, 220–222
    groups, enabling, 307
    In-Place Editor, 255–263
    input, channel strips, 376–377
    Key Editor, 265–278
        applying, 265–271
        display areas, 271–273
        multiple tracks, 274
        Step Input mode, 273–274

editing (*Continued*)
Merge MIDI in Loop option, 289–290
MIDI (Musical Instrument Digital Interface) drum tracks, 279–285
Musical mode, 222–223
nondestructive, 28–29
Note Expression Editor, 265–278
notes, 253
output, channel strips, 377–378
parts, 268–269
projects, 440
properties, 27
Sample Editor, 28, 215–225
session, Undo command, 329–330
snap points, 224–225
Tempo Track Editor, 341–345
Track Edit Groups, 6
VariAudio, 251–253
vocals, 243–253
waveforms, 217
Edit In-Place button, 196
effects, 5
applying, 144
audio
adding, 245
plug-ins, 146–149
AudioWarp, 239–241
insert, 54
inserts
adding, 82, 261
applying, 143–156
tracks, 149–154
levels, modifying, 385
MIDI (Musical Instrument Digital Interface), adding, 309–314
normalization, 234
output, routing surround sound, 418–420
plug-ins, 143–146
processing, 228–229
real-time, 228
return pathways, 55
reverb, applying, 249
sends, 54, 144, 383. *See also* sends
send to, 55
enabling. *See also* starting
automation, 403
direct monitoring, 50–51
group editing, 307
metronomes, 78, 98
entire notes, selecting, 222
Envelope dialog box, 231
Envelope process, 231
environments
audio, recording, 5
mixing, 5
multimedia production, 5
navigating, 25
EQ (equalization), 245
adding, 389–396
Channel Settings window, 391–393
controls, modifying, 391
Extended Mixer panel, 393
filters, applying, 393–395
holes, carving, 395–396
Inspector, 393
navigating, 389–390
presets, 395
State button, 207
equalization. *See* EQ (equalization)
Erase Destination option, 290
Erase tool, 176, 267

erasing. *See* deleting
errors
quantization, 11
quantizing, 429
Event bar, 189
Event Display, 173
events, 27, 157
Arranger tracks, 333–335
audio, 25–26
overlapping, 211–212
quantizing, 303–308
Sample Editor, 216
snap points, 224–225
automation, adding, 408
copying, 322–325
dragging, 61, 167
locking, 329
MIDI (Musical Instrument Digital Interface), 132, 193–194
In-Place Editor, 255–263
merging, 259–260
moving, 257–258
muting, 258
resizing, 258–259
splitting, 258–259
multiple, analyzing, 349
notes, 258–259
objects, shifting inside, 328
punch-in/punch-out, 105
quantizing, 295–308
splitting, 318–319
Transpose command, 288
trimming, 220
existing recordings, 103–110. *See also* recording
existing tracks, overdubbing, 106–107
Export Audio Mixdown dialog box, 423
exporting. *See* importing; moving
audio, 421–424
final mixes, 422, 432–434
MIDI device setup files, 123
mix-downs, 139
OMF export options, 432–434
Pool, 165–166
real-time, 141
ReWire, 140–142
surround sound, 420
Export Options dialog box, 433
Extended Mixer panel, 373–375
EQ (equalization), 393
extended panels, Control Room Mixers, 82
extending loops, 354–356
external effects, renaming, 55
External FX tab, connections, 54–56
external inputs, 79
external instrument connections, 56–57
external monitoring, 50

F

Fade In dialog box, 232
Fade In process, 231–232
Fade Out process, 231–232
faders
channels, 201
submix groups, 399
volume, 150
fades, 110
files, 29. *See also* clips; projects
backups, 431–432
deleting, 164
dragging, 90

formats, selecting, 424
importing, 90–91
media
   importing, 158
   managing, 85–94, 160
MIDI (Musical Instrument Digital Interface), importing, 92–93
missing, 163
ReWire, 137
searching, 159
sizes, minimizing, 165
stereo, splitting, 423
Fill Loop
   functions, 324–325
   tools, 355, 356
filters, 143
   applying, 88
   comb, 234
   EQ (equalization), applying, 393–395
Filters pane, 86–87
final mixes
   dithering setups, 430
   exporting, 422, 432–434
   formatting, 422
   mastering, 421–434
finding. *See* searching
FireWire, 33, 39
First Repeat of Current Chain Step button, 333
fixed tempos, configuring, 101
flattening chains, 338–339
floating-point recording, 12–13
folders. *See also* files
   adding, 123
   Pool, 157
   tracks, applying, 454–455
Folder tracks, 184–185
Ford, Mary, 103
formatting. *See also* configuration
   Arranger tracks, 331–333
   audio, 424–425
   busses, surround sound, 415–416
   CDs (compact discs), 13
   chains, 338
   channels, instruments, 113
   drum maps, 284–285
   final mixes, 422
   groove presets, 302–303
   hitpoints, 304–305
   loops, 353
   macros, 442–443
   Ogg Vorbis, 425
   OMF export options, 432–434
   projects, 61–72
   ramps, 262
   regions, 223
   ReWire, 137–139
   rulers, 191
   slices, 304–305
   templates, 439–440
   time, 191
   tracks, 13, 66–67
      instruments, 70–71
      MIDI (Musical Instrument Digital Interface), 71–72
   Workspaces, 437–439
Freeze Audio Channel button, 207, 452
Freeze command, 154
Freeze function, applying, 451–453
Freeze Instruments Options dialog box, 453
freezing quantization, 295–296

frequencies, 10
   MIDI (Musical Instrument Digital Interface), 13
   sampling, 11, 95
Frequency control, 390
full duplex, 35
Full Duplex drivers (DirectX), 35–36
full-length tracks, adding, 104. *See also* tracks
functions
   Arranger, 331–339
   Audio Mixdown, 421
   Delete Doubles, 292
   Dissolve Parts, 290–291
   Fill Loop, 324–325
   Freeze, 451–453
   Hide, 378–379
   hitpoints, 305–306
   MIDI (Musical Instrument Digital Interface), 292–293
   pasting, 320–321
   Pool, 162–166
   Quantize, 269–270
   Sample Editor, 220–222
   Snap, 269–270
   zoom, 256–257
FX channels, 184. *See also* effects
   adding, 22, 387
   applying, 381–387
   deleting, 387
   options, navigating, 381–382
   Track Sends feature, 382–386
   VST (Virtual Studio Technology), managing, 386–387

G

gain, 56
Gain control, 390
Gain dialog box, 232
Gate, 248–249
General Quantize button, 285
ghost tracks, 379
Global Automation Mode button, 174–175, 405
Glue tool, 176, 267
graphs, EQ (equalization), 392
Grid Display control, 297
grids, quantizing, 298–299
Grid Type button, 179
Groove Agent ONE, applying, 358–360
groove presets, formatting, 302–303
Group Channel tracks, 185
Group/FX tab connections, 54
groups
   editing, enabling, 307
   of events, 256
   notes, modifying, 258–259
   submix group faders, 399
   Track Edit Groups, 6
   tracks, applying, 397–399
guitars, overdubbing, 103

H

half duplex, 35
HALion Sonic SE, 6, 117
hardware
   audio, 18
   configuration, 35
   mixers, 22
headphones, 57
   Control Room Mixers, 77
height, resizing tracks, 183

Hertz (Hz), 10, 11
Hide Channels button, 371
Hide function, 378–379
hiding automation subtracks, 409–410
history
    of Cubase, 4
    Edit History dialog box, 329–330
    offline audio processing, 237–238
hitpoints
    formatting, 304–305
    functions, 305–306
    navigating, 303–304
    quantizing, 306–307
hits, drums, 282, 357–358. *See also* drums
Hold Peak option, 376
holes, carving EQ (equalization), 395–396
horizontal axis, 10
Horizontal Zoom bar, 190
Horizontal Zoom pop-up menu, 190
hosts, ReWire, 137, 138
Hz (Hertz), 10, 11

I

icons (Status column), 162
importing
    ACID loops, 240
    audio, 90–94
    files, 90–91
    loops, 364
    media files, 158
    MIDI (Musical Instrument Digital Interface),
        92–93, 124
    tracks from CDs (compact discs), 91–92
    video, 93–94
Include Chase option, 290
Include Sends option, 290
increasing values, 64
Indicate Transpositions button, 269
indicators, activity, 130–131
inflections, Compressor, 245
Info column, 161
Information line area, 172
I-Note column, 281
In-Place Editor, 255–263
input
    ASIO (Audio Stream Input/Output), 18
    busses, 20
    channel strips, 372, 376–377
    child busses, 416
    connections, 51–53
    Control Room Mixers, 76
    external, 79
    insert effects, 144
    MIDI (Musical Instrument Digital Interface), 16, 23
    Mixer, modifying, 97
    ports, configuring MIDI, 194
    signals, 47. *See also* signals
Input Routing field, 207
Input Transformer button, 195
Insert Curve field, 343
inserts
    on Control Room Mixers, 154–156
    effects, 54
        adding, 82, 261
        applying, 143–156
        MIDI (Musical Instrument Digital Interface), 310–312
        send effects, comparing, 144–146
    tracks, 149–154
Inserts State button, 197, 207

Inserts title bar, 151
Insert Velocity button, 269
Inspector, 172, 180–182
    areas, 21
    Arranger tracks, 335–336
    audio tracks, 208–209
    automation, starting, 402
    Channel section, 209–211
    controls, 206–208
    devices, applying, 124–125
    EQ (equalization), 393
    folder track settings, 454
    MIDI (Musical Instrument Digital Interface)
        Fader section, 199
        Sends section, 313
    panels, 69
    parameters, 206–208
    sends, 383
    tracks, renaming, 455
installation, MIDI
    port verification, 37
    remote control devices, 40–41
Instrument column, 280
instruments
    channels, creating, 113
    external connections, 56–57
    Groove Agent ONE, applying, 358–360
    HALion Sonic SE virtual, 117
    LoopMash2, 362
    MIDI (Musical Instrument Digital Interface).
        See MIDI
    overdubbing, 103
    plug-ins, loading, 71
    presets, 67–70
    sustaining, replacing, 105
    tracks, creating, 70–71
    virtual, 5
    Virtual MIDI Keyboards, 135–136
    VST (Virtual Studio Technology), 4
        applying, 111–119
        presets, 87–89
Instrument tracks, 184
integer values, 12
interaction, Pool, 166–167
interfaces
    audio connections, 32–34
    devices, 32
    MIDI (Musical Instrument Digital Interface), 33.
        See also MIDI
    new features, 6
    resolution, 12
interleaved formats, 66
iQ control, 298
iterative quantizing, 296
Iterative Strength control, 298

J

Jog wheel, 191–192

K

Keep Last mode, 128
keyboards
    drums, playing tracks back on, 359
    MIDI controllers, 17
    synthesizers, 4
    Virtual MIDI Keyboards, 135–136
key commands, customizing, 441–442
Key Commands dialog box, 441, 442

Key Editor, 265–278
    applying, 265–271
    display areas, 271–273
    multiple tracks, 274
    Step Input mode, 273–274
keys, 15
keywords, 159
kHz (kilohertz), 10
kilohertz (kHz), 10

L

lanes
    applying, 109
    automation, 183
    Controller Lanes, 272
    MIDI (Musical Instrument Digital Interface), applying, 134
Lane Track, 6
laps, 128
Last Repeat of Current Chain Step button, 333
Latch mode, 81
latency, 18, 35, 48
    reducing, 36
    VST instruments, 118–119
LCRS (left, center, right, and surround), 66
left, center, right, and surround. See LCRS
left locators, 129–130
length of notes, 13
levels
    effects, modifying, 385
    meters, 82
    Q (Quality Factor), 390
    sources, modifying, 97
    volume, 13
levers, 14
LFE (Low Frequency Effects) channels, 413, 419
Linear mode, 127–128
Line tool, 177, 268
    applying, 260–263
    automation, 409
linking channels, 376
Listen mode, 80
lists, adding Patch Bank, 121, 122
loading
    Beat Designer, 360
    drums
        maps, 283
        presets in Groove Agent ONE, 359
    instruments, 71
    plug-ins, 156
locations
    Define Locations, 85–86
    recording, 243–244
Locations pane, 86
locators, 129–130
Lock button, 196, 405
locking
    automation, 405
    events, 329
    tempo, 347–348
loop-based recording, 332
LoopMash2, 6, 362–364
loops, 111
    ACID, importing, 240
    applying, 351–356
    drums, 356–362
    extending, 354–356
    formatting, 353
    importing, 364
    Split Loop option, 319

loudspeakers, 10
Low Frequency Effects (LFE) channels, 413, 419
low latency, 48. See also latency

M

Mac OS X, MIDI port installation verification, 37–38
macros, formatting, 442–443
magic Q, 390
Magnifying Glass tool, 256
main areas, Sample Editor, 216–217
Make-Up control, 246
managing
    automation, 406–407
    chains, 338–339
    commands, customizing, 441–442
    connection presets, 60
    files, 160
    FX channels, 386–387
    macros, formatting, 442–443
    media, 85–94
    MIDI (Musical Instrument Digital Interface) devices, 121–124
    offline audio processing history, 237–238
    projects
        customizing, 437–447
        optimizing, 449–455
    sends, 383–386
    templates, formatting, 439–440
    toolbars, customizing, 444–445
    track controls, customizing, 445–447
    Workspaces, 437–439
manual monitoring, 49
manufacturer's websites, 37, 46
maps
    devices, 119
    drums, 282–285
    Note Expression, 276–277
    O-Note Conversion tool, 291–292
markers, Time Warp tool, 345
Marker tracks, 185
mastering, 3
    final mixes, 421–434
    overview of, 426–428
master insert effects, 144
master MIDI takes, assembling, 134–135
master takes, assembling, 109–110
matching
    pitch, 353–354
    tempo, 353
M-Audio, 34
M column, 281
measurements
    amplitude, 10
    latency, 35. See also latency
media
    browsers, 85
    files
        importing, 158
        managing, 160
    managing, 85–94
MediaBay, applying, 85–87
Media column, 158
media files, 29. See also clips
memory, 12
menus
    context, 25
    MIDI (Musical Instrument Digital Interface) options, 287–293
Merge Clipboard process, 232
Merge MIDI in Loop option, 289–290
Merge mode, 128

merging MIDI (Musical Instrument Digital Interface)
  events, 259–260
messages
  MIDI (Musical Instrument Digital Interface), 14–15
  System Exclusive, 15
metadata, adding, 425–426
meters, Show Meters button, 82
methods, monitoring, 48–51
metronomes
  configuration, 99
  enabling, 78, 98
  recording, 100
microphones, 57
  placement of, 244–145
  vocals, 244
MIDI (Musical Instrument Digital Interface), 4
  activity indicators, 130–131
  channels, 23–24, 372
  compatibility, 56
  connections, 22–25
  connectors, 15–18
  devices
    adding with Device Manager, 119–125
    managing, 121–124
    removing, 124
  Dissolve Parts function, 290–291
  drivers, 36–38
  drums
    editing tracks, 279–285
    quantizing drum parts, 285
  events, 193–194
    In-Place Editor, 255–263
    merging, 259–260
    moving, 257–258
    muting, 258
    resizing, 258–259
    splitting, 258–259
  functions, applying, 292–293
  importing, 92–93
  insert effects, 310–312
  Inspector, 181. *See also* Inspector
  interfaces, devices, 33
  Key Editor, 265–278
  lanes, applying, 134
  master takes, assembling, 134–135
  menu options, 287–293
  Merge MIDI in Loop option, 289–290
  messages, 14–15
  O-Note command, 291–292
  overview of, 13–18
  parts, converting drum patterns, 362
  ports, 22–23
    setup, 39–40
    verification, 37
  programs, assigning, 124–125
  quantizing
    applying, 300–301
    creating groove presets, 302–303
  recording, 127–136, 132–133
    configuring, 270–271
    environments, 5
  ReWire, 139
  sends, 312–314
  Thru port, 17–18
  tracks, 24–25, 184
    adding effects, 309–314
    building, 133
    converting to audio, 203–204
    creating, 71–72
    navigating, 193–204
  setup, 194–199
  Transpose command, 287–288
  values, 201
  Virtual MIDI Keyboards, 135–136
  VSTi (VST instrument), 117
MIDI Channel Settings panel, 201–203
MIDI Controller Setup dialog box, 273
MIDI Edit button, 270–271
MIDI Fader section, 199–201
MIDI Transpose Setup dialog box, 288
Minimize File option, 164
minimizing file sizes, 165
missing files, searching, 163
mix-downs, exporting, 139
Mixer
  applying, 367–380
  areas, navigating, 368–375
  audio channels, 21–22
  Common panel, 369–372
  EQ (equalization), 393
  Extended Mixer panel, 373–375
  input, modifying, 97
  MIDI channels, 200
  performance, 379–380
  ReWire, 140
  Routing panel, 375
  setup, 375–376
mixers
  Control Room Mixers, 75–84
    disabling, 57
    inserts on, 154–156
  control surfaces, 34. *See also* control surfaces
  hardware, 22
mixing, 3. *See also* Mixer
  environments, 5
  exporting, 420
  final mixes, 421–434. *See also* final mixes
  LoopMash2, 363
  surround sound, 413–420
Mix mode, 128
Mix-Stacked mode, 129
modes
  automation, 405
  Cycle, 133
  Cycle Record, 128–129
  direct monitoring, 50–51
  Keep Last, 128
  Latch, 81
  Linear, 127–128
  Listen, 80
  Merge, 128
  Mix, 128
  Musical, 353
  New Parts, 127
  Overwrite, 128
  Record, 127–129
  recording, 108–109
  Replace, 128
  Sizing Applies Time Stretch, 327–328
  Sizing Moves Contents, 326–327
  Stacked, 129
  Step Input, 273–274
  surround sound, 414
  Transpose Musical, 240–241
modifying
  automation modes, 405
  auto monitoring options, 49
  buffer sizes, 36, 43
  EQ (equalization) controls, 391
  FX channels, 386–387

input, Mixer, 97
level effects, 385
locators, 129–130
LoopMash2 mixes in real time, 363
MIDI (Musical Instrument Digital Interface), 23
notes, 258–259
numeric values, 64
Offline Process History process, 238
order of
    events in chains, 337
      overlapping events, 212
pitch, 239–241, 251–252, 353–354
programs, 15
signals, 150
sources, 97
tempo, 101, 341–349
timing, 252–253
toolbar contents, 444
modulation, 14
modulators, 143
modules, sound, 16
molecule displacement, 10
Monitor button, 397
monitoring
    audio, 47–60
    auto monitoring preference setup, 48–50
    Control Room Mixers, 77–84
    direct, 50–51
    external, 50
    methods, 48–51
    options, 79–80
monitors, loading plug-ins, 156
MonoDelay panel, 87–88
Move MIDI CC control, 298
moving
    events, 61, 167, 328
    files, 90
    locators, 129–130
    MIDI (Musical Instrument Digital Interface) events, 257–258
    tempo, 345
    tracks, 455
multichannel setups, 20
    audio track configurations, 67
    mixers, 22
    surround sound, 413–415
multimedia production environments, 5
multiple events
    analyzing, 349
    recording, 211
multiple lanes, selecting, 110
multiple MIDI channels, recording simultaneously, 132
multiple nonconsecutive events, 256
multiple ranges, selecting, 110
multiple sections, viewing, 182
multiple source tracks, 154
multiple takes, recording, 108–110, 133–135
multiple tracks
    editing, 274
    quantizing, 307–308
    recording, 132
Musical Instrument Digital Interface. See MIDI (Musical Instrument Digital Interface)
Musical mode, 219, 353
    columns, 161
    Sample Editor, 222–223
musical pitch, 13
Mute tool, 177, 267
muting. See also silencing
    MIDI (Musical Instrument Digital Interface) events, 258
    objects, 329

speakers, 418
tracks, 291

N

naming tracks, 455
navigating
    Arranger chains, 337
    audio tracks, 205–212
    Channel section, 209–211
    Control Room Mixers, 76–77
    Drum Editor, 279–282
    environments, 25
    EQ (equalization), 389–390
    FX channel options, 381–382
    hitpoints, 303–304
    Inspector, 180–182
    MIDI (Musical Instrument Digital Interface) tracks, 193–204
    Mixer areas, 368–375
    Pool, 157–160
    projects, 61–66, 187–192
    Project windows, 171–186
    Sample Editor, 215–225
    sends, 383
    Track List, 182–183
    Transport panel, 183–184, 190–192
new features, 6
New Parts mode, 127
Next Chain Step button, 333
noise. See also sound
    dithering, 430
    gates, 233
nondestructive editing, 28–29
Non-Quantize Range control, 297
normalization, 234
normal sizing, 325–326
Note Display area, 271
Note Expression, 265–278
    activating, 275–276
    controllers, mapping, 276–277
    editing, 278
    recording, 277
    tools, 6
Notepad, applying, 198
notes
    adding, 261
    deleting, 221–222
    duration, 13
    editing, 253
    events, 258–259. See also events
    pitch, 252. See also pitch
    selecting, 222
Nudge Palette, 258
Nudge wheel, 191–192
Nuendo, 4
numbers, magic Q, 390
numeric values, modifying, 64

O

objects
    events, shifting inside, 328
    muting, 329
    pitch shifts, applying, 234–236
    previewing, 161
    regions, 160
    renaming, 161
    resizing, 325–328
    types of, 27

Object Selection tools, 109, 176, 256, 267
offline audio processing, 144, 230–237
   history, managing, 237–238
Offline Process History dialog box, 238
offline processing, 227–228. *See also* processing
offline resources, Pool, 167
Offset value, 36
Ogg Vorbis, 425
OMF export options, 432–434
online audio effects, applying, 229
online downloads, 13
online processing, 227–228. *See also* processing
O-Note
   column, 281
   MIDI (Musical Instrument Digital Interface),
     291–292
Open/Close Editor button, 150
Open Process Bars button, 343
Open Process Tempo button, 343
operating systems, 31
optimizing
   Mixer, 379–380
   performance, 31–32
   Pool, 164–165
   projects, 449–455
options
   audio, exporting, 421–424
   auto monitoring, modifying, 49
   Default Location, 63
   FX channels, navigating, 381–382
   Hold Peak, 376
   MIDI (Musical Instrument Digital Interface)
     menus, 287–293
     Merge MIDI in Loop, 289–290
   Minimize File, 164
   monitoring, 79–80
   OMF export, 432–434
   presets, 89
   processing, 227–241
   Prompt for Project Location, 63
   regions, 223
   Remove Missing Files, 163
   surround sound routing, 416–417
   Sync Reference, 36
Organize Workspaces window, 439
organizing. *See* managing
output
   ASIO (Audio Stream Input/Output), 18
   busses, 20
   channel strips, 372
   child busses, 416
   connections, 53–54
   Control Room Mixers, 76
   editing, channel strips, 377–378
   effects, routing surround sound, 418–420
   MIDI (Musical Instrument Digital Interface),
     16, 23
Output column, 281
Output Routing field, 207
outputs, 144
overdubbing, 103–110
   existing tracks, 106–107
overlapping
   audio events, 211–212
   MIDI parts, 194
over-quantizing, 296
Overview line area, 172
   applying, 188–189
Overwrite mode, 128

P

pan controls, 414
panels, 25
Pan settings, 201
Parabola tool, 262
parameters, 14, 206–208
   automation, 404
   quantization setup, 299–300
   search, 159
   synthesizers, 15
parts, 27
   audio, 26–28
   drums, 282
   editing, 268–269
   folders, 455
   MIDI (Musical Instrument Digital Interface), converting
     drum patterns, 362
pasting, 221
   functions, 320–321
   loops, 354
Patch Bank lists, 121, 122
patches, 24
   modifying, 15
Patch Selector field, 118
paths, signals, 47, 312, 386
patterns, drums, 4
   converting into MIDI parts, 362
   saving, 362
Paul, Les, 103
Peak Margin Indicator, 201
Peak Meter Value indicator, 210
peaks, Hold Peak option, 376
pedals, 14
performance
   Mixer, 379–380
   optimizing, 31–32
periods, 11
peripheral setups, 31–46
permissions, sampling, 352
phantom power, 244
Phase Reverse process, 234
physical space, recording, 243–244
pianos, 14. *See also* keyboards
pitch, 13
   bend, 14
   Compressor, 245
   matching, 353–354
   modifying, 239–241, 251–252
   shifting, 228, 240–241
Pitch column, 280
Pitch Correct, 250–251
Pitch Shift process, 234–236
placement of microphones, 244–145
playback, 219
Play Order controls, 332
play order lists, flattening, 338–339
Play tool, 177
Plug-in effect selection field, 150
plug-ins
   Beat Designer, 360–362
   effects, 143–146
     audio, 146–149
     inserts, 143–156
     MIDI (Musical Instrument Digital Interface), 310–312
   instruments, 71
   loading, 156
   parameters, automating, 404
   vocals, 245–251
     Compressor, 245–247

DeEsser, 247–248
Gate, 248–249
Pitch Correct, 250–251
reverb, 249
VST (Virtual Studio Technology), processing offline, 450–451
VSTi (VST instruments), 111–119
plugs, MIDI-connectors, 15–18
points, punch-in/punch-out, 105
Pool
analyzing, 160–162
applying, 157–167
archiving, 165–166
exporting, 165–166
functions, 162–166
interaction, 166–167
navigating, 157–160
offline resources, applying, 167
optimizing, 164–165
processing, 229
populating Arranger chains, 337
ports
audio setup, 41–44
devices, 19
input, configuring MIDI, 194
MIDI (Musical Instrument Digital Interface), 22–23
setup, 39–40
verification, 37
Thru, MIDI (Musical Instrument Digital Interface), 17–18
positioning
locators, 129–130
snap points, 224–225
timing, modifying, 252–253
post-fader inserts, 149, 150
post-production microphones, 244
Post-Roll fields, 106–107
power
phantom, 244
processing, 154
pre-fader inserts, 149
preferences. See also configuration
auto monitoring, setup, 48–50
presets, 89
regions, 223
VST instruments, 112–114
preparing
for ReWire applications, 138
tracks for recording, 96
Pre-Roll fields, 106–107
Preset Name dialog box, 60
presets
adding, 123
audio tracks, 67–70
connections, saving, 60
EQ (equalization), 395
grooves, formatting, 302–303
saving, 89
instruments, 118
quantization settings, 300
VSTi (Virtual Studio Technology instruments), 87–89
Preset selection field, 150
pressure, keys, 15
Previewer pane, 87
previewing objects, 161
Previous Chain Step button, 333
Process bars dialog box, 343
processes, background, 44
processing
audio
effects, 144, 228–229
offline, 230–237

options, 227–241
post-fader inserts, 150
power, 154
VST (Virtual Studio Technology) plug-ins offline,
450–451
Process Tempo dialog box, 343
production environments, multimedia, 5
programs
DAW (digital audio workstation), 3
MIDI tracks, assigning, 124–125
modifying, 15
ReCycle, 90
Program Selector field, 197
Project Assistant, 62
templates, 440
Project Root Key button, 177–178
Project Ruler, 173
projects
Arranger tracks, creating, 331–333
backups, 165
creating, 61–72
customizing, 437–447
editing, 440
navigating, 61–66, 187–192
optimizing, 449–455
Pool, 157–167
setup, configuration, 63–66
templates, 63, 439–440
VSTi (VST instruments), 116
Project Setup dialog box, 64, 95, 188
Project windows, 21, 28, 69
areas, 171–184
arranging in, 317–330
classes, tracks, 184–185
navigating, 171–186
Prompt for Project Location option, 63
properties, editing, 27
Punch-In/Punch-Out feature, 103,
104–105, 107

Q

Q (Quality Factor) level, 390
quality of recordings, 13
Quantize button, 179
Quantize Catch Range control, 297
Quantize column, 280
Quantize control, 298
Quantize function, 269–270
Quantize Grid control, 296
Quantize panel, controls, 296–298
quantizing, 129
advanced, 296
applying, 295–298
audio events, 303–308
errors, 11, 429
events, 295–308
grids, setup, 298–299
hitpoints, 306–307. See also hitpoints
iterative quantizing, 296
MIDI (Musical Instrument Digital Interface)
applying, 300–301
creating groove presets, 302–303
drum parts, 285
multiple tracks, 307–308
over-quantizing, 296
parameters, setup, 299–300
pitch of notes, modifying, 252
Quick Controls, setup, 198–199

R

racks, amplifiers, 6
ramps, parabolic, 262
Randomize control, 298
Range Crop command, 319
ranges
    dynamic, 12
    frequencies, 10. *See also* frequencies
    multiple, selecting, 110
    Split Range option, 319
Range Selection tool, 109, 176, 223
rates, transfer, 14
Ratio control, 246
Read Automation button, 402–403
reading, Automation feature, 401–412
real-time
    audio stretching, 4
    effects, 228
    exporting, 141
Record button, 49, 397
Record Enable button, 104, 195
Record Enabled button, 49
Record icon (Status column), 162
recording
    32-bit, 12–13
    audio, 95–101
    booths, 57
    Control Room Mixers, 75–84
    Cycle mode, 108–109
    DAW (digital audio workstation), 3
    environments, 5
    floating-point, 12–13
    insert effects, applying, 152–153
    locations, 243–244
    loop-based, 332
    metronomes, 100
    MIDI (Musical Instrument Digital Interface), 13–18,
        71–72, 127–136
        configuring, 270–271
        in Step Input mode, 273–274
    multiple events, 211
    multiple takes, 108–110, 133–135
    multiple tracks, 132
    Note Expression, 277
    overdubbing, 103–110
    Punch-In/Punch-Out feature, 104–105
    quality of, 13
    ReWire, 139
    vocals, 243–245
Record modes, 127–129
ReCycle, 90, 353
reducing
    latency, 36
    sibilance, 247
Reduction control, 247
Reference Level button, 81
references, 157
regions, 25, 26, 27
    applying, 223–224
    objects, 160
Regions List, 217
Regions pane, 217, 218
Release control, 248
remapping, drum maps, 284
remote device setup, 40–41
Remove Missing Files option, 163
removing
    files, 164

MIDI (Musical Instrument Digital Interface) devices, 124
    notes, 221–222
renaming
    chains, 338
    external effects, 55
    objects, 161
    tracks, 455
Repeat command, 322–324
Repeat Events dialog box, 355
Repeat tool, 355
Replace mode, 128
replacing
    drum hits, 357–358
    Offline Process History process, 238
    sections, 104
    sustaining instruments, 105
Reset button, 40
Reset Quantize control, 298
resizing
    events, 258–259
    objects, 325–328
    Track List, 183
    tracks, 183
resolution, 16-bit, 12
resources
    freezing, 154
    Pool, applying, 157–167
    ReWire, 137–142
    searching, 121
Results pane, 87
Return Gain, 56
reverb, applying, 249
Reverse process, 237
ReWire, 45
    applying, 137–142
    exporting, 140–142
    setup, 137–139
    VSTi (VST Instrument), 139–140
rhythms, swing, 361
right locators, 129–130
ripping samples for loops, 352–353
routing
    channels, 415
    Control Room Mixers, 76
    effects in output, 418–420
    MIDI events, 117
    signals, 47
    surround sound, 414, 416–417
Routing Editor dialog box, 419
Routing panel, Mixer, 375
royalties, 352
Ruler bars, 189
rulers
    formatting, 191
    Key Editor, 272
    Project Ruler, 173
    tempo, locking, 348
Ruler tracks, 185
rules, Slice Rules section, 308
running applications simultaneously, 44–45
Rürup, Manfred, 4

S

Sample Editor, 28
    applying, 215–225
    areas, 215–217
    AudioWarp, 239–241
    functions, 220–222

Musical mode, 222–223
  regions, applying, 223–224
  snap points, 224–225
  toolbars, 217–220
sampling
  frequencies, 95
  loops, 111
  overview of, 11–12
  permissions, 352
  pitch, modifying, 353–354
  ripping, 352–353
  tempo, matching, 353
Save as Template dialog box, 439
Save Preset dialog box, 89
saving
  channel view sets, 371
  connections, 58–60
  drum patterns, 362
  presets, 89
  quantization settings to presets, 300
  toolbar customizations, 444
  VST instruments, 118
Scale Correction fields, 288
scroll bars, 173
scrubbing, 192, 219
Search button, 159
searching
  missing files, 163
  resources, 121
sections
  replacing, 104
  viewing, 182
Select Channel View Set menu, 371
selecting
  audio formats, 424–425
  entire notes, 222
  events, 256
  multiple lanes, 110
  multiple ranges, 110
  Object Selection tools, 109
  presets, 68
  Range Selection tool, 109
  VST presets for plug-in effects, 88
Select Preset control, 296
Select Send Destination field, 384
Semitones field, 287
Send Gain, 56
sending signals outside Cubase, 385–386
sends, 54, 144, 371
  insert effects, comparing, 144–146
  MIDI (Musical Instrument Digital Interface), 312–314
  Track Sends feature, 382–386
Sends State button, 198, 207
send to effects, 55
sessions
  Edit History dialog box, 329–330
  recording, 103. *See also* recording
setup. *See also* configuration
  audio
    configurations, 67
    ports, 41–44
    tracks, 205–209
  auto monitoring preferences, 48–50
  channels, copying settings, 370
  clocks, 43, 95
  devices, 38–44
  discrete mixes, 83–84
  dithering, 430
  metronomes, 99
  MIDI (Musical Instrument Digital Interface)

  ports, 39–40
    tracks, 71–72, 194–199
  Mixer, 375–376
  multichannel, 20
  multichannel, surround sound, 413–415
  new features, 6
  overview of, 3–4
  peripherals, 31–46
  presets, 67–70
  project configuration, 63–66
  quantization
    grids, 298–299
    parameters, 299–300
  Quick Controls, 198–199
  remote devices, 40–41
  ReWire, 137–139
  toolbars, 444–445
  toolsets, 5
  Track Controls Settings dialog box, 446
  versions, 6–7
  VST (Virtual Studio Technology) connections, 51–58
  VSTi (VST instrument), 112–114, 114–118
Set Up Window Layout button, 174, 188
shapes, drawing, 409
shifting
  events inside objects, 328
  pitch, 228, 240–241
Show Extended View button, 82
Show Info button, 158
Show Lanes button, 109, 196
Show Meters button, 82
Show Note Expression Data button, 268
Show Regions button, 217
Show VST Connections button, 370
Shuttle wheel, 191–192
sibilance, reducing, 247
signals
  bypassing, 385
  Compressor, 245
  modifying, 150
  normalization, 234
  paths, 47, 312, 386
  routing, 47
signatures, time, 98–101
  adding changes, 345
  deleting, 345
  moving, 345
Signature tracks, 185
silence
  adding, 221, 320
  tracks, 248
Silence process, 237
Sine tool, 262
single events, 256
single tracks, recording, 96
16-bit resolution, 12
sizes
  buffers, 36, 43
  files, minimizing, 165
  normal, 325–326
Sizing Applies Time Stretch mode, 327–328
Sizing Moves Contents mode, 326–327
Slice Rules section, 308
slices, 25, 26
  formatting, 304–305
slots, inserts, 150. *See also* inserts
snap buttons, 219
Snap function, 269–270
Snap On/Off button, 178
snap points, Sample Editor, 224–225

Snap to Zero Crossing button, 178, 223
Snap Type button, 178
soft-switching, 15
software, 45. *See also* applications; programs
    ReCycle, 90
    ReWire, 137–142
Solo Editor button, 266–267
sound. *See also* audio
    analog, 10–11
    banks, 15
    modules, 16
    surround, mixing, 413–420
sources
    clock setup, 95
    modifying, 97
space (as a dimension of sound), 11
speakers
    muting, 418
    surround sound, 413. *See also* surround sound
Split at Cursor command, 318
Split Loop option, 319
Split Range option, 319
splitting
    events, 258–259, 318–319
    stereo files, 423
Split tool, 176, 267
Square tool, 262
Stacked mode, 129
start and end points, trimming, 220
starting
    automation, 402
    metronomes, 78
    VST instruments, 116
Status column, 161, 162
Status line area, 172
Steinberg, Karl, 4
Steinberg mixers, 34
Steinberg Pro 16, 4
Step Input
    buttons, 270–271
    modes, 273–274
stereo
    child busses, 415, 416
    files, splitting, 423
    tracks, 66
Stereo Flip process, 236
straightening pitch of notes, 252
stretching
    real-time audio, 4
    time, 239–240
strings, 10
Strings channel, 21
strips, channels, 372–373, 377–378
studio channels, Control Room Mixers, 77
Studio connection tab, 57–58
studio sends, 83–84
subfolders, Pool, 157. *See also* folders
submenus, Zoom, 256
submix group faders, 399
subtracks, automation, 407
    editing, 411
    hiding/deleting, 409–410
subwoofers, surround sound, 413
support, manufacturer's websites, 46
SurroundPanner, 414, 415
SurroundPanner V5, 417–418
surround sound
    busses, 415–416
    effects in output, 418–420
    exporting, 420

mixing, 413–420
    routing, 416–417
suspending read/write functions, 407
sustaining instruments, replacing, 105
Swing Factor control, 297
swing rhythms, 361
switches, soft-switching, 15
switching effects on and off, 151
switch pedals, 14
synchronization
    inputs, 18
    MIDI (Musical Instrument Digital Interface), 15
syncopation, 252
Sync Reference option, 36
synthesizers, 14
    keyboards, 4
    parameters, 15
    VSTi (VST instruments), 111–119
System Exclusive messages, 15
systems, optimizing performance, 31–32

T
tabs, Group/FX connections, 54
takes
    master, assembling, 109–110, 134–135
    multiple, recording, 108–110, 133–135
Talkback, connections, 81
Tapemachine Style, 50
TASCAM, 34
templates
    connections, saving, 59
    formatting, 439–440
    projects, 63
tempo, 4, 98–101
    applying, 341–349
    deleting, 345
    matching, 353
    modifying, 239–241
    moving, 345
    OMF export options, 434
    ReWire, 139
    Time Warp tool, 345–348
Tempo Detection feature, 348–349
Tempo Recording slider, 343
Tempo Track Editor, 341–345
Tempo tracks, 185
Threshold control, 246
32-bit recording, 12–13
Thru port, MIDI (Musical Instrument Digital Interface), 17–18
thumbnails, viewing, 220
time
    latency, 35. *See also* latency
    pre-roll, exceeding, 106
    signatures, 98–101
        adding changes, 345
        deleting, 345
        moving, 345
    stretching, 239–240
    Transport panel, 191
    warping, 219
Timebase button, 195
Time Stretch process, 236–237
Time Warp tool, 177, 268, 345–348
timing, modifying, 252–253
Title bar area, 172
Toolbar area, 172
toolbars
    customizing, 444–445
    Drum Editor, 282

Key Editor, 266, 271
Project window, 173–179
Sample Editor, 217–220
Tempo Track Editor, 341
Toolbar Setup dialog box, 445
Tool buttons, 176–177
tools
    Audio Warp, 353
    Audition, 266
    Color, 177
    Draw, 177, 260, 267
    Duplicate, 355
    Erase, 176, 267
    Fill Loop, 355, 356
    Glue, 176, 267
    Key Editor, 267–268
    Line, 177, 268
        applying, 260–263
        automation, 409
    Magnifying Glass, 256
    Mute, 177, 267
    Object Selection, 109, 176, 256, 267
    O-Note Conversion, 291–292
    Parabola, 262
    Play, 177
    Range Selection, 109, 176, 223
    Repeat, 355
    Sample Editor, 218. *See also* Sample Editor
    Sine, 262
    Split, 176, 267
    Square, 262
    Tempo Detection, 348–349
    Time Warp, 177, 268, 345–348
    Triangle, 262
    Trim, 267
    Zoom, 177, 189–190, 268
toolsets, 5
    closing, 31
    Note Expression, 6
Touch automation, 405
Track Controls Settings dialog box, 446
Track Edit Groups, 6
Track List, 173
    controls, 206–208
    Header bar, 172
    navigating, 182–183
    parameters, 206–208
    resizing, 183
Track Pan control, 196
tracks
    adding, 185–186, 455
        insider Mixers, 376
        overdubbing, 103–104
    Arranger, 331–339
    audio. *See also* audio
        creating, 66–67
        disabling, 449–450
        Inspector, 180. *See also* Inspector
        navigating, 205–212
        presets, 67–70
        recording, 95–98
        replacing drum hits, 357–358
        setup, 205–209
    CDs (compact discs), importing, 91–92
    channels, automation, 403–404
    classes, 184–185
    click, 98–101
    Compressor, 246

controls, customizing, 445–447
copying, 203
delays, 196
deleting, 455
drums
    editing, 279–285
    loops, 356–362
existing, overdubbing, 106–107
folders, applying, 454–455
formatting, 13
FX channels, applying, 381–387
ghost, 379
Groove Agent ONE, applying, 358–360
groups, applying, 397–399
inserts, 149–154
instruments, creating, 70–71
MIDI (Musical Instrument Digital Interface), 24–25, 184
    adding effects, 309–314
    assigning programs, 124–125
    building, 133
    converting to audio, 203–204
    creating, 71–72
    navigating, 193–204
    setup, 194–199
moving, 455
multiple
    editing, 274
    recording, 132
    sources, 154
muting, 291
overdubbing, 103–110
Punch-In/Punch-Out feature, 107
renaming, 455
resizing, 183
ReWire, 137
sections, replacing, 104
silencing, 248
stereo, 66
Tempo Track Editor, 341–345
view rectangles, applying, 188
voices, creating, 20
Track Scale pop-up menu, 190
Track Sends feature, FX channels, 382–386
Track Settings section, 195
Track Volume control, 196
transfer rates, 14
Transport controls, 175–176
Transport panel, 54, 128
    customizing, 445
    navigating, 183–184, 190–192
Transpose command, MIDI (Musical Instrument Digital Interface), 287–288
Transpose Musical mode, 240–241
Transpose palette, 258
Transpose tracks, 185
Triangle tool, 262
trimming start and end points, 220
Trim tool, 267
troubleshooting
    activity indicators, 130–131
    audio alignment, 56
truncating, 429
Tuplet control, 297
24-bit resolution, 12
types
    of objects, 27
    of processing, 227–228

U

unfreezing audio channels, 451–452. *See also* Freeze
        function
unlinking channels, 376
USB (universal serial bus), 33, 39
Use Range fields, 288
utilities, closing, 31

V

values
    delay, 55
    increasing, 64
    integers, 12
    MIDI (Musical Instrument Digital Interface), 201
    numeric, modifying, 64
    quantize, drum parts, 285
VariAudio, 251–253
velocity, MIDI (Musical Instrument Digital Interface), 13
verification of MIDI port installations, 37
versions, 4
    setup, 6–7
vertical axis, 10
Vertical Zoom bar, 190
vibrations, 10
video
    audio, importing, 93–94
    Pool, 157–167
Video tracks, 185
viewing
    automation, 410
    MIDI (Musical Instrument Digital Interface), 23
    multiple sections, 182
    Play Order controls, 332
    takes, 109
    thumbnails, 220
views
    channels
        deleting, 371
        saving, 371
    Show Extended View button, 82
    track rectangles, applying, 188
violins, 4, 10. *See also* instruments
virtual instruments, 5
Virtual MIDI Keyboards, 135–136
Virtual Studio Technology. *See* VST
vocals. *See also* voices
    editing, 243–253
    microphones, 244
    plug-ins, 245–251
        Compressor, 245–247
        DeEsser, 247–248
        Gate, 248–249
        Pitch Correct, 250–251
        reverb, 249
    recording, 243–245
    VariAudio, 251–253
voices, 9
    tracks, creating, 20
voltage, 12, 111. *See also* amplitude
volume

faders, 150
levels, 13
VST (Virtual Studio Technology), 4, 22
    amp racks, 6
    connections, setup, 51–58
    Connections panel, 51–53
    Control Room Mixers, 76. *See also* Control Room Mixers
    Expression 2, 6
    FX channels, managing, 386–387
    instruments. *See also* VSTi (VST Instrument)
        applying, 111–119
        plug-ins, 70
        presets, 87–89
    plug-ins, processing offline, 450–451
    signals, routing, 47
    System Link settings, 38
    Virtual MIDI Keyboards, 135–136
VSTi (VST Instrument), 137
    freezing, 452–453
    ReWire, 139–140
    tracks, copying, 203
VST Input Channel Settings dialog box, 152
VST Instrument. *See* VSTi (VST Instrument)

W

Waveform Display area, 218, 220
waveforms, 10
    editing, 217
    periods, 11
WAV files, 90
wheels, 14
wildcard characters, 159
windows, 25
    Channel Settings, EQ (equalization), 391–393
    Computer Management, 37
    Organize Workspaces, 439
    Pool, 158. *See also* Pool
    Project, 21, 28, 69
        areas, 171–184
        arranging in, 317–330
        navigating, 171–186
        track classes, 184–185
WMA (Windows Media Audio) files, 90
Workspaces, formatting, 437–439
Write Automation button, 402–403
writing, Automation feature, 401–412

Y

Yamaha control surfaces, 34

Z

Zero Crossing button, 219
zero crossings, 178
zooming
    controls, 173
    functions, 256–257
    tools, 189–190
    Zoom tool, 177, 268